The Sociology of Globalization

The Sociology of Globalization

Luke Martell

polity

The right of Luke Martell to be identified as Author of this Work has been asserted in accordance with the UK Copyright, Designs and Patents Act 1988.

First published in 2010 by Polity Press

Reprinted 2010 (twice)

Polity Press
65 Bridge Street
Cambridge CB2 1UR, UK

Polity Press
350 Main Street
Malden, MA 02148, USA

ISBN-13: 978-0-7456-3673-3
ISBN-13: 978-0-7456-3674-0(pb)

A catalogue record for this book is available from the British Library.

Typeset in 10.5 on 13 pt Swift
by Servis Filmsetting Ltd, Stockport, Cheshire
Printed and bound by MPG Books Group, UK

The publisher has used its best endeavours to ensure that the URLs for external websites referred to in this book are correct and active at the time of going to press. However, the publisher has no responsibility for the websites and can make no guarantee that a site will remain live or that the content is or will remain appropriate.

Every effort has been made to trace all copyright holders, but if any have been inadvertently overlooked the publisher will be pleased to include any necessary credits in any subsequent reprint or edition.

For further information on Polity, visit our website: www.politybooks.com

Contents

Figures, Tables and Boxes

Figures

Tables

Introduction: Concepts of Globalization

THERE have been many trends in sociology in recent decades. These have varied from country to country. One was a concern with class and social mobility from the 1950s onwards, in part evident in debates between Marxists and Weberians. In the 1960s and 1970s, feminists argued that such debates had marginalized another form of social division, gender inequalities. Feminism grew in influence, itself being criticized for failing to appreciate other divisions, for instance ethnic inequalities, identified by those with postcolonial perspectives. In the 1980s, this concern with differences was highlighted in postmodern ideas, and the power of knowledge was analysed by theorists such as Michel Foucault. In the 1980s and 1990s, a more homogenizing idea came to the fore, globalization. This also went on to stress local difference and plurality. The themes of globalization were not new, but the word and the popularity of the idea really came to the fore in the 1980s (an early mention is in Modelski 1972).

Why did globalization become a popular idea? One reason is the rise of global communications, especially the Internet, which made people feel that connections across the world were flowing more strongly and speedily, as well as becoming more democratic. With the end of the cold war, it seemed that the bipolar world had become more unified, whether through cultural homogenization or the spread of capitalism. People became more conscious of global problems, such as climate change. Economic interdependency and instability were more visible. Money flowed more freely and national economies went into recession together in the 1970s and again thirty years later. From the 1970s onwards, one of the building blocks of the national era, the nation-state, seemed to be under threat. Welfare states became cumbersome and expensive, and economic liberals like Ronald Reagan and Margaret Thatcher led the world in rolling them back.

The first half of this introduction will look at the sociology of globalization and themes of the book. The second half will discuss the concept of globalization.

The sociology of globalization

Globalization may appear a macro phenomenon and distant, unlike micro issues that have more of an impact on daily life. Yet large-scale global processes of economic restructuring and international political power have a big impact on our individual lives. The global economy and distribution of wealth affect, for example, our chances of employment, alongside our material circumstances generally. Identity and cultural experience are forged out of global inputs, from media to music, migration and food. Which side you live on in the constellation of global political powers has significant consequences for your life chances.

For some, phenomena such as culture and people movements are what sociologists should be concerned about. Culture is sociological and has social effects, whereas economic and political issues are the preserve of other disciplines or maybe just less interesting. Culture is both important and interesting, as we shall see in this book. But so are economics and politics. Culture is affected by economic and political factors. Economic and political factors that seem distant from our lives have a large impact – for instance, mergers and diversification in the media industry and government deregulation impact on our cultural experiences as consumers. The fact that I live in a rich, developed country, one of the core powers in the world, and relatively democratic, peaceful, and free, has a great effect on my life compared to what it would be like if I lived in a poor, developing country, or one with less democracy and freedom, or more conflict and violence. A large proportion of the world's population lives in places with some or all of these problems. That I can watch cable television or access the Internet, what are cultural experiences, is not only based in economic and political factors, but also pales into insignificance next to economic and political advantages, which give me a privileged everyday experience.

Culture is important, it interests us and we are conscious of it. But economics and politics matter on a micro, individual and daily basis in ways that we often don't think about.

Some sociologists think the study of politics and economics is not really sociology. It is the territory of political scientists and economists. But this lacks a sense of an interdisciplinary role for sociology. Furthermore, sociology is the study of social structures, relations and processes, of society. Society includes the political and economic dimensions that affect such aspects as culture and migration.

This book takes politics and economics seriously, as an important part of sociology, without which globalization cannot be understood. You can't understand globalization without looking at its economic and political dimensions. And to analyse cultural and social spheres in isolation would be to overlook the economic and political power, inequality and conflict that affect them, making cultural globalization seem more equal and benign than it really is.

Some sociologists separate their studies of cultural globalization from their studies of political-economic relations. Consequently, their awareness of conflict, inequality and power in politics and economics becomes separated from the more benign, equal and cosmopolitan picture they have of culture (for instance, see Beck 2000, 2006, and Nederveen Pieterse 2004a, 2004b; for a sociology of globalization that incorporates political economy and so power, inequality and conflict, see Bourdieu 1998, 1999, 2003a).

To take an interdisciplinary perspective is distinctively sociological. Sociology has, from its founding days, drawn on economic and political perspectives and dealt with issues such as capitalism, ownership, the division of labour, economic class and the role of the nation-state. Consequently, sociology is well equipped to deal with modernity, capitalism and the state, some of the main institutions in globalization.

Some of the core themes of sociology are at the heart of this book – power, inequality and social divisions and inequalities such as class and gender. Such issues have always been central to the sociological perspective and sociology has played a key role in bringing them to the fore across the social sciences and in public life. Nevertheless, sociology does not have a monopoly on understanding these themes, and to make sense of them I will draw on economic and political perspectives.

So this book looks at some important conventionally sociological topics – migration and the movement of people, the media, culture and social movements – but it also identifies inequality and power as distinctively sociological preoccupations to look out for in globalization. Furthermore it argues that the economy, politics and war, often left out of sociology, are sociological. They are part of society and they affect society, social relations and social structures. To narrow-mindedly rule such things out from being the proper concern of sociology omits some major factors affecting social life, and especially behind power, inequality and conflict, leaving sociology with a perspective that turns away from the realities of society, especially its harsher realities.

There is a danger of fetishizing the new in recent perspectives on globalization. Old ways of sociology – such as Marxist economic determinism, or perspectives that have a 'realist' view of the state (as an actor that pursues its interests in competition with others) – are viewed by some as outmoded. Cosmopolitanism is seen as more appropriate to a new global era requiring new perspectives to fit with a world in which cultures intermingle, where foci on the nation-state or capitalist economic power are too methodologically nationalist or economically determinist, where societies are no longer neatly bounded within national borders, and global identities such as human rights and hybridity are taking over (for instance, see Beck 2006; Urry 2000).

There are problems with this advocacy of a cosmopolitan sociology:

(a) The old sociology was quite international in its outlook (Turner 2006). Cosmopolitan sociologists overstate the novelty of contemporary cosmopolitan views.

(b) Rejecting classical sociology as too economistic and statist undermines an understanding of the role of economic power and the state in globalization, leading to a picture of culture and social relations which does not show how they are unequal and power-laden because of economic and political structures.

(c) Economic and political power are omitted in a way that is theoretically elegant and pleasing, but is not empirical enough. The argument is made mainly theoretically in the face of empirical evidence that shows the role of capitalist and state power.

(d) One empirical absence in cosmopolitanism is the focus of its advocates on their own parts of the world, especially old Europe and North America, and to a lesser extent other fast-growing societies, with little attention paid to large parts of the world afflicted by poverty and war. The former fit the cosmopolitan story better than the latter, although even the former are also distinctly uncosmopolitan when it comes to things like immigration and economic protectionism.

(e) Cosmopolitanism is put forward as a fresh perspective in tune with the new global and intermixed world. There is a fetishization of the new over the old such that anything that is old is labelled outmoded, unsophisticated or out of date even if empirical evidence shows it has a stronger hold on explaining things. This categorization of something as old and outmoded is used as a way of dismissing it in place of a convincing critique of its theoretical cogency or, more importantly, empirical evidence. The important thing is not whether an argument is new or old but which is the right argument.

(f) As well as a lack of emphasis on empirical evidence there is contradiction. Some of those who reject the old approaches combine their new cosmopolitan arguments with other arguments that show the role of state and capitalist power. (Some of these points are developed more in Martell 2008, 2009, and in this book).

Themes of the book

There are number of themes running through this book.

1 Economic bases of globalization

As mentioned, many sociological studies of globalization have focused on culture and some have argued for a shift away from economic determinism. Culture has heavily shaped globalization, and globalization has a lot to do with the transnationalization and intermingling of cultures and local cultural responses to global cultures. The interaction between globalization and culture and identities is exciting, important and full of possibilities, and is discussed in this book. But it is difficult to see many areas of globalization where lying behind them are not also economic structures that affect the equality or power relations with which globalization is produced or received, or economic incentives to do with making money. My argument is not just about the economics behind globalization, but *capitalist* economics, the pursuit of profit by private owners. Other factors tailor and shape globalization and the economics of profit is not the only causal factor or one that goes in a simple unlinear direction unaffected by other forces. But it is very often a significant driving force.

2 Globalization as historical/modern

Globalization is historical. It started long before the recent years of information technology, the end of the cold war or even the end of the Second World War. It has its bases earlier, in the development of capitalism and industrialism, and in the institutions, technologies and incentives these systems brought along. These provided the biggest qualitative leap in globalization and are behind many forms of globalization today. They were not just the key starting point but also the basis for current forms. At the same time it is less plausible that globalization, or the bases for *current* globalization, started before this. While Europe and the West were still relatively backward, other more sophisticated parts of the world were practising long-distance trade, religion and expansion but these were not truly globalization.

3 Sceptical perspectives on globalization

Sociology is historically a critical discipline, and a critical but open-minded approach is healthy and in part what academic research should be about. Applied to globalization this leads to some sceptical conclusions, including doubts about whether what is called globalization really is that, or whether international structures and processes in the world match up to the criteria for globalization. What many people describe when they talk about globalization is happening. But it's not clear that it is globalization. Describing it as such gives it a meaning that is misleading as to its true character.

The sceptical view is linked to another theme of this book. Globalization is structured by power, inequality and conflict. Some play a greater role in globalization than others, and some are more integrated and others excluded. So, while there may be globalizing processes, they are sometimes not global because some people are not as influential or included as others. Structures and processes described as globalization are significant, so the study of these is important. But, as a result of the unevenness of inclusion, and because of power, inequality and conflict, these are not always 'global'. It's important to recognize the significance of international processes but also to not assume they are necessarily globalization.

4 Power, inequality and conflict

Many analyses of globalization have been critical and see it as a problematic process – to take a couple of examples, neoliberalism imposed on parts of the world by the West leading to negative consequences, or American imperialism played out through the media, exploitative multinational corporations or military power. Others in sociology, reacting against this view, see globalization as a more positive, equalizing, democratic and benign process that brings an intermingling of cultures in a new cosmopolitanism, with the generalization of positive values such as universal human rights. One of my aims is to investigate some of these latter perspectives and, in doing so, themes of power, inequality and conflict come to the fore.

This book adds to the literature on globalization by taking distinctive concerns from sociology. It has an emphasis on critical analysis, examining power, inequality and conflict in global relations. It puts arguments about globalization to the test of theoretical coherence and empirical evidence. It looks for interdisciplinary links and a holistic view, outlining important social relations of culture and migration but seeing these as not separable from political and economic structures. As well as breadth in perspective, the book is broad in the range of areas of globalization discussed, from hybrid cultures to worldwide wars. The book aims to be accessible to an audience that is relatively new to this area, but without sacrificing its own arguments.

Being critical can lead in different directions. In this book it leads to some partly pessimistic conclusions. Globalization may not be as developed as it seems. Insofar as it is, the picture is not as rosy as it might appear. The aim to solve world problems through global politics is well meant, but optimistic and hopeful. It is important to be negative if this is the most accurate conclusion to come to. But, alongside doubts about globalization and global politics, positive political arguments are put forward, for instance about how things could be made better in relation to migration, global poverty and international politics.

The book argues that it is necessary to include national politics while going beyond them. At the level of global politics consensus and commonality cannot always be achieved because of inequalities, power and conflicts of interest and ideology. A politics of conflict between different sides might be necessary. This may involve the poorer and less powerful allying internationally against the richer and more powerful. This involves a politics that is international (rather than just national or global) and conflictual (rather than cosmopolitan or consensual).

Political and pluralist perspectives on globalization

One of the striking things about the literature on globalization is that positions which see globalization happening or are sceptical about its existence do not break down along clear ideological lines. There are neoliberals and Marxists who see neoliberal globalization going on, although they may not agree on its consequences (for instance, whether it will solve global inequality and poverty or not) or whether it is good or bad. Normatively and prescriptively there are divisions between neoliberals and Marxists, and sometimes empirically on the consequences of it, but, at the descriptive level concerning the fact of whether economic globalization is happening, the split between globalists and sceptics is not along the lines of political ideology. I have outlined some political ideology perspectives on globalization in table 0.1. These will come up again throughout the book.

One issue discussed in this book is the tendency towards pluralist, hybrid and multidimensional views of globalization. Such views see

Table 0.1 Political ideologies and globalization

	Globalization happening? descriptive	Globalization Good or Bad? Normative
Neoliberals	Yes.	Good.
Globalist Marxists	Yes.	Bad (for socialist reasons).
Conservative nationalists	Yes.	Bad (for nationalist reasons).
Social democratic sceptics	No.	Bad because: (a) unequal, i.e., not global; or (b) not route to solving poverty (protectionism better).
Social democratic globalists	Yes.	Good, if subjected to global regulation.

Table 0.2 Pluralist views of globalization	
Multicausal	Globalization not just caused by one chief factor, e.g., economy.
Multilevel	Economic, political, cultural, military, environmental.
Hybrid	Mixture of inputs from East/West/North/South.
Localized	Form globalization takes varies where it is received.

globalization as operating at different levels, from the economic to the cultural or political. Sometimes emphases on multidimensionality are trying to get away from perspectives that focus mainly on economic globalization. Some views emphasize globalization as a hybrid and mixed phenomenon with inputs from many different parts of the world – one that is not just Westernized or homogenizing. For others, globalization is pluralistic and localized in its effects, with its reception varying depending on where it is received. Globalization is also driven by a multiplicity of factors rather than being reducible to single or selected causes. Globalization is multidimensional, hybrid, localized in its effects, and multicausal.

Seeing globalization in these plural ways is helpful and an antidote to monocausal, over-Westernized, homogenizing views, some of which focus on the economy at the expense of culture, or have a simplified view of its effects. Pluralistic views of globalization are an improvement on earlier sweeping general theories, less popular nowadays, which see globalization rolling out in a similar manner across the world.

But there is a danger of being pluralist without analysing if there is primacy or greater causality at some levels, and ascertaining whether amongst the plural factors some are more dominant or have a causal effect on the others. To say globalization is multidimensional is helpful and brings out its mix. But there are dangers in seeing it as an equal and hybrid mix without seeing the primacy, dominance or determination of some factors over others. It is also important not to separate off these plural factors, focusing on each as if separate from others and distracting from causal relations between them.

***

Concepts of globalization

The rest of this chapter looks at the meaning of globalization. Defining globalization is important because it affects other issues discussed in this book, such as when globalization started. Globalization is a powerful discourse or ideational force. It has an impact on how we see the world and behave. If an idea has this power it's important to pin down what it means and see if what it refers to lives up to the definition. The picture of globalization as inclusive, unifying and general makes it seem positive, whereas other definitions are more pessimistic. So it's important to identify what globalization means and how this fits with reality.

Globalization – beyond internationalization, liberalization and universalization?

Scholte (2005) argues that a new word should not restate what is already known with other terminology but has to mean something different. He rejects four meanings of globalization – as internationalization, liberalization, universalization or Westernization. These do not add anything new and do not capture what is different about globalization.

Internationalization involves the growth of transactions and interdependencies between countries. Things cross borders between states or national territories; for example, messages, ideas, goods, money, investments, pollutants and people. But Scholte says that inter-national transactions are nothing new, and that as the word 'international' captures what this describes we don't need a new word for these sorts of processes.

Scholte says that globalization is also not liberalization. The latter refers to the removal of constraints on movements of resources between countries – an open, borderless world. Liberalization involves abolishing regulatory measures such as trade barriers, capital controls and visa requirements, and is linked in part with neoliberalism. Both supporters and critics of neoliberalism define globalization in this way. Scholte says this liberalization has happened and has facilitated globalization. But liberalization and globalization are two different things. Globalization can and could take different forms, including non-neoliberal ones. We don't need the new word 'globalization' for this as this has long been debated as liberalization.

Globalization is also not universalization. This involves the dispersion of objects and experiences to all parts of the earth, global here meaning worldwide or everywhere. Examples provided by Scholte include tobacco, clothes, the state, food, education, children's toys and arms. Sometimes this gets extended into globalization as standardization or homogenization. But Scholte says there is nothing new about this. It is age-old, for instance, in world religions and trade. There is no need for new terminology for something we already have a word for.

Globalization also has to be more than Westernization. This is a particular type of universalization, of Western structures such as capitalism, industrialism, rationalism, urbanism, individualism and democracy, or put more critically, colonization, Americanization and imperialism. Again, Scholte says these are part of globalization but not the same. Globalization can go in non-Western directions. It need not be imperialist if emancipatory movements can guide it. And Westernization existed long before globalization, so let's call this Westernization and not invent a new word for it.

For Scholte, globalization is deterritorialization or supraterritorialism. These involve more than just transplanetary links. *Transplanetary* connectivity, connections between parts of the world, has been around for many centuries. *Supraterrritoriality*, however, is relatively new and breaks with territorialist geography, with territories and borders being important. In the first edition of his book Scholte defined globalization as *deterritorialization*. In the second he replaces this with the idea of *supraterritorialism*. This, he says, is because the word 'deterritorialization' suggests that territory doesn't matter any more, which is putting it too strongly.

Transplanetary relations involve links between people across the world. These have been around for centuries but are more dense now than before, involving more people, more often, and are more extensive, intensive and of greater volume. Supraterritorial relations, however, are more recent, and involve not just an intensification of links across the world but different types of global connectivity. This intensification of links across boundaries also involves the decline of those boundaries. They transcend and are detached from territory. They involve things like transworld simultaneity (e.g., people in lots of places doing the same thing, such as consuming the same brand of coffee) or transworld instantaneity (e.g., the telephone, where distant people talk to each other at the same time).

Other examples of supraterritorialism for Scholte include jet planes, telecommunications, global media, finance, ecological problems and global consciousness (e.g., sports and human rights consciousness). In such cases more is involved than compression of time over space, for instance, where communications or travel over the same distances are quicker. There are social relations beyond territorial space. The difference between time–space compression and supraterritoriality is qualitative. It involves not just an intensification of existing relations, but new sorts of relations. For Scholte, territorial domains remain important but don't define the whole framework where there is supraterritorialism.

Scholte lists examples of supraterritorialism, including communications (e.g., books, post, telegraph, phone, fax, texting, Internet, newspapers, radio, TV, film); the movement of people (e.g., tourism, migration/refugees, business travel); production processes (e.g., production that occurs in many places, global sourcing, global trade); consumption; global money/finance; global organizations (e.g., MNCs, faith-based, unions, NGOs, charities); military globalization (e.g., weapons that have global reach, war carried out from global locations); ecology (in both causes and effects); health (for instance, illnesses that spread globally); law (e.g., international laws); and global consciousness (e.g., sports competitions, global tours and events, conferences).

The problem is that these are all examples of transplanetary connections as much as supraterritoriality, and Scholte makes a number of qualifications to what he is saying, claiming that globalism has not eliminated territorialism which remains important, for instance, in production, governance, ecology and identities. The world is both territorial and global; no pure globality exists independently of territorial spaces. The global is not a domain separate from regional, national, provincial and local levels, and there is an intersection of all these. This is what Scholte says and these are quite big qualifications that seem to take the edge off ideas of deterritorialization and supraterritorialism.

Furthermore, many things described as globalization fall into the categories of internationalization, liberalization or Westernization. Scholte himself says that these are part of globalization but just not the same as them. So it's not clear how different globalization is from these as he suggests it is. The exception is universalization. Few of the processes Scholte mentions are universal. So, while globalization encompasses internationalization, liberalization and Westernization as much as breaking from them, it rarely achieves the universalization he also differentiates globalization from.

The qualifications that Scholte makes, mentioned above, undermine his concept of globalization. They suggest that globalization is intertwined with territory rather than something above, beyond and separate from it. It might be better to say that what people talk about when discussing globalization are forms of Westernization, internationalization and liberalization, but that they are not above and beyond these.

Sociologists and historians define globalization

Waters (2001: 4) mentions definitions of globalization made by Robertson and Giddens. For Robertson (1992: 8):

> Globalization as a concept refers both to the compression of the world and the intensification of the consciousness of the world as a whole . . . both concrete global interdependence and consciousness of the global whole.

Here the compression of space is mentioned. Things that are at a distance as great as ever before are, because of technological developments, nearer in terms of the speed of communications and travel. We can see media from the other side of the world or communicate with someone there as if they are in the next room. This is also sometimes called the annihilation of space (Harvey 1991), where spatial distances no longer matter because of the possibility of communicating, moving and seeing over them fully and quickly. There is a cultural emphasis in Robertson's concern with consciousness of globality. As we will see in future chapters, consciousness of globalization is, for some, as important as the reality of it.

For Giddens (1990: 64):

> Globalization can . . . be defined as the intensification of world-wide social relations which link distant localities in such a way that local happenings are shaped by events occurring many miles away and vice-versa. This is a dialectical process because such local happenings may move in an obverse direction from the very distanciated relations that shape them. Local transformation is as much a part of globalization as the lateral extension of social connections across time and space.

Here worldwide relations are seen as becoming more intense, with a stress on the importance of interactions between the local and global, in which the local is not just shaped by globalization but may react to it in an alternative way.

Waters (2001: 5) sees globalization as a social process in which the constraints of geography on economic, political, social and cultural arrangements recede and people become increasingly aware of this and act accordingly. Like Holton, mentioned below, Waters sees globalization as a process rather than an end, and he emphasizes culture and consciousness and the effect it has on action.

Holton (2005) defines globalization as:

1 Interconnection – the intensified movement of goods, money, technology, information, people, ideas and cultural practices across political and cultural boundaries.
2 The interdependence of these activities across boundaries, and convergence and integration, for instance, in prices and markets. Globalization must be more than movement that is episodic, or involves few people (e.g., as in early trade), or has few consequences for those not involved in it.
3 Holton also sees globalization as involving consciousness and identification of the world as a single place, for instance, as in cosmopolitan culture, religions and environmentalism. There are overlaps here with Robertson's consciousness-focused definition.

4 Holton emphasizes agency and process in globalization, as opposed to it being seen as an external or fixed structure.

Held et al. (1999) have what they call a transformationalist view. This sees globalization as: new but not unprecedented; open-ended – it may go in many different directions; and varying in the form it takes by place and class and over time. This is compatible with local, regional and national relations continuing but interacting with globalization and taking global forms or forms affected by globalization. Globalization transforms human affairs by linking together and expanding human activity across regions and continents. It involves:

1 The *stretching* of activities across frontiers so activities in one part of the world have significance for others in distant regions. There is transregional interconnectedness and a widening of networks.
2 World relations become regularized with the consequence that there is an *intensification* or growing magnitude of interconnections, interactions and flows across societies and states.
3 The *speeding up* of global interactions and processes as a result of the development of transport and communications. The global diffusion of ideas, goods, information, capital and people is faster.
4 The *impact* of distant events is magnified. Local developments can have big global consequences, so the boundaries between domestic and global affairs become blurred.

Held et al. show that globalization is complex. It includes numerous processes rather than one activity or end, and involves both agency and structure, the input of actors into making it and external constraints on them. It is differentiated in the sense that it develops to different extents and in varying patterns in different areas. It is aterritorial, in that it can involve deterritorialization (where the stretching of activities goes beyond being coterminous with territories) but also reterritorialization (where globalization becomes established in regions and subnational areas, and even encourages nationalism). Some significant complexities and qualifications are added to the concept of globalization here.

Held et al. distinguish between *flows*, which are movements of things, people, symbols, tokens and information across space, from *networks*, which are regularized or patterned interactions. This involves an important distinction between things moving across space and those movements becoming established or even a system.

Held et al. also make some important qualifications about what globalization is not. They argue that globalization should not be confused with interdependence, integration, universalism or convergence. It is not interdependence because, they say, that involves symmetry rather than hierarchy and there is plenty of the latter in globalization; not integration because that implies shared community and that does not exist; not universalism because globalization is not shared by all people or communities in the same way; and not convergence because this assumes growing homogeneity and harmony, while globalization could lead to conflict.

So this is a complex definition of globalization with some similarity to the points voiced by sceptics about globalization. Some of the complexities and qualifications they add make what they describe something less than what others might see as globalization.

The historians Osterhammel and Petersson (2005) also stress regularization and stability in global relations as a prerequisite to globalization. They say that globalization is different from imperialism. While the idea of empire is revitalized in some concepts of globalization – for instance, those that stress American power – globalization is also more global and postcolonial. It includes the inputs of non-imperial sources, and involves the end of self-contained societies. They make the distinction between: (1) world history, which is the study of different civilizations, their internal dynamics and comparisons between them; (2) global history, which is the study of contacts and interactions between societies; and (3) globalization, which may grow out of some of those contacts and interactions.

Globalization grows where the contacts and interactions become networks and interaction spheres. Not all interactions become networks. This requires longevity, and sometimes institutional reinforcement so that they gain the sort of stability also found in hierarchical organizations. Osterhammel and Petersson say institutions such as diplomacy and trade help to turn interactions into networks. Other factors in globalization they mention include range, importance, intensity and speed. These are enabled by technology and organizational and institutional support. The durability and frequency of relations affects whether interactions become a stable network, and this can be restricted by space, or frozen or reversed. As such, globalization is a process rather than being fixed or static at one moment. For Osterhammel and Petersson, the features that fit their definition started about 1500 or so and became established in the mid-eighteenth and nineteenth centuries.

The concept summarized

When the definitions of globalization supplied by these authors are put together, what does it all add up to? Globalization involves the compression of space such that distance is less of a factor than it used to be in terms of knowledge, communication and movement. Geography and territory is undermined and things start to develop at a level that is more than, and above, inter-national relations. What more has to happen for this to become globalization?

1 Globalization needs to be *global in distance*. Long-distance or transnational extensions of economy, politics and culture that are regional are not global because they do not extend globally. It would be a lot to say that to be globalization something has to reach every part of the world but it is reasonable to say that it needs to reach all continents and most parts of those continents.

2 Globalization needs to be *globally inclusive in inputs* as well as reach. So something that extends ideas or products from one part of the world to another is merely the extension of one part of the world, e.g., Westernization. Again, it would be a lot to say that absolutely all parts of the world need to have an input of equal weight. But globalization, to be 'global', needs to have inputs from across continents and many countries within them, rather than be just a one-way or very unequal process from one place to another.

3 There needs to be *interdependency rather than just interconnection*. So, if a stoppage of trade in luxury goods such as jewels or silk has no significant repercussions, maybe this is not real inter-dependency. But if a decline in trade has significant effects for the exporting society's workers and economy, or for the access of the receiving society to goods, then there appears to be an interdependency.

4 There needs to be *stability and regularity* in relations so that, rather than being intermittent or temporary, these establish a structure or system.

5 Some other aspects could be added to make a more demanding concept of globalization – for example, that it needs to involve *more than elites and include the masses*, or that there needs to be not just globalization but also global *consciousness*. People need to not be just doing things globally but have an awareness of the globe as one place.

As we shall see when we look at the history of globalization and sceptical perspectives on globalization, the use of such criteria leads some to decide that what is taking place internationally is not globalization. At the same time these are tough criteria – it would be difficult for anything to ever match up to all of them fully. If you see globalization as a process moving towards such criteria, rather than as an end, then globalization may well be something that is going on.

Does defining globalization matter beyond the issue of just decid-ing when something is globalization or not? This is not just a question of academic definition. There are other things that make defining globalization important. One is that it ensures we see the power, inequality and conflict in globalization. Seeing some situa-tions as globalization – as inclusive, integrated, two-way and globally extended – gives an impression of inclusivity and equality that is inaccurate. Questioning whether phenomena meet the definition of globalization helps to show the power, inequality and lack of inclu-sion in the processes being outlined.

At the same time saying that certain things are not globalization, such as flows of capital or multinational corporations, is not to deny their existence or importance. What is being described by globalists may not be globalization but may still be happening and significant, and thus something which should be studied and analysed carefully. This is why globalization is important even if you don't think it is happening!

Practical note on reading chapters

You can read this book by looking at chapters on areas of most inter-est to you and not reading the others. However, while individual chapters stand alone they are overlapping and interlinked. To avoid repetition, I have sometimes only mentioned briefly in some places issues that are developed more in other chapters. At the same time, some issues are of such significance in more than one chapter that they are explained to some extent in more than one place.

Further Reading

The literature on globalization is enormous. I have not tried to give a full range of references in the chapters of the book. However, at the end of each chapter I have given some suggestions for further reading. These are primarily for those who are relatively new to globalization and would like to go a bit further on any of the topics.

Held et al.'s (1999) *Global Transformations* is quite an old book, but remains a substantive and complex introduction to areas of glo-balization, with a historical perspective and both theoretical and empirical information. It argues for a transformationalist perspec-tive, in between more globalist and sceptical views. It has a useful companion reader edited by Held and McGrew, *Global Transformations Reader* (2003).

Larry Ray's (2007) *Globalization and Everyday Life* is a more recent, compact discussion of some of the key themes in the sociology of globalization.

Robert Holton has written a number of books, such as *Globalization and the Nation-State* (1998), *Making Globalization* (2005), and *Global Networks* (2007), which illuminate issues in a concise way.

Scholte's *Globalization* is a good book at an introductory level. It is quite descriptive and I am not convinced by the case it makes for globalization, but it is useful as a starting point (2nd edn, 2005). Another short readable book that brings in key themes, with a cultural emphasis, is Malcolm Waters's *Globalization* (2nd edn, 2001).

The news magazine *The Economist* has a mostly neoliberal point of view, but is also fairly open-minded. It is very informative on international affairs. It includes coverage of economics, conflict, politics and poverty left out by some sociologies of globalization.

Sociological perspectives which have a cultural and positive view of globalization have been mentioned in this introduction. For a powerful critical view from a sociologist who brings in politics and economics whilst also paying attention to media and culture, see *Acts of Resistance* (1998), *The Weight of the World* (1999), and *Firing Back* (2003a), by the French writer Pierre Bourdieu.

Perspectives on Globalization: Divergence or Convergence?

PERSPECTIVES on globalization have been separated into four waves. Three waves initially identified in discussions of globalization were globalist, sceptical, and post-sceptical or transformationalist (e.g., Held et al. 1999 and Holton 2005). More recently it has been argued that there is a fourth perspective that goes beyond these. However, the three waves need to be looked at again rather than seen as redundant or out of touch. The fourth wave is important, but not as novel or effective as its advocates argue.

Contributors to the third wave defend the idea of globalization from criticism by second-wave sceptics. They also try to construct a more complex and qualified theory of globalization than provided by the first wave. But the third wave defends the idea of globalization while including qualifications that unwittingly reaffirm sceptical arguments. This has political implications. Third wavers propose globalist cosmopolitan democracy, but their arguments in practice bolster a sceptical view of politics. The latter involves inequality and conflict, nation-states and regional blocs, and alliances of common interest or ideology, rather than cosmopolitan global structures.

Globalization theory, seen to have emerged about the 1980s, is said to have begun with strong accounts of the globalization of economy, politics and culture, along with the sweeping away of the significance of territorial boundaries and national economies, states and cultures. Ohmae (1990, 1996) is often picked out as an example of this approach, and other proponents are said to include writers such as Reich (1992) and Albrow (1996), as well as discourses in the business world, media and politics (Hay and Marsh 2000: 4; one example is Blair 1997). The first wave in globalization theory is said to have a 'hyper' globalist account of the economy where national economies are much less significant, or even no longer exist, because of the free movement of capital, multinational corporations and economic interdependency. Reduced political restrictions on the movement of money and technological change in the form of the computerization of financial transactions, mean that large amounts of money can be moved almost instantly with little to constrain it within national boundaries. Many corporations are seen now to be multinational in their ownership and worldwide production facilities, workforces and consumers, from Coca-Cola and McDonald's to News Corporation. Consequently, the global economy has opened up, integrated and included more parts of the world, although whether this has been a positive thing or not is debated. Marxists and economic liberals have agreed that the world is globalized, while disagreeing on whether it is a good thing (e.g., Sklair 2002; Wolf 2004).

The globalist perspective is sometimes seen as economistic (Held et al. 1999: 3–4), with economic changes having political and cultural effects. Nation-states lose power and influence or even sovereignty because they tailor their policies to the needs of mobile capital. Social democracy and the welfare state are curtailed to fit in with the wishes of business interests (e.g., Gray 1996; Cerny and Evans 2004). Nation-states are superseded by international organizations such as the United Nations and International Monetary Fund, social movements that are global, or even a global civil society (e.g., Gill 2000; Keane 2003). Globalization is said to lead to homogenized or hybridized global cultures, where national differences become less marked as people consume culture from around the world rather than so exclusively from their own nation (e.g., Tomlinson 1999). This is facilitated by global electronic communications, such as the Internet, globalized TV broadcasts, migration and tourism. The role of new technologies has made globalization seem to some a relatively recent thing, perhaps of the post-1960s' or post-1980s' period (e.g., Scholte 2005). Economically, politically and culturally, globalists see transnational, global, forces taking over from nations as the main sources of economy, sovereignty and identity. For some, this means that social science has to move away from methodological nationalism, even from ideas of society, to more cosmopolitan and global perspectives on social relations (e.g., Beck 2006; Urry 2000; but see a response from Outhwaite 2006).

Then, it is said by writers on the three waves, there was a more sober set of accounts. These reacted with scepticism to argue that globalization is not new and that the processes being described are not very global either (e.g., Hirst and Thompson 1996; Krugman 1996). Sceptics argue that globalist perspectives can be quite abstract and thin on empirical substantiation, making sweeping claims about processes as if they affect all areas of the world evenly and with the same responses. The sceptics see evidence of the continuing role of nation-states, within their own boundaries and as agents of globalization, through which they both maintain and lose power. In the case of core countries, for instance in North America and Europe, states continue to be very powerful in global affairs. National identities have a history and a hold on popular imagination that global identities cannot replace, evolving rather than being swept away. There may even be evidence of a resurgence of nationalism as old nations come under challenge, but from strongly held smaller nationalisms, for instance in the former Yugoslavia, Sri Lanka and Canada, as much as from transnationalism (e.g., see Smith 1990; Kennedy and Danks 2001).

Sceptics want to test the claims of globalism against evidence, and when they have done so have sometimes found it wanting. They are also concerned to see whether globalization is received evenly and with the same response everywhere and, not surprisingly, have found signs of differentiation in its spread. Sceptics tend to see the global economy as not globally inclusive. For instance, areas of sub-Saharan Africa are much less integrated than the powerhouses of East Asia, Europe and North America. Global inequality is rising and protectionism still rife, for example, in Europe and the USA in response to imports from growing Asian economies. As we shall see, sceptics argue that the global economy is inter-nationalized and triadic rather than global, and that its internationalization in recent years is not unprecedented. In fact, it may even have been more internationalized a hundred years ago than now. It is questioned whether globalization or free trade, insofar as it really is free, is the answer to global poverty. Liberal policies and integration into the global economy may have helped some parts of the world, such as China, India and other parts of Asia. But in these places protectionism and state intervention have also been part of their success. Other parts of the world, Africa, for example, have fallen prey to greater inequality and poverty while globalization has progressed. They are increasingly less likely to stand a chance against stronger competitors in the open global economy which some see as the solution to their problems (e.g., Wolf and Wade 2002; Kaplinsky 2005).

Politically, the effects of globalization are uneven – states have gained as well as lost power in processes of globalization. Many states are more powerful than others globally and some are able to continue with more social democratic policies despite hyperglobalist perspectives that see globalization requiring compliance with neoliberalism (Mann 1997; Mosley 2005). This suggests nation-states retain autonomy and sovereignty in some ways, and unevenly so. Bodies like the UN seem to be as much inter-national as transnational, composed of nation-states and driven by them. Global bodies can be seen as being determined by the balance between competing interests as much as above such interests. This happens in cases of global governance from the UN Security Council to agreements on global warming, nuclear proliferation and international justice. The UN is seen as the tool of the most powerful nations, who bypass or exempt themselves from its rules when it doesn't suit them, and who use such bodies to impose their will for their own benefit when it does (Zolo 1997, 2002).

Culturally, it is said that nations respond to globalization differently. McDonald's may have proliferated around the world, but the ingredients vary to fit in with local customs (from shrimp burgers in Japan to kosher burgers for Jewish customers). Depending on location, the consumers of individual outlets are either mainly working class or middle class, while eating customs vary from fast to leisurely in different contexts. From France to parts of the Middle East not everyone responds positively to the globalization of American culture. In fact, in some places, a retreat to fundamentalism and greater rather than less nationalism are seen to be notable reactions to globalization (Robins 1997). It is the culture of one nation, America, that is often talked about in relation to cultural globalization, as much as culture originating from all around the world (Beck et al. 2003). As such it is not very global. There have even been (flawed) predictions of clashes of culture arising from globalization, against hyperglobalist assumptions about the homogenization or hybridization of culture (Barber 1996; Huntington 1996).

There has been another set of reactions alongside and in response to the sceptics. There are those who share the concerns of the sceptics about evidence and differentiation but despite this can't help but see globalization before their eyes, moving ahead at unprecedented levels in recent times. Economic interdependency, for instance, is seen as having grown significantly so that national economies are no longer contained within national territorial boundaries. Third-wavers have been keen to critically reassess the claims of globalism, but without throwing the baby out with the bathwater (e.g., Held et al. 1999, and Held and McGrew 2003, who call themselves 'transformationalists'). The outcome of this has been a departure from some conclusions of sceptics, with instead a more complex picture of globalization in which globalization is seen to occur without just sweeping all away, as hyperglobalists have pictured it.

The global nature of structures such as finance, environmental problems, drugs and crime, and developments in international communications and transport, have led to more global political forms. National economic, political and cultural forces are transformed and have to share their sovereignty with other entities of global governance and international law, as well as with mobile capital, multinational corporations and global social movements. But they are not removed. Globalization may have a differentiated effect depending on type (e.g., economic, cultural or political) or location where it is experienced, while still being a force. Global inequality is seen as having moved from a simple core-periphery shape to more of a three-tier structure, including a middle group of more successful economies from Brazil to China. All of these involve both the continuation and transformation of existing structures, something in between what is described by sceptics and hyperglobalists.

Globalization's future may be uncertain and open-ended. It could take different forms (perhaps more neoliberal or more social democratic) or even be reversed, rather than the future being unavoidable globalization or just continuity with unaffected nation-state structures. With recognition of uncertainty comes an acknowledgement of the importance of agency in deciding what happens to globalization, rather than an assumption that it is predetermined or inevitable as suggested in some first-wave accounts (Holton 2005).

In short, the third-wave contributions are critical of hyperglobalism and wish to formulate a more sophisticated picture but feel, contrary to scepticism, that globalization is changing the world. They do not go as far as the sceptics in that they say that real significant changes have happened. Third-wavers acknowledge the reality of globalizing changes and so defend a globalist position but one that is modified to be more complex than that of the hyperglobalists.

Table 1.1 summarizes the three waves. These are models. Individual contributors do not always fit only into one wave, and, as we shall see, although the third wave presents itself in one way, when looked at more closely it seems to actually reinforce the sceptical wave it seeks to criticize. So the emphasis in this table is on models of the three waves. The reality of this is explored subsequently (see also Held et al. 1999: 10).

Beyond the second wave?

Kofman and Youngs (1996) made an early outline of perspectives on globalization but discussed two waves rather than three. In their outline, transformationalist and sceptical views are combined. This relates to a problem I wish to highlight, that third-wave theories reinforce the scepticism they seek to undermine. I will focus here more (but not only) on economic and political dimensions of globalization that are a main emphasis of authors I am looking at here and will discuss cultural dimensions more fully in chapters 3 and 4.

The first wave is seen by those in the second and third waves as exaggerating the extent of globalization, and arguing for globalization in an abstract and generalizing way which does not account enough for

Table 1.1 Three waves in globalization theory			
	Globalists	Sceptics	Transformationalists
Globalization	Globalization; globalization as causal.	Globalization is a discourse; internationalization as effect of other causes.	Global transformations, but differentiation and embeddedness.
Method	Abstract, general approach.	Empirical approach.	Qualitative rather than quantitative approach.
Economy	Global economy; integration, open; free trade.	International economy; triadic, regional, unequal; state intervention and protectionism.	Globally transformed; new stratification; globalized but differentiated.
Politics	Global governance or neoliberalism; decline of nation-state; loss of national sovereignty.	Nation-states, regional blocs, international; power and inequality; political agency possible.	Politics globally transformed; nation-states important but reconstructed; sovereignty shared
Culture	Homogenization.	Clashes of culture; nationalism; Americanization; globalization differentiated.	Globally transformed; hybridization; complex, differentiated globalization.
History	Globalization is new.	Internationalization is old.	Globalization old but present forms unprecedented.
Normative politics	Global governance or neoliberalism; end of social democratic welfare state.	Reformist social democracy and international regulation possible.	Cosmopolitan democracy.
Future	Globalization	Nation-state, triad, conflicts, inequality.	Uncertain, agency; left or right; continued, stalled or reversed.

empirical evidence or unevenness and agency in globalization. Third-wave theorists try to distance themselves from both more radical globalists and outright sceptics. They defend an idea of globalization, and so distance themselves from the sceptics. But they do so in a more complicated way than put forward in the first wave. However, in doing this they add qualifications and complexities that actually bolster second-wave sceptic arguments. This is not always the case and there are some differences between third-wavers and sceptics. But if it transpires that third-wavers are confirming the second wave, intentionally or not, then it is important that the sceptical view is validated rather than seen as less adequate. Getting a correct understanding of what the third wave is actually saying is important to understanding globalization properly.

There are political implications to this. In reaching globalist conclusions, albeit more complex ones, and arguing they have shown the flaws in scepticism, third-wavers like Held et al. conclude that globalist forms of politics such as cosmopolitan democracy, discussed in chapter 10, are the most appropriate way for directing globalization along more progressive paths. This is against the sceptical analysis of politics that has a more realistic view of a world where such global forms are not possible. This is because of the superior power of advanced states, especially rich core states, the conflicting interests and ideologies of global actors, and the importance of politics at the level of nation-states, regional blocs and other alliances.

Sceptics stress power, inequality, conflict and the importance of the nation-state. These point to a politics other than, or in addition to, global democracy. This might involve states. Or it could involve alliances below the global level between states with similar objectives or interests, for instance a shared antipathy to neoliberalism or US imperialism, and with global social movements that have related objectives. This is rather than, or as well as, global universal structures in which common agreement may not be possible and which are liable to being hijacked by more powerful actors. If third-wave analysis leads more in the direction of the sceptics' findings than it says it does then an analysis of global power inequalities and nation-state power in political strategy, of the sort highlighted by the sceptics, should become more part of the picture and the outlook for global democracy seems more problematic.

To look at the implications that third-wave arguments have for the second wave, I need to set out in more detail some of the claims of the second wave. Hirst and Thompson (1996) are frequently cited as leading proponents of the sceptical point of view and have engaged directly in discussions with third-wavers, for instance in Paul Hirst's debate with David Held (Held and Hirst 2002).

Hirst and Thompson's analysis of globalization claims are mainly economic and use empirical data to test an ideal type of globalization. The ideal type they use is, they say, an extreme one. But it represents what globalization would be if it were occurring, and they say it is one that shapes discussions in business and political circles. What are their main points? (See Hirst and Thompson 1996: ch. 1.)

- There has been internationalization of financial markets, technology and some sections of manufacturing and services, especially since the 1970s. This puts constraints on radical policies being pursued by national governments. Internationalization allows investment to flee across national boundaries more easily, something it may well do if confronted with a radical left government where it is invested.

- The current internationalized economy is not unprecedented. The international economy was more open between 1870 and 1914, its international dimensions are contingent and have been interrupted or reversed in the past. Hirst and Thompson's data shows high levels of trade and migration before 1914, much of which was reversed in the interwar period, showing how globalization is not going along an evolutionary or predetermined path, but one that can stop or go into reverse.

- Greater international trade and investment is happening but within existing structures rather than as part of a new global economic structure. What is happening is between nations, i.e., international, especially between dominant states or regions, rather than something which has extended globally or gone above and beyond nations or the international or inter-regional.

- Transnational corporations (TNCs) are rare. Most companies are nationally based and trade multinationally (i.e., MNCs rather than TNCs). There is no major tendency towards truly global companies. A company may be based in one country and sell its goods or services abroad. But this makes it a national company operating in the international marketplace, rather than a global company.

- Foreign direct investment (FDI) is concentrated amongst advanced industrial economies, rather than any massive shift of investment and employment occurring towards third world countries. The latter remain marginal in trade. Exceptions to this are some newly industrializing countries (NICs) in Latin American and East Asia.

- The world economy is not global. Trade, investment and financial flows are concentrated in the triad of Europe, Japan and North America. Something that falls so short of being inclusive on a worldwide scale cannot be seen as a global economy.

- The G3 have the capacity to exert economic governance over financial markets but choose not to for reasons of ideology and economic interest. They have an ideological commitment to unfettered finance or find that they benefit from it. This is the reason for any restraint in economic governance rather than because it is impossible. States, by themselves, or in regional or international collaborations have the capacity to regulate the global economy and pursue reformist policies if they choose to do so.

- Radical expansionary and redistributive national economic management is not possible because of domestic and international requirements, such as norms that need to be met to satisfy international financial markets. Capital would flee if governments were to pursue policies that were too radically socialist. Governments and other actors have to behave differently because of internationalization. But globalization theory leads to excessive fatalism, and the injunction that neoliberalism is unavoidable because of globalization is as much ideological as an actual inevitability. Politicians say that neoliberalism is inevitable as much to justify policies they are ideologically committed to as because they really are inevitable. Reformist strategies at national and international level are possible, using existing institutions and practices.

Hirst and Thompson argue that in some respects the world economy *is* very internationalized (see also Hirst and Thompson 2000 on the 'over-internationalization' of the British economy). But they use the word 'internationalization' rather than 'globalization' and argue that evidence of the former is used to justify claims about the latter. They see the world as internationalized rather than globalized because of conclusions such as those mentioned above: for instance, that there are distinct national economies and companies; that internationalization of the economy is restricted to advanced economies and the triad rather than being worldwide; and that internationalization is happening within existing structures rather than creating new global ones that go beyond national or inter-national structures.

Let us look now at the third perspective on globalization. This tries to maintain a globalist outlook, one that does not retreat from globalist claims as the sceptics do, but that attempts to outline a more complex globalism than the one outlined by the first wave of hyperglobalists.

Held et al. – transformationalists, a modified globalism

I am focusing here on Held et al.'s transformationalism. Held et al. distance themselves from the sceptics. But they also argue that globalization is more complex and uncertain than first-wave hyperglobalists claim. Held et al. advance a third perspective, transformationalism, which outlines a more complex picture of globalization (e.g., Held et al. 1999; Held and Hirst 2002; and Held and McGrew 2003).

Elements in Held et al.'s arguments go in different directions. They defend globalization theory by putting forward a modified version of it. But the qualifications and complexities they add confirm claims of the sceptics. As such, they do not undermine scepticism or support globalization as much as is claimed. Let us look at examples of what Held et al. set out as the transformationalist position and at what they criticize about scepticism. According to the transformationalist position (Held et al. 1999: 7–14):

- Contemporary globalization is part of a long-term historical process but is unprecedented. There was trade and migration, for instance between Asia, the Middle East and fringes of Europe, in pre-modern times. But technological and political changes since the Second World War have led to an unprecedented growth in the extent, velocity, volume and intensity of, for example, global media communications, economic interdependency between countries and international political organizations.
- Globalization involves transformative change and is a driving force behind changes reshaping the world. There are not clear distinctions between the domestic and the international in economic, social and political processes. For instance, aspects of national culture such as media, film, religion, food, fashion and music are infused with inputs from international sources so that national culture is no longer separate from the international. This is a transformatory driving force because this globalization changes people's life experiences.
- Economies are becoming deterritorialized, global and transnational. This is happening through, for example, the mobility of capital across national boundaries, the role of multinational corporations and interdependency between different nations' economies.
- While they are legally sovereign, nation-states' powers, functions and authority are being reconstituted by international governance and law, by global ecological, transportation and communications developments, and by non-territorial organizations such as multinational corporations (MNCs) and transnational social movements. The nation-state is not a self-governing, autonomous unit and authority is diffused. Held et al. also say that states have become more activist and their power is not necessarily diminished but is being reconstituted. This is unlike the globalists' claim that nation-state sovereignty has ended, or what is regarded as the sceptics' position that nothing much has changed.
- Territorial boundaries are still important but the idea that they are the primary markers of modern life is more problematic.

Economic, social and political activities are locally rooted but become disembedded from territory or reterritorialized in new forms of localization and nationalization. So a company may have roots in a particular territorial area but become detached when its workforce is internationally located or its products sold internationally. It is reterritorialized in the new places the workforce is located or where its products are tailored for markets in different areas. Types of music start off from a locality but can become disembedded as they are performed or sold globally, or take on global influences. They influence or spread into other types of music globally, or to other national places where fusions of music then create new forms of local or national culture in that area, i.e., new forms of localization and nationalization.

- Transformationalists say they do not reduce the world to a single, fixed, ideal type, as other perspectives do, and that they recognize it is contradictory and contingent. They feel that globalists and sceptics reduce the world to global or non-global types respectively, without realizing how contradictory it is, with aspects of both types alongside middle elements where, for example, cultures may stay national but what the 'national' is becomes changed by global inputs – so a mixture of the national *and* global. And they see globalists or sceptics as suggesting inevitabilities when whether the world becomes more or less global is not predetermined but is open to going in different possible directions.
- Sceptics are said to see the world as a singular process when actually it is differentiated with different patterns in different areas of life. So, for instance, some types of globalization (e.g., finance) may be more globalized than others (e.g., corporations), and some countries in the world (for instance, those with more inward investment) may experience the impact of global finance more than others.
- Held et al. argue that sceptics are empiricist because statistical evidence is taken to confirm, qualify or reject the globalization thesis when more qualitative evidence and interpretive analysis is needed. Migration or trade, for example, may (arguably) be no more globalized now than in the *belle époque*, in terms of quantitative indicators such as value of goods exchanged or numbers of people on the move. But the qualitative impact of migration and trade on economies, politics and culture could be greater. Quantitative indicators of limited change do not necessarily demonstrate lack of qualitative impact.
- There is a global system that most societies are part of, but not

global convergence or a single world society. National societies and systems are enmeshed in interregional networks. But
this is different from global integration, which does not exist,
because it implies too much singularity, and from convergence, which would involve homogeneity. For example, there
is global economic interdependency but that does not mean
there is convergence on economic factors such as prices or
interest rates.

- Globalization involves new patterns of stratification across
  and within societies, some becoming enmeshed and some
  marginalized but in new configurations that differ from the
  old core-periphery of North–South and first world–third world
  classifications. It follows that globalization is not universalization because globalization is not experienced to the same
  extent by all people. In place of the core-periphery model of
  global inequality there is now one that shows a middle group
  of developing countries in Latin America and Asia. These have
  grown significantly and become more integrated into the
  global economy, so lifting themselves out of the periphery.
  But others, some African countries, for example, have become
  more left out. So a bipolar model is replaced by a more complex
  stratification with greater inclusion of some but also exclusion
  along with greater polarization between the top and bottom,
  revealing the uneven effect of globalization.

- Transformationalists claim that, unlike hyperglobalists and
  sceptics, they recognize the direction of globalization is uncertain rather than teleological and linear with a given end-state.
  Instead of globalization being destined to sweep ahead, or the
  status quo being the predetermined future, transformationalists say that what will happen internationally is open and could
  go in a number of directions, depending on factors such as the
  choices of big corporations and governments or the influence
  of civil society and social movements.

- Government strategies for dealing with the globalized world
  are said to include neoliberalism, the developmental or catalytic state, as well as more outward-looking approaches based
  on international regulation, an approach to government action
  favoured by global cosmopolitan democrats such as Held et
  al. (Held and McGrew 2002). The openness in the paths that
  globalization could take in the future mean governments have
  a number of options to influence that direction, including
  economic liberalism, greater state intervention in guiding the
  future of economies and societies, or global governance of the
  world economy and global problems.

Transformationalists and sceptics compared

How much does this transformationalist third wave rescue globalization in a modified form and undermine the sceptics? Let us go through some of Held et al.'s points.

There are differences between the transformationalists and sceptics: on definition (should the processes they see be defined as internationalization or globalization?); on history (is current globalization unprecedented or the period between 1870 and 1914 the most globalized?); and proposals (divergence between seeing nation-states and international blocs or global democracy as the bases for future political action).

Hirst and Thompson are accused of attacking an ideal type to undermine the case for globalization. Hirst and Thompson agree this is what they do. But their ideal type is what globalization would be if it existed, and they use it to assess whether it does. This seems right if you are testing the extent of globalization. But I want to leave aside models and compare what Hirst and Thompson say *is* going on in the world – internationalization – with what Held et al. say is happening, i.e., global transformation. Then we can see if there are differences in their understanding of the world. We can do this by going through the transformationalist points outlined above.

Held et al. say that contemporary globalization is historically unprecedented but that there are earlier pre-modern forms of globalization. This means there are precedents for globalization but none as intense, extensive, fast and of such great volume and impact as at present. Sceptics and transformationalists agree that globalization is long-running. But there is a difference between Hirst and Thompson's view that its heyday was the 1870–1914 period and that it is less intense now, and Held et al.'s view that the current period is the most advanced.

Held et al. argue that there are not clear differences between domestic and international processes. This is something sceptics agree with. As can be seen from the summary of the sceptics' position above, they see domestic economies as internationalized, for instance, in terms of finance, trade and investment. Where there is a difference is on whether international processes are characterized as 'global' or not. But their view of the interpenetration of the national and international does not mark transformationalism off from scepticism.

Held et al. argue that economies are becoming deterritorialized, global and transnational. This sounds like a more radical position than that of the sceptics, but they qualify this with the view that territorial boundaries are still important. Economic, social and political activities are locally rooted and become territorially disembedded or reterritorialized in new forms of localization and nationalization. How different is this from the sceptic position that there are national economies trading internationally, and companies with local bases whose production, trading and investment activities go on beyond this location? The emphasis on deterritorialization and disembeddedness goes beyond the sceptical position, but the idea of rootedness and reterritorialization reaffirms rather than rejects sceptical arguments.

The view of nation-states that Held et al. have is of agents, legally sovereign with their power as much reconstituted as diminished, who are activist, but with authority diffused, and lacking self-governing autonomous powers. For example, a nation-state may have reconstituted itself as a part of regional and international organizations, resulting in both its authority and self-governing power being diminished by this and by global economic pressures. But it is still legally sovereign, taking an active role in reconstituting itself in a more globalized world in a way which maintains or enhances its powers. This is said to be unlike the sceptic position that nothing much has changed. However, this distinction from the sceptical position is problematic for three reasons.

First, the claim that nothing has changed is not one that the sceptics make. They say a lot has changed, in the *belle époque* period, and the 1970s and 1980s, but that this does not mean we live in a globalized era. They argue that there have been big transformations in the international economy, although within existing structures. Companies have to act differently and the norms of international financial markets restrict what it is possible for nation-states to do, for instance, ruling out radical macro-economic policies.

Second, sceptics agree that nation-states lack complete sovereignty and have to share this. For instance, they outline the role of international organizations, international finance and constraints on radical redistributional politics. Their qualification is that this is not new and is partly reversible. But they agree there is not clear sovereignty and that this has to be shared.

Third, they agree with the view of the activist state. But the transformationalists' emphasis on this gives credence to the sceptic case that nation-states are important actors on the world stage, with the power at national and international levels to determine the form that globalization takes. Sceptics argue that nation-states have the autonomy to affect the future of globalization. Held et al.'s outline of alternative strategies, such as neoliberalism, the developmental state, the catalytic state and cosmopolitan democracy, reinforces the view that nation-states have some autonomy and power to determine the future, in the way that Hirst and Thompson argue. Transformationalists and sceptics are not in complete harmony on the role of the nation-state in the global or international world. But qualifications in the transformationalist analysis affirm arguments of the sceptical case as much as rebutting them.

For Held et al., one difference between transformationalists and sceptics is that the former recognize the multidimensional, contingent and contradictory nature of the world and its uncertain direction, whereas sceptics see it as singular and linear with a given end-state. But this misinterprets the sceptics. Hirst and Thompson argue that internationalization has varying effects in different parts of the world, with much activity concentrated in advanced economies, while other areas of the world are less integrated. They state that internationalization is not linear but is subject to reversals, such as that after the *belle époque*. They argue that the idea that globalization is predetermined and inevitable is a myth used to justify neoliberal policies, the reality being that nation-states, individually or organized internationally, have the power to alter the course of internationalization. The claim of difference from scepticism made by transformationalists is based on a misunderstanding of what sceptics say. What transformationalists argue on these points seems to be in accordance with the sceptics and to confirm rather than undermine their case.

Finally, transformationalists argue that there is a single global system in which all societies are enmeshed, something that appears to differ from the sceptic position that claims significant activity in the international economy is concentrated in the triad of Japan, the EU and North America, with some NICs up and coming into this sphere, and other parts of the world much less integrated. However, the differences are smaller when it is considered that transformationalists outline a situation in which, while there is a world system, there is not global convergence or a single world society, that they see stratification across and within societies involving some becoming enmeshed and some marginalized, and in which globalization is not universal because it is not experienced to the same extent by all. The unevenness of integration into the global system comes closer to confirming rather than breaking with the sceptics' outline, which leads the latter to the conclusion there is no global economy because of such patterns of inclusion and exclusion.

The politics of globalization

So, attempts to rebut scepticism and defend a modified globalism seem to actually share ground with the sceptics' analysis. This raises doubts about the reality of globalization and reaffirms sceptical claims. Rhetorically, transformationalists are stronger in defending globalism, despite such commonality with the sceptics, and this may be partly what leads to one area of significant difference. Transformationalists remain committed to a globalist outlook, and their prescriptions of a politics which can respond to globalization puts strong emphasis on cosmopolitan global democracy (see Archibugi and Held 1995; Held 1995; Archibugi 2004). This involves global political fora in which different communities and interests participate to reach agreements on issues which have a global character and cannot be solved purely at national levels. Human rights and war, ecological problems, drugs and crime, economic instability and inequality are seen as global rather than national, and require global coordination or interventions to be solved. Cosmopolitans look to global fora or international interventions, based in global cosmopolitan consciousness, to solve such problems.

Sceptics whose analysis does not lead to globalist conclusions do not share this faith in global politics (for example, see Zolo 1997 and 2002). Sceptics do not believe that powerful Western states will be willing to put up with the political equalization that global democracy would allow. They will resist political equality and inclusivity and try to maintain their superior power in global fora. They will use global politics against others when in their interests and evade being subjected to it where it is against their interests. There are conflicts of interest and ideology, and over resources, between nation-states, increasing as a consequence of problems such as climate change. Solutions to global problems would have to involve the interests or ideologies of some being favoured, while those of others were opposed. There are no win–win solutions to such problems. So conflict is more likely in global politics and the cooperative consciousness on which cosmopolitanism relies is unlikely.

An example of these issues has been the role of the USA in international politics. It has tried to maintain its power against equality in international institutions (e.g., in the UN Security Council) and has used those international institutions as a basis for pursuing its interests against others, but has exempted itself or bypassed them when they are not supportive (e.g., in the war against Iraq). It has supported or undermined international agreements (e.g., on global warming, international justice and rights, and nuclear proliferation) on a selective basis, depending on its ideology and interests. A sceptical view, that sees the international sphere as important but affected by power, inequality and conflicting interests, suggests that global cosmopolitan politics is unlikely.

Cosmopolitans are well intentioned and right to be concerned about issues such as ecology, rights and inequality. They are correct to see such problems as global and often requiring transnational solutions. But if cosmopolitan politics is unlikely or undesirable for the reasons mentioned what might an alternative political solution of such issues involve?

For sceptics, the future lies in nation-states acting alone, or, because such problems are transnational, acting together multilaterally – for instance, in regional blocs or alliances of the like-minded rather than globally. This involves not universal or global agreements, but bilaterally and multilaterally agreed blocs and alliances between those with shared objectives, interests and ideologies. It may be better for states and other political actors to ally transnationally with actors who are like-minded and have shared interests, rather than trying for cosmopolitan consciousness at a global level where many have opposed interests and ideologies and are more powerful. This is a politics that works more with the reality of divisions, antagonism and state alliances than the global commonality and agreement required for global cosmopolitan democracy. Such alliances could be forged, for instance, between states or movements that see themselves as anti-neoliberal or anti-imperialist, such as left-wing governments in Latin America and other places, the non-aligned movement, or the global justice movement (e.g., see Gill 2000; Gills 2000; Motta 2006).

International institutions exist and have to be engaged with, so such actors should participate in them. But these institutions also represent particular as much as global universal interests and are seen as a tool for the powerful as much as for equality and democracy. As such, politics has to operate outside as well as inside such institutions, with agents forming alliances with each other using what resources they have (e.g., energy resources and human expertise) for mutual assistance, in a politics of conflict (rather than cosmopolitan universality) against powerful forces where these preserve inequality or lack of democracy, or are amongst those who transgress human rights and whose policies lead to ecological problems or war.

This politics is neither statist nor globally centralist (although it uses both levels). It does not ally scepticism about cosmopolitan politics with anti-interventionism, pacifism or inertia. It favours activism and intervention transnationally in issues of global concern and relevance, but through recognition of conflict because these issues involve conflicting rather than common interests and objectives. This can be done internationally beyond the state through bilateral and multilateral blocs of actors with common agendas and interests where they exist, or can be forged, rather than through either the isolated state or global universals. This is an alternative to both statism and centralism/globalism, operating at both these levels but also at a level in between of conflictual politics and selective transnational multilateralism.

The differences between sceptics' and transformationalists' political prescriptions stem more from the transformationalists' globalist conclusions than from the substance of their arguments which in practice often share similar ground with the sceptical approach. Transformationalists give a picture of: unevenness of integration; inequality, stratification and power; nation-states (albeit reconstituted ones) for whom there are different possible activist strategies; and reterritorialization and regional blocs. On this basis, the politics of cosmopolitan global democracy they favour seems unlikely. Their analysis shows up inequalities and conflicts that would make it difficult for global agreements to be realized. These are often between nation-states that remain, according to their outline, powerful actors. The more appropriate political conclusion from such a picture of the world order is one which recognizes inequality and conflict, nation-states and regional or multilateral like-minded blocs, as identified by sceptics as more likely structures in future politics.

The fourth wave in globalization theory

For some, the three waves debate is old hat. What matters is less what is happening in the world and more globalization as a discourse or ideational development (Cameron and Palan 2004; Bruff 2005; Scholte 2005). What we *think* about globalization is more important than globalization itself. We interpret the world as globalizing, whether it is or not. This may even have a self-fulfilling effect. Because we think the world is globalizing we act as if it is. Globalization then has an ideational force on us. Furthermore it starts to happen when we behave in a globalized way because of what we think as much as because of what is actually there. Whether globalists, sceptics or transformationalists have got it right in describing globalization is not that important. The fourth wave in globalization theory analyses globalization as a discourse.

This approach is influenced by post-structuralist, postmodern and social constructionist perspectives, as well as by the work of thinkers like Foucault. Post-structuralism and postmodernism emphasize the role of symbols and consciousness of the world as much as the world itself. The emphasis is on signifiers (the symbols which signify something) as much as on signifieds (the objects the signifiers refer to). What we experience and so believe and act upon is in discourses or ideas about society, which mediate between us and the world, and, in effect, are the world itself as far as we experience it. It is from discourses that we know the world or through which our experience of the world is constructed.

For Foucault, discourses such as psychiatry or medicine create bodies of knowledge through which we interpret and understand society and which consequently constitute the world for us (e.g., Foucault 1979). So knowledge and those who construct and control it, psychiatrists and doctors, for instance, are very powerful. The labelling of mental illness or homosexuality, for example, provides categories for making sense of the world. People only become mentally ill or gay when discourses classify them in these ways. Before such discourses and classifications were used to label people in these ways madness and homosexuality were not understood and so effectively did not exist as such.

This signifies a shift from economic and political perspectives on globalization to ideational ones. Symbols, consciousness and cultures are seen to have their own force rather than being determined purely by, for instance, the capitalist economy. Ideas are detached from politics and economics, having an autonomy and power of their own. So discourse approaches involve in part a reaction against economic determinism. The ideational perspective is idealist as opposed to materialist in terms of where it sees causality coming from and plays a greater role in understanding globalization for such disciplines as anthropology, media studies and sociology than for disciplines such as economics and political science. The former put more of a stress on subjective meanings in explaining social life, as well as studying objective structures themselves.

From this point of view, one of the key developments in the history of globalization was the popularization of the idea of globalization itself in the 1980s onwards as much as any actual processes of globalization. This was more important than whether globalization started in the pre-modern era, with capitalism, after the Second World War or whenever. When we developed a consciousness of globalization, rather than globalization itself, is the important thing. At this point people started to move away from national identities to global identities, and global imaginings led to globalization. People interpreted the world as globalized and acted in accordance with this.

There is a parallel with nationalism. Nationalism as an idea helped to promote territorialist ideas of the world and the nation-state. Nations are imagined communities (Anderson 2006). People believe in nations and national identities. When we look for criteria that define a nation or national identity we often think of aspects such as shared history, language, religion or ethnic identity. Yet there is no nation in the world that has a single shared form of any of these. All nations have members who come from different parts of the world originally and so have different histories through their ancestors. All have more than one language, even if one is dominant, and are multi-religious or multi-ethnic. So nations are artificial constructions that hold together because we believe in them as myths rather than because of an objective reality to them. They are discourses rather than realities. And the discourse constructs us as nations.

The key argument is that with the arrival of a discourse of globalization, it becomes a new symbolic experience. Having more plural and hybrid identities made up of sources from around the world, which make us think of ourselves more as people with global identities than national ones, allows other things to develop – such as global governance. If we see ourselves as having global identities we can identify more easily with such global forms. Here global imaginings precede and help constitute substantive globalization. Ideational types underpin political and economic forms of globalization.

However, discourses of globalization may be based more in real globalization and economic and political interests than arguments that stress their autonomy and power to construct the world allow. The idea of globalization is facilitated by real globalizing developments that make discourses of globalization and the idea of global identity a possibility – migration, global media and the Internet, for example. These enable us to have identities which are diasporic or hybrid, or not connected to nationality or multi-nationality at all – e.g., as a woman, a member of the peace movement, a worker, religion or our sexuality, for instance – and they bring us into touch with identities, culture and media beyond the national level. So real developments of globalization facilitate the discourse of globalization.

Here a discourse of globalization is based in the reality of globalization, rather than it being purely ideational. The social constructionist idea about the world being made in our discourses about it, rather than in objective reality, can also be allied with a power analysis as it is in Foucault's theories. Discourses of reality determine what can be known and how we know the world. So constructions of globality determine how we make sense of the world and act within it. Power over discursive constructions is an enormous power to have. It is power over truth. Foucault saw this as positive rather than negative power, or power over life rather than over death, because it creates the categories through which we positively make sense of the world rather than being a prohibitive power as law and the judiciary are. For some, this power over the mode of production of ideas is more important than ownership of the means of production of material things that Marx highlighted. The former may have taken over from the latter in importance in what is sometimes called a post-industrial or information society (Kumar 2004).

Discourses about global neoliberalism lead business people and politicians to see the world as governed by the movement of capital and multinational corporations, and to make business or policy decisions in accordance with these apparent structures and imperatives. For instance, politicians may lower business taxes or weaken regulations to protect workers and the environment because they believe the world is constituted by the free movement of capital and that they need to take such neoliberal policy decisions to keep capital in their country.

There is a danger in putting forward ideational perspectives over economic ones. Discourse theories are often set up as a sophisticated step forward from crude outmoded economic determinism. But economics may be the decisive factor that brings ideational discourse to the fore. Economic expansionism creates global media and structures on which global imaginings are based and from which they also develop. There is real globalization behind the idea of globalization as much as the idea constituting reality. It may be a desire to expand business opportunities abroad that leads corporate leaders to stress globalization and free trade as a necessity we must go along with. There are ideational drivers to globalization but they are based in material economic expansionism or interests.

Economic liberalism, for instance, or global human rights, are ideas that justify Western expansionism, economically or politically. Furthermore, they disguise something beneath the surface of what they say. For example, economic liberalism involves a huge discrepancy between more wealthy and powerful nations and those less so. Free trade gives the richer and more powerful the freedom to compete openly with those at a large competitive disadvantage to them. So free and open trade disguises something less than free and open. Global human rights involve Western and individualist values (which, as with free trade, Western advocates adhere to inconsistently, depending on whether it favours their interests or not). Other parts of the world stress collectivist or economic ideas of rights, such as the right to food and water, more than individual or political rights. Or they see other values, such as collective obligations or economic equality, as above individual rights. So what appears to be a universal idea that stresses the rights of all disguises a Western idea that contrasts with alternative values in non-Western societies. Global human rights, important as they are, disguise their own lack of globality and rights.

Globalization involves economic and/or political projects to which meanings are attached to gain the consent or acquiescence of groups in society, legitimating or justifying them through categories such as 'globalization'. So they are rooted in underlying political-economic objectives and interests. As we have just seen, some disguise inequalities and power as equality and freedom.

If discourses and political-economic relations were put into a causal hierarchy where you saw which was rooted in the other you may find that discourses are rooted in political and economic interests. So an explanation of them would have to emphasize the political-economic basis of discourses as much as the discourses themselves. As such, discourse and ideational arguments do not break so much with political and economic analysis as it may at first appear, or as is sometimes claimed by them.

Ian Bruff's (2005) outline of ideational perspectives reacts to the importance of political-economic understandings by bringing them more into discourse analysis. For him, from the discourse perspective the idea of globalization influences how reality is understood. A complex and multidimensional world is open to going in different directions and which it does may be affected in part by how globalization is perceived. It does not matter if the sceptics are right about globalization if discourses of globalization are effective and create the reality of globalization.

But Bruff argues for a neo-Gramscian perspective which brings in an economic grounding for discourses of globalization, explaining why they happen on the basis of material interests. Gramsci was an Italian Marxist who wanted to get away from overly economically determinist understandings of the world by developing the idea of hegemonic ideologies that could mobilize people and dominate understandings of the world. In doing so, he rightly showed that ideas, and not just economics, are determinant. But he maintained his perspective of seeing these as linked to material interests and agents in society rather than just being free-floating and unrelated to economic and political bases. For Bruff, there needs to be more cross-pollination along these lines between Marxist materialist critical theories and the critical theories that come from discourse and ideational analysis.

Bruff also tries to bring agency in. He argues that globalization is not an external force out of our control, but a discourse which is produced and to which we can provide alternative accounts. The aim is to look at which groups and interests are invoking the idea of globalization – from capital that will benefit from free trade reforms, to governments that want to invoke external global pressures as a reason for reducing the amount spent on welfare. There are many discourses about reality, and looking at the power behind them helps in understanding why some are selected and retained and implemented in different circumstances.

So the ideational perspective on globalization is brought out by Bruff, combined with agency and political economy, rather than making the latter redundant and overlooking their importance for understanding discourses, where they come from and what interests they represent. Agency and contingency at the level of ideas are combined with causality in material and economic interests, capital accumulation and expansionism. Different meanings may be negotiated according to the circumstances or according to which social groups win the battle for power in determining the evolution of capitalism and the hegemonic meanings we use to understand society.

Bruff's analysis is an antidote to first-wave globalist theories, explaining how globalization is in part an idea and that interests lie behind the idea. It is less clear how far discourse theories of globalization are an alternative to the sceptics, though, as much as a development of or supplement to the second-wave approach. As with the third wave, the fourth wave reaffirms scepticism and reinforces it as much as breaks with it.

Bruff argues against second-wave approaches on the basis that whether globalization is a fact or not is less important than the meanings people attach to it to signify it. But the sceptics make a similar point, that globalization is as much a justification for political projects as an external inevitability. An important part of the critique of discourses of globalization is not just to show they are discourses but to test whether they are accurate. Because people can construct discourses about the world does not mean that any one construction is equally as true as any other. If it can be shown they are not an accurate representation of reality, something the sceptics try to assess, this is part of the struggle over discourse. It recognizes discourse as important but engages with trying to test and establish different representations of reality.

So Bruff develops or adds to scepticism rather than showing it to be redundant. Sceptics also see representations of reality as discursive and ideological and as used to (mis)represent the world as globalized to achieve economic and political ends, such as neoliberal policies. These interpretations are contingent and sceptics play a part in the process of shaping the discursive debate, in this case by empirically showing globalization to be a representation rather than a reality. Rather than fourth-wave discourse theories surpassing second-wave sceptics, these perspectives should be allies in critical analyses of globalization.

Further Reading

Held et al. (1999), in *Global Transformations*, and Held and McGrew (2003), in the introduction to *The Global Transformations Reader*, argue for a third-wave transformationalist perspective. They outline the first, second and third waves or perspectives on globalization. Others, such as Holton (2005), also provide outlines of the three waves. As I have argued above, third-wave transformationalists like Held et al.

argue that they are putting forward a more sophisticated version of the globalization thesis, but, when we look at the detail of what they say, they may as much be unwittingly affirming second-wave scepticism.

Hirst and Thompson (1996) put forward a sceptical perspective, theoretically sophisticated and backed up with hard empirical evidence on globalization, or the lack of it, in the economy. Dicken's (2007) *Global Shift* also tries to assess economic globalization theories against hard empirical evidence and comes to some sceptical conclusions. Mosley (2005) has written a concise and persuasive article about the limits of the view that state policy is determined by globalization.

Bruff's (2005) article is a good example of a fourth-wave approach and has the advantage of emphasizing discourse but also embedding it in material interests. Cameron and Palan (2004) also emphasize the discourse approach in talking about globalization as an 'imagined' economy

The History of Globalization: Pre-modern, Modern or Postmodern?

Mᴜᴄʜ of this book is about recent and contemporary globalization, since the mid-twentieth century and after the 1980s, with the end of the cold war and the rise of information technology. However, for some such a focus is too short-sighted. It overlooks that globalization is older. From one perspective its history goes back to the rise of industrialism and capitalism. For others even this is too recent, not to mention too Eurocentric. A longer-term view shows globalization going back centuries before this and emerging in its earliest forms from the East rather than as a process of Westernization.

One concern of this chapter is to look at how far back globalization or globalizing tendencies go. Another is to see in what period we can find the bases for current globalization. This seems like a similar question to the preceding one, but, as we shall see, they potentially have different answers. It could be that the first signs of globalization started a long time ago, whereas the institutions and structures that underpin current globalization are more recent.

The periods I will be looking at are:

1 Pre-modernity – before about 1500.
2 Early modernity – c.1500–c.1800.
3 Modern industrialism – c.1800–1914.
4 The world wars and in between – 1914–45.
5 Late modernity – 1945 onwards.
6 Contemporary or recent developments – from the 1980s onwards.

A number of themes relevant to globalization are raised by looking at its history. There are conceptual issues. How globalization is defined affects in part when it is located in history. Arguments about Euro- or

Western-centrism in globalization studies come up in discussions of the history of globalization. These also connect with discussions about whether globalized culture should be seen as homogenized or hybrid. Debates about the relative weight of Eastern or Western inputs into the history of globalization raise issues of power and inequality, which are central to this book.

Globalization as pre-modern

For those who view globalization as pre-modern, movements over long distance are very old. People moved in search of food, land, slaves, to escape persecution or pursue trade well before the sixteenth or seventeenth centuries, and the centuries after that when industrialization and the rise of capitalism occurred. What moved were not only people but also the ideas that came with them and goods that were traded. Empires were pursued, religions spread with the movement of people, people themselves migrated and economic exchange extended.

The ancient world's Greek and Roman empires grew, as did a Muslim empire around 800, covering a large area that has remained Muslim since, as well as a Chinese dynasty, covering areas that remain as China now. There was a temporary, destructive Mongolian empire in the thirteenth century that extended Eastwards, Southwards and West as far as Central Europe and the Middle East. These empires were often held together as much by centralized military rule as cultural incorporation of local populations.

Before the industrial capitalist era, religions such as Christianity, Islam and Buddhism spread over distance to areas where they are often still evident today. Examples of long-range trade include the silk route between China and the Mediterranean, migration and trade in people, art and luxury goods between Arab regions, the Near East, South Asia and Africa. There is evidence of long-distance regional travel and resettlement, but not of a sort where settlers maintained relations with the lands they had left or which involved established and durable relations and structures of migration. Other Asian empires followed in the 1500s with extensive trading over distance within them, while Western states developed in the meantime.

These pre-modern extensions were regional rather than global in extent, and temporary. But voyages of discovery in the fifteenth and sixteenth centuries, such as Columbus's, extended over greater distances. A lot of this occurred before the Western expansionism associated with globalization, whether the European imperialism of the French, Spanish, Portuguese, British and Dutch or the later Americanization of the world economy, politics and culture of the twentieth century. Longer-term historical perspectives stress the East and the movement of Eastern ideas and trade Westwards.

World systems theory (e.g., Wallerstein 1974, 1980, 1989) has stressed the earlier days of global relations and links, although within world systems theory there are differences. Frank argues that the world system is about 5,000 years old (Frank and Gills 1993). As long ago as that, long-distance trade existed, together with market exchange and capital accumulation. These define this period as the early core of capitalism. So what appears to be a system that rose some time between the sixteenth and nineteenth centuries, with capitalism, is said from this view to have happened much before then. Furthermore, the trade, exchange and accumulation took place in the East rather than the West and, as we shall see, some of this fed into later Western capitalism, revealing the non-Western origins of the world system. Wallerstein, however, stresses more a sixteenth-century start to capitalism. Frank focuses on long- distance exchange. It was not until later that production and finance as well as trade were globalized as part of the development of capitalism.

Janet Abu-Lughod (1989) also goes back beyond 1500 and what she calls 'European hegemony' to look at relations across distance in earlier periods. She argues that looking for globalization's origins earlier on shows it as coming from Asia and so undermines Eurocentric and Western-focused views of globalization. Abu-Lughod's research suggests that Chinese, Indian and Islamic worlds were exporters of innovation to others. So what later became the West was actually quite Eastern in its inputs, and West and East are not as polarized as sometimes portrayed when the East is seen as the 'other' to the West (see also Frank 1998 and Hobson 2004). As can be seen in figure 2.1, Abu-Lughod identifies eight overlapping circles of long-distance exchange going from China to Western Europe. There is interdependency between the circles so changes in each circuit affect the others.

Commentators such as Hopkins (2002a), Nederveen Pieterse (2004a) and Scholte (2005) emphasize different phases of globalization, with earlier ones coming in the pre-modern era and other globalizations taking a different form developing later. Hopkins talks about *modern globalization* after 1800, *proto-globalization* from 1600 to 1800 and *archaic globalization* before that (see also Holton 2005: ch. 2). I will come back to modern globalization. Key points about *archaic globalization* are raised by Hopkins. He identifies phenomena such as trading, and diaspora that developed from this, as well as empires and religious movements spreading across wider regions. This led to interconnections between parts of the world and, as relations developed between them, to interdependency. As we shall see, the difference between interconnections and interdependency is important. These long-

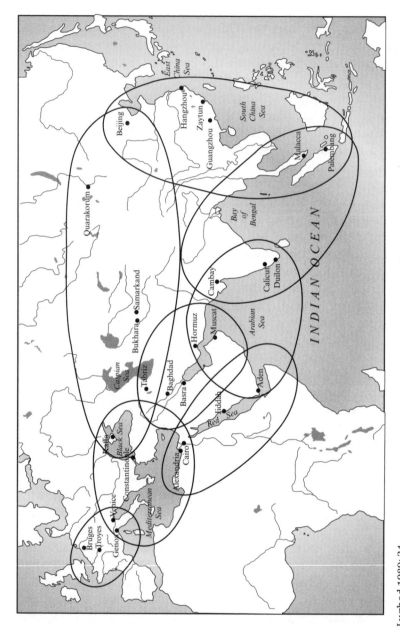

Source: Abu-Lughod 1989: 34

Figure 2.1   Circles of pre-modern trade

distance networks were African and Asian as much as European. The key actors were kings, warriors, priests and traders, from Marco Polo to Genghis Khan. At the same time Hopkins stresses that these were mini-globalizations, and that some of them collapsed or became more insular, such as outward extensions by the Chinese. He outlines these mini-globalizations as episodic and ruptured, with empires sometimes overreaching and having to retract.

Nevertheless, the mini-globalizations left a *legacy that was taken up in many cases by the West*. Some of this was integral to what became more Western-based globalization, for instance, in its monetary system and regulation. Coins, paper money and complex bureaucracy were legacies from China. Monetary policy and commercial credit came from Chinese and Arab mini-globalizations. The Arabic numeral system allowed the double-entry bookkeeping system that is central to accounting, while maritime regulation came from the East. These developments are central to systems such as capitalism and bureaucracy that define modernity and modern globalization. So there were Eastern origins to institutions that later became central to European globalization. These pre-modern extended relations were not really globalization, for reasons I will come back to. But to say so is not overly Western-centred because it is compatible with acknowledging that later Western-dominated processes on a more globalizing scale were not purely Western. The Western world that dominated later globalization was made up of these inputs from the East. In fact this has increased further with modern globalization as the West has encountered other inputs from the East, whether cultural (e.g., film, food and music from many parts of Asia) or economic (e.g., the rise of China).

There are important themes in these observations by Hopkins that are worth stressing. One is this emphasis on *Eastern origins*, providing an antidote to more Western-centric views of modern or postwar globalization as coming from Europe or America. This emphasis shows earlier Eastern origins to long-distance links, but also Eastern inputs into what was later to become the West, and establishing the basis of Western globalization.

A second issue is to do with distance. Many of these were mini-globalizations. They did not operate over a *global distance*. They were confined to Asia, North Africa, the Middle East and parts of Europe. The Americas do not emerge as an area reached by globalization (or its basis) to any major extent until later. So, if globalization has to be global in reach, and as such to include transatlantic or trans-oceanic relations, then what happened in this era was not globalization, even if it was reaching outwards in this direction.

Third, there is another issue of definition to do with *interdependency, stability and regularity.* Globalization has to involve more than communication or mobility from one part of the world to another. It also requires interdependency between those parts so that they mutually affect one another, and regularity or stability so the relations between them that are established are enduring (see Osterhammel and Petersson 2005; Holton 2005). To move from one part of the world to another without maintaining ongoing relations with your origins could be argued to not be globalization. There are global movements but not enduring global relations. Or, if globality involves connections but between two things that do not affect each other, that is, are not interdependent, that too could be said to fall short of globalization.

I can make a telephone call from England to Delhi, but this is a connection and it does not follow that there is interdependency between the two callers. What may sound like globalization, the international telephone call, may not really be so. Interconnection involves links but not necessarily the relations or mutual dependence that are a necessary part of globalization. Furthermore, there is the issue of regularity or consistency of relations. When people talk about globalization they generally mean a system or set of relations rather than one-off, intermittent or short-lived movements or communications. An interaction is not necessarily a relation or a network. There needs to be some sort of enduring constancy for something to be globalization.

So several elements of defining globalization are relevant here – (1) global distance; (2) going beyond interconnections to interdependency; and (3) enduring stability in relations rather than intermittent and short-lived contacts or movements. Some of the more regionally limited forms of trade, mobility or religious movements of pre-modern Eastern globalization did not extend over global distances, so cannot be seen as globalization, even if they created forms which were adopted by the West and later featured in more global globalization. Hopkins suggests that what occurred in archaic globalization was not that enduring but more intermittent and reversed. So there were globalizations that were mini, i.e., regional rather than global, and short-lived processes of extension and retreat rather than enduring or stable relations of interdependency.

Nederveen Pieterse (2004a) distinguishes between ancient, modern and contemporary accelerated globalization, and emphasizes its long running nature. He argues that seeing globalization as old avoids a Eurocentric or Western focus and shows that it is intercultural rather than Western dominated. For him, global culture is hybridized rather than homogeneous.

Nederveen Pieterse argues that *disciplinary perspectives* have an impact. Economists and sociologists who are preoccupied with capitalism and industrialism, if not exclusively so, and political scientists whose focus has been on the politics of the modern nation-state, although again not exclusively, tend to see globalization as modern. This is because their foci, capitalism, industrialism and the nation-state, are products of the modern era. Nederveen Pieterse says that anthropologists and historians who have less of a primarily modern focus see the longer-running origins to globalization.

This involves some of the things mentioned above – ancient population movements across continents, long-distance trade and the mobility of culture and world religions like Buddhism, Hinduism, Christianity and Islam. Nederveen Pieterse mentions the diffusion of technologies and knowledge, such as agricultural knowledge, military technology, numeracy, sciences and philosophies. Much of this came from East to West long before West to East became the pattern for globalization, and Asian economies were the central ones earlier on. This is not to say that more recent developments are not significant. Globalization has a long history, but contemporary globalization is accelerated, in terms of volume, speed and diversity of flows and networks. Nederveen Pieterse's perspective on globalization, as old but recently accelerated, is echoed by others such as Held et al. (1999).

It is important to draw attention to earlier Eastern origins of processes over long distances that preceded Western modernity and fed into it. This is a corrective to overly Western-centred and historically short-sighted views. But Nederveen Pieterse makes some qualifications to this picture. Having said that there were early long-distance processes, he argues it is open as to whether these should be categorized as globalization. He claims that because modernity united fragments of the world this gives the impression that globalization developed along with modernity, while earlier periods lacked the unity for this. He says that there is asymmetrical inclusion or hierarchical integration in globalization. If this structure to globalization is acknowledged it is difficult to see it in terms other than those in which the West or North are more dominant than the East or South. A view that tries to bring in the East in a more equal role historically has to be seen in this context of modern Western or Northern domination. Nederveen Pieterse's qualifications suggest that early forms might not have been globalization, that it was modernity that brought a more unified globality and that globalization operates on a basis of unequal inclusion. This gives a more qualified view of premodern globalization and Eastern inputs.

Scholte (2005) also distinguishes between phases of globalization, suggesting that earlier forms were more emergent than achieved. He says that from the 1850s to the 1950s globalization was 'incipient', and after the 1960s it was 'full scale', but that up to the eighteenth century it was more 'emergent' (1st edn, 2000), or in a state of 'intimations' up to the nineteenth century (2nd edn, 2005). Scholte says there were circumnavigation and world religions but these lacked the technology at that stage to allow the development from international links to supraterritoriality at a global level above and beyond nations and the international. Capitalism was mostly territorialized – with capitalist relations, including trade, going on mostly within regional areas rather than globally. International finance was mostly bilateral, that is, between individual countries rather than global, and slow in moving. Globalization was more an idea than a reality, and more contemplated by an elite than more widely. Very little globalization existed in the arenas of communications, markets, production, monies, finance and organizations. Scholte's emphasis on globalization properly taking off focuses on a quite late stage, the post-1960s' period, and on the importance of IT.

Was there pre-modern globalization?

What are we to make of the view that globalization occurred in the pre-modern era or has pre-modern origins? Questions to ask about pre-modern globalization are what the scale, intensity and impact of the interconnections were – how far did they extend, how strong and full were they and how far did they change the economy, society, politics and culture?

1 These older globalizations were *not global* in extent. Historians have shown phenomena such as long-distance trade, religions, and empires, but the distances were mostly regional rather than global. In the pre-modern era there was not, on a large scale, the trans-oceanic reach that would have allowed these to be global. This was partly because technology did not make trans-oceanic movements of people and ideas easy. There were no international political bodies of the sort that became common in the twentieth century.

2 As well as extent over distance, there were limits to extent in terms of the *proportion of the population* involved. Levels of interaction were confined mainly to agents of the processes concerned – such as merchants, traders, priests and the military – and therefore were restricted to certain sections of the population. At this stage, selected sorts of products were traded, often more luxury items, whereas in the contemporary era vast swathes of types of consumer products are traded globally. Furthermore, in the pre-modern era, the technology and wealth needed to maintain global relations were limited but, as

capitalism and industrialism grew, the capital and industrial technology to provide the basis for globalization also developed, for instance, technologies of mass production, global transportation and communication.

3 *Consciousness was not global*, at least beyond elites, and there was not transcontinental consciousness of the whole world. Global consciousness in Europe was confined mainly to elites and even then incomplete. Islamic knowledge was more of the East and Middle East and less of the Americas. The Chinese knew of Europe, but less about Africa and the Americas.

4 Movements from or connections to other parts of the world do not alone constitute globalization, but at most could be called only a thin form of globalization. A movement from one place to another can occur without a *system or ongoing relation* between the two places being developed. Furthermore, connections between parts of the world can exist without *interdependency* occurring, so that events in one area would not be dependent on or affected by events in another area. A migration from one part of the world to another might be a global movement but not necessarily one in which relations are maintained between the migrants and their place of origin, just as the international telephone call involves a connection between two people without interdependency or an ongoing relation. However, in the twenty-first century, economic events in one part of the world, for example, frequently have a significant effect globally. Some areas are dependent on others for quite basic and fundamental resources, such as energy and trade. Historians of pre-modern extensity do not portray interdependency of this sort arising out of global movements and connections. And globalizing tendencies were episodic and intermittent, rather than regularized in a more enduring form with a system through which the economy, politics and culture were organized.

5 I mentioned two questions at the start of this chapter. First, to what extent could pre-modern extensions be called globalization? We have seen that they were not, even if they temporarily went in a globalizing direction. The other question concerned the extent to which they were the *basis of later globalization*. This is as interesting as the argument about when globalization first happened. The two are not the same thing because there could be pre-modern globalization but without it being the basis for current globalization, as the retraction and reversals of globalization during the earlier period effectively ended globalization at that time. Apart from this, the form that current

globalization has taken is grounded more in structures and bases from a later period.

Although there were globalizing movements in pre-modern times, the basic infrastructure of current globalization was mostly developed in the modern era. Capitalism and then industrialism created the incentives, wealth and technology to turn limited globalization into more fully blown sorts, global in distance, more inclusive and established over time. Eastern influences constituted in part what became the West, which then became the more dominant basis for globalization. But, as we will see, the basis of globalization was laid in the modern era. Capitalism, industrialism, global transportation and communications technology and the nation-state – all these developments began in early modernity and took off more fully and widely with the development of industrial modernity.

Early modernity: proto-globalization

A subsequent phase of globalization that Hopkins discusses, after archaic globalization, is *proto-globalization*. He identifies this with the pre-industrial period 1600–1800 and distinguishes it from modern globalization post-1800. It is significant that Hopkins distinguishes pre-industrial from industrial globalization. This suggests that capitalist forms in the early modern pre-industrial period were not alone sufficient to establish globalization. They needed to be accompanied by industrial technology that could allow and facilitate the globalization encouraged by capitalism. Capitalism alone was not enough to fully establish globalization. It also needed industrial technology.

A key argument of this book is that the economic motivations of capitalism are key (but not solely so) to understanding the spread of globalization. At the same time there is an emphasis on technological developments making this spread possible. The former contains incentives for globalization and the latter the technology that allows these to be fulfilled. So Hopkins's distinction of proto-globalization in the period of emerging capitalism, from previous less global forms, is important in recognizing the importance of capitalist economic motivations. But so too is his distinction of modern globalization of the industrial period, from pre-industrial capitalist proto-globalization, in showing the importance of industrial technology.

While proto-globalization, for Hopkins, covers the pre-industrial period of 1600–1800, it may make sense to start this period in *c.*1500 and recognize some important developments that were to continue on a grander scale from 1800 onwards. The period from 1500 or so onwards was an 'in-between' time when Asian extensions of economy and culture were still important and some significant industrial technologies and forms of European imperialism were developing, before industrialization really took off in the eighteenth century onwards. During this period, explorers and colonizers extended globally, for instance, to the Americas, and the slave trade transported millions across the Atlantic and other areas. Naval power allowed trans-oceanic movements. So movements were not restricted to land and could be more global. Many people fled religious persecution, notably from Europe to the Americas, while scientists and map-makers tried to exploit the possibilities of globalism. These sorts of developments meant people were conscious of globality and wanted to collect information about other parts of the world – so there was a developing global consciousness.

Trading states such as Britain, backed up by state and military power, extended economic links globally. Indian, Persian, Arab, Muslim and Hindu knowledge was used as a basis for European botanical classification systems and Western medicine. Spices, cloth and tea were exported from the East by European trading companies, while silver came Eastwards from Spanish colonies in America. By the mid-eighteenth century capitalism in Europe and North America was becoming more dominant over the primarily mercantile trading of India, China and Arab countries. As well as naval travel, modern weaponry such as gunpowder and firearms were making this possible, often before 1600, alongside continuing empires in the Asian and Islamic worlds. Communications were improving, too, with the invention of the printing press. Before radio, TV or the Internet, printing enabled wider distribution of information than spoken or handwritten forms, and on a scale that made it into mass media. With these developments of the technologies for mechanized war and mass communication, the foundations of globalization were established.

Modern globalization

If globalization has to be global rather than regional, involving not just the movement of people, goods or ideas from one part of the world to another but also the establishment of interdependencies, then the modern era may be a better place to look for globalization than the premodern period (see authors such as Osterhammel and Petersson 2005, O'Rourke and Williamson 1999 and Bayly 2004). This period of globalization involved the expansion of the West, capitalism and imperialism backed up by the nation-state and industrial technology. These were all developments primarily of the modern era from the 1500s onwards expanding over time as industrialization developed in the eighteenth century. I will be brief on modern and postmodern globalization as these periods are covered through the rest of the book.

Capitalism involves an economy in which private ownership dominates, and the market is the primary mechanism for determining the production and distribution of goods to people, for profit and in response to market demand. This is in contrast to socialism where the economy is predominantly publicly owned (e.g., by the state) and production is planned by a public body to meet what the planners decide is socially needed in society. For world-systems theorist Wallerstein, the capitalist expansion of the West goes back centuries to cross-border agrarian and mercantile capitalism around 1600. For others, the major steps were more recent, with the nineteenth-century expansion of European commerce and empire, when imperialism, the nation-state and industrial technology were more available as bases and agencies for globalization than in earlier periods.

Capitalism started before the nineteenth century, although it was during this century that it started to globalize more fully, partly because industrial technology and the modern nation-state were behind it but also because capitalism had developed the strong economic motivations to accumulate wealth, alongside the capital to back this up. *Industrial technology* provided the means for long-distance travel and global communications, as well as advanced weapons to back up military imposition. It allowed the mass production of goods that could be sold globally. Steam power used in ships and trains allowed for global transportation of goods and trade. Larger-scale and more accurate firearms led to a firepower gap between core states and others. In other words, important technologies were of mass production and consumption globally, transportation and war. Alongside these developments, the laying of trans-oceanic cables across empires, and trade and the telegraph allowed for speedy international communications, while the development of international news agencies allowed rapid worldwide news reporting. The movement of communication, information and finance could be separated from the movement of people and done instantaneously. Further developments such as the Internet allow even greater scope and volume of instant global communication.

Marx and Engels' *Communist Manifesto* described in 1848 what later became called globalization. This is in contradiction to those who say globalization started 100 years or more later, and for whom old theories are backward and out of touch and only new ones capable of understanding the new global times (Beck 2000, 2006).

> The need of a constantly expanding market for its products chases the bourgeoisie over the entire surface of the globe. It must nestle everywhere, settle everywhere, establish connections everywhere.
>
> The bourgeoisie has, through its exploitation of the world market, given a cosmopolitan character to production and consumption in every country. To the great chagrin of reactionaries, it has drawn from under the feet of industry the national ground on which it stood. All old-established national industries have been destroyed or are daily being destroyed. They are dislodged by new industries, whose introduction becomes a life and death question for all civilized nations, by industries that no longer work up indigenous raw material, but raw material drawn from the remotest zones; industries whose products are consumed, not only at home, but in every quarter of the globe. In place of the old wants, satisfied by the production of the country, we find new wants, requiring for their satisfaction the products of distant lands and climes. In place of the old local and national seclusion and self-sufficiency, we have intercourse in every direction, universal inter-dependence of nations. And as in material, so also in intellectual production. The intellectual creations of individual nations become common property. National one-sidedness and narrow-mindedness become more and more impossible, and from the numerous national and local literatures, there arises a world literature. (Marx and Engels 1998: 39)

To grow and develop, capitalism needed raw materials, new markets and sources of labour. The search for these led it beyond localities to a more global reach. This is not just something that capitalists decided to do. It is inherent in the dynamic of capitalism that looks wherever it can for profit. One way this happened was through *imperialism and empire*. The firepower gap and the role of the nation-state were important factors in this. Economic expansionism was behind imperialism, and it was imposed by Western powers on other subjected countries in a way that was exploitative and involved social injustice. The motivations were primarily economic, but not only, and this is not to say that the economy itself as an impersonal structure caused imperialism. Economic and political actors, such as states, were agents of economic globalization, often using military force. So economic motives were pursued by military and political forces as much as by economic actors and by active human agents rather than impersonal forces. The aim was to open up the world to trade ('free' trade insofar as this can be free when enforced down the barrel of a gun by states with huge economic advantages over their competitors), find new markets and new sources of raw materials. Cultural socialization where necessary or desired was pursued, as well as economic objectives, although not wholesale in all cases or through all sections of subordinated populations.

Main imperial powers were the Spanish, Portuguese, French, British and Dutch, variously from about 1500 onwards. Technologies of naval power and modern weaponry helped them to impose their will globally. Naval power that was initially concerned with exploration and commerce also became involved in war over subjected colonies. Battles across seas between the competitor imperialists occurred in many international locations, in Europe, Canada, India and the Spanish colonies. British and Spanish colonies in the Americas fought for independence in the eighteenth and nineteenth centuries, and later so did colonies in Africa and Asia.

Mass migration in the tens of millions occurred, especially in the late nineteenth and early twentieth centuries. Migrants were often permanent, but maintained connections with their countries of origins which encouraged ongoing global relations rather than just global movements. The amount of world trade increased dramatically, although this was mainly focused within North America, Europe, Australia and New Zealand. Large volumes of goods were transported globally as a result of mass production, combined with modern technologies of transportation and communication. This led to the development of global markets and a form of integrated international economy, signified by convergence in prices and wages. The world economy appeared to be interdependent as different parts affected others and they began to move in tandem. In the twentieth century this was symbolized by the global economic depression of the 1930s. In short there was global migration and an increasingly integrated international economy as the nineteenth century and early twentieth century developed.

Hopkins (2002a) distinguishes the modern period of globalization from others. He says that globalization shifted from being Eastern to Western, and developed from European and then North American expansionism in the nineteenth and twentieth centuries. Three areas of modern globalization can be picked out. First, Hopkins identifies economic and technological developments. These include free trade connected with imperialism, changes in production and communications technology which allowed mass production and globality, and transport improvements which allowed the global movement of goods and people.

Second, he identifies the nation-state as a key agency. The nation-state is a product of the modern era and differs from previous political systems such as feudalism and monarchies. It was often behind what designed, financed and militarily enforced globalization through imperialism. Furthermore, the nation-state itself has become globalized as more societies around the world have adopted it as a political form. In some cases this has happened because non-Western societies have had this form foisted on them by imperialism and colonization. Subsequently, independence movements identified anti-imperialism with control of the state. The nation-state is an agent and part of globalization as much as something undermined by it.

Third, Hopkins identifies international organizations that have developed with globalization. This does not conflict with the emphasis on the nation-state. Such organizations have often been created and constituted by nation-states. International organizations are both governmental and non-governmental, and range from examples such as the Red Cross to the League of Nations and the UN, the International Labour Organization, World Health Organisation, International Atomic Energy Agency, World Trade Organization and International Monetary Fund. These were created to deal with issues such as security and social and economic affairs across national boundaries. They are constructed by and composed of nation-states and dominated by some of them more than others.

For Waters (2001), politics in the nineteenth and twentieth centuries was a matter of internationalization as much as globalization, and as much about international relations between states as the global agencies above and beyond these. World economic bodies, international relations, war, alliances, diplomacy and colonialism continued beyond nation-state boundaries but between nation-states or in forms composed of them, rather than by transcending nation-states, relations between them or their input. Politics was international but not yet global.

Hirst and Thompson (1996) take a similarly sceptical view of the world economy as international rather than global. The most internationalized period was between 1870 and 1914, and internationalization has rolled back since then. This *belle époque* saw migration at its heights, facilitated by colonialism, economic integration and an open economy. But Hirst and Thompson urge against seeing the world economy as globalized. Transnational corporations are actually multinational – nationally based companies operating internationally. Foreign direct investment is concentrated among advanced industrial countries. The global economy is not out of control. The richest states could control financial markets and impose greater regulation in the global economy, but choose not to for reasons of ideology (neoliberalism) and economic interest (they gain from a liberal global economy). Globalization writers are right to talk about international forms of economy, politics and culture, and globalizing tendencies, but Hirst and Thompson are also right to show the power and inequality in this and how it limits and undermines full globalization.

For Giddens (1990), globalization is a consequence of modernity that he sees as inherently globalizing. Modernity is a product of the West, first Europe and then more North America, especially the USA, so globalization is about the expansion of the West. Giddens describes this as the 'disembedding' of markets, capital and labour movements from local ties, rules, religions and traditions. Such institutions and actors become detached from a basis in localities and so also from the rules and regulations about how they should behave, together with local norms and values. They are more footloose and free, or at least more integrated into the rules and norms of the global rather than local sphere. States are seen as the main actors behind the capitalist expansion of globalization, and they have the use of military force, a fact emphasized by Giddens who says it has been underplayed by sociology in the past. Big corporations are also important actors in spreading economics globally. What results is a changing global division of labour, with interdependence between its parts, made more complex by the shift from a split between first world and third world to one that includes newly industrializing countries that have broken away from the third world, creating intermediate strata. Cultural globalization is brought about by new technologies of communication and by the media they carry. Giddens here roots globalization in capitalist expansionism.

What conclusions can we make about *globalization in the modern period*? First, there were key developments economically of capitalism, technologically of industrial technology and politically of the nation-state. These were behind a shift from long-distance movements of the pre-modern period to global systems. Capitalism expanded to make money and industrial technology developed transport and communications that allowed this to develop globally. The nation-state became more prevalent and facilitated globalization organizationally, including through military power, and has been a constitutive element in globalization as much as something undermined by it. Military power was used to back up imperial expansion in the colonial eras, the cold war and by the USA in the post-cold war period. States have facilitated trade and been behind changes in regulations that allowed free trade and the movement of capital alongside the growth of big global corporations.

Second, what happened in this period was the expansion of transnational movements from regional to global extents. For instance, the Americas and Africa were incorporated into imperialism, trade and migration. Third, they shifted from being episodic, reversed and non-regularized to being stable systems and structures that were established and continue in many forms today to underpin contemporary processes of globalization. This does not mean they are fixed for ever or that they will continue to take the same form. But economic, technological and political developments led to more regularized, stable and established global relations rather than movements and processes that could halt and, when they did, reveal an absence of more constant systems or structures behind them.

Fourth, many of these shifts of modernity – the capitalist economy, industrial technology, the nation-state and the global economic, political and cultural forms they established – are at the basis of more recent globalization. You could not say the same about pre-modern Eastern-originating globalization that fed into what became the West but that did not itself establish the transnational forms underpinning contemporary globalization. The forms of economy, industry and state that underpin current globalization developed later. It also cannot be said that postmodern globalization broke from modern globalization to make something new. It built on it, speeded it up, increased its volume and established new possibilities within it. Modern rather than pre-modern globalization underpins the contemporary globalization that builds on, rather than breaking from, modern globalization.

Fifth, running through these developments is power – of imperialism, capitalist corporations, states and military force. Agents behind these have greater power than others and globalization is unequal, so unequal that it may be misleading to describe it as globalization. Some are integrated while others are more outside, so that its extent is not global. Furthermore its main agents are more national, international or regional than global actors. So the power and inequality involved suggests a more sceptical perspective which questions how far the structures and processes described really are globalization. This is not to say there aren't important expansions beyond nations and international economic, political and cultural forces, as described by globalists, but that these are sometimes not globalization. To say that they are globalization can only be done by glossing over power imbalances, inequalities, and limits of inclusion and integration.

Globalization in the late twentieth/early twenty-first centuries

Much of the rest of this book focuses on the twentieth and early twenty-first centuries, so I will restrict the outline here to some key points and their relation to the history of globalization. As we have seen, the period of 1870–1914 was seen by some to be a heyday of globalization. There was a period of disruption to globalization between 1914 and 1945 (although Osterhammel and Petersson 2005 argue that the common view of this period as deglobalizing can be exaggerated). Two world wars created enormous blips in the development of the world economy, politics and culture in which many nation-state powers, albeit some of them being expansionist, were engaged in conflict at horrendous human cost. This was on a world scale and involved international alliances, but hardly in a spirit of global unification. In between the wars, economic depression drove many states to protectionism and regionalism and away from a free-trade economy. At the same time, the depression was in part a consequence of the interdependence of economies globally.

After the Second World War, the world was divided in two ways, an East–West capitalist–communist divide and a North and South divide between rich developed countries and developing countries, many of them breaking free from colonialism, and fired by anti-imperialist nationalism. But, despite East–West and North–South splits, the communist and capitalist blocs were extended on an international scale and for newly independent countries this was a chance to participate in world society on their own terms. A period of openness to immigration in some places was followed in the 1970s and afterwards by greater restrictions on people movements. International economic and political organizations grew and after the 1980s the world changed from a bipolar split to one more dominated by a single superpower and the spread of capitalism. This was also a phase where the growth of the Internet and the significance of IT increased in huge leaps, with especial implications for communications and finance. This post-1945 period was characterized by both divisive and globalist aspects.

Hopkins (2002a) characterized earlier periods as archaic, proto- and modern globalization. He talks about the later twentieth century in terms of *postcolonial globalization*, and highlights shifts in power from advanced states through the growth of supraterritorial organizations and regional integration. This includes organizations such as the EU and World Bank, but also transnational identities such as diasporas, for instance, of Chinese and Indians. Additionally, culture globalizes across the boundaries of states, through the Internet, in popular culture of a transnational sort, and through the global media, intercultural fusions, hybridization and creolization.

Hopkins argues that decolonization involves a move away from Western domination to a more prominent place for postcolonial states, agents and culture. Postcolonial perspectives attempt to show the input of actors beyond the powerful Western core. There is a risk of underestimating Northern and Western power in doing so. At the same time there is potential for agency from those who can organize politically as an alternative to this core. And the postwar period saw a huge rise in the world economic order of major Asian states such as Japan, China and India, initially often by pursuing policies outside the global economy. China continues to grow and develop at speed, the implications of which economically, politically, environmentally, culturally, and maybe militarily, are in full flow and yet to further unfold.

Scholte is one of those who locates full-scale globalization not so much in the modern era as in the post-1960s period. In the first edition of his book (2000) he refers to this period as full-scale globalization. In the second (2005), he talks about it as contemporary accelerated globalization, a weaker term, implying that it involves a speeding up of something already there rather than a new era in itself. It is in the 1960s, Scholte says, that communications, markets, production, money, organizations, environmental problems and consciousness all became global, primarily because of developments in electronic communications.

The merging of telecommunications, computing and the Internet has allowed the transmission of information instantly, whether through direct communications such as email or the transferring of money or documents, or through media such as web content. Globalization has been identified with different sorts of developments in the past – imperialism, capitalism, industrialism or the end of the cold war, for instance. IT is emphasized as the key development in this perspective on globalization as more recent.

A stress on IT is often accompanied by an emphasis on culture and communication as the defining feature of this era of globalization, as opposed to economics and politics as the prime sites of globalization in previous eras – say, economics, with the rise of capitalism and industrialism and politics in the postwar period alongside the growth of international organizations (e.g., Waters 1995). An emphasis on culture, especially on culture becoming mixed, fits in with post-modern rather than modern perspectives, the former emphasizing symbols more than materiality, and highlighting the pluralization of identities and culture.

In contrast to the postcolonial characterization mentioned above, some perspectives see this as another *imperialist* era, rather than *post*-imperialist, with globalization being transmitted in this way (Holton 2005: 48). Rather than the European empires being the source of imperialism, in this later period it happened first through the American and Soviet empires during the cold war up to the 1980s, and then more singly through US imperialism after the collapse of the bipolar divide. In the first phase both sides tried to extend their values – whether liberalism and democracy or international socialism – through wars in places like Vietnam, Korea, Afghanistan and Latin America, as well as in African countries – either fought directly by them or through proxies. Or they propped up regimes, often dictatorships, that aligned with them, for instance, as the USA did in Latin America.

The USA and the Soviet Union also attempted to promote their perspectives ideologically, through consumerism and politics in the case of the USA or by means such as art, culture and state propaganda from socialist countries. America became the major world power economically, politically, militarily and in terms of the attraction of its culture (at least, as it appeared in Hollywood films). It was able to mass-produce its culture for a mass consumer audience, and people in many other parts of the world found its values appealing. A one-sided dominance in cultural exports, from movies to pop music and TV programmes, meant that cultural globalization seemed more like Americanization than globalization.

After the collapse of communism the picture is more unilinear. It is important to stress the role of power and avoid falling into too uncritical a view of the democratizing and equalizing effect of globalization. At the same time, the view of the postwar cold war and post-cold war periods as imperialist needs to take into account the effects of reverse flows. While Western or capitalist corporations are dominant in the production and distribution of media and culture, there are exports from East to West of media, culture, goods and services, as well as migration. Politically speaking, the movement is also not all one way. Parts of the world beyond North America and Europe form their own collective or regional organizations, alliances or bilateral links, for example, in Asia and Latin America. These provide alternatives or opposition to the USA economically, or even politically. Some include Europe in this category of counterweights to US power.

I have mentioned that perspectives on pre-modern globalization see it as intermittent, *reversible* and not established on a regularized systemic basis. We have seen that Hirst and Thompson view globalization in the early twentieth century as at a peak which was reversed in the interwar period. There are also signs in the postwar period of globalization being accompanied by de-globalization and reverses (see Holton 2005). After the early twentieth century, some reversals of globalization were in migration and free trade. There were rises and then falls in migration with political restrictions on immigration in rich countries after the 1970s. There was a turn away from free trade during depression in the 1930s and, at the turn of the twenty-first century, world trade talks frequently broke down. Big powers feeling the competition from other parts of the world resorted to protectionism, for instance, the USA, EU and China, in industries such as steel, farming or garments. Many developing countries that were successful in growing economically, from Latin American to East Asia, did so by pursuing strategies that were not initially based on integration into the global economy but by substituting their own products for imports, or by protectionism. In other words, they did it at first by keeping out globalization.

After 1945 many global organizations were set up, from the United Nations to the World Bank and International Monetary Fund, but many have attracted criticism, for instance, for being ineffective or inconsistent in the face of human rights abuses, war, or crimes against humanity, or for imposing policies favoured by the developed world on developing countries. Regional economic organizations such as the EU and ASEAN, as much as global ones, have turned out to be significant in the world economy. From governments such as the Castro regime in Cuba after 1959 to Chavez in Venezuela after 1999, to the social movements of the 1960s and the anti-globalization movements thirty years later, there were examples of politics against imperialism and globalization.

At the same time part of the backlash is itself global. Holton (2005) describes the reaction to globalization as in part *re-globalization*, but in a different direction. So the reaction against globalization may be expressed as a part of global civil society, or by transnational social movements against global corporations or states. Some of these are reacting in response to issues that are global, such as climate change, global poverty, 'free' trade and human rights. Or it may be from alternative transnational networks, such as regional economic blocs or political or bilateral alliances by countries with shared interests or ideological approaches. Re-globalization with a different content may also emerge in diaspora, culture, music or religion. So anti-globalization may be alternative globalization or re-globalization as much as a retreat from the global.

The postmodern era, meanwhile, has produced technologies in the form of IT and the Internet. However, what is a pathbreaking and exciting leap *technologically* needs to be separated from whether this creates a qualitative leap for *society*. The Internet, and IT more generally, allow mass instant communication of information, but much of this was available on a mass or instant basis before, via the telegraph, telephone, radio or TV, for instance. This is not to say there have not been qualitative shifts, in the technology itself, the changing nature of the networked world of finance and the ability of Internet users to become producers of content, for example, through blogs. But, although not introducing the era of mass immediacy, in terms of social relations, and access to audio and visual media and information, the Internet makes much easier and quicker a lot of what was already available in mass form.

One important part of the 'postmodern' era as far as globalization goes may be the development of the idea of globalization itself. 'Globalization' as a term only began to become common in the 1980s, even if some of what it evokes had been recognized for much longer than this. But globalization as an ideational force became important at this point, such that people began to interpret the world as globalized because the conceptual apparatus for seeing it this way then existed and was a public idea. This may well then have started to influence people's behaviour as well as their thought, with business people or politicians making decisions appropriate to a context of globalization because that was what they believed to exist and to be a constraint. Or they used globalization as a discourse to justify as necessary, decisions that they favoured for other reasons, such as an ideological commitment to neoliberalism or the economic benefits to be made from reducing restrictions on capital and trade. Something like imperialism may become defined as globalization. Once it becomes the latter, this disguises the power, inequality and conflict involved in it. So globalization as an ideational force became important in this more 'postmodern' period.

Conclusions

Pre-modern globalization was not globalization. It was regional in extent and did not create the systemic interdependent structures of a global sort that have been established in modern globalization. It did feed into what was later to become the West that was behind modern globalization. However, it did not create the global structures that are behind globalization now. The latter is based more on the global structures that came with modern capitalism and industrialism.

It is in the modern era that globalization has become more global rather than regional and with more systemic and regularized structures and relations. In this period globalization became more worldwide and interdependent rather than just interconnected. The motivations of the capitalist economy, industrial technology and the nation-state, all modern institutions, were behind this. Furthermore when you look at contemporary globalization you can see it is established on the basis of modern globalization – its economic expansionism, technology of transport and communication, and political state bases.

The late twentieth and early twenty-first centuries featured the imperial blocs of the cold war, the end of the cold war and the rise of information technology. The world has become less bipolar and more of a connected unipolar place. However, US imperialism and the Internet did not build globalization. They have established global forms on the basis of capitalist economic expansionism, the development of industrial technology and the state. Things have changed, globalization has expanded and new possibilities in it have been created by developments such as IT. But these are extensions to the globalization of the modern period, through its institutions and technologies, rather than a break from it to a new era of globalization.

Globalization is *complex*. There are different spheres in which it occurs or is based – economic, political and cultural, for instance. Which of these you look at may alter your view of when globalization started. What you use to measure globalization will affect where you see it starting. If you focus on free trade and price convergence, you might see the start of global forms and convergence in the mid-nineteenth century (e.g., O'Rourke and Williamson 1999). If technologies of communication are important, globalization may be based more in the twentieth century. If the imaginings of something global amongst sections of the population are decisive, then earlier than the modern era may be a good start date, or the 1980s onwards if you are looking for globalization as an ideational force. It is important to be open to the differentiation of globalization and to varying perspectives.

At the same time, it is important to make an interpretation and not drift into a relativistic perspective where there are a number of different equally valid views. Globalization is often talked of as interdependence and integration across the economic, political and cultural spheres of society. If you look at it this way, then before the modern period this was not established. In the modern period, the economic, technological and political forms for this were formed. In the postmodern period, globalization has extended and built on these. So globalization is primarily a modern creation.

A focus on modernity historically, and on Western power as behind globalization, need not imply a Eurocentric or Western-centric view. The West has taken on Eastern inputs historically, and Eastern and Southern inputs and agency are important now. But not to acknowledge Western power does a disservice to the South and East, and glosses over power, inequality and exploitation created by the West. The South and the East need to be brought in as important agents and not reduced to something 'other' and passive, but not to an extent that glosses over Western power and attempts to dominate and exploit them. Following from this, if globalization is not universal or spread evenly, then the question arises as to whether it is (yet) globalization or, rather, the spread of things from certain parts of the world internationally, unequally and not universally.

This chapter has brought up some of the *conceptual* issues raised in the introduction. When globalization started and whether it exists depends, in part, on how you define it. I have argued that it makes sense to define globalization: (1) as worldwide rather than regional; (2) as beyond movements and connections, and where regularity and systems and structures occur; and (3) where connections turn into things that have mutual effects worldwide, interdependency. On such a definition, globalization was not achieved in the pre-modern period, even if there were globalizing processes then. It was in place before the postmodern era. The foundations of worldwide interdependency were established in the era of modernity. However, power and inequality have made globalization uneven and unequal in its integration and inclusiveness. If globalization is to mean universality, and equal or even integration, it has not been achieved, and may well never be.

Further Reading

Osterhammel and Petersson's (2005) *Globalization: A Short History* is a concise, readable book that puts globalization into historical perspective and sees its origins primarily in the modern period.

Janet Abu-Lughod's (1989) *Before European Hegemony: The world System AD 1250–1350*, and Frank and Gills's (1993) *The World System: Five Hundred Years or Five Thousand?* both date the origins of globalization earlier. I have argued above that they make a good case for early long-distance movements, but that globalization cannot be dated this far back.

There are some useful and interesting edited collections on global history – Hopkins's (2002b) *Globalization in World History*, which has a good introduction by Hopkins, Gills and Thompson's (2006) *Globalization and Global History*, and Hopkins's (2006) *Global History*.

Jan Aart Scholte's (2005) *Globalization: A Critical Introduction* sees globalization as something much more recent than these other contributions.

CHAPTER 3

Technology, Economy and the Globalization of Culture

IN this chapter and the next one, I will look at the extent to which globalization has changed culture and at how globalized culture has become. These are not necessarily the same because a culture that has been changed by globalization may not become globalized. There can be other responses. For instance, the effect of globalization on culture can be to turn it away from globalized forms to more fundamental or national responses.

I will look at what shape culture takes if it is globalized. This too is not a straightforward question because a globalized culture can take different forms. It can become homogenized – globalization may lead to uniformity in culture worldwide. It could become hybridized, culture becoming mixed up with different global inputs. Or it could become heterogeneous, with cultures living side by side. It could be something else or a combination of these.

I will come back to these questions on the effect of globalization on culture in the next chapter. To understand such changes it is necessary to look at what may be behind them. In this chapter I will look briefly at some historical forms of the globalization of culture, and then at technological and institutional changes behind contemporary cultural globalization. Wider themes of the book are reflected in these discussions – globalization as historical and modern; the economic bases of globalization; power, inequality and conflict; and the need to subject claims about globalization to open-minded but critical scrutiny.

Some contributors argue that culture has been overlooked in globalization studies in favour of politics and economics, or is reduced too much to them (e.g., Rantanen 2005; Beck 2000). This is surprising because there is a large literature on cultural globalization, such as early books by Robertson (1992) and Tomlinson (1999), and later ones such as those by Waters (2001), with a wide literature in this area (see Hopper's 2007 overview). This is not to mention general books on globalization that nearly always feature media and culture (e.g., Held and McGrew 2003). Furthermore, it is difficult to understand cultural globalization without looking at the political and economic infrastructure for it. This does not mean reducing culture to economic determinants, but rather seeing the role of political and economic factors in it. If there is a problem, it may be that some studies of cultural globalization tend to detach culture from politics and economics too much, so leaving out the way that power and inequality in those spheres affect global media and culture.

It is possible to have a broader or narrower definition of culture. Culture is often associated with the media or values, but it can include *goods, commodities and services*. These include things like clothes, food, music, or the car someone owns, if they have one. All of these are part of culture and for many people define their identity. Culture includes not only what norms we hold, and media, but also other things we use and buy. In the case of the West, culture is quite consumerist and commodified.

Culture includes *information, communications and media*. This is a definition people are more used to. Culture here is the sort of media we watch or listen to, or the type of books, magazines or newspapers we read. It is about information and the communications we consume. An aspect of American culture is Hollywood film and the ideas and symbols it reflects or encourages in American society. When people talk about culture being globalized they are often thinking about music, film or TV programming that spreads around the world and is received by many people.

Culture includes *norms and values*. This is not separable from the previous types of culture that reflect or influence norms and values. Culture is composed of our beliefs. This can include religious or political beliefs, for instance. Some countries might be characterized as liberal countries because of the generalized adherence to ideas about rights and liberal democracy. Some could be characterized as Christian, Jewish or Muslim because of the dominance of these religions' values in the value systems of the country.

So culture is about more than just media. It is also about what we believe and do. There is a distinction here between media and other aspects of culture. These are interrelated because culture may be affected by media, or media may reflect culture. But they are also not identical and it should not be assumed that globalization of the media is replicated in global cultures. The distinction between culture and media, whilst not absolute in reality, is significant.

Power through the media and over culture should be distinguished from economic, political and military power. The latter come through wealth and income, control over the state apparatus, or force and coercion. Media power involves influence over symbols, meanings and information, and over values, attitudes and knowledge. Some of these forms involve observable power – money, the state office someone occupies or the weapon they use to coerce you, for instance. Some involve less observable power. This is especially the case with the media which influence what people think, and set the agenda of what is known and talked about in society. This is more hidden. This can make it more effective and dangerous and difficult to counter.

At the same time, media power and influence over information and ideas is not separable from economic, political or military power. If you have wealth, political power or the means of coercion you can use these to control the media and influence knowledge and ideas. Having the wealth to establish ownership across the media, or the political or coercive power to censor it are important parts of media influence. Some feel that culture and media are reduced too much to political economy. But political and economic dimensions are important even if culture cannot be explained only in terms of them.

The history of cultural globalization

Most of this chapter and the next will focus on modern and contemporary cultural globalization. But what forms of cultural globalization were there before this? I have discussed historical forms of globalization in chapter 2. The literature on pre-modern globalization discusses long-distance *trade*. This involves the transportation of goods that make up culture, for instance, precious stones or cloth, and the intermingling of cultures over distance when traders meet each other. Religions, empires and politics are further examples of long-standing types of cultural globalization (e.g., see Held et al. 1999).

World religions include Christianity, Islam, Confucianism, Hinduism, Judaism and Buddhism. These can be found across regions of the world. One way they become globalized is through people adopting religions from elsewhere. For example, Buddhism, Christianity and Islam have spread beyond their places of origin to areas where people convert. Another way involves diaspora, peoples dispersed from one part of the world to others. The globalization of Judaism is an example of this. For centuries Jewish people have scattered around the world, to escape persecution but for other reasons too, and formed diaspora and the globalization of the Jewish religion. Islam and Christianity have spread through military conquest and cultural influence. Islam spread through North Africa, the Middle East and Southern Europe, often through armed force, and Christianity too has often followed conquering armies from Christian countries. What followed military conquest was cultural influence. So there was a dynamic of military force and then conversion.

Literacy, writing and printing aided the spread of religion and other forms of culture. Religious texts and norms could be disseminated in written and mass printed form. As we shall see throughout this chapter, such technological and institutional developments are important in the spread of culture. We shall also see that culture does not diffuse equally. Religions have spread hierarchically or unevenly. People who can read are more likely to be from higher classes and so religion has penetrated more strongly amongst such groups, at least initially. Some people in countries that adopted Christianity or Islam kept to their local belief systems and religious practices (e.g., Abercrombie et al. 1980). And globalized religion has often been more regionally than globally spread in the past. The globalization of some religions I have mentioned, for instance, to the Americas as well as to Asia and Europe, came later, as we saw in the last chapter was the case with trade.

Empires have also been linked to the spread of global culture, from the Chinese, and Greeks and Romans, to modern European imperialists such as the Spanish and British. American expansionism is also associated nowadays with the globalization of American media and culture, although whether it is an empire is open to debate. Historical empires involved the military imposition of political authority over a broad territory populated by diverse social, ethnic and national groups. Sometimes this was accompanied by the cultural socialization of elites and the extension of literacy. In ancient empires imperialism was linked to the spread of theatre, drama and poetry. The British pursued an imperial educational policy, a British school system, textbooks and curricula, use of the English language, and the education of colonial elites in the UK. In parts of its former empire elements of this live on. Under the auspices of imperialism communication, technologies such as international telegraph and submarine cables were built, for example, by the British to their colonies.

A closer look at empires historically shows unevenness and stratification in the diffusion of culture. Empires have been more political and military than cultural. Empires have ruled, but how far they have actually governed across their territories, and how far down their rule penetrated is open to question. It is likely, as I have said, that cultural practices such as local religions continued, and that cultural socialization penetrated more to elites than the wider public. In many cases the British were happy to have an empire that was political, military and economic, attempting to ideologically incorporate local populations only if they were a threat. Empires have sometimes been more about the imposition of power, including culture, than the emulation or diffusion of culture. With contemporary technology, this may be less the case – the penetration of culture globally is more possible with modern communications technology.

I have defined culture as including values and norms and these include political values. It is possible to see the globalization of culture in the form of *political ideology*. Socialism is a global ideology that has been adhered to across the world. It had a hold in the twentieth century in Central and Eastern Europe and the Soviet Union, parts of postcolonial Africa, Latin America and countries in Asia from China to Vietnam and Korea. There are societies which were not socialist but where socialism has attracted support, for instance, in Western Europe. At the same time socialism has taken localized forms and there have been different types, from Marxist-Leninist and Maoist to social democratic and more pluralist and decentralized (Wright 1987).

Liberalism has also been a globalized ideology. In fact, globalization is sometimes described in terms of the replacement of a bipolar divide between capitalism and communism at the end of the cold war by a unipolar world geared around liberalism, economically and politically, and around its global spread. Fukuyama (1989) has argued that we are at an 'end of history' where communism has died as an alternative to capitalism that people believe in, even if in material terms it hangs on in some places. Liberalism has won the ideological battle, even if it is not yet established everywhere in practice. This means liberalism as an economic system with private ownership, competition and free markets, rather than state ownership and planning. Politically it means liberalism as pluralist multi-party competition and the protection of the individual from the state.

Socialism has collapsed in many places as the governing system. But it is not dead in terms of support and its analysis of power, inequality and contradictions in capitalism. Big corporations are some of the most powerful actors in the world and maintain their power to make a profit, often through relations of domination and exploitation that reproduce inequality. Inequalities and conflicts are part and parcel of capitalism and cause problems for it, as well as being part of its dynamism. Such an explanation is common, including amongst non-socialists, and comes out of the socialist analysis of capitalism. Socialism has public support, including in post-communist countries where former communist or socialist parties get significant votes in elections. In alternatives to neoliberal globalization and American power, there are socialist elements to the criticisms and alternatives that are proposed. Problems of global inequality and poverty, ecological crisis and economic instability have been attributed to economic liberalism. Liberalism has become more popular in the late twentieth and early twenty-first centuries, but socialism still has a hold analytically and ideologically.

Technology and the globalization of media and culture

Economics, technology and history in global communications

Several themes of this book apply to the globalization of culture. As we shall see, the globalization of culture is structured and stratified in a way that involves power, inequality and conflict. Modernity and the importance of economics are also evident. Technological change has been a key factor behind the globalization of culture and media. Many of the technologies of cultural globalization have been of the modern industrial era. I argued in chapter 2 that the clearest qualitative leap for globalization was in this period. Modern cultural and communication technologies, from the printing press to the television, may be qualitatively more significant than the IT developments of the 'postmodern' era, although this is not to say that the latter have not been important.

Economic incentives have been behind technological change, especially under capitalism where profits can be made out of developing communications technologies and the globalization of media and culture for sale. Economics is an important underlying factor, as I will argue throughout this book. Economic motivations are not the sole factors or impersonal and out of control, but are often primary. People will develop new technologies and media because of the financial gain that can be made from them.

Often economic motivations only turn into globalization if *technology* (as well as other factors) allows them to. The rise of capitalism created a force for globalization. But it was when technologies of communication and transportation developed under *industrial* capitalism that globalization could take place. Capitalism developed in the sixteenth century or earlier and had an outward-looking economic impetus that could be fulfilled when the rise of industrial technology from the eighteenth century onwards provided the means for this. Economics is a driving force, but technology is a vital enabler for this economic driving force.

Technology itself is not determinant. There is not a dynamic of change inherent in it. *Economic and other factors* have to allow the technology to develop – so they are the determinant forces. Economic gain, or political or scientific institutions favourable to technological developments, have to exist. Depending on whether such bases are there, in some places globalizing technology may develop; in other places not. The combination of capitalist motivations and industrial technology provided a significant phase in the globalization of the media.

There were *pre-modern or pre-industrial developments* in communication that were important. Postal communications in Roman and medieval times were an early form of the movement of information.

The development of printing in the late fifteenth century allowed writings to be mass-produced and disseminated across wider geographical areas. And trading relations, established for economic reasons, promoted by political authorities and backed up by military power, provided a basis for lines of communication along which culture and media as well as goods could be transported.

Important to cultural globalization is not just technology that transmits media and information but also technology for the *transportation of people*. This is significant culturally because people take their culture with them, especially if they are moving on a longer-term rather than transient basis, as in tourism. They experience global culture in the places they go to. Or they have global culture brought to them by the movement of people from abroad to their locality. Host communities' cultural configurations are changed by the movement of people into them.

The development of *naval travel*, and the transition from sail to steamships, was important in the global movement of culture via people because it allowed global and trans-oceanic movements beyond regional and land-bound constraints. More recently *jet travel* has been important in developing means of transport that can take people great distances quickly. Jet planes allow people to travel from one side of the world to the other within a day, rather than over longer periods in propeller planes, or weeks or months by sea. In these cases diminishing costs then become important in mobility developing across classes. Most people in rich countries can now afford to travel quickly globally on at least several occasions throughout their life.

Some qualifications to this picture have to be made. The movement of people is uneven. In chapters 5 and 6 I will look at longer-term migration and will only mention tourism here. *International tourism* has increased significantly but also unequally. People from richer countries make up a disproportionate number of those who travel and their expenditure is stratified by wealth. Furthermore, a lot of transnational tourism is regional, for instance, by Asians within Asia and Europeans within Europe.

In 2007, the countries that had the most tourists visiting were, in order: France, Spain, the United States, China, Italy, the UK, Germany, Ukraine, Turkey and Mexico. These are predominantly European and North American states. The Asian examples are large countries and there are no African or South American destinations in the top ten. This gives some sense of the inequality in tourism. About 80 per cent of international tourism is within the same region and about 20 per cent to other regions. So not only is there inequality in global tourism but its globality is limited (UNWTO 2008).

We can see, in tables 3.1 and 3.2, the skewed nature of tourism

Table 3.1 Tourism arrivals

	1990 millions	2007 millions	Market share 2007 %	Receipts 2007 %
World	436	903	100	100
Europe	262.6	484.4	53.6	50.6
Asia and Pacific	55.8	184.3	20.4	22.1
Americas	92.8	142.5	15.8	20
(North America)	(71.7)	(95.3)	(10.6)	(14.6)
Africa	15.2	44.4	4.9	3.3

Source: Data from UNWTO 2008

Table 3.2 Tourism departures

	1990 millions	2007 millions	Market share 2007 %
World	436	903	100
Europe	252.7	502	55.6
Asia and Pacific	58.9	181.9	20.1
Americas	99.8	149.7	16.6
Middle East	8.2	27.8	3.1
Africa	9.9	26.7	3.0

Source: Data from UNWTO 2008

arrivals and departures. The figures show that international tourist movements are increasing, but also how unequal such movements are. The data do not show internal variations within regions but I have included North American arrivals in table 3.1, as well as the Americas as a whole, to give one example of such variation.

I mentioned that it was under British imperialism that some global technologies for the transmission of media and information were established, and this leads us back to the globalization of culture in the form of symbols rather than people. European imperialist powers established *underwater cable systems* across oceans in different parts of the world, for instance, from Europe to Asia and Australia. This allowed communication to be separated from the transportation of people. Communication could be done through cables speedily, almost instantaneously, rather than at the speed of people transportation by ship. It also allowed fast communication across seas. It was less regionally constrained by land, more trans-oceanic and global. This led to the internationalization of the telegraph system where messages could be sent by signals such as Morse code. More recently, the use of fibre-optic cable has vastly increased the amount of information that can be sent in this way.

International telephone calls and the possibility of making phone

Table 3.3 Global telephone access		
	Fixed telephone lines 2007 per 100 inhabitants	Mobile subscribers 2007 per 100 inhabitants
World	19	49
Europe	41	110
Oceania	36	78
Americas	33	72
Asia	16	37
Africa	3	27

Source: Data from ITU 2008

calls through wireless, cable and satellite technology, have been significant. There have been big increases in the use of international telephone calls but significant inequality in access to them. Wireless and satellite technology and the advance of mobile telephony have the potential to equalize things, to some extent, because they do not require a fixed infrastructure of wires and cables. In poor parts of Africa, for instance, people can make mobile phone calls, for personal or business reasons, send or receive money with their mobile phones, or rent out mobile calls locally. The figures in table 3.3 show how mobile telephone access is much higher than fixed-line access in Africa. Nevertheless, within the context of increasing international access to telephony, the figures below show inequalities.

These figures disguise further divides within these regions. For instance, North African access to telephony is much higher than in sub-Saharan Africa. Sub-Saharan Africa (excluding South Africa), has an average telephone density of 1 per cent, while in North Africa (Algeria, Egypt, Mauritania, Morocco, Tunisia) it is 11 per cent. Almost three-quarters of the continent's fixed lines are in six of Africa's fifty-five countries (ITU 2008).

While talking on a telephone enables global communication, it is less a mechanism for transmitting *culture* globally than radio, cinema or TV. *Radio* is a medium for the global transmission of music and news, amongst other things, and was so before the spread of television. It was especially important in the development of pop music and youth culture from the 1950s onwards. These, especially in Anglo-American and Westernized forms, were globalized through this medium. Wireless radio can be received where there is not a fixed infrastructure of wires and cables, including in more remote or poor parts of the world. It has been an important channel for dissident communication. For instance, in the Second World War it was used as a propaganda, intelligence or disinformation tool by different sides, in Eastern Europe in the anti-communist movement before 1989, and in pirate radio stations. At the same time there are inequalities in access to production and consumption in radio.

Cinema and TV are some of the most important media for transmitting culture globally. Wireless radio was important in disseminating music, news and culture but has been overtaken by TV. In some rich developed countries the ownership of televisions rose from about 10 per cent of households at the start of the 1950s to about 90 per cent at the end. There are soaps and reality TV shows, and events like the Olympics, World Cup and Iraq War, that are viewed in many parts of the world. Technological changes such as satellite and cable allow a greater volume of information to be received, in particular, more TV channels. This allows for a broader global range of television to be broadcast into people's homes but also narrowcasting. Rather than watching a small number of general channels, people choose from a far greater number of channels with narrower coverage – e.g., channels dedicated to either pop videos, sport, news or soap operas. So it leads to a more global spread in the range of TV received, but increased narrowness in type of television watching. Cinema, as we shall see, tends to be dominated by American productions and so by American values and lifestyles, but not without competition from other parts of the world

Fibre-optic cable and then satellite and digital technology have been important developments. They allow larger volumes of information to be sent. As well as allowing more TV channels to be received, computer Internet connections can send and receive not just Internet and email but also large volumes of information such as video and audio. Digital technology allows for the convergence of communications technologies, so that telephone, TV, radio and Internet information can be sent quickly and in great quantities through the same means. Satellite technology allows instantaneous and long-distance technology but without, as mentioned, the costs or restrictions that come with fixed cables.

The digital and Internet era

A technological development much emphasized in discussions of globalization is *the Internet*. The Internet is global, or potentially global, and involves more or less instant access to information or communication. Although there is great inequality in access, there are also poor parts of the world where it is available relatively inexpensively. The Internet integrates telecommunications, computing and media technologies. Computers that were used to process information unlinked with other computers now have such connections worldwide and do more than just handle information or word process. They are a means of communication and for fetching information and media, written, visual and audio, globally. It gives people across the world access to common global information, although in countries such as Cuba, North Korea or China use of the Internet, or areas of it, is restricted. In China, for instance, searches for terms such as 'human rights' or 'democracy' and on specific websites are limited (although some of these restrictions can be circumvented). Internet availability is globalizing rapidly, although still very uneven. In terms of economic motivations behind the rise of the Internet, advertising revenue is a key factor. Much Internet content is funded by adverts rather than consumer payment.

The Internet of the early twenty-first century is relatively unregulated by governments and a qualitatively different aspect is that those with Internet access *can contribute* as well as receive information, without extensive financial or institutional backing, for instance, through blogging or participating in the interactive dimensions of sites. People who are consumers or users can also become producers of content. Sites such as Blogspot and WordPress provide free resources that people can use to publish blogs and sites such as MySpace and YouTube allow people to post video or music for free. Individuals can publish their own websites. Many corporate or political sites provide fora where users can contribute.

In US politics political bloggers are an important group perceived to have an impact on the electoral fortunes of candidates, for instance, in presidential nomination campaigns and elections. Wikis are an example of the democratizing and equalizing potential of the Internet. The online encyclopedia Wikipedia can be edited by any user with Internet access. It has become an important source of information for many people. The consequence could be poor-quality information, misuse and chaos, and many question its reliability. But it provides useful information, diverse and critical views, with openness to users to define that information. The public can be active producers of content, independent of institutional backing, and not just passive users. At the same time, there is a question mark over whether independent producers of content change the agenda of public discussions and so provide a qualitatively different experience for Internet consumers.

Authors such as Castells (2000, see also Holton 2007) see the access and horizontal networking that the Internet allows as part of a developing *network society*. People can communicate and organize via the Internet themselves, rather than this being organized through hierarchical or bureaucratic forms or states, political organizations or corporations. Networks are a form of mutual civil society organization and communication that is an alternative to organization via the state or the market. Individuals and groups can counter cultural imperialism via the Internet, providing their own meanings and information. It has been a means for networking organization used by global social movements and some see networking as generalized beyond this to, for instance, types of work organization.

There are criticisms of the idea of the network society, and Castells is conscious of its inequalities. There is a digital divide between those who have access to the Internet and those who do not. Sub-Saharan Africa is mostly outside this network society at present. And the network society exists alongside and intertwined with one where the economic and political power of corporations and states wield disproportionate power and where such organizations make the most important decisions that affect economics, politics and people's lives.

Some of the big media corporations buy up Internet companies and fora where networking has developed, colonizing such areas themselves. The democratizing element of the Internet has to be weighed up against the counter-movements of large corporations into Internet industries. News Corporation, for example, acquired MySpace. Google, whose motto is 'don't be evil', has gained increasing control across the Internet, in part by buying up other smaller companies, such as YouTube. And companies such as Microsoft and Time Warner have also diversified into ownership in the Internet sector.

Potentially the Internet can be equalizing and democratic in the access it gives to individuals to contribute and be heard. That large swathes of content and functions on the Internet are free to the user is important and increases the range of things which Internet users as consumers can access. But whether the Internet provides a leap forward in access to culture for *consumers* greater than that provided by radio, TV or film, or than the innovations produced by printing, trans-oceanic cables, the telegraph and the telephone is questionable. These allowed instant or mass communications. Mass instant communications and access to information were available before the Internet which has provided a quantitative increase in these rather than a new qualitative shift to them for the first time.

The Internet is faster, providing greater ease of access for consumers to information than provided by previous forms of technology, and its speed increases the volumes of information that can be reached. News, reference information, banking, shopping, music and video can be accessed with greater ease and convenience, more quickly and broadly. But as this information could be obtained before the Internet, albeit more awkwardly and slowly, the Internet is a great resource for radically improving access, rather than establishing access that was not there before, a *quantitative improvement rather than a qualitative shift* in such areas. Similarly, social networking on the Internet, for instance, on MySpace and Facebook, often adds a virtual dimension to already-existing real-world relations, rather than adding new forms or types of relations.

From a sociological point of view, the key thing is not what is new and exciting about the *technology*, but what is *socially* novel about it and how it changes society or creates new forms of social experience. Technologically, the Internet is revolutionary. But it does not necessarily follow that its social impact is transformatory and this has to be considered separately. The qualitatively different thing is that the Internet provides new access for ordinary people as producers to publish content independently of financial or institutional backing. The change for consumers of culture, compared to previous media technologies, is more quantitative than qualitative.

The technology of global media and culture as modern, economic and unequal

For Rantanen (2005: 26), media and communications moved from oral, to handwritten, to printed media in the early days of modernity. From the nineteenth century they shifted to wired electronic, then to wireless in the twentieth century, and to digital technology from the 1990s onwards. This has changed communication from slow to mass-produced and faster, at the speed people can move, then to immediacy since the nineteenth century, with electronic communication. The space that can be covered by communications has moved from local to global. For Rantanen, the most significant developments have been electronic and digital innovations in the modern and postmodern eras respectively. These have made media and communications immediate, mass and global.

Many of these developments have made the world a 'smaller' place, a 'global village' where time and space seem to have shrunk. Distances are just as great but the time taken to get from one place to another, communicate or receive information has been so reduced that places which are just as far away in physical distance are much closer as far as speed of communication and transport is concerned. A letter which could take weeks to be transported from one side of the world to the other by sea and land could go by plane in a few days or hours, and was replaced by the email which is almost instant. Goods or people which had to be transported around the world over weeks or months can be sent by jet in a few hours or, if goods in the form of information, almost at once.

Modern industrial technology made a leap forward for cultural globalization. It enabled communication to be trans-oceanic rather than restricted to regional land masses. It increased the speed and volume of people movements, separating the transmission of information and culture from the mobility of people to make it more immediate. There was a break from regional and pre-modern cultural movements. More 'postmodern' technologies have been dramatic but have built on this type of cultural globalization and made it possible to expand and democratize it, rather than themselves introducing fast mass global transmissions of culture. These are more a product of the industrial age than the post-industrial one.

There had to be an incentive for these forms of technology to be developed and generalized. The incentive was money. These were developed and popularized by companies, with the backing of states, for profit. So capitalism as well as industrialism is a key factor. The themes of this book relating to the significance of the modern era of industrialism and capitalist economic incentives apply here.

Similarly, themes of power and inequality are relevant. The technologies I have discussed involve inequality and power in production and dissemination. Large corporations and wealthy states have a disproportionate role in the production and distribution of culture and media. A significant proportion of media that is transmitted is Western and especially American, for instance, in cinema, TV and pop music. Consumers in rich countries have greater access to media technologies such as TV and the Internet. So, in the globalization of culture, structures of power and inequality are reinforced. The Internet has the capacity to democratize this, at the level of production as well as consumption, but this has not yet been realized on a global basis, as poorer people and those in less affluent countries are under-represented in contributing to and accessing the Internet. Within richer countries, the content of blogs or sites where video, audio and information are shared by ordinary people do not generally have the same capacity for dissemination as that produced by states, corporations or others with organizational and financial backing.

The figures shown in table 3.4 on Internet access are crude measures, as there is significant differentiation within the regions mentioned. For instance, Internet use is about half in sub-Saharan Africa of that in Africa as a whole, and half in South Asia of that in East Asia (UNDP 2008a: 276). But they give an illustration of inequalities in communications and media, especially between Africa and the rest of the world. Internet

Table 3.4 Internet users per 100 inhabitants, 2007	
World	22
Oceania	45
Europe	42
Americas	41
Asia	17
Africa	5

Source: Data from ITU 2008

access is not only important for the transmission of culture but increasingly also for business success. Inequality in Internet use is not just a form of cultural inequality but also affects economic life opportunities.

Sociology has long focused on divisions and power relations in social processes. Seeing globalization as structured by inequality and power shows how short of globalization many of its processes fall. Some actors are more at the core in terms of power over them than others, and some are more integrated into globalization, while others are more excluded. This is at the levels of production, distribution and consumption. Globalization is a process and many of these patterns may change, but at present they show power and inequality to be undermining globality.

There have been leaps forward in the globalization of culture. The transmission of culture to global extents has significantly increased in the industrial era. The extent of globalization of culture and the significant implications this has for identity in some parts of the world should not be underestimated. At the same time, inequality in production and consumption makes it difficult to support theses of cultural globalization instead of more sceptical ones that highlight internationalism (between some nations) over globalism, and the role of inequality, power and variation globally in production and consumption. Inclusivity into cultural globalization is uneven.

Furthermore, analyses of inequality and power bring out another theme of this book, the *importance of economics*, because power and inequality is structured partly according to wealth. The production of technologies of cultural globalization has been pursued where there is an economic incentive to do so. Their distribution in the world has been uneven according to demand, which depends on who has the purchasing power to afford them, and where the economic benefits of introducing them are. Technologies of cultural globalization have developed where it is profitable, and unequally, according to who can afford to produce the technologies or buy them as users. As a result, there are patterns of inequality in the production and distribution of technologies such as TV and the Internet and their content. This shows up in geographical concentrations in production and use. There are national or continental variations in the spread of the technology of cultural globalization and urban/rural and class divides in access and take-up. These often reflect economic wealth, income and power.

Institutions, corporations and the global media

New technology has contributed to the globalization of culture but changes in institutions and regulation of the media have also been important. Issues of economy, wealth and power are relevant here. (McChesney 1999, Held et al. 1999, Thompson 1995, McPhail 2006, and Flew 2007 are amongst those who have contributed overviews of this area.)

The development of *international news agencies* in the mid-nineteenth century allowed for the gathering of news from around the world for domestic consumption. Such agencies provide a global dimension to news even where newspapers themselves remain mostly national or sub-national. Global news agencies include Reuters, the Associated Press, United Press International, Agence France Presse, Bloomberg and Dow Jones. Many come from core Western states and their staff act within the mainstream values and concerns of those countries. To a large extent, they collect and deliver news that reflects the news agendas of such countries rather than of those more at the periphery. People can also watch TV channels that cover international news and broadcast it to audiences around the world, for instance, CNN, BBC news channels and Al-Jazeera.

The dominance of *English* and a few other languages has made it easier for culture to be globalized. Information can be put in a language that is accessible to many globally. Ten to twelve languages are the first languages of about 60 per cent of the world's population (De Swann 2001). English, French, Spanish and Portuguese are especially globally spread, because these countries extended globally in their imperial days. Others such as Arabic, Hindi, Russian and Chinese are widely spoken, because they have spread beyond one country or because of the sheer size of the main countries they are spoken in. English has developed as the primary global language in business, politics, academia, science, advertising, popular culture and the Internet. This helps producers of culture to communicate on a worldwide basis, although there are millions of people who cannot speak or read English.

Regulatory changes have had an effect on the globalization of culture. After the *end of the cold war* media that stressed collective, nation-building and political or public objectives, in Soviet-bloc and socialist states, but also in Western states and the anti-communist US, shrunk relative to media more determined by market, corporate and trade influences. With the collapse of socialist states and deregulation in the West, the latter has become more dominant in ownership, production and content. Western media have gained access to post-socialist states that they were denied during the cold war (McPhail 2006).

Since the 1980s there has been movement of European TV and cable away *from government ownership or control*. This has entailed a shift from goals that stress public service and the expressing or shaping of national culture towards an emphasis on profit, consumer ratings and advertising as greater determinants of content. There has been *deregulation* of cross-media ownership in many parts of the world, especially from the 1980s onwards, so that companies can diversify and obtain ownership in a range of types of media. Someone who owns one type of media takes ownership in others, or companies from different areas of media merge. Foreign ownership of media has been relaxed. As a result more of the media are concentrated in fewer private hands. Trends in media ownership have been towards privatization, deregulation, mergers, diversification and concentration of power.

This involves *horizontal integration* (McChesney 1999), control extending within or across sectors, and its concentration in fewer hands. So corporations can own media across book publishing, newspapers, music recording, TV production, TV stations, cable channels, satellite TV, film production, cinema theatres and the Internet. *Vertical integration* involves the same firms gaining ownership of both the production of content and its distribution. So companies that own Hollywood studios that make films may also control TV channels and TV networks that show them. The separation of production and distribution provides protection against accumulation of power in the media because distributors can decide whether or not to show content that comes from producers. Neither party has complete control. But companies that control both decide what is produced and can also make sure that this is what is distributed. They also control the distribution of content from producer competitors. Many of these actors are global players, doing these things across the world with large overseas sales.

Examples of large global media corporations include News Corporation, Disney, Viacom, Bertelsmann, Sony and Time Warner. Most of these are American, with the exception of Japanese Sony and the German Bertelsmann. All are geared around seeking profits internationally. Rupert Murdoch's News Corporation is an example of a company that has benefited from the technological changes and deregulation I have mentioned. Murdoch has ownership stakes in media from TV cable and satellite networks and TV and film production, through newspapers, magazines, book publishing, radio, Internet media and sport. For instance, he owns 20th Century Fox movie production and Fox TV channels, a number of other cable and satellite channels such as those offered by Sky, a number of major newspapers, including several of the main national papers in the UK and Australia, publishing interests such as HarperCollins, and websites including MySpace. He is involved in these media across the world, from Australia, the UK and the USA, to China. Rupert Murdoch has openly conservative political views, which his media products tend to reflect or not depart from too much.

Disney owns motion picture studios and distribution networks,

ABC TV, a number of cable channels, such as ESPN, TV and radio stations, book publishing interests, websites and theme parks. Many of these sell and distribute worldwide. Time Warner has ownership in film, television, broadcasting and cable, music, publishing, Internet provision and telecommunications. It owns subsidiaries such as Time Inc., AOL, Warner Bros., Time Warner Cable, CNN, HBO, Turner Broadcasting System and the CW Television Network. Many of these ventures are international in their reach – CNN for example. Viacom owns MTV, CBS, and other TV interests, Paramount Pictures, and Blockbuster. It has ownership in motion pictures, TV, publishing, and video distribution internationally.

Cultural imperialism and homogenization

While more companies can enter media ownership, an overall effect is that fewer owners monopolize control globally and across sectors, so there is increasing control of the media in a smaller number of powerful hands. More of the media is in private as opposed to public hands, with the result that private profit dominates over public service as the dominant ethos of media companies. Another effect is the reduction of competition. Interlocking directorships across companies and mergers reduce competition in media industries, allowing more companies to monopolize more within and across sectors. There is less space for alternative media with different perspectives and for media from countries beyond the core.

Ownership in the media has been heavily dominated by one nation, the *USA,* along with others such as *Japan and the EU countries,* and much TV programming and cinema globally is American. There is transnational ownership and reach in the media, and a shift from national to global media markets. But these have been biased to certain countries. There is inequality in production and consumption, for instance, in TV ownership and access to other media.

There have been attempts to protect domestic media and cultural industries, for example, from Hollywood, through restrictions or quotas on the showing of foreign films, or subsidies for domestic products. This has occurred in countries such as Norway, Denmark, Spain, France, Mexico, South Africa and South Korea. But the overall trend has been towards opening up markets to foreign competition. To some extent it depends how a country views media, as economic goods to be traded freely without restriction or as symbols that express national culture, history and identity. The US and core countries tend to favour the former (although their globally traded goods express quite specific identities), while others see the latter as the chief concern, eroded by free trade in the media, and not something to be left to whatever direction the market moves in.

US productions make up 50 per cent of films shown in Europe despite measures to protect domestic film industries. Only France shows more of its own films than US movies, 40 per cent French as against 33 per cent US. Some other European countries show about 20 per cent of their own films at home – France, Italy, Germany, the UK and Russia – but still much less than the American share. Other European countries fall much further behind 20 per cent. Between 1995 and 2000, EU exports of TV to the US were 6 per cent of the value of US exports to Europe. So, against what is economically and culturally one of its strongest competitors in cinema and broadcasting, Europe, the US dominates (Unesco 2005: 47–8).

A shift from state to private ownership, a free market in the media and the breaking down of constraints on ownership and production seem good things. They overcome restrictions and state control and increase media freedom. But while freedom of speech is very important, so too is the democratic safeguarding of public culture (in the form, for instance, of ensuring quality, minority content or indigenous culture) and it's not clear that a 'free' media delivers openness and freedom so much as monopoly control and less freedom and pluralism. Government regulation can protect the media from the concentration of control in a small number of private hands, while deregulation can increase this possibility.

Supporters of the idea of a *New World Information and Communication Order* (NWICO; see ICSCP 1980) have argued that media globalizing through the market threatens national autonomy and equality across the world in the production and content of information (see also Bourdieu 2003b), with the result that 'culture is in danger'. A deregulated global media can undermine states' attempts to maintain collective identity, promote public concerns or egalitarian measures, or find space for messages from the perspectives of their own society through greater control over the media. Such an argument can be misused by governments to justify censorship and transgress individual freedom. But it also provides an alternative to liberal and free market justifications for a globalized media that in practice is dominated by big corporations and Western content. And it can be made within a perspective that favours democracy and free speech. Arguments for the free movement of global media are often in effect supporting the skewed flow of media from the US and Western core countries, with the values of those countries wrapped up in this. To correct and equalize this, and make a truly free and open media, requires regulation and restrictions on monopolies which erode space for alternative and less powerful media. While a free market can allow monopolies, regulations to restrict monopolies can protect diversity, alternatives, national autonomy and equality from Western media power.

For commentators like McChesney, the growth of large Western media corporations leads to less open and equal competition, and to US *cultural imperialism and increasing homogeneity* (McChesney 1999; Hermann and McChesney 1997; also Schiller 1969; Tunstall 1977). Technological and institutional changes that I have discussed result in a similarity of foreign media content comprising a large area of domestic media and culture across many countries. The effect is a form of unofficial censorship of content and distribution, and a reduction in alternative views, by a small number of actors from selected countries. Speech is legally free. This is very important. People will not go to prison for questioning Western programming. But a smaller number of companies, often from the US or other rich countries, dominate the media. They are in it to make money so produce media content that sells. There is a convergence around commercial programming of a similar sort. The outcome is that difference and criticism globally is reduced and there is an increasing uniformity in tastes and cultural experiences.

For McPhail (2006), this is *cultural imperialism* in which core nations have power over semi-peripheral and peripheral nations. In media terms, core nations include many in North America and Europe, along with others such as Japan and Australia. Semi-peripheral nations include China, India, Russia and a number in Latin America. Peripheral nations include developing countries in Africa, Latin America and Asia. Nations are stratified by their significance in media production, trade in media, access to media such as TV and Internet, and how featured they are in media coverage, a lot of which is affected by factors such as economic development and literacy. Core-, semi-periphery, and periphery distinctions can be made on economic, political and military matters as well, and sometimes nations fall into similar categories in a number or all of these areas. As far as the media go, core nations make large profits from selling TV, music, film, books, magazines and newspapers, as well as from the infrastructure for transmitting these – technology, software and companies, for instance. Content is dominated by the economic, political, social and cultural values of the West, and by its preoccupations in terms of matters like culture, lifestyle and sport. Countries more at the periphery become dependent on, and recipients of, core nations' media infrastructure and content.

Cultural imperialism follows from previous forms of military, religious and mercantile imperialism over many centuries. Where political and military colonialism has passed by, it has been replaced by economic and cultural imperialism or electronic colonialism. This involves the domination of media from core countries over more peripheral powers that are dependent on the media investment and infrastructure coming from the core and thus are subject to the media content transmitted through these which may threaten local cultures. In one way, this is more of a threat than political or military forms of colonialism because it can involve changing the attitudes and ideas of those subject to it. In response to this, nationalist and protectionist measures occur in an effort to preserve national cultures.

There are *reasons to question* the extent to which media is increasingly controlled by multinational corporations (Flew 2007: 80–90). Deregulation and technological change have allowed for greater competition, for instance, in broadcasting, as well as monopolies. The Internet has provided alternatives and plural sources of media. Often, multinational or global corporations are predominantly national corporations with overseas operations. They are trading internationally, but not worldwide or with integrated activities at either ownership, production or consumption levels. For Flew, News Corporation may be the only media corporation that is close to being genuinely global. Time Warner and Disney earn over three-quarters of their revenues in North America and less than 15 per cent of their assets are foreign. Where they have overseas operations, control and content is maintained at the national base. Hollywood films are made and distributed throughout the world, but they are national in the important senses that they are owned and controlled in the US and bear the imprint of American values and culture. The same could be said for other examples such as CNN. Media corporations may have overseas operations and consumers but in a relation of dominance over them, or through outsourcing rather than genuine integration or the transfer of control and skills. Some of the most transnational media corporations, which are often not the largest, are based in Europe where their transnationality is more to do with the openness of EU borders than globalization and with being based in small countries where overseas operations are necessary to expand profits.

However, as with many globalization arguments, what is being described is possibly not globalization but is still of *international significance*. Awareness of this significance is as important as awareness of the lack of qualities that would symbolize true globalization – that is, inclusivity, spread and integration. There is abundant evidence of media systems which are not national ones for national audiences and certainly are not global, but which involve nationally or multinationally based MNCs, trading internationally, with huge power over the production, distribution and consumption of media content, meanings and information. The wealth earned by such organizations is then returned to their core countries and contributes to further spreading their ideas. While not properly globalized, they are disproportionately powerful in relation to other states, groups and individuals who also have a culture, meaning or message they wish to get through. These MNCs may not be worldwide and may be detached from a domestic national focus in terms of profit, control or content, but they are international and powerful. At the same time, the fact that such corporations are not genuinely global is important. This is because the companies involved are owned in one area, have relations with other parts of the world that is more to do with export than integration and whose content reflects this less-than-global bias. They are less than global due to the power differences and inequalities they encapsulate and which underly their significance, and to describe them in terms of globalization hides this.

Further Reading

Thomas McPhail's (2006) *Global Communication* is a readable book full of useful information on the globalization of the media. It puts forward a perspective which sees globalization of the media as cultural imperialism and uses world-systems theory to show the inequalities between core and periphery areas of the world as far as media goes, although it occasionally itself lapses from sticking to this perspective.

Terry Flew's (2007) *Understanding Global Media* is a substantial and more advanced overview, with quite an encompassing content and balanced use of a variety of theoretical perspectives.

John Thompson's (1995) *The Media and Modernity*, especially chapter 5, looks at the globalization of media within the context of a social theory of the development of modern media more generally.

Robert McChesney (1999), 'The New Global Media: It's a Small World of Big Conglomerates', *The Nation*, 29, also in Held and McGrew's (2003) *Global Transformations Reader*, and online, is a bit dated but a short and punchy summary of some of the key issues. McChesney is author with Edward Hermann (1997) of *The Global Media*.

Similarly, Bourdieu (2003b), in a short, powerful, polemical piece, warns that the autonomy of culture is in danger because of neoliberal globalization.

CHAPTER 4

The Globalization of Culture: Homogeneous or Hybrid?

Homogenization, Westernization and clashes

WHETHER or not technological change and deregulation have created what can be called global media corporations, they have allowed the growth of international corporations that have concentrated great media power in their hands. What sort of effect do these technological and regulatory changes and institutional structures have on the content of globalized culture and identity in society? Does it lead to the sort of cultural imperialism and homogenization that authors such as McChesney (1999) and Schiller (1969) talk about?

I wish to look at a number of conclusions about what form the globalization of culture takes in society and its effect on identity, including: homogenization; Westernization; clashes of culture; hybridization; localization and contextualization of global culture; heterogeneity; coexistence of cultures; and inequality in production and consumption of culture. Some of these interpretations overlap with one another.

The tendency in global cultural studies has increasingly been to dismiss the homogenization thesis in favour of more localized and hybrid perspectives. Nederveen Pieterse (2004a) is one prominent advocate of the view of globalization of culture as hybridization. It is right to bring out the complex nature of cultural globalization, and the idea of homogenization by itself is too simplistic. This recognition parallels shifts from globalist to transformationalist perspectives discussed in chapter 1. But some of the insights in the homogenization perspective are important and the thrust of its argument should not be ruled out. To do so runs the risk of bringing in too much of a benign view of world culture as pluralistic and mixed, as if dominant power and hierarchy does not have a big effect. I want to argue that phenomena such as hybridization, heterogeneity and localization show a homogenization perspective to be too simplistic. But more recent perspectives that favour hybrid and pluralist pictures over homogeneity can go too far the other way. Hybridity and pluralism is happening within the context of cultural imperialism, so homogenization and conclusions which represent the latter perspectives need to be revised rather than rejected, and to be rescued from those who see them as too simplistic and crude.

All of these perspectives agree that transformations in culture and the media have gone beyond national boundaries and national cultures. Culture extends across borders and in doing so brings the same or similar cultures to many parts of the world, even if without the same consequences everywhere. This process has been accelerated and expanded by changes I have discussed in technology, deregulation and corporate ownership. It forges new forms of culture, identity, consumption and style, from dress to food and music, in the everyday life of individuals.

The *homogenization perspective* is sometimes known as the McDonaldization thesis (see Ritzer 2007), referring to the fact that consumer products such as McDonald's burgers have spread around the globe. This is linked to the idea that a small number of big media conglomerates dominate the marketplace, replicating similar types of culture worldwide. Because such culture originates in these big, mostly Western or capitalist corporations, it is seen as cultural imperialism or *Westernization* – homogenization in the image of the West and dominated by Western media.

Much of the culture referred to by the homogenization thesis is consumer culture – food and drink, media and other consumer products. It is seen as coming from the West or the US especially, and if from the East then from a sort of high-capitalism in countries such as Japan or South Korea, and eventually perhaps China too. Although it has long been commonplace for images, genres, media and cultural content to go from these Western and capitalist countries to other Western or capitalist countries, especially to the young, increasingly these are now exported to other parts of the world and other generations.

From this perspective, there is a homogenization, convergence or sameness of cultures. People are more and more watching the same sorts of TV programmes, from CNN news to the Disney channel, MTV, ESPN, American soap operas from cable and satellite channels, video games, as well as consuming the same products, such as Coca-Cola, in the same sorts of places like McDonald's and Starbucks. All these products are made by American corporations.

If you watch TV outside America it isn't unlikely that you will come across US TV shows like *The Simpsons*, *Friends*, *Sex and the City*, *ER*,

Seinfeld, *Frasier*, or *Everybody Loves Raymond*. The largest audience for a TV series was for *Baywatch*, with 1.1 billion watching weekly in 1996, more than one in six people in the world. The show has been seen on all continents except Antarctica, in 148 countries and translated into forty-four languages (*Guinness Book of Records* 2008). A channel like MTV is adapted for local audiences, but there is still a great deal of sameness across its local outputs, dominated by American and Western English-language pop music, or local music influenced by Americanization. This crowds out space for local musicians and especially for those who pursue non-Americanized or non-Westernized types of music. CNN, for instance, has a very wide international reach while broadcasting quite an American perspective on the news. Even where programmes themselves are not globalized, their format may be, for instance, in the case of some reality TV programmes or soaps.

I argued in the last chapter that media globalization might be best seen as the internationalizing of national media. Because of the limited global scope of the biggest media corporations in overseas assets and sales compared to their domestic involvements these should be seen as national corporations with international operations rather than global. At the same time we have seen that this internationaliza-tion is not necessarily as localizing or indigenizing as it appears on the surface. What is going on is something *between globalization and localization* – international but less than global, but internationalizing national products from a source as much as adapting them in a mean-ingful way to the local circumstances they are distributed to.

Diversity, alternative views or local products get squeezed out as these big firms monopolize markets, through competition or buying out competitors. This mostly Western culture may come into tension or conflict with local values. It can have images or messages which are counter to or not supportive of the values of local ways of life, whether politically, as in places like China, or culturally.

One thesis is that globalization leads to *clashes of cultures*. A promi-nent advocate has been Huntington in his book *The Clash of Civilizations* (see Huntington 1996; Barber 1996). Globalization brings cultures into contact and proximity, for example, through global media or migration, and this causes friction and conflict. For instance, Western political values are seen by the Chinese government to clash with their beliefs and security, and efforts are made to prevent access to them or to human rights activities. Western liberal ideas of the role of women, sexuality or the family conflict with ideas beyond the West in the traditions of other cultures and religions, and also within the West, for instance, in fundamentalist types of Christianity. Potential political outcomes of this include a desire for closure of some cul-tures from others, as well as regionalization and rivalry (Nederveen

Pieterse 2004a). The clash often highlighted is between the West and Islam, although Huntington referred to a number of religions and linked Islam with Confucianism. Conflicting values are said to occur between Western and other countries, or within Western countries. Cultures sometimes do have different norms and values that are contradictory. But there are problems with the clash of cultures thesis.

Many of the problems of cultures clashing are to do with *political or economic differences* rather than cultural differences. Conflicts between Western and Islamic groups are often connected with the situation of Palestinians in Israel. The Muslim world has tended to side with the rights of Palestinians to their own state, while the USA is seen to be a friend of Israel and insensitive to the cause of Palestinians under occupation. Other aspects of American foreign policy are a source of conflict, such as the overseas stationing of troops or invasions of Afghanistan and Iraq. Muslims within Western societies sometimes feel they are victims of racism or scapegoating, disenfranchized and excluded, and members of a group on the receiving end of economic, political and military power. Tensions result from this as much as from cultural differences, between Western and other countries, and within Western countries such as the UK, France and Germany. There is a danger that attributing these differences to culture may involve the demonizing of Islamic culture or values, and a thesis of irreconcilable differences between cultures, on a false basis, when divergences are connected with remediable issues of foreign policy, politics or economics.

Second, the clash of cultures thesis can *overestimate the differences between cultures* and underestimate those within them. Non-Muslim Westerners and Western Muslims have lived together in peace for a long time. In fact there is often an intermingling of these cultures. Many Muslims living in Western societies mix their Muslim faith, culture and identity with values and culture from Western societies, for instance, in consumption, music, media, fashion, sport and socializing. They have hybrid identities of the sort I will come back to shortly. There is cultural intermingling rather than separation. This is not to say there are not differences in norms and values between liberalism and capitalism on the one hand and Islam on the other. But the record of liberal and Muslim cultures has often been one of coexistence. There is no clear evidence that such cultures must clash because of their differences or that cultural differences are the source of conflicts that do happen.

Third, the clash of cultures thesis *underplays the internal differentiations of cultures* it refers to. The West is divided. It was especially divided, for instance, over the Iraq War. And there has been constant division amongst European countries regarding how close to America they are on issues such as foreign policy, economics and culture. Western Christianity has serious internal divisions, for instance, over sexuality and abortion. Similarly, Islam has its own historical internal conflicts, for example, between Sunni and Shi'a Muslims.

Localization, coexistence and the hybridization of cultures

There are also criticisms of the homogenization thesis. These can lead to an alternative view of the globalization of culture as involving hybridization rather than clashes or a common type (Nederveen Pieterse 2004a).

There are *exceptions* to the homogenization thesis. For instance, the Indian film industry is dominant in its own country over Hollywood film and is an exporter to other parts of the world – a globalizer as well as an alternative to globalization at home. India makes about 700 films a year as compared to about 400 a year made by the USA (and about 600 made ever in Africa). Its exports go beyond diaspora communities in places like the USA, the UK and the Middle East, to countries like China and Japan (UNESCO 2005). In many countries, film, TV content, food and music of local origin continue to be the main staple over imports from overseas that come with the globalization of culture, and these local products are popular too.

It is important to make a *distinction* between media and culture. What I have emphasized is media such as TV, radio, music and the Internet. Much of this is produced commercially and sold and distributed through cable, satellite or wireless signals. Culture is broader than this and includes values and beliefs, for instance, of a political or religious sort, alongside ways of life and traditions. These cannot be completely separated from media – quite often they are bought and sold or transmitted through the media. But they are broader and not reducible to it. So where there is Western domination and homogenization in the media there may not be so in broader culture. For instance, people in societies beyond the Western core receive and consume Western media – American TV shows and films, for instance. In this sense the media is globalized and homogenizing. But cultures in such societies may not be Westernized or homogenized, and often maintain their own religious and family cultures, despite a Westernized media. Globalization of the media is not the same as, and need not imply, the globalization of culture.

Focusing just on media, I have mentioned how the *proliferation of forms* of media and narrowcasting can go against homogenization. People get media from different sources – TV, radio, the Internet and so on. Some of these sources – for example, with the proliferation of TV channels following developments in cable, satellite and digital technology – carry greater volumes of information. With the multiplication of channels, many of them specialize in a specific type of content – e.g., news, sport or comedy. So people's exposure to culture may be quite global but also narrower in the genre, type or origin they choose to watch. The variety of sorts of programmes produced increases so narrowness and diversity in viewing are outcomes as much as broader and more homogenous experiences. But, although many of the TV channels are dominated by Western media, the success of alternative new channels such as Al-Jazeera shows that such diversity also creates the opportunity for a variety of contents.

Another criticism of the homogenization thesis is that it has a *passive view of the receivers of culture*. The hypodermic model of the media sees it as having a content that is injected into the audience. The message can be decoded by a media analyst who identifies its meaning and effect on the audience. Studies of the media as causing violence sometimes adhere to this model.

But *audiences* are active readers of culture. They read it in different ways, come to different interpretations of what they see, and are accepting, critical or antagonistic. Often this is because of the *varying contexts* they come from which have different values and norms through which readings of culture are made, leading to different interpretations and reactions. A limitation of content analysis in media studies is that it makes assertions about what the content of media are (for instance, in literature, films or TV news) and about what meanings or effects it has, but without putting media into their social context or seeing the active role of the reader or viewer. What media mean depends not only on what is in the media (the film or literature, for example), but also in what happens to it when it enters different contexts within which it may be read in varying ways. If content is looked at less in the abstract and more sociologically, as embedded in its social context, it is clear that its meaning is variable.

With active audiences coming from diverse contexts, the meaning of media and culture is mediated by national or local cultures. There will be differences in the uptake and reading of Western culture in different circumstances, and varying degrees of openness to or sympathy with it. This implies some degree of autonomy on the part of listeners, readers or viewers in making an active interpretation of what they see, hear or read rather than just passively accepting a message. In some cases this will lead to conflicts and tensions between localities and the incoming culture. This perspective, which focuses on the active role of the audiences and their context, has more of an ethnographic and anthropological aspect to it than the more political/economic approaches of the cultural imperialist school. The latter tend to focus on the generalization of the media, with less attention to context and people's own readings of it.

In fact, Western media and cultural producers are well aware of difference and adapt their products to local audiences. *Localization* happens on the part of the producer as well as the consumer. For instance, to return to the McDonaldization theme, McDonald's produce different kinds of burgers for different contexts, shrimp burgers in Japan, kosher burgers for Jewish areas and halal meat for Muslims. Whether McDonald's has a mainly working-class or middle-class clientele varies from country to country. In some places it is a fast-food restaurant, but in others a place where consumers go for a long, more social meal. MTV produces different versions of its broadcasts for different areas of the world. Formats for soaps and reality TV shows are taken on but adapted for the national context. In these and many other ways, Western culture is adapted for different local circumstances. This process has become known as glocalization, the localization of globalization (Robertson 1992; see Sassen 2007 for a different view of local spaces in globalization).

TV audiences often watch local TV even when given the choice of American imports. A stronger version of the localization thesis is that local alternatives *to* globalization, as well as local versions *of* globalization, become *revived and reasserted*. In part this is a turning away from global integration and negative resistance to homogenization. At the same time it is a turning to a more positive identity locally or nationally. The French, for instance, try to protect their own music and film industries by restrictions on the import of foreign (i.e., American) TV films and pop music, and by resistance to the Anglicization of the French language. Nationalism can be stirred up as a reaction to globalization which is seen as a threat to national identity in terms of the outside culture it brings in, whether through cultural influences such as Americanization or, it is alleged, immigration. In France, attacks on McDonald's have been part of a nationalist reaction to Americanization, demonstrating how national cultures may be revalidated or reasserted in the face of globalization of culture. The same is said of other tribalist or fundamentalist identities, such as religious or ethnic ones. There is a combination of clash of cultures and localization perspectives in examples like this.

The rise of the Internet and political blogging alongside the growing access of a greater variety of TV stations allows for the expression of alternative or oppositional views to Western globalization. Middle Eastern media like Al-Jazeera express views sceptical of America and the West, rather than being incorporated by them. Bloggers who can make their views publicly available without corporate institutional platforms or extensive finance can criticize the West from outside or within it. Cable, satellite and the Internet make it possible for such channels and blogs to be available internationally. This means there are forces that are oppositional to cultural imperialism.

Nations that continue to have a significant hold or are reasserted under globalization include not just nation-states, but also (as Scholte 2005 argues) *sub-national* nations (such as the Scots, Basques or Tamils), or *ethno-nations* (such as the Kurds, a shared ethnic group who live across parts of Turkey, Iran and Iraq, as well as Syria and Armenia, aspiring to their own state). Or it includes *transworld nations* such as the Chinese or Indians who have home nations but are also a global nation spread around the world – a diaspora. Intranational nationalism as well as religious fundamentalism (for example, Hindu, Jewish or Christian) has been attributed to a resistance to globalization. Because it is in relation to globalization it is part of the processes of globalization, both negative resistance to it and positive aspiration to an alternative identity.

Diaspora preserve their cultures in nations they migrate to. So, even in the heartlands of Western culture and not just in places it is exported to, diversity rather than homogeneity survives. The US is a diverse country with many languages, religions and cultural groups, as well as being a major manufacturer and exporter of global culture. In its own home such a globalized Western culture exists alongside diversities of culture, whether of food, music, language, media or belief. And America is not the only country that has such cultural pluralism even if it has more than most.

Additionally, Western countries such as the US *import culture* more generally. Pop music in the West often contains influences from Latin America, Africa or Asia. Film is not just a question of Hollywood exports. Imports to the West from India, Hong Kong and East Asia, China, Japan and South America are important. In most Western countries you do not have to travel far to buy wine or food from many countries of the world, hear languages other than a country's primary tongue, or come across diverse places of worship from religions whose main homes are outside the West. There are reverse cultural flows, from East to West and South to North, as well as the other way round.

The forms of consumption, style, culture and identity that result are *hybridized*, in the way that a hybrid plant is made up of a combination of other plants. Different combinations of plural inputs create a new synthesis or mixed culture. Sometimes culture like this is described as creolization, from the idea of languages made up from two or more languages with new elements emerging not directly from either of its parents but from what the combination has produced. Waters (2001) puts it that this involves not just the bringing of the centre to the periphery, in global terms, but also the periphery to the centre. Just like homogenization, this is constituted by the mobility of goods, information, media products and people from around the world.

The USA has a hybrid culture, a multi-lingual, multi-ethnic nation of immigrants, mostly arrived in recent generations and who far outnumber the indigenous population. Some studies focus on global cities such as London and New York (Sassen 2001), where there are diversities of ethnicities and cultures that feed into one another so that over time generations become more hybrid. Different cultural inputs become combined in people's individual or social identities and cultures. In global countries and cities, hybrid mixes include city kids listening to rap or bhangra, talking a lingo that includes, say, European, Asian and Caribbean dialect, or Europeans and Americans adopting Japanese culture such as manga and films. Japanese culture includes a mix of collectivism, loyalty and Confucianism with a hyper hi-tech capitalism. There is hybrid music that combines Western pop, hip-hop, and Asian and Latin influences. Western films such as *Kill Bill* explicitly adopt influences from Asian film. And there are young Muslims who hold to their religion and traditions but are also enthusiastic participants in Western consumer culture, music and sport.

The mixing of cultures produces new forms of identity, or third cultures (Beck 2000), or, as Nederveen Pieterse (2004a) puts it, *mélange* culture. There is integration but with diversity rather than homogeneity. This not only differs from homogenization but also from models of *multiculturalism or heterogeneity* which see cultures living side by side rather than becoming mixed into new forms. Multiculturalism models of different cultures, maintaining their difference but living peacefully adjacently, contrast with assimilationist models where cultures are expected to conform to common norms and values. Hybridization stresses interculturalism more than multiculturalism. Rather than assimilation or a multicultural coexistence of cultures, there is hybridization. There is a mix instead of side-by-side pluralism, which creates a diverse pot rather than convergence to homogeneity. What is created is hybrid cultures but also hybrid identities in individuals.

While this involves borders being fluid, it *may not mean nations or national identity being dissolved.* Nations are reconfigured by taking on the hybrid identity they have imported and created. In each nation this identity will be different from elsewhere because of the specific historical, economic, political and cultural links each nation has with others, always different according to the nation in question. This is not to mention other factors such as language similarities, geographical proximities, specific economic situation or political cultural history, taking forms varying by nation and influences, that affect the type of hybridity that develops in each case. Each nation will have its own hybridity, not replicated in other nations with their own different varieties of inputs. The transformation of UK identity, for instance, is effected by the particular countries that are its former colonies and that it has links with, ties with the USA, and its membership of the European Union. Other nations have other channels of integration into globalization that are different from this. This fits with transformationalist perspectives outlined in chapter 1, which see identities, such as national identities, as not eroded or swept away but reconfigured or transformed into new hybrid forms, distinct from other nations but also including their influences and cultural inputs.

Studies of the *history of globalization* argue that, before modernity, the advanced civilizations of the East made important contributions to what became the modern West. Historians who put this point of view are trying to correct Eurocentric views of the West as dominant, pointing out that it has drawn on the East and was preceded by a period of geographically extended trading and religions before modern industrialism and capitalism. So the West is not all powerful and there is hybridization within it, from pre-modern periods as well as from contemporary Eastern influences Westwards. If the West is being hybridized now, this is being done to something that was already hybridized on the basis of Eastern influences into Western modernity.

An argument that fits with both homogenization and hybridization perspectives is that *identity has become displaced away from locality or from being clear* (Robins 1997; Beck 2000; Bauman 1998). Globalization leads to identity being constituted from outside rather than from the local community. This may make people feel disenfranchized or disorientated. They have lost the roots for their identity or culture in what is local, familiar and feels under their control. Communities lose the capacity for meaning generation (Bauman 1998) and globalization leads to individuals' or communities' dissociation from their locality because much of the meaning in their identity or culture comes from distant or overseas culture and influences. Or there is confusion resulting from different or incompatible messages from varying global inputs. For Beck, this involves 'place polygamy', the global being incorporated into personal life. There is a multi-locationality or inner mobility to personal identity. This may be disorienting, because there is too much diversity for people to have a clear identity. On the other hand it does not have to be negative. Globalization leads to a wider diversity of inputs from around the world into culture and identity. Identity can be seen as a process and the diversity of possibilities and inputs as exciting and an opportunity. It can allow more 'reflexivity' or self-reflection over numerous life and identity alternatives, and more choice, rather than just following traditional patterns or singular possibilities (Giddens 1990).

Beyond hybridization

This is all plausible and logical. The idea that culture is being homogenized with the West just imposing the same everywhere through globalization is too simplistic. It does not recognize complexity, or the autonomy of people to be able to define their own cultures even if subjected to more powerful actors such as big media corporations. Seeing cultures in a process of intermingling with one another, rather than reduced to just one of them, seems to fit better with reality and is more plausible through recognizing plurality and autonomy. It also seems better, in terms of both reality and theory, than the perspective that sees cultures as clashing. Despite some conflicts between certain cultures, generally it does appear that cultures often interpenetrate and mix without clashes. Similarly, when cultures meet it seems they do not simply coexist next to each other in hermetic enclaves. They may intermingle and create new hybrid cultural forms as a result.

Is this the case? One possibility may be that what we are seeing is not a form of hybridity where cultures intermingle in communities or as individuals, to create new mixed third cultures, but *heterogeneity* where combinations of cultures live alongside one another rather than become mixed. In global cities sometimes people follow their own religions and value systems separately, with migrants relying on support from their community rather than the host society. People may live in separate groups in the same neighbourhood alongside other ethnic or cultural communities rather than intermingling with them to create new cultures. People can work in different places, watch different media, socialize in different places, and have their own social and political organizations. This may be the case for older more than younger generations. But it may be possible that what happens is not the fusion of different world cultures into new ones, but the coexistence of world cultures alongside one another – heterogeneity rather than hybridity, elements of multiculturalism as well as, or rather than, interculturalism.

There are other reasons to express scepticism about the hybridization thesis. For one thing *hybridization and homogenization need not be mutually exclusive.* If hybridity is increasingly found around the world, from Shanghai to Bangkok, London and New York, then hybridity is becoming generalized and homogenized. We might find the same sorts of hybridity in many places. In the West we may find food, electronic goods and religions from the East, with the same happening in the East, alongside Western TV programmes, hotel chains, and food and drink products and outlets. Globalization is not the same the world over. But in different parts of the world hybrid mixes may have similar contents. Hybridity is generalized in recognizable mixes around the world. Instead of a homogenization of Westernization there is a homogenization of hybridity.

Hybridization is quite an old thing. The hybridization thesis sometimes seems to assume that discrete cultures are becoming intermingled in the era of globalization of the late twentieth century. Hybridization is happening with, for example, modern Western media being exported, and with migration from the East to the West. But all cultures are hybrid and what is being hybridized is itself already hybrid. Migration is not an aspect of the late twentieth century alone and neither is transnational cultural influence. Nations are constituted by such hybridity, and it goes back a long way. An associated criticism is that not only is hybridization not new but that to propose it as a theory is, as such, stating the trivially true. To put it another way, we live in hybrid societies and the challenge is to ask questions about the terms on which hybridization occurs, which actors have the most power in the mix, and what form it takes empirically in different places. In fact, the pluralist picture of hybridity lends itself to an optimistic picture where many cultures contribute in a cosmopolitan mix (Beck 2006), and this distracts, as such, from questions of power and influence in this mix.

A further criticism is stronger than this. It suggests that hybridization is exaggerated and is something that some sections of society experience but that is more confined to them while being less experienced by others – *hybridization is an elite experience* (e.g., see Friedman 1999). Those who write about cosmopolitanism are the types of people who experience hybridization and are writing about themselves more than about the rest of society. The people who talk about hybrid and cosmopolitan cultures are often international academics living in rich countries where they have the resources to visit many countries and mix with people from different cultures and backgrounds. Their world is one of international conferences, holidays, jet trips and hotels in diverse global cities worldwide, and the consumption of culture from different parts of the world. They often live and work in particularly hybridized places, universities and metropolitan global cities, and research, write and talk about hybridization. Others in the hybrid elites include international business people and politicians. The emphasis, then, is on hybridization as an elite experience, often a benign one if you are in such privileged positions, and not so much shared by others. Not only is hybridization confined to this elite but the discourses they create about the way the world is gives them the power to create the misleading idea that society more generally is hybrid.

There is an element of truth to this picture but it underplays the extent to which *hybridization is more widely experienced*. For those more rooted and fixed in terms of actual physical mobility, global cultures can be experienced where migration brings it to their locality. This is more the case in some places than others. But about half the population of the world live in urban areas (UN 2007: 3) and many cities are global hybridized cities, so it is not an unusual experience. The other means by which non-elites experience hybrid culture is through the media. Music, films and news, not to mention food and consumer goods, are part of the lives of non-elites, and hybridity is experienced here also. In rich countries many people experience global diversity through travelling and tourism.

The difference is not so much that hybridity is confined to elites but that *experience of it happens on different bases*. For some, hybridity is experienced voluntarily, with autonomy, through the power of influence by creating discourses about it or inputs into it as mobile citizens. For others, experiences of hybridity are more involuntary – for instance, through migration to find work, flee war or persecution as in the case of labour migrants and refugees (Bauman 1998). This is not chosen, even in much economic migration. Most people would rather not break up their families and leave their communities to ensure a reasonable standard of living. Those who do are less active agents in defining hybridity or constituting their own situation within it, and more lacking in autonomy as citizens of hybridity. They are reacting to it in terms of mobility, or are recipients of it through the media that is controlled by powerful people.

Once you insert *politics, economics and power* into the picture of hybridity it looks different. Proponents of hybridity as a description of cultural globalization tend to paint a benign picture of a plural and exciting mixing of cultures from around the world. This is a helpful corrective to over-homogenized images of Westernized global culture. Globalization is not just one-way homogenization. But it gives a positive and pleasant picture partly because the analysis stays at the level of culture. Once underlying power to manufacture and distribute culture, and the economic weight that allows actors to have disproportionate power in this comes through, the image is less equal and diverse. The globalization of culture may be more than a one-way street but the two or more ways culture travels do not all have the same power.

There is a reason for *pushing economics out of the picture*. The case sometimes given for this is as a reaction against Marxist economic determinism that is seen to be crude and simplistic. Rejecting this justifies a focus on culture that leaves out the factor of economics being determinant. However, this can separate culture from the economy, with the result that relations of economic power and inequality that affect culture are left out. When culture is seen separately from economics the influence of economic power and inequality is not considered, so things seem more benign and plural. Power, inequality and conflict in the production and consumption of media and culture are left aside, or added as a qualification or side dimension rather than something that structures society. Bringing economics back in gives a more realistic picture of the inequality of, in this case, culture and can be done without the crude impersonal determinism that critics reduce economic influences to.

For instance, as we saw in the last chapter, much of the media we consume is produced and distributed by a small number of corporate actors. This squeezes local and diverse global producers and distributors. What may seem equal and plural is less so once this aspect of the picture is introduced. This is not to say that hybridization does not happen but that the basis on which it does is structured by power and inequality, albeit with space for those less powerful to have an input. So the music, film and TV programming that we see are affected by the wealth and power that produces and distributes this content. Hybridization occurs within such a context and is skewed by it.

Nederveen Pieterse, an advocate of the hybridization perspective, does *reply to some of these criticisms*. On the idea that hybridization is old and trivially true as a description of contemporary reality, he argues that, while the reality may be old, consciousness of it is not. He says purity claims have been strong for a long time and consciousness of hybridity is new and important. His claim is that talk of hybridity is not just the preserve of intellectuals and cosmopolitans, but in practice goes across all classes and has done so for a long time. And, if hybridity is done on power and inequality terms, then so is the world of maintaining boundaries, the opposite of hybridity, and hybridity is often produced by ordinary indigenous people.

There are some fair points here, but overall this does not overcome the fact of unequally distributed *power and inequality* in the production and distribution of media and culture. There may be hybridity as a result of the globalization of culture but in a situation where some actors have greater power, through ownership of production and distribution, to influence what is made and disseminated. This means some forms of media in the hybrid mix get greater exposure. Robins (1997) emphasizes hybridization but with an acknowledgement that there are also processes of homogenization, reaction and conflict, defensiveness, particularism and inequality in media and culture. This is important in recognizing hybridization as a more complex picture than simple homogeneity or a process of Westernization. But it also suggests that the concept of hybridization as an alternative to such perspectives is too simple. It retains a recognition of power, inequality and conflict, and of hybridity but within a context of homogenizing processes.

Sometimes hybridization perspectives are motivated by *postcolonial* concerns to stress the agency and role of non-Western inputs historically and more recently. It is important that non-Western culture is not viewed as passive and powerless, or as something other and different from the West. There are reverse cultural flows from East to West, with the West being Easternized as much as the East is Westernized. However, there is a danger of doing a disservice to non-Western cultures and economies by glossing over the way they are subordinated to Western power, culturally, politically and economically (for a related argument, see Dirlik 1996). It may be better to see hybridization as a development within the dominant power of the West and the process of homogenization, rather than as something that overturns the latter. Hybridization should be a reason for revising homogenization perspectives rather than rejecting them.

Conclusion

We have looked in this chapter and the previous one at the globalization of culture. This has a mixture of characteristics, including *homogenization and hybridization*. Recognizing hybridization provides a corrective to over-homogenized perspectives. Globalization, in the form of travel, migration, media and consumption, has created dynamic and exciting hybrid cultures, styles and identity through dress, food and music, to take just some examples. But hybridization should be seen within the context of processes of homogenization and Western power, rather than as overturning perspectives which emphasize these.

There are reasons to be *sceptical* about how globalized the globalization of culture is. This is particularly the case when we look at *economic* factors and relations of *power and inequality*. Global media corporations are especially powerful and it is not clear they are global but, rather, national corporations, from particular places more than others, operating internationally. The extent of world inclusivity and integration in global culture, whether in the production, distribution or consumption of it, is questionable.

Culture cannot be separated out from power and economy, so looking at culture in the light of these should not be dismissed as crude or too determinist. Culture is produced and distributed globally when there is money to be made from it. It is often, but not always, commercial. The most powerful actors in the commerce of culture are big corporations who, exploiting technological change and deregulation, are able to monopolize more of this in a smaller set of hands in rich countries.

It is in the era of *modern capitalism* that technology allowed culture to become mass and global. Pre-modern technology did not allow for this. Postmodern technology, such as the Internet, has expanded, speeded up and opened out the mass and global character of the media that was established by modern industrial technology, rather than creating it in the first place. Power, inequality, economy and modern capitalism are important parts of the story of globalization in the spheres of culture and media.

It is not only media and symbols that move across national boundaries and create these hybrid mixes. It is also people, and it is the movement of people across national boundaries that I will be looking at in the next two chapters.

Further Reading

Jan Nederveen Pieterse's (2004a) *Globalization and Culture* makes the case for the hybridization perspective in a concise, readable and evocative way.

Terry Flew's (2007) book *Understanding Global Media*, listed as further reading for the last chapter, is also relevant here. It covers issues to do with the structure of the global media and what forms the interaction of globalization and culture are taking, whether homogenized, hybrid or otherwise. It is balanced and substantial, well grounded in a variety of theoretical perspectives and areas of study.

Paul Hopper's (2007) *Understanding Cultural Globalization* provides an accessible overview of perspectives and studies on this topic.

John Tomlinson's (1999) *Globalization and Culture*, is an older and theoretically inclined but useful survey of perspectives on the globalization of culture.

Friedman and Dirlik are critics of cosmopolitan and hybrid perspectives on culture – for instance, in Friedman (1999), and Dirlik (1994), amongst others.

Robins's (1997) 'What in the World's Going on' is a bit dated, but provides a brief and evocative discussion of globalized culture, giving a picture of hybridization in combination with homogenization, conflict and power.

Global Migration: Inequality and History

Dɪscussɪoɴs of globalization often focus on economic globalization, neoliberal globalization, global politics or global media and culture. These include the movement of money, information or symbols. However, a key sort of global movement is of people themselves. This is what the next two chapters focus on.

A theme of this book has been that the causes of globalization are often based in economic motivations and material interests. This chapter argues that this applies to migration, but that economic bases are more complex than in simplified versions of economic determinism rejected by critics. Looking at economic dimensions also shows unequal aspects of migration. This chapter draws out historical and modern dimensions of migration and, with the following chapter, highlights ways in which there may be reasons to be sceptical about the globalization of migration. Migration is often constructed as a problem, but the next chapter argues that the evidence is that it is as much a solution as a problem. Hostility to it is as much to do with prejudice as reason.

Causes and types of migration

There are many forms of migration. These are different but related and vary over time in significance. Often types of migration are classified by cause. Migration can also be classified in terms of how it is received by host societies. I will discuss the effects of migration in the next chapter.

One distinction is between *legal and illegal* migration. A great deal of time is taken up by immigration agencies in assessing whether immigration is legal and in acting to counteract illegal immigration. Governments decide what form of migration is illegal and on what basis migrants can be defined as refugees and so allowed into a country or not. Hundreds of people die each year in attempts at illegal migration, crossing the border from Mexico to the USA and trying to get into EU countries from Africa, to take two prime examples. This results partly from inequalities between nations that drive people to escape poverty or conflict and pursue a better life, but also because legitimate means are closed off so they resort to illegal and dangerous routes. Making migration illegal is not just about definition; it has serious human consequences. As we will see later, a tragic dimension of this is that it is not clear that migration would rise to unmanageable numbers if more of it were to be made legal and free. Many who suffer and die because they have to take illegal paths may do so unnecessarily.

The distinction between *voluntary and forced migration* may seem to have become outmoded with the abolition of slavery. However, there is continuing forced migration. In many rich European countries there are involuntary migrants who have been transported by people traffickers and kept against their will. Forced migrants include those in sex work or domestic work. Sometimes they are persuaded to come to a country under false pretences, by someone who poses as a boyfriend or by the promise of a different type of work from the one they end up doing. Once they have migrated they may be kept by force or threats, or because of debts they have incurred as a result of paying to move and which they have to repay before they are free. It is estimated that there are 27 million slaves worldwide (Bales 2004). Most are women and children, forced into manual labour and prostitution by abduction, coercion, threats, deception or debt, in all continents and most countries in the world. Migration that is forced is also more general than this. It includes the migration of refugees and people displaced by conflicts, natural or environmental disasters, chemical or nuclear incidents, famine, or development projects where people are forced to leave their homes by states who wish to build or develop the area where they live. These are other types of migration where people move because they have to.

Another distinction is between *smaller- and larger-scale migration*. This is important because from evidence of geographically extensive migration, over long global distances, it may appear that globalization is taking place. But if this is mainly on a small scale, then what is geographically extensive is not so socially inclusive. This can be the case in military-led globalization, for instance. It is also sometimes said to be the case for current globalization which is claimed to be disproportionately done by elites such as business people or international academics, while others are more fixed and less mobile, and less cosmopolitan in their experiences. We should be aware not only of distances over which people move but also of the inclusivity regarding who moves.

Some international migration is *more permanent and other types more temporary*. This is important because it has implications for questions such as citizenship or identity. If people are moving on a more permanent or long-term basis then the issue of their citizenship in a new country or of changing national identity arises, something that is less the case with temporary residents. Temporary migrants may include those who go somewhere for an abbreviated time to earn income and then return home. Or it can include international students visiting a foreign university for anything between part of a year and a few years, or visits by tourists and business people, or by academics going to other universities on research trips or to conferences. In OECD countries (thirty mostly rich states), the number of international students rose by 50 per cent between 2000 and 2005, especially in the USA, UK, France and Australia. Approximately 2.5 million temporary labour migrants entered the area in 2006, about three times the number of permanent labour migrants but growing at a slower level than permanent migrant entries. Between a fifth and a half of immigrants into OECD countries leave within five years of arriving, whether to return home or move to a third country (OECD 2008: 22–3, and 'Essential Material' section').

Much migration is *labour or economic migration*. It involves people looking for work or better economic conditions, or being sought by employers. This can be legal or illegal, voluntary or involuntary, small-scale or mass, permanent or temporary. Much postwar migration from colonies or former colonies to current or former imperial powers was brought about by such powers seeking labour, as well as people seeking work and better economic conditions. In a number of European countries labour migrants make up 30–50 per cent of permanent migrants (OECD 2008: 22). Female migration into, for example, domestic work or other paid employment in rich countries has been of this sort. Most migration within the European Union is temporary labour migration, with workers from Eastern Europe seeking work for a few weeks or months in Western or Northern Europe and then returning home before possibly migrating again to richer countries at some point for another temporary period of earning income. This may well change in the EU, with migration from countries such as Poland, Romania and Bulgaria to Northern Europe becoming more long-standing. Where states limit migration, and there is no state that does not, economic migration is often more restricted than, say, migration to escape persecution, war or human rights abuses.

Other forms of migration involve *refugees* or those seeking asylum. They may be escaping from religious persecution, especially at some of the heights of mass migration in history, for example, from Europe to America. Or it can involve people fleeing political persecution or war. Wars in Africa, Afghanistan or Iraq, for instance, have been sources of refugees. Some of the most prominent debates in rich countries have concerned the distinguishing of 'genuine' asylum seekers from those using asylum to justify migration for other reasons such as economic, say, of immigrants from Mexico to the US or from Africa to Europe looking for better conditions of life. This is not accepted by governments as a basis for refugee status, even though economic factors can sometimes be as threatening to the security and health of migrants as conflict or persecution. Media coverage of refugees and asylum seekers has been out of proportion to the numbers who attempt it and has whipped up public animosity towards migrants, who even if they do not fit the technical criteria for asylum are often fleeing great hardship. One consequence has been that migrants who are fleeing adverse circumstances, whatever they are, then also face hostility in the place where they are seeking security. Furthermore, it gives the impression that refugees are flooding from poor to rich countries. In fact most flee across the nearest border to neighbouring poor or developing countries, who already have their own problems, greater than those faced by the richer developed nations, and who bear the brunt of ensuring the safety and well-being of their new guests. Asylum in OECD countries declined in 2006 for the fourth consecutive year, the largest receiving country being the USA with 41,000, while Canada, France, Germany and the UK received in the 20–30,000 range (OECD 2008: 22). When the geographical size and wealth of countries like the US and Canada are considered, these are small numbers to absorb.

Another factor is *family reunion or chain migration*. Migration leads to further migration. Migrants may move to countries where previous or current generations of their family have settled. Family migration makes up 70 per cent of permanent migration into the USA, 60 per cent in France, and in the OECD generally makes up 44 per cent of permanent migration compared to 14 per cent being labour migration and 12 per cent humanitarian (OECD 2008: 22, and 'Essential Material' section). Some literature on migration pays attention not just to causes such as war, hardship and persecution but also to *migration systems* and networks. Whether migration happens lies not just in external circumstances but also in whether migration systems exist which allow such causes to carry through to the movement of people. Such systems can arise out of previous migrations. Overseas family or community links provide conducive locations for migrants to go to, and legal reasons that give them an entitlement to migrate (e.g., marriage or family in the country they are moving to). Cultural ties may exist between the country people leave and the one they go to, where culture from the former has previously been located and established in the destination country. Ties arise out of migration that facilitate further migration.

Other aspects of migration systems include postcolonial links, or agencies that facilitate migration. Imperialism involved forms of globalization, often militarily led and economically motivated. People from imperial powers moved in large numbers to colonies, and many refugees from colonies were escaping the war and violence of colonization. These links have then been the basis of postcolonial movements. For instance, labour from former colonies later moved to former imperial powers. This was the case in colonial migrations, for example, from Britain to Asia and Africa, and then later from such places to the UK, and from other former colonies to the colonial power, such as from North Africa to France or South America to Spain. Where channels of trade and investment are set up there may be migrations of managers or experts from one country to where the investments have been made. In this way, causes of migration may be facilitated by further enabling factors such as community or family links or existing lines or agencies of migration.

Another triggering or enabling factor is *geography or proximity*. Transport is cheaper and easier to somewhere close, so proximity enables migration. Much international migration has been across nearby borders. Historically, technologies that can transport people long distances at an affordable cost have made a difference. Developments of naval transport, including the steamship, and of planes, especially the jet plane, alongside the growing affordability of these for some people, have facilitated global migration. They open up people movements beyond landmasses to trans-oceanic, and so more global, travel, with increasing speed and beyond elites.

Technologies of communication are important. These enable potential migrants to gain knowledge about possible destinations. In some cases the picture is glamourized, possibly by stories from previous migrants or from commercial images of potential destinations. Communications technology allows migrants to maintain contact with families and communities at home. So the availability of international telephone calls, email and the Internet has been important in allowing migrants to maintain relations in real time, quickly and relatively affordably with home communities, insofar as such technologies are also available there. This makes long-distance migration seem more of a possible prospect.

Political factors are important. A significant factor is whether border controls are tight or relaxed, which will vary from place to place. Within the European Union, for instance, borders are *relatively* relaxed and people can move around in search of work. But boundaries to migration into the EU are very restrictive. This is the result of political decision-making and treaties by governments that have opened some borders through mutual union agreements, while maintaining tight control over others. In some places restrictions on migration have been as much on people migrating out as in, notably in some communist countries of the twentieth century, for instance, in Eastern Europe and intermittently in places like Cuba.

Economic causes of migration

This book argues that economic factors and material interests are key motivations behind globalization. Economic explanations for migration, or globalization in general, are easy to dismiss. The economy is an impersonal force – how can it cause things? Don't actual agents such as individuals or states make decisions about whether migration happens or not? If it is all about economics, how come people often do not move when wages in their country are lower than in other countries they could migrate to? Surely individuals are not just economically rationally calculating beings. They also have loyalties, emotions and make non-rational and less individualistic calculations. Non-economic factors seem to play a role.

However, economic explanations for globalization need not be as crude as such criticisms imply. Stressing economic motivations does not necessarily mean that the economy is the cause of globalization. The facilitating of globalization by governments or states can be economically motivated, to find labour or contribute to production and growth, for example. In situations like this economic factors come in without the economy itself being determinant. Globalization can be economically driven but by agents rather than impersonal structural forces, and by actors outside the economy, such as political actors. It may be economic motivations or interests rather than the economy that are the key factor. Economic explanations can hold without there being a crude economic reductionism (for a discussion of economic theories of migration see Massey et al. 1998). What are key features of economic explanations for migration and how is a good economic explanation different from crude constructions of it?

1   Economic *motivations* are the key factor I am stressing, rather than the economy itself. An explanation based on the former need not see the latter alone as necessarily determinant.
2   A focus on motivations also means that actors make decisions, rather than the explanation being one that involves external impersonal economic forces or structures. So economic explanations are compatible with *agency* and cannot be written off as structurally determinist. It may be that economic structures, such as investments or inequalities, affect migration.

But there is also a role for agency in motivations to move, whether on the part of migrants, governments or other people who make decisions about people mobility.

3 While economic motivations are a factor, it can be *non-economic actors* that have them. For instance, governments, households or individuals are actors in migration as well as the economy or economic entities like corporations. Governments, for example, might encourage immigration for the economic reason that they need labour or taxpayers to support an ageing population. Individuals or households may decide whether to take up the economic opportunities of migration. Migrant social networks, or 'social capital' (relations of trust and reciprocity), amongst immigrant communities also play a part in business opportunities, housing and employment being provided for later inward migrants. Such social or human capital can be converted into economic capital. Economic explanations cannot be dismissed for reducing everything to the economy because explanations in terms of economic motives are compatible with non-economic actors and networks being important.

4 Economic explanations do not need to assume *individual rational economic* actors as in rational choice or neoclassical explanations. Actors can include states and households. And an economically motivated decision may not happen only in response to the economic motivations. A decision by a family member to migrate to seek a higher wage can also be affected by emotional family bonds or politically enabling factors. Family bonds might prevent them migrating, or alternatively make it easier if these are weak. So an economically motivated decision need not be a rational individual choice alone.

5 Although economic gain can be made from migration because of income differences between countries, this is not a sufficient basis on which to predict migration. Economic causes cannot be measured in objective criteria alone; they also have to be *subjectively perceived* by the actors involved. Economic explanations cannot be dismissed because there is a failure of actors to migrate in economically advantageous situations, as other intermediary factors must be considered in such situations. Often wage differentials exist, which are a key driving force behind migration decisions, but they have to be perceived, and seen to be decisive against other factors such as the costs of upping roots or migration being politically possible. At the same time, that it is more complex than can be predicted from comparative economic indicators alone does

not mean that economic factors are not still the motivating force in such situations. Once other factors are taken into account, it might be the possibility of a better wage that is the main motivating factor to move.

6 Economic motivations are filtered through *other factors such as political obstacles to migration and networks that facilitate migration*. So economic motivations do not translate automatically into migration. They have to be perceived, and are affected by such factors as government policies which encourage or inhibit emigration or immigration, networks for migration, demographic factors (such as an ageing population in receiving countries), costs and risks of migration, proximity and distance, colonial or postcolonial links, and channels of investment. Stressing underlying economic motivations as significant does not mean they are the only factor or sufficient by themselves. At the same time, the role of other factors does not mean that economic factors are not significant and prevalent. It shows they are filtered through other intermediary influences, but this fact does not negate the importance of economic motives.

7 Once economic motivations and other intermediary filtering factors are taken into account, then, *at the level of individuals and households*, there are different circumstances in the face of similar economic motivations. Consequently, whether migration occurs or not will vary even if common economic motivations exist. On one level, this means that an analysis based on economic motivations is complex. At the same time, while economic motivations may lead to varying migration decisions across individuals and households and you cannot therefore predict outcomes from economic data alone, this does not mean that economic factors are not key motivating forces.

8 Where economics is *not the most proximate or direct incentive* it can be a factor underlying what is. For instance, refugees from wars migrate to escape physical danger rather than for economic reasons, but it is possible the war could have been caused by economic motivations or material interests, for instance, the desire to secure access to precious resources such as oil or water. In such cases, economic motivations may not be the direct cause of migration but can underlie the causes that led to it.

9 Economic motivations can be linked to a *variety of economic circumstances*. They may involve push factors in the country of origin and/or pull factors in the receiving country. They may

be linked to wage differentials between countries, employment opportunities, the possibility of remittances, or general
economic buoyancy or prospects in sending and receiving
countries. So economic explanations cannot be dismissed
if, for instance, wage differentials between countries do not
lead to migration from one to another. There are various
sorts of economic factors that are motivating factors, not
just obvious ones such as wage differentials or employment
prospects.

10 Furthermore, the question of *degree and extent* is important.
Whether different economic opportunities between countries
become factors in migration does not only depend on the existence of these, but also on the degree of difference. Migration
is a risky, complex and costly business. Small economic gains
may not be sufficient to encourage migration. Migration for
economic reasons depends also on degree and extent.

So economic motivations for migration are complex. Economic
explanations cannot be dismissed by making them crude and simplistic. Showing how economic reasons for migration are complex does
not diminish their importance. Economic well-being as a motivating
force has been a major factor in migration, from pre-modern plunder-
ing and trading, through to European imperial migration to colonies
in pursuit of economic expansionism, European migration to America
in search of a better life, the slave trade, postcolonial migration to
Europe in the postwar period, Asian migration more recently to
America, and Latin American migration to the Northern hemisphere.
These examples have been dominated by economic expansionism or
by the movement of people in search of better economic opportunities. They frequently involve the poor looking for better material
prospects or the rich trying to increase their profits. As such, economic
causes of migration are also bound up with inequality, something
which I am arguing in this book is a central feature of globalization.

The history of migration

What I have discussed above are different types of migration. Many of
these are classified by cause – such as economic, imperialism, seeking
refuge, reunion and coercion. So type and cause overlap. How have
these varied over time (see Held et al. 1999 and King 1995)?

As we saw in chapter 2, many *pre-modern* long-distance movements were across Asia and even into the Middle East and Europe.
This provides a corrective to pictures of globalization that see it as

predominantly emerging from the West. Chinese civilization pursued imperial expansion. Armies from North of the Great Wall, such as the Mongols, penetrated into China, Europe and the Middle East. There was Islamic expansion from the Middle East by conquest and settlement into Africa, Southern Europe, the Balkans, Malaysia and Indonesia. To this day, these are Muslim areas or places that show signs of earlier Islamic expansion. Regional movements took place within Africa and South America. In Europe, Greek and Roman armies were regionally mobile. There was a slave trade across the Mediterranean, and conquering by Celtic and German tribes. There were Barbarian invasions of Rome, transnational movements of Vikings, Jewish diaspora and the migration of skilled labourers. So mobility over what would now be transnational distances happened in pre-modern times, although this was regional rather than global.

It was *in the modern period after 1500* that migration became more global. Much of this was connected with European empires, and with the global economic interactions and movements that followed. In the early modern period between 1500 and 1800, migration became geographically more extended, although less inclusive in the numbers and breadth of social classes involved. In the nineteenth century movements grew significantly, and some see the period between 1870 and 1914 as the highpoint of global migration. In 2005, there were 185 million documented migrants, the largest recorded figure, but proportionally lower than the nineteenth century when 10 per cent of the world's population were migrants compared to 2.9 per cent today (Dicken 2007: 447). Between 1880 and 1920, about 30 million people left Europe for the Americas and Australasia. This was a period of global imperialism and later there were greater restrictions on immigration. Between the wars there were big falls in migration and in the postwar period it became more complex, in ways I will come back to. But by this stage it had become quite organized and gone beyond land-based migration to more global trans-oceanic movements.

A key development in global migration was *European imperialism* and ensuing migration. Numbers are not certain and until the nineteenth century may have been smaller than later periods. But movement was often in search of economic expansionism and led to European domination in many parts of the world, by powers such as the Spanish, Portuguese, French and British. This penetrated to Asia, Africa, Oceania and the Americas, so was trans-oceanic and global. In extending to the Americas and Oceania, it stretched to areas beyond the reach of pre-modern globalization. Such places maintain the legacy of these migrations in language, architecture, ethnic mixes and links with former colonial powers. In the late nineteenth and early twentieth centuries, there was mass global migration as the means of transport improved and people sought better lives. Between 1850 and 1914, about 40–50 million people migrated, mostly to the Americas but also to Oceania. Many came from Europe, with some from Asia. This slowed down with the world wars, interwar economic depression and the beginnings of political restrictions on immigration into the USA.

Another basis of large-scale migration was the movement of *slaves* from Africa to the Americas and Middle East between the sixteenth and nineteenth centuries. A great deal of this was for labour in plantation economies established by Europeans. It is estimated that about 4 million slaves moved to the Middle East and between 5–20 million to the Americas, such as Brazil and the Caribbean. The ethnic composition of the Americas now is heavily affected by this history. With the end of slavery, *Asian labour* replaced slave labour. Sometimes the movement of Asian labour was involuntary, conditions were poor, and the debts incurred in migration were so large they had to be worked off over long periods, or never at all, before workers could move again. Labourers came from countries such as India, China and Japan, and moved to the USA and European colonies. In fact, large numbers moved within and across Africa and Asia. Less discussed movements to South East Asia and the Far East were almost as large in number as cross-Atlantic movements (McKeown 2004).

Much of this migration was labour migration for economic reasons. I am arguing throughout this book that economic motives are often behind globalization. This does not mean that economic structures are an impersonal force. Social and individual actors are agents in these processes, some with more power than others. Cultural and political factors are also important, for instance, with governments promoting or restricting migration and affecting the economic circumstances that are behind it. But economic motives are often behind migration, be it the search for new resources, markets or cheap labour on the part of governments or economic actors, or for a better material life by individuals or families.

Economic factors are not *always* dominant. The *world wars* lessened economic and labour migration, and resulted in migration to flee conflict rather than for economic reasons. Russians fled the revolution in their country, Armenians fled Turkish persecution, Greeks left Turkey for Greece, Germans returned after the Second World War, Palestinians left the newly founded state of Israel, and there was migration between the partitioned India and Pakistan, to take some examples. In the interwar period, depression brought an end to international migration on any significant scale as economic opportunities globally diminished, and countries like the USA had started to implement restrictions on immigration. In the *postwar period* migration became more mechanized and politicized. Travel by ship and plane became faster and, over time, cheaper. Migration became an issue the state got involved in, organizing, facilitating and directing it towards certain ends. The state is sometimes portrayed as responding to migration. But it often has an active role in encouraging it, filtering particular sorts of migration of people with certain characteristics and skills, and regulating and restricting according to factors such as economic policy.

After 1945, much transnational migration was regional, of the displaced returning. Western European countries suffering labour shortages, and in some cases major restructuring, turned to overseas labour recruitment from colonies, former colonies or other locations. This included migration from Southern Europe, Turkey, North Africa, Asian countries such as India, Pakistan and Bangladesh, and the Caribbean. The migration from colonial powers to colonies was reversed, with migration being actively organized by states. Other common migration phenomena followed, with family members migrating to reunite with those who had relocated. Later policies were concerned with restricting immigration and dealing with race relations problems that arose after migration. In some cases, such as the UK, citizenship was actively extended to the new migrants. In others, Germany, for instance, it was more difficult to obtain.

In the mid-1960s, there was migration to North America and Australia, but economic problems in the 1970s led to a decrease in labour recruitment and Western European countries started to impose restrictions. Immigration increased to oil-rich countries in the Middle East, much of it regional from neighbouring countries rather than global. Asian migration switched away from Europe towards North America, Australia and the Gulf. Economic developers in Asia such as Japan, Singapore, Taiwan and Brunei became labour importers and some migration was by people fleeing wars, in Asia, Africa and the Middle East. Immigration to the USA shifted in origin from Europe to immigrants from the Asia-Pacific region, as well as from Central and Southern America. Between 1945 and 1995, there were about 25 million legal immigrants to the USA, and perhaps another 10 million who were illegal. The population of the USA increased from 50 million in 1880, through to 75 million in 1900, 248 million in 1990 and about 300 million in 2009. Immigration into Western Europe, North America and Australia in the postwar period has totalled about 100 million, with the peak period being 1965–85.

Migration from Europe diminished, while more people emigrated from Africa, Asia and Latin America, countries that had previously been destinations rather than origins. African migration has been to colonial states, such as France, but much has been regional within

Africa rather than global. This has been in part migration to states with resources such as oil or gold, for instance, Nigeria and South Africa, or by those fleeing from wars, for example, in Sudan and Congo. Latin America has changed from a region of immigration to one of emigration, especially to the USA, Southern Europe (for example, to former colonial powers, Spain and Portugal), and within the region.

The *collapse of communism* in Eastern Europe in 1989 led to the end of restrictions on emigration from communist states. Soviet Jews moved to Israel. There were post-communist movements of Central and East Europeans from countries such as Poland to the West. This was facilitated by EU membership and the partial relaxation of movements on labour within the EU. Some of this has been temporary or intermittent – with migrants going to richer West European countries to earn money for a period, then returning home, perhaps making other trips for work at later dates. There were also refugees from wars in the former Yugoslavia. Other types of migration that have grown in this postwar period have included tourism, a direct result of cheaper travel, especially jet travel, for all classes in rich countries. Business travel has increased, along with an increase in international students and student exchanges. This has occurred both within regions, for example, Europe, and globally, a key example being that of Chinese students travelling internationally to countries like the USA.

Trends in migration

Castles and Miller (2003) have tried to summarize contemporary trends in migration. One is *globalization*. More places have become countries of origin or destination for migrants, so there has been a wider global inclusion of those involved. Migration has also become more global in extent, as well as just regional, although a large amount continues to be regional.

A second trend is the *acceleration* of migration. There has been a growth in the volume of people moving, but this is in comparison to the slower interwar period. Whether migration in recent periods has been greater than the *belle époque* of 1870–1914 is contested. Calculations need to allow for the rising size of the world population, which partly explains the numerical rise. From the 1970s onwards, many countries imposed restrictions on immigration, which has reduced the number of refugees since the early 1990s, demonstrating that governments can affect migration.

Migration has become *differentiated*, meaning there is more variation in types. Much migration in the 1950s/1960s was in search of manual work. But with the expansion of the service sector, especially but not only in rich countries, more migration is post-industrial rather than to manual manufacturing work. This connects to migration becoming more *feminized*, as service-sector work has a disproportionately larger number of women workers. A shift from unskilled manual work migration to more professional and elite skilled worker movements occurred in the 1980s and 1990s. This has been associated with a brain drain, for instance, of scientists from Europe to the USA, or of doctors and medical staff from developing countries to developed world health services. There are many forms of migration in and out – for instance, labour migration, refugees, temporary or permanent, international students and business people, with ensuing forms such as family reunion. Return migration is also a trend today, many Greeks returning from the US, and Turks from Germany, for example.

Finally, migration has become more *politicized*. Domestic politics have become more oriented around migration issues – restrictions on immigration, with debates about assimilationist or multiculturalist responses to migration and about the basis of citizenship for immigrants. Parties highlight immigration policies to win votes, normally seeing a conservative and restrictive discourse as the most electorally beneficial. Some parties base their politics primarily on an anti-immigration stance. Racism and policies to counteract it have become politicized issues. Immigration has become more linked to security by politicians, especially in the post-9/11 era. Bilateral and regional policies on migration have been sought, for instance, within the EU.

A number of themes of this book have been raised in this chapter. There has been *globalization* of migration, in the expansion of countries involved in sending and receiving and in some of the distances travelled. It was in the *modern* period that regional migration of the pre-modern period became more global. Much migration is marked by *power and inequality*. Migration has been from more powerful states to ones that they have subjected to their power, or from poorer states to richer ones. The former was about *economic* expansionism, while the latter was dominated by economic motivations, the search by poor people for an improvement in the material conditions of life. What the world looks like now and recent migrations are shaped by *history*. The characteristics of countries are marked by the migrations that have happened in and out of them over centuries. Recent migration is sometimes connected to historical migrations, for example, through postcolonial links or family reunion. Meanwhile the regionally limited nature of some migration, and inequalities in and restrictions on it, should remind us to maintain some *scepticism* about the extent to which what has been discussed is truly globalization.

Further Reading

Castles and Miller's (2003) *Age of Migration* is a leading textbook on international migration.

A more advanced overview of theories of international migration with foci on different areas of the world is Doug Massey at al.'s (1998) *Worlds in Motion: Understanding International Migration at the End of the Millennium.*

Messina and Lahav's (2006) *The Migration Reader* is a useful selection of articles with a politics and policy emphasis.

The chapter on migration in Held et al.'s (1999) *Global Transformations* is useful. The journal *International Migration Review* is very relevant as is *The Journal of Ethnic and Migration Studies.*

For a grand and historical view, see Dirk Hoerder's (2002) *Cultures in Contact: World Migrations in the Second Millennium.*

<http://www.iom.int/> – the website of the International Organization for Migration, with useful resources on migration.

CHAPTER
6

The Effects of Migration: Is Migration a Problem or a Solution?

So far, I have looked at causes, types and patterns of migration. In this chapter I will focus on the effects of migration primarily, but not only, on host countries. In the public and political discourses of rich countries, migration is often more about immigration than emigration and is frequently seen as a problem. This chapter will look at the extent to which discourses about immigration as a problem are right or not. Looking at it with an open mind, there are powerful moral and practical arguments for migration. Given countervailing evidence, hostility to migration must be as much to do with racism and intolerance as with rational argument.

Citizenship systems

How nations receive migrants varies. Commentators identify a number of citizenship systems. Different countries have different systems for integrating migrants when they arrive. These also vary over time so countries may adopt one system in one period and then shift to other ones later. Equally, states may combine aspects of more than one system at any one time.

One response to migrants in some receiving countries is the *guestworker* system. This involves migrants being welcomed into a country to work but without full citizenship rights. To get citizenship requires family links. So it is based on blood relations, which means it is often effectively based on shared ethnicity. Residence or employment in the country, even over a long time, does not qualify migrants to citizenship. Contribution to the country does not count and sometimes people who have been born in a country and are second- or third-generation immigrants do not qualify for citizenship. This leads to a differential and exclusionary experience. Migrants are workers, but as guests, and they are differentiated from those who are full citizens by kinship. The experience of Turkish migrants in Germany until recently is one example of this system, and it has also been identified with countries such as Switzerland, Austria and Belgium.

An alternative system is one that offers citizenship to migrants on grounds such as *residence or employment* over time. Citizenship is linked more to contribution or participation. This system characterizes more the experience of migrants from colonies or former colonies into countries such as France and the UK, and includes the experience of subsequent generations. Migrants and their children are legally less differentiated from longer-term residents and citizens and there is less of a racial element to citizenship status.

So one distinction is between situations where migrants gain citizenship or where their status is more as guests. Another is between systems in which migrants are expected to conform to the dominant norms and culture of the society they are joining or where it is seen as appropriate for cultures to exist alongside one another. This is the difference between *assimilationist and multicultural approaches*. Most major immigration countries have at one point or another been assimilationist. Immigrants are expected to conform to domestic laws, learn the host country's language and, in societies like France, conform to secular requirements in public institutions like schools, such as a ban on wearing religious items.

Multiculturalism is a system where cultural differences are accepted, albeit within an accepted common set of laws. In countries like Australia, Canada and Sweden in the 1970s and 1980s, the model was that immigration was permanent and citizenship assured alongside the acceptance of cultural pluralism. However, where this is a model it is not always realized in practice as fully as it is expressed as an ideal. And in many countries that have had a multicultural model the debates have shifted more to assimilationist requirements in areas such as language, citizenship tests and secularism.

Castles and Miller (2003) argue that a new model of citizenship is needed to deal with the extent of global migration. Increasingly, people have multiple national backgrounds or identities. They may be the children of parents of two different nationalities. They may have lived, worked or studied in a third or fourth country. Consequently, their national belonging is not clear. It is often multiple. Or they do not feel they have multiple nationalities so much as none at all – an experience beyond any national identity. Much of this has arisen because of migration by their parents and themselves. Castles and Miller suggest that existing models of citizenship are appropriate in cases of primary citizenship of one nation, and maybe for dual citizenship. But in an era where people have multiple national identities, or even a supranational identity above and beyond this, a *transnational model of citizenship* makes more sense. This means not just increasing the number of national citizenships that people can hold, but identifying a model beyond nations where people are identified with transnationality. Transnational identifications are further made possible by global communications and media, global businesses, and diasporas which form global nations and global social movements, such as the women's movement. These, it is argued, generate global consciousness and identity (Beck 2000; Glick Schiller et al. 1992).

Despite this, plenty of evidence can be seen of racism and nationalism in Europe, a place where transnational citizenship is said to be developing, and elsewhere, including violence against ethnic communities, electoral support for anti-immigration parties, and subnational identities within nation-states. The latter can be found from the former Yugoslavia to Sri Lanka, and in secessionist movements throughout the world. There are differences of identity along tribal, religious or ethnic lines. For some, these sorts of nationalism and other group identities are a reaction to globalization and so also part of it. Authors like Anthony Smith (1990) doubt whether global identity can develop because of the lack of a single global culture. Societies vary, for instance, by religion, and between religious and secular, and collectivist or more individualist cultures. Values such as human rights and democracy, claimed to be universal, are actually quite Western in the form they are globalized. There is no shared global history (except of world wars and global imperialism which involved a divisive experience of conflict and exploitation rather than unification). Myths of shared identity are mobilized at more national levels, and in nationalisms within nation-states. There is a lack of an 'other' against which global identity can be defined. The existence of the other is partly what binds together national identity – for instance, in the case of the US against putative external threats such as communism or 'axis of evil' states and terrorism. There are conflicting economic and political interests between states which in practice divide as much as unify them in a global consciousness. These are evident in negotiations over issues such as climate change, nuclear proliferation and world trade, global issues where global consciousness might be expected to be to the fore. So there are reasons to be doubtful about the extent of transnational identity and consciousness in the world.

Another structure for receiving immigration and participation is beyond the state and legal or political responses, in *networks and social capital* in society. Social capital involves relations of trust and reciprocity between people, enabling them to achieve their goals or create integration and community (e.g., Bourdieu 1984; Halpern 2004; Putnam 2001). If there is social capital in institutions like democracy, education and the local economy, then they work better. Without trust and reciprocity, these need regulation and policing which is more costly. This links to migration systems discussed in the last chapter. A migration system facilitates migration, but it also affects the experience of migrants joining a new society and how they are supported or integrated there.

Migration systems include networks between migrant groups and their home country. These facilitate transnational movement by migrants in a destination country, providing economic, social, political and moral support for further migrants from their home. Friends, relatives and others originally from the home country help with the integration of migrants in the search for employment or housing, emotional and social support, community, political representation, and resources such as knowledge and financial assistance. This reduces the costs, economic and otherwise, and the risks of migration. These relations of trust and reciprocity, social capital, play a part in the decision to migrate, the process of migration and the adjustments required after arrival.

Migration systems and social capital are about membership and participation on arrival as well as causes and reasons for migration. They involve a level that is to some extent independent of government, although networks may engage with government and legal bodies. Networks are formed in civil society by migrants themselves. Government intervention in regulating flows, by encouraging, discouraging or directing it in particular channels, is diluted by the existence of such functions in social networks beyond the state. In fact, government policies facilitate and open up networks by including family reunion as a basis for immigration and citizenship. So migration networks create potentially perpetuating and cumulative drivers behind migration that have some independence from corporate or government elites, in civil society and amongst migrants themselves. A potential, but not necessary, consequence of strong social capital in migrant groups is a bounded solidarity in which such members of groups may be integrated with each other but maintain relative separation from surrounding society.

Effects of migration

One implication of migration is to raise questions about citizenship. Citizenship models have to be constructed to fit with migration. There are other ways in which migration has effects on the source or destination countries. I am including references to the UK context below, to concretize matters, and because Britain, as well as being a country

I am familiar with, is an interesting example of a nation of migration, partly because of its postcolonial links and membership of the EU.

Debates over the effects of migration are affected by prior pro- or anti-immigration stances. Racism and xenophobia cloud judgements on the effects of migration. They lead to exaggerated perceptions of *the scale of migration*. People born abroad made up just under 12 per cent of the total population in OECD countries in 2006. Significant as migration is, even in a globalized era the vast majority of people stay put. Migration is inhibited by the ties of family, friends, community and work, combined with obstacles such as cost and political barriers. Surveys reveal that 97.5 per cent of the world's population live in the country of their birth (UNHCR 2000: 280). This leaves 2.5 per cent who do not – a significant figure, but not consistent with 'floods' or other tidal metaphors used to describe migration. Opinion surveys consistently show that people overestimate the scale of migration into their country. For example, over 50 per cent of Americans perceive the foreign-born population in the US to be at least twice as large as it really is (Pew Research Center 2006: 30).

Many included in figures for migrants entering countries are not in those countries at any given moment. For instance, many migrants within the EU move temporarily for work and return home. Amongst asylum seekers in the UK there is a return rate of about 80 per cent. So immigration numbers are not the same as the number of immigrants in the country. Furthermore, where immigration is measured by numbers of migrants born abroad, some of those are at birth citizens of the country they then emigrate to. They are counted as immigrants but are also those who are regarded by the media and politicians as home workers whose jobs are being taken (see Legrain 2006, 2007).

Data on the countries of origin of immigrants clashes with the media picture. In the media image in the UK, as well as that propagated by politicians and amongst the public, immigrants appear to be mostly from India, Pakistan and Bangladesh, often Muslim, or from the Caribbean and most recently from Poland. Yet the biggest immigrant group in the UK consists of the Irish, rarely mentioned as taking British jobs or placing a burden on the welfare state, although they have suffered discrimination. Amongst other main immigrant groups in the UK are Germans, Americans, Italians, Australians and French. These rarely appear in the talk by media, politicians and the public of the dangers of migration, perhaps because they are predominantly white and Christian.

When political obstacles to migration are eased, as with the relaxation of barriers within the EU, the predicted volume of movement does not occur. Many in rich states overestimate their attractiveness to those in poorer countries. Extrapolating from situations where obstacles to migration are relaxed, such as the pre-1914 period and

Table 6.1 UK immigrants by country of birth, 2001		
Origin	Numbers	% of population
Ireland	494,850	0.87
India	466,216	0.82
Pakistan	320,767	0.56
Germany	262,276	0.46
Caribbean	254,740	0.45
USA	155,030	0.27
Bangladesh	154,201	0.27
South Africa	140,201	0.25
Kenya	129,356	0.23
Italy	107,002	0.19
Australia	106,400	0.19
Hong Kong	94,611	0.17
France	94,128	0.16
Total 7.5% of people in Britain born abroad		

Source: ONS 2001

more recent EU cross-border migration, Moses (2006: 172) estimates that open and free migration globally would lead to population movements of between 5 million and 205 million annually out of a world population of over 6 billion. The mid-point between these two figures is about the level of current migration. These are rough estimates but they suggest that the actual or potential scale of migration flows is not overwhelming.

The *free movement* of capital across national boundaries is sometimes exploitative and creates economic interdependency. This can cause instability and economic depression, as with the post-2007 financial crisis, and in the best of times constrains the freedom of democratically elected governments to set policy. This freedom of movement is generally accepted or celebrated. But the movement of human beings, frequently in search of better life chances, attracts hostility often on the basis, as we shall see, of dubious evidence. Philippe Legrain (2007) is an exception as a neoliberal who favours the free movement of both capital and people, the latter seen as bringing benefits for the former and the economy at large.

There is also a paradox, or hypocrisy, in that states that express confidence in their liberal institutions and freedom of their citizens do not extend such liberalism to other world citizens as far as policies on migration go. Liberal governments are rightly vociferous critics of states, such as socialist states in the past and present, from the GDR to Cuba, who have limited the movement of citizens out of their countries. At the same time, the expectations that liberal states place on others to allow free outward movement are contradicted and undermined by their limits on allowing free movement in.

This book emphasizes *power, inequality and conflict* in globalization. Some of the reasons for migrants pursuing better life chances are based in global inequality and poverty. Most of the resistance comes from rich developed states against immigration from poorer developing countries. As we shall see, it is difficult to regard this as anything other than factors such as political expediency or prejudice, pursued despite their harmful consequences for migrants, because empirical evidence does not show migration to be the threat it is said to be. There has been a long tradition, from the earlier days of the twentieth century, of states being reluctant to take in migrants fleeing hardship and danger even when they have known what the fate of such migrants would otherwise be.

Political divides over migration are complex. Advocates of open migration range from supporters of free market capitalism, such as Legrain, to many in the anti-globalization movement who are critical of the way the free movement of capital works but call for the free movement of people and ideas. Opponents can be found in less liberal strands of both the right and left.

Arguments for free migration are often based on *liberal* concerns for freedom. These are important, but my reasons for favouring freer migration are more to do with inequality and the poverty of those who wish to migrate. Such reasons tend to come from those with an egalitarian or socialist perspective. *Socialism* has had internationalist strands, which stress the commonality and unity of humans, regardless of national background. This stress on all people as equally important, and against putting national interest and the interests of humans of your own country or race over others, is behind arguments for open migration. People should not be treated differently because of the accidental fact of where they were born and because this happened not to be within the borders of your own country. However, it is not necessary to be a socialist to argue for equal status for all humans regardless of whether or not they are part of your nation. If the reason for obligations to others is based on their need, rather than on place of residence or birth, then citizens in rich countries have greater obligations to foreigners than to their 'own'.

I think the strongest arguments for migration are to do with the *needs of migrants* – the economic hardship, exploitation or persecution they are escaping and the opportunities migration gives them for a better life. Such concerns are rarely mentioned in debates on immigration that focus on the effects for receiving societies. We will see below that the evidence for such effects being negative is problematic. Contrary to the public image, there is not only a moral case for migration, but there are reasons to suggest it is beneficial for *receiving societies* too. Nevertheless, arguments for migration on the basis of the needs of migrants, which often involve basic economic or physical security, are sufficiently compelling regardless of whether or not there are benefits for receiving societies. More detailed empirical evidence for arguments of the sort discussed in this section is laid out by authors such as Harris (2001), Moses (2006) and Legrain (2006).

Perhaps the most radical effect that migration has is to *constitute nations*. Many nations have been made over time by centuries of immigration (or emigration). In the modern era, countries like Australia and the US have been constituted by mass immigration. Such states had pre-existing native populations, killed in large numbers and leaving the survivors marginalized, following migration from Europe and other parts of the world. Big shifts in migration have made or radically reformed these nations.

Arguments against immigration are insensitive to these sorts of histories. The migrations from which such nations were formed often resulted from those fleeing persecution or economic hardship, and who desired a better life. This better life was pursued alongside the subjection of indigenous populations in receiving societies. But the opportunities available for people also led to the creation of dynamic, modern, affluent and diverse societies. A historical perspective on the way that migration can provide such opportunities is often marginalized in contemporary debates on the effects for receiving societies.

The *economic consequences* of migration are not clear-cut or predictable. These vary according to factors such as the source or destination countries, the volume of migration and what type it is. Researchers in richer states tend to be more interested in its effects on their countries as destinations than on the nature of the *sending countries*. And the consequences for sending countries should not be separated from those of its members who are the migrants seeking better chances in life.

Many migrants go to rich countries to flee conflict and persecution (for instance, from war zones in Africa or Asia), or to escape poverty by seeking wages hugely superior to those in their home country. The search for a better life, against a background of violence, poverty or poor standard of living, is rarely a theme in public discussions of migration in rich countries. The responsibility of humans to humans (regardless of the arbitrary accident of their country of origin) also infrequently crops up in this context.

One consequence of migration can be a reduction in unemployment in source countries, and of its economic consequences, such as the costs of support for the unemployed and of conflict. Migration increases remittances back to the host country. These can make very substantial contributions to sending countries' economies, more than overseas aid in some cases. The biggest recipients of remittances are India, Mexico and the Philippines. Annual remittances to Latin America and the Caribbean are greater than Foreign Direct Investment and development aid combined. In some countries they are greater than or comparable to a sizeable chunk of export earnings or Gross Domestic Product (Dicken 2007: 508). Migrant remittances to the least developed countries were $13 billion in 2006 compared to net aid of $28 billion and FDI of $9 billion (UNCTAD 2008a: 7–8). This offsets the loss of tax income from migrants. Remittances bypass governments, going straight to individuals and families. Rejecting immigration involves also rejecting this channel of aid by individuals and families themselves. Self-help alternatives to government paternalism are something that critics of immigration favour in other contexts but disregard in connection with migration.

If emigration results in a shorter supply of labour in some areas, this strengthens the power of labour in the sending country to secure gains such as higher wages. Emigrant workers can also gain skills and access to contacts, capital and markets that may benefit their home country. A serious problem for source countries can be the loss of skilled workers, for instance, in the case of doctors and medical staff leaving African countries for better wages and conditions elsewhere. This should not be downplayed. But 'brain drain' can also have benefits. As well as remittances, people gain skills from migration and will bring them home if they return. And, if they can afford it, better opportunities might be offered by governments or employers to keep skilled workers at home or attract replacements.

The majority of studies focus on the consequences of migration for *receiving countries*. An anti-immigration argument is that migrants *take the jobs of domestic workers*. However, migrant workers tend to go where there are vacancies rather than competition for jobs. In receiving countries they are often focused at the higher and lower end of the skills hierarchy, where it is either difficult to recruit skilled workers, or they are willing to accept low-paid, low-status work with poor conditions in, for instance, food services, health, or care for the elderly. Often it is difficult to find local workers to do these jobs. Migrant workers who take them can be highly skilled professionals and hugely over-qualified. From the postwar period onwards, immigration from poorer parts of the world has solved labour shortages in a number of rich countries.

Sometimes this work is temporary and undertaken by migrants on short-term visits, as is the case with some migrant workers in the EU. It can be informal and less regulated, so more open to exploitation and danger. The idea of wages being forced down or jobs being taken from home workers receives more attention than the poor conditions of work experienced by many migrant workers. The British government is keen to restrict immigration to more skilled workers, which is puzzling when the unskilled often fill gaps the British do not wish to. Or they provide cheap services such as domestic labour to the richer and more skilled, enabling these local skilled workers to do their own jobs, as is also the case in the US.

The alternative to bringing in migrant workers may not be more jobs for 'home' workers, but instead the exporting of those jobs to low-wage workers in other parts of the world. Critics of immigration give a false choice between home workers or migrants taking their jobs. But there are other possibilities. Those jobs could not be created in the first place if the migrant workers were not there to take them, or the jobs that migrants take could be exported if immigration was restricted (Sriskandarajah 2006).

There is evidence that migration can lead to *decreases in wages* in receiving societies. Because more workers are chasing the same number of jobs employers can cut wages, secure in the knowledge they can find labour willing to accept the lower wage. However, this is by no means general and usually affects unskilled sectors of the workforce rather than others. UK Bank of England evidence in 2006 showed that while wages in some sectors were falling (as will always be the case in a large complex economy), average wages across the economy were on the rise (Blanchflower et al. 2007; also see TUC 2007; Reed and Latorre 2009).

Furthermore, it is the employers who make the decision to cut wages. Wage reduction is not a product of migration itself, although this is how the issue is constructed by the media and politicians. And, if migrants' wages rise, this would result in an overall benefit from the viewpoint of all human beings being equal. Often studies of this phenomenon are concerned only with effects on the host country labour's wages, rather than on wages for migrant workers, as if it is only the former that matters. All are not equal human beings the way this story is told.

In fact, immigration can also contribute to higher wages in receiving countries. It provides labour that enables sections of the economy to expand, for instance, the construction industry in some places, which leads to economic growth. The wages of migrant workers are spent on goods and services, boosting other industries' fortunes, and providing tax revenue for services such as health and pensions. A government report in 2007 suggested that immigration boosted growth in the UK by up to £6 billion a year (Home Office 2007; TUC 2007). This has a positive effect on employment, wages and tax revenue.

Many rich countries have the *demographic problem of an increasing proportion of elderly people in the population* which puts a burden on health care and pensions, alongside a smaller proportion of younger workers to pay the taxes that fund these and meet the needs of the labour market and economic growth. Migration can fill such gaps. Migrant workers provide income that can be taxed to support public services for the elderly and others. When they spend their income they increase consumer demand and stimulate the economy, so feeding into factors that create more jobs and so further taxable income.

For Julian Simon:

> If we consider both the sending and the receiving countries as part of the same world, then – and on this every economist agrees – the overall effect of migration on the average standard of living of the world's people is positive. (1989: 299)

The reason for this overall effect is that migrants in general go from situations where they are unproductive to ones where they are more productive. The match between supply of labour and demand for it improves when there is more leeway for the former to move to meet the latter, leading to greater efficiency and productivity. This is not to say that in some contexts and for some groups migration, like any other social phenomena, does not sometimes bring economic losses. Nothing else could be expected of a complex phenomenon. But *overall*, with all groups and contexts taken into account, the effect is positive. Remittances can increase the home country's income, the migrant and his or her family may gain in income, and both the receiving country and the international economy may find economic growth boosted by migrants' economic productivity, with public services gaining from additional taxable income.

If rich countries do not perceive such benefits, as a result of prejudice rather than rational analysis, and choose to see on balance negative effects, then there is still a reason why open migration might be of benefit. Open migration can create an *incentive for rich country governments to help solve economic imbalances* between richer more attractive countries and poorer ones that migrants try to escape. Open migration can be an incentive for the richer states in the world to help solve the problems of poorer countries that people are trying to flee. Additionally, the past colonial involvements and economic exploitation by the richer states mean they often bear direct responsibility for this anyway, not to mention the responsibility of humans to other humans.

The anti-immigration lobby argues that immigration puts pressure on *public services*, such as welfare and education and, because immigrants are bent on committing crime, on the police. However, this is a one-sided argument. As we have seen, demographic change has led to increased pressure on public services. Many migrants into European countries or North America are labour migrants, so they support themselves financially rather than calling on welfare, and pay tax which finances these public services. Migrant workers are often relieving the pressure on public services that comes with demographic change and an ageing population. Here, the picture is two-sided, with the pressure on public services by migrants, such as it is, being seen against the extra tax revenue that migrant workers supply to support such services.

Furthermore, anyone who has visited a British hospital will know that migrant workers provide a large proportion of both the lowest-paid and the most skilled workers in the UK health service. They are providing the labour as well as the tax base for public services. The conflict and social problems that are said to have resulted from immigration are also cast into doubt by empirical evidence. Research by the UK police force in 2008 concluded that immigration has not led to an increase in crime, putting a burden on the police force, contrary to public misinformation which is encouraged by the media and politicians for whom such stories provide, respectively, readers and electoral support (Dodd 2008).

Another consequence that arises in situations of migration is *racism and the unequal treatment of immigrants*. This is often portrayed as a consequence of immigration but, rather than being a product of the process of migration, is a product of the reception of migration by host countries. In many countries some immigrant communities are the poorest sections of society, with lower employment and educational opportunities, and are subjected to racism and discrimination, sometimes to the extent of violence. However, this is not predetermined and is complex. Many immigrant groups are successful in such areas and racism and discrimination are not inevitable. They are the products of agency and can be countered.

Similarly, conflict and a *decline of community and trust* is sometimes associated with immigrant or diverse societies (e.g., Putnam 2007). But, again, this portrays immigration rather than the reaction of the host community as the problem, which implies policies of restricting migration, whereas if the reaction of the host community is seen as the issue this suggests policies geared towards dealing with hostility and intolerance.

Problems like this are not inevitable. They can be solved. And there are *political consequences* of migration. Some of these involve defining the terms of citizenship in receiving societies as discussed above, as well as promoting, restricting or determining the shape of immigration and the relation of public services to migration. Political actors such as states and governments react to migration but they are also constructors of it. They institutionalize migration and are mechanisms for organizing, facilitating, encouraging or restricting it. Governments and political parties make migration a political issue, both as governments or states acting on it and as political parties constructing it as an issue to mobilize electoral support. This can be through mainstream parties bringing up migration as an issue, or explicitly anti-immigration parties, or parties of immigrants.

These points are relevant mostly to receiving societies. Migration may also have positive effects *politically for sending states*. Migration to escape dictatorship and authoritarianism could pressurize regimes and encourage nations to opt for more democratic systems to regain loyalty amongst their citizens. Open migration can also encourage receiving countries who perceive immigration to be a problem to help rectify drastic imbalances of power and wealth between them and sending societies, these being a major factor behind migration from poor to rich countries.

Even attempts to question immigration have revealed its lack of significant negative effects. In 2008 a *report from the UK House of Lords* argued that the economic case for migration into Britain was mistaken (House of Lords Select Committee on Economic Affairs 2008; Wakeham 2008). Yet the report concluded that evidence on the effects of migration into the UK is neutral or mixed rather than negative. It stated that, while GDP has increased with immigration, GDP per head has stayed the same. This is not exactly a damning conclusion on the economic effects of immigration. The report bemoans that immigration leads to job vacancies. Migrants spend their wages, which creates demand for goods and services and therefore more jobs to provide them. But it's difficult to see how the new vacancies created in this way could be a problem, except within a framework of prejudice against immigration. The Lords' report concludes that the effect of immigration on low wages is slight, while the effect on the wages of the more skilled is positive. It argues that the tax contribution of immigrants is positive but small. The report also states that it does not find any significant economic losses resulting from immigration into the UK. With enemies like these, who in the pro-migration lobby needs friends!

Stories about immigration tell that it takes workers' jobs, brings wages down, drains public services and provides a source of crime and conflict. But, as we have seen, the evidence contradicts the myths. As this evidence is available to everyone, it can only be assumed that politicians and the media choose not to look for it or to disregard it because it differs from their motives.

And it suits the purposes or prejudices of the media, politicians and the public to direct the blame to immigration for factors such as low wages arising from a surplus of workers, when in fact, in this example, those who set the low wages are the employers. Many such stories are promoted by parts of the *media* that use them to promote sales, for example of newspapers, by appealing to popular prejudice. Politicians raise fears about immigration to appeal to popular concerns and thus to win votes. The irony of this is that politicians have also encouraged migration through colonialism, labour recruitment and EU integration. The persistence of the media and politicians in encouraging negative interpretations of immigration, despite the unreliability of the information these are based on, has consequences in terms of stirring up racial hatred, intolerance and violence against immigrants. At the same time, these are not just problems of elites. Politicians and the media appeal to anti-immigrant sentiments because these exist amongst the population at large – it is a public phenomenon and not just an elite one.

I have focused so far on primarily economic and political aspects of migration. None of this touches on the *cultural impact of migration*. Alongside culture that the media brings from around the world, migration is also a contributor to dynamic and diverse cultures. Culture in rich receiving countries has been enhanced as a result of migration – through food, music, religion, values, film and media, or in a range of other day-to-day areas. Witness the dynamism and entrepreneurialism in a country of immigration like the USA, as well as the economic, cultural, social and political contributions of immigrants, from the oldest to the most recent, in global cities such as New York and London. As we saw in chapter 4, globalization through the media and migration has contributed to new hybrid identities, with diverse and mixed forms of consumption, style and culture, whether in dress, food, music or other lifestyle influences.

This undermines arguments that migration reduces diversity. Such arguments equate diversity with national diversity and say that national differences are being eroded by the globalization of culture via the media and migration. In fact, national diversity tends to be maintained by migration because it often has a varying content in each country, related to that nation's specificity. In Britain, migration is linked to its colonial past and membership of the EU, so the forms this takes in the UK differ from those of other nations without colonial pasts and with links to different countries worldwide. Furthermore, those who criticize migration for eroding national diversity are placing too much emphasis on diversity of national differences. Within nations, diversity is increased by migration.

Societies are plural entities that are always in a state of process. Attempts to argue that their meaning or identity will be undermined by immigration take a fixed moment and do not see that societies continually change over time, and that migration in and out is one of the elements in this process. Often the society into which migrants are entering is made up of centuries of migration itself. In the UK, you could be led to believe that postwar postcolonial immigration or EU immigration at the turn of the twenty-first century were the first the country had experienced. Yet the majority of citizens of this country were then the descendants of centuries of migration from Roman, Germanic, Viking and Norman invasions, to mention just some overseas inputs from the past, as well as more recent migrations from Ireland, and of Jewish refugees amongst others.

Holding on to the fixed moment of national identity at any given moment sometimes involves a form of racism. It takes that moment as real and true, in an arbitrary way, as there will have been many such moments through history – all different, but this one chosen because it is the latest. In this way, anything different becomes 'other' and alien, purely on the basis of such difference and not because of any inherent qualities. Definitions of identity are not only too fixed on a specific historical moment, but that moment is also often a construction or caricature rather than a reality. The fixed identity that is sometimes appealed to in the UK, implicitly or sometimes more explicitly, is of a white, Protestant society. Not only does this choose British identity at an arbitrary point without justifying this, but it also detracts from the reality of how Britain was at this point by creating a false and imagined picture.

Further Reading

The further reading listed at the end of the last chapter – for instance, Castles and Miller's (2003) *Age of Migration* – are relevant to further reading on the themes of this chapter too.

Messina and Lahav's (2006) *The Migration Reader* is relevant to both this chapter and to chapter 5.

Nigel Harris (2001), *Thinking the Unthinkable,* Jonathon Moses (2006), *International Migration*, and Philippe Legrain (2007), *Immigrants: Your Country Needs You*, outline the benefits of migration.

Reed and Latorre's report (2009) looks at the economic effects of migration for the UK.

The Global Economy: Capitalism and the Economic Bases of Globalization

ECONOMIC globalization is a theme throughout this book. This chapter is primarily about what economic globalization is, how determinant it is, and whether or not it is happening. It argues that globalization is often economically driven, even in many cases where on the surface it may seem to be cultural, political or military. It discusses arguments that it is too reductionist or economically determinist to put an emphasis on the role of economics. The next section sets out a case for economic causality in globalization and the others look at concrete instances of economic globalization.

The economic bases of globalization

From pluralism to economic determinism

Many perspectives on globalization see it as hybrid, occurring at different levels, with inputs from around the world and varying in its effects where it is received. It is seen as driven by multiple rather than single or selected causes. Globalization is mixed, multidimensional, localized in its effects and multicausal. Much of the stress on multiple causes is a reaction against economic determinism, especially Marxism, which is seen to reduce political, cultural and social phenomena, including processes of globalization, too much to economics.

Being pluralist about the factors behind globalization is important. Explanations of globalization should not be too economically determinist but should recognize the variety of causes alongside the autonomous impact of culture and politics on the economy and society, and that they themselves are not just determined by the economy. For instance, globalization is not only about the spread of neoliberalism but also of culture. How globalization is received in different places, whether economically or culturally, depends on the culture of that place. This means that it takes different forms in different places. Anti-economism and views of globalization as plural often go together.

The mission statement of the journal *Globalizations* says that:

> *Globalizations* is dedicated to opening the widest possible space for discussion of alternatives to a narrow economic understanding of globalization. The move from the singular to the plural is deliberate and implies skepticism of the idea that there can ever be a single theory or interpretation of globalization. Rather, the journal will seek to encourage the exploration and discussion of multiple interpretations and multiple processes that may constitute many possible globalizations, many possible alternatives.

One sphere of society cannot be the only one that drives globalization. However, giving a pluralistic mix of reasons as an alternative to monocausality is not by itself adequate. Often some causes are more dominant and some have more of an effect on other influences than the alternatives. It is necessary to look not just at the plurality of causes and influences but also to see if some are more dominant. Many parts of society and causes of globalization are interlinked and my argument is that the economy can often, but not always, be seen to be the driving one.

I say this not because of a pre-given Marxist economic determinism, but because empirical evidence suggests this is often the case. Other chapters discuss how. Culture is often economically driven, expanding globally because of attempts to sell and make a profit from it. War is sometimes a battle over the resources to fuel an economy. Politics can be driven by the attempt to maximize the wealth of a society. Migration can be in pursuit of better economic circumstances or in reaction to factors like wars that have economic bases. The economy is not the only casual factor in any of these spheres and there are many instances where it is not the primary one. But if you look at globalization in practice economics is often behind it in different spheres of society, even if this is not the only factor and is combined with other factors such as politics or culture, which are sometimes behind the economics or shaping the path it takes.

What economic determinism is and is not

Even if the economy is often seen to be dominant, this does not have to imply conclusions that critics attribute to this perspective or that may seem implicit in it. Economic explanations in the way I am arguing for them do not mean: (1) that the economy itself is necessarily determinant; (2) that economic forces are impersonal structures as opposed to being driven by agents with choice; (3) that political and cultural factors do not also have causal power within the context of economic causality; (4) that economic forces are *always* determinant; or (5) that economic determinism leads to homogenization. These are important clarifications, within the context of economic motivations being primary causes behind globalization.

My emphasis is on economic *motivations* rather than the economy. If globalization is driven by economic incentives this does not necessarily mean it is caused by the economy as a structure, or by economic actors. For instance, key actors in economically motivated globalization can be states or governments. These are political rather than economic agents but might be motivated by a desire to secure economic benefits within their territory. So, while economic motivations are driving factors, the economy or economic actors may not be. It can be political actors who are the drivers, out of choice and not because they are forced to be.

As such, economic determinism does not necessarily mean that society is shaped by *impersonal economic structures* out of its control. This could sometimes be the case, but economic motivations are often the creation of actors such as governments or corporations. They deliberately and actively promote their economic aims. This could be changed by these or other actors putting different goals in their place. To see globalization as driven by economics is compatible not only with non-economic actors being behind this but also with agents and choice, rather than impersonal structures being the determining forces.

Focusing on economic motivations does not negate the impact that *politics and culture* have on economic globalization. If economic motives are behind globalization, such motives can be pursued in more ways than one. The shape economic globalization takes varies often in accordance with culture or politics. The political institutions and traditions of a country may affect the reception of globalization, and it takes different forms according to the local cultures where it is received. That economics is politically and culturally embedded, partly explains why economically driven globalization does not have a homogeneous outcome everywhere. At the same time, economic incentives may still be the driving forces behind globalization, albeit taking different forms according to political and cultural embeddedness. The latter does not disprove the former, and I will provide some examples in this and other chapters.

To say that economic incentives are a primary force behind

globalization does not mean that they are necessarily *always the primary force in all areas*. For instance, domestic politics and policies may be determined by forces other than economic ones, such as cultural aspects. In the US, socially conservative religious values have a strong influence on politics. Religious values are important in the politics of Islamic countries too. Gender inequality and the globalization of it is often perpetuated by economic motives – women workers from the developing world provide cheap labour in rich countries, for example. But the gendered dimension of this cannot be explained by economics and partly needs to be accounted for in terms of patriarchal culture and ideology.

Sociologists are sometimes reluctant to accept explanations that put a primacy on economic causes. Why is this?

1 One reason may be that they confuse arguments about economic motivations with the thesis that the economy is causal. As we have seen, economics can be a motivation without economic actors necessarily being the key agents (even if they often will be), and without impersonal economic structures being the determining force or non-economic spheres such as politics or culture being irrelevant. Economic causality can be dismissed if it is seen as impersonal, structurally determinist or oblivious to politics or culture. But economic determinism need not imply such a crude approach as this.

2 Another reason may be a continuation of attempts in the postwar period within or against Marxism to break with the reduction of everything to economics. This goes back to Weberian arguments for status and party as factors in the struggle for power in society, as well as economic class, and for cultural as well as economic factors as being behind the rise of capitalism (see Parkin 2002). Within Marxism, there have been debates involving figures such as Gramsci and Althusser who tried to put more emphasis on culture and ideology relative to the economy (see Larrain 1983). Sociological anti-economism is related to debates within and against Marxism.

But as we have seen: (a) stressing economic motivations is not the same as reducing causation to economic forces only, or to impersonal structures rather than actors; (b) ascribing economic motivations can involve pointing to non-economic actors such as states as key figures in pursuing them; and (c) prioritizing economic causation does not mean that economic motivations are always dominant, unaffected by political and cultural factors, or homogeneous in their effects. Political forces can underlie such motivations or take things in another direction. And, as we shall see, economic motivations can be important but embedded in culture or shaped by it, resulting in it taking different forms in different places – for instance, the way capitalism develops in different regions due to varying cultural and political set-ups. Economic motivations may be primary amongst globalizing forces but cultural particularity can prevent homogeneity or convergence when political and cultural factors take them in different directions.

None of these complexities detract from the significance of economic causality. They show that if economic motivations are primary this is not the same as reductionism to impersonal forces, as roles for agency, non-economic forces and diversity are included in outcomes. But they show the form that economic motivations take. They do not show that the economic is not determining or imply a return to pluralism. They show the agency and role of politics and culture in economic determinism, but do not deny the fact that economic motivations are often a primary determinant. And these complexities to the theory do not minimize the role of economic causality because globalization takes different forms in different places, or is taken in varying directions by non-economic actors or contexts. Economic causality still explains globalization in many cases. It shows why some forms of globalization may happen rather than others. And it helps

---

Box 7.1 Economic causes of globalization

1   Being *pluralist* about the multicausality of globalization is good but not good enough. We need to look at relations between causes and see which are more dominant or have a causal effect on the others.

2   Empirical *evidence*, rather than theoretical presuppositions, shows economic causality behind the globalization of culture, migration, politics, war and so on, in ways outlined in the chapters of this book.

3   Economic determinism does not mean that *the economy itself* is necessarily determinant – economic causes may operate through other agencies and spheres, corporations, governments, and so on.

4   It is not the economy I am saying is determinant, but economic *motivations*.

5   It is not the economy as an *impersonal structure* that is the determinant but active agents making economically motivated decisions.

6   That economic motivations are often primary does not mean they are the only causal factor. There may be *other causes* at the same time.

7   It also does not mean that they are *always determinant*. Sometimes other factors will be more important, e.g., culture.

8   Economic causality does not mean that globalization will be *homogeneous*. Different decisions are possible on the basis of the same economic motives, and location and political and cultural factors may lead to differentiation in the way globalization turns out.

9   Despite such complexities to economic explanations of globalization, there is still *economic causality* and it is important to identify it. Seeing the economic causes behind globalization helps us to know the determinants of it, to explain it, understand the agents and interests involved and who is most powerful, make predictions, understand the relative weight and mutual effects of different causal factors, and to do more than see globalization as simply caused by multiple factors.

us to identify the key powers behind globalization, their motivations and, therefore, what sort of directions globalization could be pushed in. Maintaining the sort of economic determinism I am arguing for here tells us about causes, directions and power in globalization.

Economics is causal. But it is possible to be more precise than this. The sort of economics that is often behind globalization is capitalist economics (Sklair 2002). This is based around profit for privately owned business (as opposed to socialist economics which is geared, in theory at least, to provision for social need by publicly owned corporations). In chapter 2, with its historical focus, we saw that, while there were pre-capitalist transnational forms of trade, people movements and culture, it was with the economics and technology of the industrial capitalist era that transnational relations of a globalized sort developed. The economics of capitalism, private profit for private owners, and the wealth the state could gain from this, provided the motivations for economic globalization in the early modern period, and for the development of the technology that allowed that globalization to develop. There are several dimensions to economic globalization.

Economic interdependency

One aspect of economic globalization is interdependency. In previous chapters I argued that true globalization occurs if it involves not only interconnections between two areas but also interdependency, where they are not just linked but also affect one another. One aspect of economic globalization is that the world is interdependent such that economic events in one part of the globe can have effects in many others.

In the 1970s, OPEC, a group of oil-producing countries, put up the price of oil. The cost of this vital energy supply quadrupled. This led to inflation (rising prices) in many countries. The cost of manufacturing and transport rose because of the higher price of oil on which these depend. Because production and transport became more costly, profits dropped, companies made people unemployed, and consumers who were unemployed or making less profit had less money to spend, which affected other industries selling to them. The cost of state support for the unemployed rose, there were fewer people in employment paying the tax needed to support unemployment benefits and so on, in a cycle of effects throughout the economy. There was inflation and economic stagnation in many countries and a loss of confidence, with insecurity on the part of investors about developments in the world economy and whether it was safe to invest.

So what happened in one place had global ramifications – because of the dependency of other parts of the world on what happened in oil-producing nations, and the host of other interdependent factors affected by the cost of oil

In 2007 there was a world 'credit crunch' rooted in the collapse of the 'sub prime' US mortgage market. Mortgage lenders in the US lent money to poorer people, some of whom were unable to pay off these loans. Banks and other lending institutions globally became short of funds because they could not obtain repayments of loans, or they could not borrow money from institutions that were short of cash as a result of lending to people unable to repay. Borrowers such as individuals, banks and companies therefore found loans and investment harder to come by – the 'credit crunch'. This led to a loss of confidence amongst investors and borrowers, reluctant to pursue economic activity if there would not be enough money to fund it. This had global repercussions. With less access to investment and less spending by consumers, economies around the word went into recession, with companies going out of business and people losing their jobs. As countries that export goods could not sell so many of them in affected countries, they too were drawn into economic difficulties. Governments had to pour money into the banking system to provide money for investment. Some banks went out of business and savers lost their money or their savings had to be guaranteed by governments. As confidence in business success declined, the price of shares in companies went down, with companies losing a source of investment when people became reluctant to buy these, and shareholders losing money on their shares. So what would seem like a small problem, a blip in one section of the mortgage market in one country, showed up the interdependency of the global economy because of its knock-on effects elsewhere.

While economies are strongly affected by domestic circumstances – such as national government policies, culture and attitudes – external economic factors have a big influence too. These include demand from overseas for exported goods, inward investment from outside, stability and confidence in the economy further afield, the cost and availability of energy supplies like oil from overseas, and events such as wars or climate change which can in part be out of the hands of the nation affected and can affect the economy.

In this way, national economies are integrated into the global economy, even though the extent and type of this may vary from nation to nation. For instance, nations like Germany are globalized because they are big exporters of manufactured goods, while others like the UK are integrated as significant importers and exporters of Foreign Direct Investment and cultural goods. Nevertheless, there is an interdependence between what happens within the national economy and what happens in the rest of the world. But, as we shall see, this does not mean simple globalization of the world economy.

Capital mobility

Another important area of economic globalization is capital mobility. Money can be moved more easily across national boundaries as result of *technological* and *political* changes. Technologically, it has become possible to integrate finance into computer networks. Money now takes an electronic and virtual rather than a paper form, with the result that enormous amounts can be sent instantaneously from one side of the world to another. Politically, since the 1970s and 1980s, regulations to restrict the movement of capital globally have been relaxed in line with more neoliberal policies, and there are fewer legal constraints on the movement of money across national borders.

Different kinds of money are moved. Transnational corporations invest beyond their home country, for example, by subcontracting work or setting up their own branches elsewhere, or by spending money on technology or labour in overseas countries. Or investment can be in stocks and shares in companies around the world. There can be direct investment that comes with influence in the company, or more speculative investment in shares without a direct role in running the company.

The movement of capital has big economic consequences but also political and cultural implications, which I will mention here and discuss in other chapters. One *political* implication is connected to the fact that governments cannot rely on money to stay in their country. Capital can move around to look for the best investment, the cheapest workers and the most relaxed environmental regulations. Governments have to work to keep money in their country, or to attract mobile capital in competition with other states. This reduces the strength and autonomy of governments in terms of what policies they can pursue, as their policies are now determined in part by the need to be attractive to global capital. This changes the balance of class forces globally – it makes capital more powerful in relation to the state or labour (Crouch 2004). Policies pursued by government are more likely to be neoliberal because, on the whole, this is favoured by businesses – lower taxes, lower public spending, and fewer regulations on companies. The theory of the 'competition state' argues that socialist or social democratic policies have consequently become more difficult to follow. It also suggests that democracy suffers because power shifts from elected governments to unelected financiers.

Additionally, it is claimed, there are *cultural* implications of capital mobility. Big corporations that originally had more of a domestic focus are becoming more involved globally. Corporations such as News Corporation, Coca-Cola and McDonald's have activities across the world. So a capitalist, Westernized or even Americanized culture, which reflects the dominant origins of many of these businesses, becomes globalized. This leads to a homogenization of world culture that irons out national differences and diversity, although there are alternative perspectives to this which were discussed in chapter 4.

MNCs and FDI

A key factor in economic globalization is said to be the role and rise of multinational or transnational corporations (MNCs). The distinction is that a transnational corporation goes above and beyond nations and takes on a global character independent of national origins and ties. In fact, corporations at this level of transnationality or globality do not appear to exist – there are international or multinational corporations, but perhaps not global or transnational ones. I will return to this point. MNCs are involved in the sort of capital mobility mentioned above that involves direct investment more than indirect investment or speculation in stocks and shares. They are investing in their own operations or in subcontractors abroad.

What makes a corporation multinational? There are a number of dimensions to this. Its ownership may be multinational. It can be owned by shareholders from different parts of the world. Its investments and assets could be multinational. It may have factories or investments in labour in many different countries. Its production might be multinational, taking place in different countries – perhaps its headquarters in Europe or the USA, while its production facilities or data-processing activities may be in an Asian country with lower production costs or looser environmental regulations, and its customer services, call centre or its IT support perhaps in Southern India. It may subcontract or outsource some of its work to companies in other countries or have its own branches or subsidiaries there. To the extent that some sorts of operation stay in some parts of the world (e.g., higher managerial operations in more developed countries) and others in other parts (e.g., production, data-processing or customer services in developing countries), then there is an international division of labour.

Its trade and consumers may be multinational. It could sell its TV programmes or its burgers or soft drinks in countries across the world. Coca-Cola, for instance, is a product that is difficult to avoid, from the richest American cities to the some of the poorer cities and most remote areas on the other side of the world. So global consumer-ism of products on global markets has grown. An MNC is one that has multinational dimensions in such areas – (1) ownership and invest-ments; (2) production and labour; and (3) trade and consumption.

Nike, the US sportswear company, is an example of a globalized company which outsources to distant localities. It has its headquarters in the US, while its products are made by globally dispersed partners who get their materials and equipment from local suppliers or from other partners or Nike. Nike's suppliers are global, from South Asia to Latin America to Europe, but focused in East Asia. It sells its prod-ucts in different parts of the world. The US computer company Dell sources its parts from around the world. Components are transported between units in different international locations, and assembled in places from the US to Lebanon, Ireland, Poland, China, Malaysia, India and Brazil, before being shipped (or flown) to customers glo-bally. Customer support is based in locations worldwide, in North and Central America and several countries in Asia.

Many MNCs have arisen out of *merger and diversification*. We saw this in chapter 3 in the case of media corporations such as News Corporation and Time Warner. Mergers and acquisitions happen where compa-nies buy or combine with other companies; with diversification, they branch out into different areas of activity. A media company may be involved in just publishing or perhaps TV, but through mergers and acquisitions begins to take an interest also in the Internet, cinema or newspapers, and in operations in other countries. A consequence of this is that sometimes powerful corporations have grown through buying out the competition and gaining control over large areas of the media. In 2007, the global value of mergers and acquisitions was $1,637 billion, a 21 per cent increase on the previous record in 2000 and a major factor behind cross-border FDI (UNCTAD 2008b: 3).

There are estimated to be 79,000 MNCs with 790,000 affiliates. *Industries* such as motor vehicles, pharmaceuticals, telecoms, utilities, petroleum and electronics make up 60 per cent of the activities of the largest 100 MNCs. General Electric, British Petroleum, Toyota and Shell head the list of the biggest global TNCs in terms of foreign assets owned, followed by Exxon Mobile, Ford and Vodafone. These are all US, Japanese or UK (and one jointly Dutch) companies. In 2006, 85 of the top 100 TNCs had their headquarters in the US, Europe and Japan. Five countries (the United States, the United Kingdom, Japan, France and Germany) accounted for 72 of the top 100 firms. In 2006, there were six companies from developing economies (China, Hong Kong, Malaysia, the Republic of Korea, Singapore and Mexico) among the top 100 (UNCTAD 2008b: 27).

The operation of MNCs cannot be separated from the role of *Foreign*

Table 7.1 FDI flow by region (2007, millions of dollars)		
	Inflow	Outflow
EU and more developed Europe	848,527	1,216,491.5
North America (US and Canada)	341,494	367,605
Africa	52,982	6,055
Latin America and Caribbean	126,266	52,336
Asia and Oceania	320,498	194,794
SE Europe and CIS	85,942	51,227

Source: Abridged from UNCTAD, 2008c, annex B: 253–6

Direct Investment (FDI). As mentioned, FDI involves the investor taking a role in the company's running, as opposed to indirect investment in stock or shares in which there is not that role. Often it is MNCs which are doing the foreign direct investment. Global FDI inflows rose in 2007 to reach $1,833 billion, well above the previous all-time high set in 2000. A large proportion of FDI comes from developed countries and is often in other developed countries or at best in newly industrializing countries. In 2007, the largest recipients of FDI inflows were the US, the UK, France, Canada and the Netherlands. The poorest countries only get to see a small proportion. FDI may be multinational but the unevenness of integration into patterns of FDI makes it difficult to see it as global. When richer parts of the world attract much more FDI than poorer parts of the world, with the latter being much less integrated and included, FDI is less global than regionally focused (UNCTAD 2008b: 1).

The information from UNCTAD in Table 7.1 shows that the three core economic regions contain the majority of the world's inward and outward FDI flows. EU and US flows both ways dwarf those in Africa. Flows in Asia and Oceania are dominated by China and India. Taking into account the huge populations of these two countries they fall well behind the EU and North America. Furthermore, Glyn shows that FDI makes up about 13 per cent of the share of capital stock in national economies, often in particular sectors of the economy more than others (2004: 6). So, as a portion of national economies, it is far from dominant. The spread of FDI around the world and its role in national economies are both short of global.

MNCs develop primarily in the search for profits. As already discussed, economics and especially capitalist economics are a driving force in globalization. MNCs look for cheaper labour, expanding markets, buying off the competition, getting more of a monopolistic grasp of the market in their area, diversifying into new areas of production and consumption and becoming bigger and stronger. All of these are geared towards seeking profit and lead to greater multinationality. The capitalist economics of profit drive globalization.

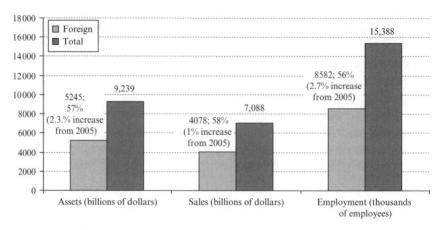

Source: Data from UNCTAD 2008c: 27

Figure 7.1   The world's 100 largest TNCs, 2006

MNCs are often seen as a threat from globalization to the nation-state. I will discuss this in chapter 9. My focus here is on its economics. *Does the MNC demonstrate globalization?* To be a form of globalization there are some characteristics it could have. It could be a form of company not identifiable with national locations but with an identity above and beyond nations – transnational and global. There could be convergence amongst MNCs to a typical global form rather than variation linked with national territories. Are MNCs beyond nations and globalist? Are there signs of convergence in the global economy?

The United Nations Conference on Trade and Development (UNCTAD 2008c) has calculated the transnationality of the world's largest MNCs by the proportion of their overseas assets, employment and sales. In 2006, the largest 100 TNCs had over 55 per cent of their assets, sales or employment abroad, as shown in figure 7.1. So these are very international companies and there is an upward trend in their internationalism. But the other 40 per cent or more of their assets, sales and employment are in their home economies. So these are still nationally rooted companies. This can also be seen from the list of top TNCs in figure 7.3. These have identifiable national affiliations that, furthermore, are concentrated in the core regions of the world.

Hirst and Thompson argue that these are less transnational companies than national companies trading internationally. Profits from overseas involvements are often returned predominantly to the home base. The national base of a company may have an effect on the way it behaves and what makes it successful. There are different types of capitalism in different places, so national location can make a difference to company behaviour. National requirements matter and we should

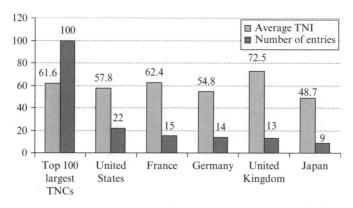

Source: Data from UNCTAD 2008c: 28

Figure 7.2   Comparison of TNI values (Transnationality index) by region, 2006

guard against assumptions about global convergence in capitalism or MNC behaviour.

UNCTAD's index of top MNCs shows an upward trend in transnationalism and some countries, as we can see in figure 7.2, have some very international MNCs. The figure shows the domination of some countries of origin amongst MNCs. There is a transnationality of around 50 per cent in many cases. This means companies may be international, but still with strong national bases.

UNCTAD's data on the locations in which MNCs are investing and participating shows that transnationality is not very global in reach (figure 7.3). There is inequality in the favoured locations of MNCs. The most favoured are either rich developed countries or transitional or newly industrialized countries at the upper end of development. There are no African countries amongst the most-favoured locations of the top 100 TNCs, nor amongst those favoured by the top 100 TNCs from developing countries, not even if you go far beyond the top 20 locations listed in figure 7.3. Globalization is not looking very global here, because of its unequal spread and the inequality it is reinforcing.

Finance

Finance is often said to be the area of the economy which has been most globalized, even by commentators who are otherwise sceptical about globalization (Hirst and Thompson 1996). This is in part because of information technology – money often consists of figures in networked computers rather than physical money or goods that have to be transported. As such it has been especially affected by

For largest world TNCs

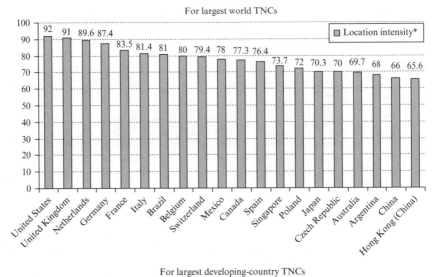

For largest developing-country TNCs

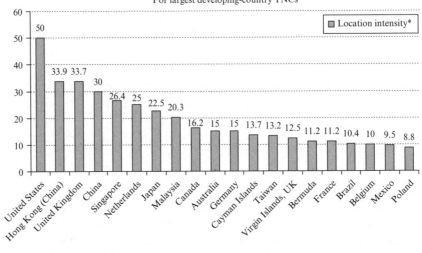

Note: * Location intensity is defined as the number of TNCs with at least one affiliate in the host country, divided by 100, excluding TNCs in their own countries from their countries' own figures.

Source: Data from UNCTAD 2006: 35

Figure 7.3 Most-favoured locations of top 100 TNCs

developments in information technology and least restricted by the limitations of transport which slow down the movement of people and goods. Furthermore finance is less tied by local cultures than people or goods. People have roots (such as family and friends) and cultures that affect their ties or mobility, whereas finance is a virtual entity that does not. Similarly goods are often wanted (or not) in local areas according to local culture and tastes whereas money has more universality. This is not to say that finance is not affected by restrictions and boundaries to do with culture and politics but that it is less so than people and goods.

Finance is vitally important because economic activities depend on money to fund them and money is the basis of exchange and transactions in economies. States are keen to try to control or attract capital as investment affects the wealth of an economy, economic growth and employment and, hence, where relevant, governments' electoral prospects.

Finance is also of concern, (a) because of its capacity to evade state control and move across boundaries and to places where it can exploit more relaxed regulations, and (b) because the highly global and interdependent world of finance is, as a result of this, very volatile. Finance is central to the world economy. So lack of predictability (with the consequences this has for confidence and therefore investment and stability) and financial crises have very significant consequences for the world economy and hence for people's individual lives, as we saw in the post-2007 financial crisis.

Susan Strange (1997) has described the world of global finance as casino capitalism. This is because much financial activity is gambling. It is often not about long-term planned investment in enterprise, but short-term buying and selling of shares to make money from them while they are on the up, then to dispose of them when they appear to be a risk – speculation. The distinction between speculation and investment is not clear-cut – what is speculated often finds its way into investment in production. But much of it involves making money out of money, rather than out of production, and is invested in a way that is not concerned with long-term planning.

About 90 per cent of international financial flows and foreign currency transactions are speculative rather than in trade and production. The amounts are huge and growing fast in proportion to trade in goods and services. In 1973 the ratio of foreign exchange trading to world trade was 2:1; in 1980, 10:1; in 1992, 50: 1; and in 1995, 70:1 (Dicken 2007: 380). Since the 1970s, there have been a number of key developments in financial services. They have been deregulated or liberalized. One consequence of governments being less involved in regulating and controlling finance is that financial markets have become less domestically confined and more internationalized, especially in response to international trade, the spread of MNCs and the institutionalization of savings (Dicken 2007: 383). Deregulation and internationalization have increased competition and shaken up the financial services industry. Lack of regulation allowed the irresponsibility of financial institutions that led to the post-2007 financial crisis.

Financial globalization has been accelerated, not just by deregulation (a political factor) but also by developments in IT (a technological factor). As mentioned above, money is often virtual, especially the large amounts moved around in financial services, and takes the form of electronic symbols moved in massive amounts instantly and globally on computer networks with the click of a mouse. Money is essentially information moved through computers on networks.

There has been a concentration of activities in different sectors of finance in a smaller number of companies, as a result of mergers and acquisitions. One feature of the concentration of financial activity is that, although finance is globally mobile, its activities are geographically concentrated in places such as Japan, European countries like Switzerland, the UK, France and Germany, and the US (Dicken 2007: 391). The world's major financial centres are in London and New York, and to a lesser extent other sites such as Tokyo and Frankfurt, with financial companies concentrating in such places even if they have global operations (see Sassen 2001).

Despite the geographical bases of global finance, since the 1960s and 1970s it has become more transnationalized with domestically based banks setting up overseas operations and distant branches. Banks have adapted to fit in with development of the operations of multinational corporations operations beyond their home countries (although MNCs branches often use local banks), with US banks raising money abroad for lending at home and elsewhere or US dollars being held in overseas banks – what are called Eurodollars. Oil-exporting countries lent their wealth abroad from the 1970s. Many of these developments accelerated, especially from the 1980s onwards. Accountancy firms have had to transnationalize to adapt to these processes, and being a global firm has become a selling point for financial companies, albeit with recognition that sensitivity to local circumstances needs to be part of the image.

One problem is volatility. Money moves so fast that there can be big shifts in international finance that reduce stability and confidence. High levels of interdependency and velocity mean that an upheaval in one place can quickly carry over to other places.

Nevertheless, even in this massive globalized industry, the role of the nation-state as regulator is not dead. One consequence of deregulation and the mobility and insecurity that can follow is that states step in to control this situation. For instance, they can limit the involvement of institutions in different functions across financial services and restrict foreign ownership.

But corporations try to avoid such regulation. There is an industry providing advice on loopholes in regulation, as well as recommended locations where regulations or taxes are lighter, to which operations can be moved. Some of these 'offshore' locations are islands, such as the Cayman or Virgin Islands, although it is often as much a question of being registered in such places as being physically located there. Many are onshore but offering the same advantages. Some governments have relaxed limits on cross-ownership and foreign involvement, one example being the 1986 'Big Bang' in the UK. Regional blocs have pursued financial deregulation too – for instance, across the EU single market. The post-2007 financial crisis prompted calls for greater regulation of finance, but it is not clear whether the political will exists amongst the most powerful states to pursue this significantly at a global level. Many of them believe in economic liberalism and see this as being in their interests. Responses have often been national, using government intervention in banks and the injection of money into the economy rather than tighter controls.

Free trade and protectionism

Economic globalization is often discussed in relation to world trade. Trade involves the exchange of goods and services and, if it is globalized, across national boundaries. As we saw in chapter 2, it was long-distance trade from Asia to the Middle East and Europe that provided evidence of pre-modern transnationalization. This was not globalized. It was too narrowly confined to some parts of the world and not worldwide. The extent was quite limited and it did not involve relations that are regularized and interdependent, of the sort characteristic of modern globalization, rather than merely interconnections or intermittent relations. Some point to intense global trade in the period before the First World War.

A key concern is the way trade across the world has grown and become more globalized. This is said to have brought poorer developing countries into the global economy, helping them to grow economically by selling their goods. Another consequence is cultural globalization. With increasing trade globally more of us are consuming goods and services, and so culture, from other parts of the world. For some, as we saw in chapter 4, this leads to homogenization as more people worldwide consume similar globalized cultures, or to hybridization as we are exposed to a mix of diverse global inputs.

Major debates and negotiations are over *free trade and protectionism*. Protectionism is where trade is regulated by governments to protect or favour their own industries. Tariffs or quotas may be imposed on imports of some goods so that domestic industry is protected from competition. Subsidies or other forms of assistance can be given to home industries to assist them against competition from overseas. This is the opposite of free trade because some actors are being given advantages over others or open trade is being restricted. At regional (e.g., EU) or world (e.g., WTO) level, states try to forge agreements to prevent blocks on free trade or special assistance for domestic industries. This is in order to promote open competition in the world economy. However, negotiations are often difficult and lengthy, and states retreat from free trade when they fear their own industries will be exposed to tough competition, for example, in the cases of US steel tariffs, EU textile quotas and farming subsidies, and Indian and Chinese agriculture.

A key issue is whether free trade can help get the poorest countries out of poverty. I will return to this in the next chapter, but debates on this issue are not as clear-cut and honest as they appear to be. The impression could be that there are protectionists and free traders, and that the latter promote free trade against the former. In theory, the aim of free traders is to help poor countries get a foothold in the world economy to trade their way out of poverty without unfair competition from rich countries who limit imports or provide special help for their own industries. This is good for rich countries, too, whose industries benefit from competition, making them more dynamic and also provides openings in the markets of developing countries that are required to drop restrictions on imports or special assistance for their own industries.

In fact, the picture is more complex and instrumental than this. Some promote free trade where they feel it will be to their benefit, but are protectionist regarding their own industries. For example, in 2008, the US objected to protectionism and ended trade negotiations when some developing countries wanted tariffs on agriculture to be activated if imports threatened their domestic industries. Yet the US heavily subsidizes its own farmers, giving them an advantage in world trade. Free traders are selective about where they are willing to liberalize, instrumental self-interest being the guiding criteria on this issue.

Trade blocs have been established – for instance, the EU, NAFTA, Mercosur and ASEAN – ostensibly to encourage free trade between members. But often these are protectionist towards outsiders. What appears to promote free trade and openness involves closure and protectionism, often on the part of the rich, for instance, in Europe. This is against the poor, whose development is blocked by exclusion from the economies of the developed world. Although these blocs are built to help countries respond to globalization, they frequently build walls or special help which restrict globalization. Trade liberalization talks under the auspices of the WTO were intended to overcome such protectionism, but have been fraught with difficulties.

World free trade, beyond the more regionally limited forms of the pre-modern era, grew with industrialization and in the later parts of the nineteenth century. The main imperial power, Britain, expanded trade globally, in its own extensive colonies and beyond. There has been debate about this but British imperialism was motivated to a significant extent by economic objectives (Porter 1996).

Often primary products from the non-industrialized world (products from industries such as agriculture, fishing, forestry and mining which are used as the raw materials for other industries) were exported to the imperial nations. Europe then exported manufactured goods. There was not much trade between primary producers but a lot between industrialized countries. In this case, a large amount was genuinely global in distance – between imperial powers and colonies, and richer and less developed countries. The interwar period was one of worldwide economic depression and nations responded by limiting imports and subsidizing exports, to protect their national economies. The emergence of the US as the hegemonic power enabled it to press its own interests – and a free trade system where it could trade openly with an advantage over others was ideal.

In the postwar period the US pursued the spread of free trade transnationally, but both the US and USSR built special trading relations with their favoured capitalist or communist friends. GATT (the General Agreement on Tariffs and Trade, later to become the WTO) was established with the aim of promoting free trade and limiting protectionism. Tariff reductions and world trade grew, with a growing share for the EU and Japan. Although developing and newly industrializing countries' shares of world trade increased in the 1950s, most trade then and now involves industrialized countries, as opposed to between industrialized and non-industrialized nations as in earlier periods. About 85 per cent of world exports come from the triad of North America, Europe and East and South East Asia, and largely go between them. About 85 per cent of world Gross Domestic Product comes from the same three regions (Dicken 2007: 39). This leaves Latin America, Africa, and other parts of Asia quite marginalized.

This sort of outcome is a core concern of this book. Trade has not been truly globalized despite being international, as some areas participate more strongly than others. And globalization, if that is what it is, is unequal. Some are more at the core, powerful, integrated and benefiting to a greater extent, while others remain at the periphery, excluded and receiving little benefit. These factors encourage the sceptics' conclusions about globalization, and certain perspectives on the benefits of global trade for the poor that will be discussed in the next chapter.

National location and varieties of capitalism

We have seen above that, while many MNCs are international, there is a substantial extent to which they are embedded in their domestic economies, even in the case of some of the most transnational of MNCs.

But how significant is it to be nationally embedded? MNCs could be nationally located but converging to a common global type. National locatedness could be significant in terms of the proportion of activities located in home economies. But this may not be the significant force in their global behaviour. They could remain uninfluenced by their national location, being footloose and converging in a competitive global economy, following the common norms of multinational companies. But the evidence suggests this is not the case. National location is not just quantitatively significant. It shapes and affects how companies and economies develop, and leads to a world in which diversity and difference coexist with global convergence and commonality. Sociological insights about the social embeddedness of economics and capitalism are illuminating here, and lead to sceptical conclusions about economic globalization.

Literature on diversities of capitalist behaviour compares types of capitalism such as Japanese and/or East Asian, or European and Anglo-American (Albert 1993; Hutton 1995; Hall and Soskice 2001). There is also a literature on welfare regimes along similar lines, adding Scandinavian types (Esping-Andersen 1989). Within these regional types there is significant national diversity.

Differences in company organization are linked to the national environment within which companies operate. Japan is seen to be a more collectivist and less individualistic society than, say, the US or the UK, emphasizing loyalty to nation, family or firm. This, it is argued, is reflected in company behaviour, where there are strong and longer-term relations within and between firms, and between business and the state. Japanese capitalism is said to have risen on the basis of state intervention and a collectivist culture. In Newly Industrializing Countries (NICs) in East Asia, such as South Korea, Taiwan and Singapore, the state has played an important role in promoting development, alongside stronger relations within and between firms and the state. Social market capitalism in Germany and Scandinavian countries is based on collectivist norms and arrangements, for example, corporatist decision-making between business, government and workers, longer-term relations, less of a primary focus on shareholders, and more extensive welfare.

In Anglo-American countries and some post-communist states, the emphasis is competitive, with aggressive behaviour between firms, combined with a belief that the state should keep out of the economy rather than try to guide it. Shareholders are regarded as more important and planning tends to be short term. Competitive individualism and liberalization of the economy is considered key to the dynamism of Anglo-American capitalism.

As globalization increases, such comparative differences may decline, with firms from different parts of the world learning from each other. But MNCs may also adapt their operations to fit in with national differences where workers or consumers are located – the localization of globalization. Work organization may be adjusted to local cultures and norms, and goods or services to fit with what consumers in specific areas are used to or want, meaning that even the most transnational MNCs will be affected by changes to organization or practice as a result of having bases in other domestic economies. Adaptation of this sort reaffirms difference as much as global homogeneity or convergence.

Anglo-American capitalism is based around an ideal of a deregulated free market economy. This is the form said to be at the centre of globalization, being generalized around the world. However, the success of the other types suggests that globalization in the form of the spread of neoliberalism is not as pervasive as it may seem and that Anglo-Americanism cannot claim superiority. Participation in the global economy, for instance, in the shape of German exports (Germany is the world's largest exporter) or the rise of East Asian economies, has come as much through non-neoliberal government and collectivist forms. The varieties of capitalism show that global convergence is not the shape of the world economy, and countries are integrated into the global economy on the basis of non-neoliberal forms. We will see in the next chapter that protectionism and state intervention are as much part of the story of developing countries that have grown and integrated into the global economy as the globalizing neoliberalism they are often recommended to follow.

There are other distinctive forms – in the huge economies of India and China, for example. China is an increasingly major actor in the global economy, experimenting with pools of capitalism while under the control of a strong centralized Communist Party, and providing another model of capitalism differentiating as much as homogenizing the world. The post-2007 financial crisis has led to calls to reduce the deregulated approach to finance, which would mean a move away from Anglo-Americanism. But this may underestimate how influential and successful models other than Anglo-Americanism have already been and overestimate the will of some major powers and financial institutions to move away from an economically liberal model and regulate finance more strongly.

What I have discussed so far indicates that, despite ongoing multinational, international or transnational – even globalizing – processes, there are reasons why this may not amount to globalization. This is more than just an issue of academic definition. Globalization implies global extensiveness and inclusion. If the structures and processes that have been described are restricted to some, mainly the richer, more powerful and more privileged, this cannot be globalization and concerns more than a matter of definition. It is about understanding the power and inequality involved in globalization and its limited reach and inclusiveness.

This reinforces some of the conclusions of sceptics about globalization that were discussed in chapter 1 (Hirst and Thompson 1996). They argue that:

1 Internationalization of the world economy is not new. It has existed since the 1860s. The 1870–1914 period was the most open and integrated and more so than the present.

2 The world economy is internationalized but it is not *global* for the following reasons.

3 Transnational corporations are rare. Most multinational corporations are nationally based companies trading internationally.

4 Trade occurs primarily within and across three richer regions of the world – Japan and East Asia, Europe and North America. NICs and developing countries are outside this core. This does not meet the criteria of an integrated, converging and inclusive world economy.

5 Globalization is an unequal process – capital is mobile, internationalized and powerful but labour is less so.

6 There has not been a shift in investment to less developed countries. FDI stays mostly within the developed world. Globalization is unequal and not inclusive – in other words it is not global.

7 Governments of rich core states have the power together to regulate financial markets but they don't because: (a) it goes against their ideology of economic liberalism; (b) because of divergent interests which make it difficult to agree on regulation; and c) because some see regulation of finance as against their interests. But this means that globalization is not inevitable – it is a political choice that could be reversed.

Conclusions

Economic globalization raises key themes of this book. The economy is important to understanding other types of globalization. I have argued for seeing economic motivations as primary forces in globalization. Concrete cases of this in culture and politics are discussed in other chapters. It is economic motivations that are important rather than impersonal economic structures. However, despite the importance of economics, and the significant force of economic motivations, political or cultural factors cannot be excluded.

Power and inequality play a large part in the international economy and restrict globalization. In addition, they are important themes in sociology and a sociological perspective also shows how the embeddedness of global corporations in national societies makes a difference.

Since the development of industrial capitalism, from the end of the nineteenth century onwards, there has been an internationalization of the economy globally, and of capitalism. The modern world economy is more global than pre-modern forms were. This has a lot to do with capitalist incentives and technology developed with industrial capitalism. The world economy is interdependent. Instability or changes in one place have repercussions internationally. Multinational corporations have spread, finance has been globalized and capital is mobile. And many of these developments have increased because of deregulation and new technology.

But there are reasons to question whether the world economy has been globalized. This is not just an issue of academic definition but to do with power and inequality. Multinational corporations are more national and international than transnational, with distinct national bases, and are disproportionately located and owned in the rich developed world, notably in selected areas.

Varieties of capitalism in the world show a sociological embeddedness to the global economy and affirm sceptical conclusions. If globalization is measured by convergence, there are national variations in capitalism and different routes to economic success, some of which are more statist and collectivist than based on liberalization and open competition.

Pre-modern transnationalization was based in part on trade, as was the globalized *belle époque* world economy before the First World War. But trade is not open and inclusive. It is most intense between the richest developed economies: not a signifier of a globalized economy, but of an unequally inclusive and unintegrated one in which the rich remain to the fore in terms of dominant corporations, trade and FDI.

Nation-states compete and protect themselves in the global economy, for instance, in world trade talks and in trying to attract investment. Economic blocs have grown, led by nation-states. These are regional rather than global and some of the richer blocs dominate trade and investment.

Although discourses of economic globalization are used by corporations and politicians to justify decisions, these do not reflect the actuality of globalization. Globalization is not inevitable. As a discourse it can be countered, and states and other actors can, if they choose to, regulate the world economy to make it more stable, under collective human control and equitable.

If the reality is less than globalized and the discourse affirming globalization can be contested, then nation-states have the power to counter economic globalization either alone or in alliances with other like-minded states. They could maintain welfare at home or construct cross-border regulations or taxes on capital, for example, on financial transactions. These could be used for purposes of redistribution to poorer nations or for environmental protection. A critical or sceptical attitude to theories of economic globalization is not destructive, but the basis for such positive political possibilities.

Further Reading

Peter Dicken's (2007) *Global Shift* is a clear, accessible, user-friendly book, and also analytical and critical with its own arguments. This has been through a number of editions – it is worth trying to find the latest one.

Hirst and Thompson's (1996) book, *Globalization in Question?*, was an early attempt to empirically test the economic globalization thesis, leading to a convincing critique. The book has had two editions and there is a third version by Bromley and Thompson.

David Held et al.'s (1999) *Global Transformations* is quite old in the context of globalization debates. However, chapters 3, 4 and 5 give a useful and systematic overview of global forms of trade, finance and production, with valuable historical information and conceptual and empirical detail. Also see the Perraton and Goldblatt (1997) article in *New Political Economy*, 2/2.

UNCTAD release a *World Investment Report* every year. It contains informative data and descriptions of the latest trends in areas discussed in this chapter. The reports can be downloaded free from their website.

Global Inequality: Is Globalization a Solution to World Poverty?

G LOBAL inequality is the main reason to take an interest in globali-zation. Many academics who comment on globalization focus on its effects on developed countries, especially in North America and Europe. Despite the fact that the topic is global, some pay little attention to less developed parts of the world. In such places, poverty combined with huge and sometimes growing inequalities in relation to the rest of the world are part of global relations and have cata-strophic human consequences. In fact, some academic commentators, often focusing on culture and Europe or North America, see globaliza-tion as equalizing and democratizing so are critical of the economic foci or perspectives that see it more characterized by inequality and power.

Hundreds of millions of people in the world live in comfort. They do not have to worry if they will find sufficient food, have a home or avoidable health problems. They take for granted such basic necessi-ties. On top of this they have luxuries, from cars to washing machines and TVs, audio equipment, computers, mobile phones and so on. They have good salaries in nice houses in peaceful, democratic countries amongst the richest in the world.

Many of us in such nations are aware of enormous disparities of wealth and income globally, but rarely think of or take action on such matters and may be unaware of their scale. Members of educated elites in developed countries are preoccupied with their own lives, complaining these are not good enough or that others are better off. A moment's serious thought about the condition of vast numbers, far more numerous, further away and far worse off, should end those complaints. Some complain that not enough is done by politicians and corporations to help the global poor. But when many people themselves do not give this more than a passing thought that's not really surprising.

A main focus in this chapter is on the extent of *global inequality and poverty*, which we will see is more complicated than it seems. Poverty and inequality are different things and there are varying forms of each. Quite a bit of the debate revolves around measurement. How you measure them can make quite a difference to what conclusions you reach regarding improvement or deterioration in conditions of, say, free trade and, therefore, whether you consider free trade or whatever variable is looked at to be the best route in solving them.

Even if you can agree on the evidence about the scale of inequality and poverty, it is possible to disagree on what factors might lead to improvement. People can study successful countries and attribute their success to different factors – to economic liberalization and opening up to world trade, or to state intervention and protection from the world economy.

A main concern in this chapter is to assess the extent to which *globalization* is a solution to world poverty and inequality or even, perhaps contrary to immediate intuitions, a hindrance. Globalization in this context usually means *neoliberalism* and free trade globally, with the integration of poor countries into a world economy of open competition, imports and exports. As we will see, there is some disingenuousness in discussions of these matters. Debates are often between right-wing-inclined neoliberals and left-inclined commentators who favour more of a state-interventionist and semi-protectionist approach in some places. But some who support free trade, in practice demonstrate opposing behaviour when free trade is not in their own interests. Consequently, another critical view from the left is that free trade would be a good thing if all actors were equal participants – free trade could be good if it was really free.

Economic inequality is a matter of *sociological importance* and sociologists should be interested in it. As mentioned in the introduction, power, inequality and conflict have been central themes of sociology, including inequality in wealth and income. One of the aims of this book is to pursue these traditionally sociological concerns in relation to globalization. Such themes involve economics. Power, inequality and conflict are often, but not entirely, bound up with economic power, alongside inequalities in wealth and income and the effects of these on life chances, and shaping other spheres of society such as culture and politics. Conflict is often over economic interests or the pursuit of resources or economic gain. So global inequality taps into core sociological concerns. To look at the economic dimensions of these is not a step away from sociology – it is central to making sense of the sociological concern of inequality. In fact, the sociology of development is a sub-field of the discipline that has long been interested in global inequality.

There are *different types of inequality*. One is economic and can be along the lines of either income or wealth. There are other inequalities, for example, in education or health. These are sometimes tied to economic situation because a poor country or person is likely to have poorer education and health and less good institutions and services in these areas, although this does not always follow as Cuba has shown. But cultural and political factors are also significant in inequality – such as whether education is culturally valued, if this is the case for both genders in society, or the ways in which government invests in it. There are also cultural inequalities, for instance, in mass communications. Significant parts of the world economy are becoming more reliant on the Internet and mobile telephony, so people's access to such technologies affects their life chances. And inequalities may be experienced differently by different social categories. For example, there are gendered dimensions to global inequalities.

Finally, as far as introductory issues go, it is worth mentioning the role of *China and India*. We will come back to this later in this chapter. These are two huge countries that contain over a third of the world's people. The world population is about 6.7 billion, China's is about 1.3 billion and India's 1.1 billion. They are way ahead in size of the next largest country, which is the USA with about 300 million people. They are also two fast-developing countries that have grown a lot, with positive consequences for beating poverty. China especially is becoming a major global power. General figures on developing countries are heavily affected by the inclusion of these two large growing places. The key issue at this point is that it is important to disaggregate developing countries when looking at global inequality and poverty. This is not to make the situation look worse by focusing only on those that have not done so well. It is because stratifications amongst developing countries are complex and they should be looked at in that light. It is important that everyone is not falsely lumped together and that the different routes and outcomes in different places, both good and bad, are understood.

Globalization and the poor

Globalization for the poor countries of the world often means their integration into world trade and the exchange of commodities and services in the global economy. It is argued that this will allow them to trade their way out of poverty – that in a situation of open competition rather than protectionism they can sell goods and services to bring in income to overcome it. The liberalization of trade restricts other countries from protecting their own industries with tariffs or quotas on imports, or with subsidies that give them an advantage over others. If such forms of protection are removed, then the poor can trade freely without being blocked or disadvantaged and this can help them out of poverty. As part of the deal, they also have to bring down their own tariffs, quotas and subsidies.

One way in which poorer countries have become integrated into world trade has been on the basis of what is sometimes called the *Washington Consensus*, pursued through organizations such as the World Bank and International Monetary Fund. This refers to an approach where such organizations or richer states provide financial support to poorer countries to deal with crises or stimulate development, in return for those countries meeting certain conditions – hence that it is sometimes called 'conditionality'. The IMF have called this 'structural adjustment' because countries are required to make structural changes to their economy or public sector as a condition for receiving the financial help.

The sorts of changes required often involve liberalizing and opening up to the world economy. Governments are expected to deregulate their economies so that companies are free to compete and develop, less burdened by expensive or time-consuming regulations. This allows businesses to flourish freely to the benefit of the country's economy. Trade should be liberalized with fewer subsidies, tariffs and quotas distorting or restricting free trade, so bringing developing countries into world markets where they can thrive from the gains to be made. Finance should be liberalized to allow the free movement of capital, so encouraging investment. State companies and public services should be privatized to improve incentives to make profits, efficiency and competition.

Governments are expected to put a priority on lower inflation. This tends to lead to higher interest rates. If it is more expensive for consumers or businesses to borrow money because interest rates on loans are higher, then they may spend less. This will keep prices down. Businesses have to keep prices down to attract customers who are reluctant to spend because of the interest charged on borrowing money.

Governments are expected to lower public expenditure. Higher public spending can lead to higher taxes and the diversion of funds from private investment into the public sector. So lower public spending can promote private business, which should benefit from lower taxes (because taxes pay for public spending) and more investment. Governments are expected to end price subsidies on basic goods. These are introduced to make goods more affordable to the poor, but the ending of subsidies is argued for on the basis that they protect businesses from overseas competition and inhibit free and open trade.

With open competition and free trade, the industries of poorer countries will have the incentive to improve and compete on the global market and so, in the long term, this will contribute to activities that will pull their countries out of poverty.

Economic liberals have defended such policies on the basis that, while they can have a short-term harsh impact, in the long term they contribute to the adjustment of a developing country's economy into one where restrictions that inhibit business are lifted. This also benefits the companies of rich countries because the easing of tariffs and quotas gives them better access to markets and investment in poor countries. It provides more business opportunities for them too. Governments and companies in rich countries tend to support free trade.

The Washington Consensus has been much criticized, by both the anti-globalization movement and insiders such as George Soros (2005) and Joseph Stiglitz (2003), such that some people argue there is not a Washington Consensus any more (see Broad 2004), although, as we shall see, a belief in trade liberalization is still widely adhered to, albeit with double standards. Some of the effects of neoliberal policies in developing countries have been higher unemployment, poorer public services and a higher cost of living. These have followed from loss of protection for home businesses, lower public spending and the ending of price restrictions. Protests and unrest have followed. For many, such policies are imperialistic, using money to force developing countries to pursue policies favoured by rich donors. They benefit the rich countries, by giving them access to previously protected markets of poorer countries. Furthermore, opening the businesses of poor countries to competition from such hugely advantaged states, with reduced assistance from home to level the playing field, is as likely to damage as benefit them by making them more dynamic and competitive. Structural adjustment policies might actually make poverty and inequality worse.

While it is argued that global institutions and advanced states are no longer so strongly tied to the sorts of structural adjustment policies expected as part of conditionality, because of the problems I have outlined, assistance from rich countries does still come with such ties. Help for developing countries from the G8 is conditional on liberalization and democratization, for instance, in the case of the 2005 Gleneagles agreement to provide such assistance.

Whether liberalization or protectionism are helping or adversely affecting poor countries is an empirical matter. It also depends on whether inequality or poverty are looked at and how these are measured. I will move on to such empirical questions now. I will focus on the commonly used measure of income rather than, say, wealth, education or health. This is because income is a good indicator of basic capacity to subsist and is linked to some of the other factors and to life chances.

Global poverty

There are reasons to be positive about progress in tackling global poverty. While the number living in absolute poverty increased between 1820 and 1980, the World Bank says that between 1990 and 2000 an extra 864 million people rose above $1 a day income (World Bank 2002).

The amount of $1 a day refers to the purchasing power in other countries that is the equivalent of a dollar in the US – that is, the same amount of goods in other countries that $1 would buy in the US – and is often used as a definition of the poverty line. If $1 a day will buy you a small loaf of bread in the US (leaving aside water, accommodation, electricity and other expenses), the $1 measure in other countries is of this purchasing power. It is not what the dollar is worth in terms of exchange rates, but the equivalent of what $1 would buy you in America, the loaf of bread. Calculating poverty by using the $1 a day purchasing power index is controversial, but is as likely to underestimate poverty as overestimate it. In 2008, two World Bank economists estimated that $1.25 was a better indicator of poverty (Chen and Ravallion 2008), and $2 a day is also sometimes used.

The 1990–2000 improvement was despite the growth of world population, a fact that might be expected to lead to an increasing number below the poverty line. To put it into perspective, the world population in 2000 was 5.1 billion. So 864 million fewer in poverty is a real achievement. The proportion living below the poverty line was a decrease from 27.9 per cent of the world's population to 21.3 per cent (Kaplinksy 2005; World Bank 2002).

But, despite this improvement, the picture is still bleak and there are some especially bad sides to it. The number of people below the $1 a day poverty line exceeds 1.2 billion. More than one in five people in the world are in poverty on this definition; 2.8 billion live on less than $2 a day (UNDP 2003). In 2005, 36 per cent of people in less developed countries were living on less than $1 a day and 76 per cent on less than $2. The proportion of people living in poverty is falling slowly, but the numbers living below the $1 and $2 lines were larger in 2005 than in 2000 (UNCTAD 2008a: 2). It is difficult to see the attitudes of many in the rich world as reflecting any noticeable awareness, real concern or willingness about this fact.

Many of the 1.2 billion at the $1 level spend about half their income on food, a much greater proportion than the rich, leaving half for water, education, health and shelter. Between 2006 and 2008, the price of basic food rose by 28 per cent, leading to 40 million more people suffering from hunger. There are 963 million people, 14 per cent of the world's population, who, according to the UN, do not have enough to eat (UNFAO 2008).

Most of the improvement in poverty has been accomplished in China, although there has been rising intra-country inequality, including within China, and in other parts of Asia. Between 1980 and 2000, absolute poverty in India declined by 100 million. In China, it went from 250 million in 1978 to 34 million in 1999, a huge decrease (Wade and Wolf 2002). But those living below the poverty line increased in Africa, Latin America, Eastern Europe and Central Asia. If you leave out China and other growing East Asian countries, the proportion of the world's population living below $1 a day stayed stable and the absolute numbers grew (because of the growing world population). The picture is especially terrible in sub-Saharan Africa, where poverty below the $1 line increased from the already high position of 53.3 per cent to 54.4 per cent between 1985 and 1990. Between 1990 and 2002 there was no significant improvement in this region (UNDP 2007: 11). At the end of the 1990s, 74 million more people in this region were in poverty than at the start (UNDP 2003: 41). This does not mean that the improvement in China and parts of Asia is not a success worth investigating for lessons on how it can be done. But it does mean that the picture is a mixed one and that in some parts of the world an already very bad situation has become worse.

There are about 195 countries in the world; 54 countries were poorer in 2003 than in 1990. In 21, more rather than fewer people were going hungry and, in 14, the number dying before the age of 5 had increased. In the 1980s, 4 countries experienced reversals in the UN human development index (which measures life expectancy, health, education and standard of living) but this went up to 21, becoming worse in the 1990s. In the 1990s, development assistance from the rich declined, debt in poor countries increased and the price of primary commodities, which many poor countries export, continued to drop.

A half of Africans live on less than $1 a day, one third in hunger, with about one sixth of children dying before the age of 5, a situation that is not improving. In 1990, you were 19 times more likely to die before the age of 5 in sub-Saharan Africa than in a rich OECD country. By 2003, this had increased to 26 times more likely. Because of population growth, the numbers in these situations are growing. In 2000, 4.5 million children died before the age of 5 in sub-Saharan Africa and 3.6 million in South Asia – making up 76 per cent of global

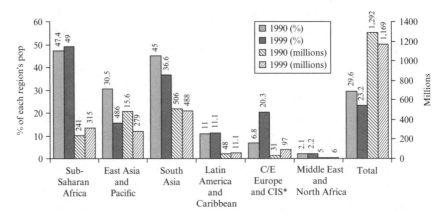

Note: * Calculated on $2 a day, seen to be a more appropriate measure of poverty for this region.

Source: Adapted from UNDP 2003: 41

Figure 8.1   Share and number of people living on $1 a day, 1990–1999

mortality by 5 that year. Life expectancy at birth is 49.6 in sub-Saharan African countries and 79.4 in high-income OECD countries, with a world average of 68.1. It is in the low 40s for countries like Sierra Leone, Zambia, Mozambique, the Central African Republic, Angola, Zimbabwe, Lesotho and Swaziland. In some of these countries, 70 per cent of people do not live until 40, and in many sub-Saharan African countries life expectancy is on the decline because of HIV/AIDS, other diseases and factors such as injury (UNDP 2003 and 2008a).

These figures should be looked at in the context of academic commentaries which are dismissive of analyses of globalization focusing on economics and inequality for being out of touch, reductionist or too negative. The alternative picture of globalization they put forward is of the spread of global human rights and cultural cosmopolitanism.

Figure 8.1 outlines changes and unevenness in poverty. It shows how there have been improvements in some parts of the world in the 1990s, while things either remained the same or deteriorated in others. As you can see the situation has worsened in sub-Saharan Africa, and in Central and Eastern Europe and the former Soviet states in the post-communist period. In East and South Asia, which include China and India, things have got better.

Climate change is a globalized phenomenon that accentuates poverty. It is caused by carbon emissions predominantly from some of the most industrialized and largest-growing countries, but has damaging effects especially on the lowest emitters, particularly sub-Saharan African countries. The latter are the poorest and most vulnerable, who rely most on fertile land and water and are where such resources are most scarce. Loss of land or water as a result of climate change undermines development and leads to conflict over the scarcer resources, for instance, in Sudan. This is bad in itself but also for growth. The twenty-one least developed countries, mostly in sub-Saharan Africa, produce less than 0.5 per cent of the world's carbon emissions but suffer the effects especially harshly. The US, China, Russia, India, Japan, Germany and Canada produce up to 60 per cent of the world's emissions. The USA produces 20.9% of the world total. China and India as more recent developers have not historically been principle contributors to the carbon emissions that have led to the current situation, and their output is partly a product of the sheer scale of their population (UNDP 2008a: 310–13; UNDP 2008b: 5). Solutions to climate change need to be global with as many countries as possible, especially the main carbon emitters, agreeing together to limit emissions.

Global inequalities

Inequality is different from poverty. Inequality can rise while poverty falls – the poor can get richer whilst gaps between the poor and the rich get bigger. In cases such as China and India, relative to some richer parts of the world this is what has been happening. For 'trickle-down' theorists there may be a link between these occurrences. If the rich have incentives to make money they will innovate and produce goods which bolster wealth in society more widely, resulting in goods which, eventually, when they are popular enough, become affordable for the poor and provide them with jobs manufacturing them. At the same time, if poor nations are successful in growing economically then they become wealthy enough to provide markets for rich countries that grow even richer. Inequality can help to reduce poverty and become greater when the poor get better off.

You can be against poverty but for inequality. Inequality can be defended on the basis that the rich deserve more because they have worked harder or been entrepreneurial, or that it is necessary for improving the overall wealth of a society – for instance, in the way just mentioned, providing incentives for people to do dynamic, entrepreneurial things that end up being good for the economy and for everyone. For some, the key factor is poverty and if this decreases while inequality increases their response is 'so what'. If the poor are getting better off it doesn't matter if the rich are getting richer at a greater rate. There is no basis for complaint against this other than envy. Objections to it imply we should stop the rich getting richer even though the poor are getting richer too (Wolf in Wolf and Wade 2002).

Others are against some inequalities – because they are based on unjust factors such as luck, inheritance or exploitation rather than real effort or talent, for instance. They can be seen as bad if rich people have resources that if redistributed could prevent the poor from being poor. Or inequality can be seen as bad because it leads to adverse social consequences, such as unhappiness amongst the poor at the unachievable ends others have attained. This can undermine solidarity and social capital in society, and lead to crime to achieve what cannot be gained through accepted means. Another result is conflict between the rich and poor, or the use by the former of their position to exert power, gain unfair advantages or reproduce inequality, exploitation and exclusion. This then undermines democracy, which requires some degree of equivalence in capacities to participate (on the effects of inequality, see Wilkinson 2005; Wilkinson and Pickett 2009).

My key point here is that inequality and poverty are different and need to be evaluated separately. One issue is how globalization affects inequality within countries, and it should be remembered that there are very poor people in rich countries and very rich people in poor ones (for more information, see Kaplinsky 2005: 39–43; UNDP 2003: 40). However, my main concern is with inequalities between countries. There are two ways of looking at these. The first compares countries with countries. The second compares inequality taking into account country populations and by individuals. The second is better for seeing how unequal individuals are in the world and, being about individual people, is the one we should be most concerned with in human terms. But the first is important because it shows how different countries are doing in relation to one another.

Looking at it *country in comparison to country*, there has been growing inequality in the globalizing years since 1980. There has been rapid growth in Asia, while African and Latin American countries have not grown or have grown slowly. So the rich and the growing developing countries have pulled away from others, leaving greater inequalities. Before this period the differences were less marked.

These are comparative rates of growth. When measured in absolute income terms rather than growth rates the difference is greater (Wade and Wolf 2002). A developing country with incomes of $1,000 a year growing at 6 per cent will not be keeping up with a developed country with incomes of $30,000 a year growing at 1 per cent. Growth rates are closing but absolute income differences at the end of it all are getting bigger, because of the much higher starting incomes of the developed country. Fast-growing huge countries, such as India and China, are closing the gap with middle-income countries like Mexico, Brazil, Russia and Argentina, but not with very rich countries in the EU, North America and Japan.

This tells us about country comparisons. The other way of measuring global inequality *takes into account population*, rather than just comparing two countries and disregarding their population size. This gives a better sense of the proportions of the world's population in terms of equality with one another, rather than just country to country. Looking at it this way shows that global income distribution is more equal (Milanovic 2003).

Much of this equalization is due to rapid growth in China and, to some extent, India. If China is set aside then inequality has risen since the 1980s. This is not to downplay the significance of growth in China. This country has a huge population and has been growing rapidly with significant positive effects on global poverty. But elsewhere the picture has been more problematic, so the effects of China should not allow us to gain an overall rosy picture or to minimize the significance of other less positive stories. Within China the benefits of growth have been unevenly distributed. There has been an increase in big internal inequalities during the period of rapid growth, with the east coast urban areas, for instance, becoming richer and other rural areas falling behind.

The figures below show some global inequalities.

- The income gap between the fifth of the world's population living in the world's richest countries and the fifth in the poorest countries grew from 30:1 in 1960, to 60:1 in 1990, to 74: 1 in 1997.
- The richest 5 per cent of people receive 114 times the income of the bottom 5 per cent, the richest 1 per cent receive as much as the poorest 57 per cent.
- The 25 million richest Americans have as much income as nearly 2 billion of the world's poorest, that is getting on for a third of the world's population. The richest 2 per cent of the world's population owns more than half global household wealth; the bottom half own 1 per cent.
- Many of these factors have got worse rather than better over time. In 1820 Western Europe's per capita income was 2.9 times Africa's and in 1992 it was 13.2 times as great.
(Based on UNDP 2003)

Out of a world population of over 6 billion, 1.6 billion people live without electricity, with 45 per cent of these in South Asia and 35 per cent in sub-Saharan Africa. And 33.2 million people are living with HIV or AIDS, up from 29 million in 2001, 22.5 million of whom are in sub-Saharan Africa.

In short, things have improved a lot in China and some other Asian countries. By including them in this comparison, global inequality appears to have decreased. But looking beyond China, which should not be allowed to overshadow other parts of the world, and comparing the top and bottom of the world in income terms, global inequality increased during the 1980s and 1990s.

Global inequality used to be characterized in terms of core and

Table 8.1 People without access to electricity, 2004	
Total	1.6 billion
South Asia	706 million (45%)
Sub-Saharan Africa	547 million (35%)
East Asia	224 million (14%)
Others	101 million (6%)

Source: Data from UNDP 2008b: 28

Table 8.2 Spread of people living with HIV or AIDS, 2007	
Region	% of world's HIV/AIDS sufferers in each region
Sub-Saharan Africa	68%
South, South-East and East Asia	14%
Latin America and the Caribbean	6%
Eastern Europe and central Asia	5%
North America	4%
Western and Central Europe	2%
Middle East and North Africa	1%
Oceania	<1%

Source: Adapted from UNDP 2008b: 18

periphery or the first world of rich capitalist countries, the second world of socialist countries and the third world of less developed countries. With the collapse of most socialist countries, this threefold categorization changed to first world and third world. But with the rise of newly industrializing countries and with some developing countries growing ahead of others, binary categorizations of developed–less developed, core and periphery and first and third world have become less applicable. World inequality has become more complex.

There is what could be called a new international division of labour or a *new stratification in global inequality*. Countries like China, India and some other Asian countries have pulled away from the most poor through rapid growth, although sometimes with inequality and poverty inwardly increasing in places. There have been notable Asian successes, such as China, South Korea, Taiwan, Japan at an earlier date, and India. Hong Kong and Singapore, and more recently Malaysia and Thailand, have been successful. Often these have had significant export-oriented growth, so there has been a globalizing element to it.

Other successes have been Chile, the Dominican Republic, Mauritius, Poland and Turkey, who have become more integrated into global markets and benefited from foreign investment. South American NICs such as Brazil, Chile and Mexico have grown, often through import substitution, where countries develop industries in areas where they used to import goods. Industries that are big in NICs include textiles and clothing (e.g., China and India), cars (Japan and Korea) and electronics (Japan, China, Korea, Hong Kong, Singapore, Malaysia, Brazil and Mexico). At the same time, as we have seen and will discuss further shortly, some areas of the world, especially in Latin America and Africa, have stayed poor or become more poor and unequal in relation to the rest of the world. The developed world (itself stratified amongst its different nations) has moved ahead, with NICs and fast-developing countries growing rapidly away from poverty, while the poor and less developed have fallen behind.

Gender inequality and globalization

Some authors draw attention to the gendered nature of globalization (Acker 2004; Moghadam 1999; Chow 2003). Women have been a resource for globalizing capitalism, drawn into production as low-wage labour, for instance, in the employment of migrants in domestic work and childcare in rich countries. Labour migration of women has overtaken that of men because of the entry of women into jobs such as nurses, nannies, domestic workers, catering and waitressing, where rich countries often recruit from poorer countries. Some women go into sex work, sometimes through human trafficking, involving deception or force, with workers then being trapped by coercion, debt or stigma. Sex work in women's home countries is linked to global tourism. A lot of work for women is in export-processing zones, free trade zones and factories producing for world markets. The globalization of trade has benefited women who are employed in factories producing goods for export, for example, in textile and garment industries, electronics and pharmaceuticals. Frequently, women's work is in the informal sector, home work, small unregistered companies or self-employment. More women have broken into global professions too.

New work opportunities have increased employment for women, enabling those in developing countries to earn income and gain independence from patriarchal structures and household and family relations. But sometimes it has been forced or exploitative in conditions or pay. The globalization of production and rise of the multinational corporation and outsourcing have led to the employment of women whose labour is cheaper and who are seen as less likely to resist poor conditions. But this means poor working conditions and insecure employment. Much women's work in global industries involves long hours, is part-time, temporary, flexible, insecure, casual, home-based and poorly unionized. It can be low paid and demeaning.

Often women's entry into globalization jobs is not accompanied by a redistribution of domestic responsibilities, so they are carrying a double burden of paid labour and domestic labour. There has been a feminization of unemployment – women's unemployment has risen higher than men's. Women have been affected by the unemployment that results from cheap imports in unequal trade liberalization. Domestic workers can be undocumented or illegal immigrants, isolated in employers' homes, with little basis for protection against exploitation. The work is often unregulated, so the women work long hours for poor pay and can be harassed or locked in by debt to their employer. More flexible home-based work may seem desirable for workers, but is often less organized, more isolated and easier to exploit.

Structural adjustment polices such as privatization, deregulation, cuts in public spending, and opening up to foreign trade and investment have affected women especially adversely (Moghadam 1999; Pyle and Ward 2003). One reason is that women tend to have disproportionate responsibility for areas such as education and health where families have to compensate for falling public expenditure. Because of the loss of price controls and fuel subsidies they have to go out to work to earn extra income while continuing their domestic responsibilities. This can be work in the informal sector, domestic or sex work, as well as microfinance or migration to richer countries for employment in the sort of jobs abroad mentioned above.

Moghadam (2000, 2005), who stresses contradictory effects of globalization for women, looks at the development of the *global women's movement* as a part of globalization. The globalization of politics and INGOs, and of human rights discourses and ideas of gender equality, have allowed women's organizations to grow globally. Trade unions have become more involved in employment in sectors where conditions are poor. While a great deal of globalized women's work is poorly protected, unions have increasingly tried to participate in such areas, sometimes through the activism of women workers themselves. Moghadam sees transnational feminist networks and women's world conferences as a logical outcome of the capitalist world economy and universal gender inequality, albeit in varying extents and forms in different places. Women establish solidarity around a common identity globally, across national or other identities that separate them. Globalization exposes more women to education and information, as well as to connections with women from different countries. There is also an economic dimension to women's global movements, in trying to secure more equality in the face of exploitation. I will look at the development of global politics and global social movements in some of the following chapters.

Is globalization the solution?

If some countries have been successful and others have fallen behind, what has been the basis for the success of those that have grown and can we learn from this to see what might help those who have been less successful? In particular, are globalization, greater liberal openness and integration into the global economy and world trade, and a break with state and protectionist approaches, the solution? Is the poverty and inequality of the poorest countries proving enduring because of globalization, or is it because globalization has not gone far enough?

Commentators such as Wolf (2004) and Dollar and Kraay (2001) argue that more globalization is the solution. For the World Bank, globalization decreases poverty and the poor's situation is residual. In other words, the benefits of globalization have not reached them yet, or they have not yet been integrated enough into it. There have, it is argued, been great successes from openness to the world economy, for instance, in China, India, Vietnam, Uganda, Mexico, South Korea and Taiwan. Places like China and India are pulling millions of people out of poverty by participating in globalization. The problem is that others are yet to be sufficiently incorporated in the same process. The losers are those who have been excluded and who need to be more included.

Economic integration decreases poverty and less developed countries need to export manufactures more, especially in industries that are labour intensive because this will increase the numbers of workers in employment and so their incomes. Marketization and deregulation will stimulate exports. It will open up overseas markets to the industries of poor countries and push them into a competitive context in which they can rise to the challenge, will have to be dynamic and entrepreneurial to do well, and can use what specific advantages they have in their own countries to succeed. As countries become more productive, integrating into the global economy and looking for overseas markets, they will gain their own specialisms and niches in which they have specific resources or capabilities. They can gain income from these and, as other countries get richer, especially big countries like China, there will be more demand for food and raw materials from them, which will pull the poorer into the sphere of growing countries. This will not end the story. The poorest countries then need to take advantage of demand for their goods, and ensure peace and good governance. But globalization in these ways is what will form the basis for their success.

Dollar and Kraay – trade, growth and poverty

This is the theory. How much evidence is there to support it? A key article by Dollar and Kraay (2001) is worth focusing on because it makes a case for globalization as a chief factor that has led to growth, lifting countries out of poverty, and criticisms of this study show some common points against the globalization thesis. As we shall see, there are methodological issues, about what countries you look at and how you measure globalization, and these affect what conclusions are reached. Some critics of Dollar and Kraay make the strong suggestion that their measures could have been chosen to support pro-globalization conclusions that they already were committed to. In quite a few of the debates on this issue, methodology and measurement on the one hand and ideology on the other seem to be interlinked.

Dollar and Kraay compare data on 100 countries and focus on post-1980s globalizers such as Argentina, China, Hungary, India, Malaysia, Mexico, the Philippines and Thailand. They say that trade as a proportion of gross domestic product (GDP) has increased a lot in such countries, compared to non-globalizers in the developing world, and this has helped the poor. Looking at liberalizing countries that are opening themselves up to world trade seems to suggest a link between trade, growth and the reduction of poverty. Non-globalizing countries, those with lower levels of trade, do not have such levels of growth (see also World Bank 2002).

However, there have been criticisms of Dollar and Kraay's research, which argue that globalization looked at more completely is not as good for growth and poverty as Dollar and Kraay's article suggests. In fact, maybe even the reverse (Rodrik 2000; Nye et al. 2002; Samman 2005; and Kraay's 2006 reply). The main points that critics have made are as follows.

1 *Choice of countries and dates.* Some critics question Dollar and Kraay's choice and categorization of countries and dates to compare. They argue that these lead to misleading conclusions that support their case. A different choice of globalizing countries and dates leads to different conclusions (Rodrik 2000; Samman 2005). Rodrik says that Dollar and Kraay left out countries from the globalizers that on their own criteria they should have included, and included some that did not fit their criteria. He carried out Dollar and Kraay's exercise using places most consistent with their selection criteria for globalizing countries. This leads, he argues, to a different choice of countries whose growth is unimpressive, less than Dollar and Kraay's

globalizers, and slower in the globalizing 1980s and 1990s than in the 1960s and 1970s. So a correct choice of countries using Dollar and Kraay's own criteria does not support the thesis that globalizers did better in terms of growth. Nye et al. (2002) also suggest that the time periods Dollar and Kraay use are mismatched. If you use comparable time periods, the finding is that non-globalizers defined in terms of changes in tariffs out-perform globalizers in rates of growth.

2 *Tariffs rather than trade.* Another problem is that Dollar and Kraay use growth in trade as an indicator of globalization. On the face of it this seems to make sense. If a country's trade with others is growing then they are more involved in the global economy. Increasing international trade is a sort of globaliza-tion. However, trade growth is not necessarily caused by liberal or globalist policies. It could be caused by non-globalizing factors such as subsidies, quotas and tariffs, measures which protect against global competition rather than opening up to it. Rodrik and Samman suggest that tariff reductions are a better measure of globalization because they involve policies that are liberal and open up a country's economy more globally, rather than boosting trade by protectionism. If you look for links between increases or reductions in tariffs and growth, you find different conclusions to Dollar and Kraay's. In fact, Dollar and Kraay say that 'we recognize that growth in trade volumes may also reflect many factors other than trade liberalization' (2001: 7), and that 'changes in reported tariff rates are not accompa-nied by any change in trade volume' (p. 3). In other words, they say that more liberal openness to the global economy may not be what is behind greater trade.

Samman and Rodrik look at tariff levels and trade volume and show there is not a link between reducing tariffs and trade growth. In fact, countries that have cut their tariffs appear not to do better than those who have not. Those with lower cuts in tariffs have bigger increases in growth than globalizers with bigger cuts. As we shall see below, China and India increased overseas trade significantly whilst maintaining quite protected economies. So trade growth does not seem to be an indicator of openness to the global economy. In fact, it may provide a good argument for protectionism in some cases. Globalization in trade is not caused by globalization in policies.

3 *Does trade cause growth or does growth cause trade?* Dollar and Kraay say that there is a link between increasing trade volume and growth. But it could be growth that leads to more trade, rather than more openness, measured by trade, which leads

to growth. In fact, as we shall see below, some countries grew before they became more open to the global economy. And in some cases their growth was, as just mentioned, due to the opposite of liberal and open policies, through initially protectionist measures. So Dollar and Kraay say that something globalized, trade volumes, is connected with growth but on the basis of their evidence it is quite plausible that growth, perhaps based on non-globalizing factors, led to greater trade, an argument against globalization causing growth. In fact, Dollar and Kraay (e.g., Kraay 2006) argue that the trade and growth link may not be causal and that there may be other third factors altogether involved in trade volume increasing and in economic growth, although this takes some of the emphasis away from the links between trade, growth and the erosion of poverty that they suggest.

4   *Levels or increases in tariffs or trade.* Dollar and Kraay's focus is on globalizers, defined as such because of increases in their trade volume and reductions in tariff levels. However, while these countries may have fast-changing trade and tariffs, the level of tariffs and trade they have reached reveals they are quite non-globalized despite such increases. Some of those with fast-increasing trade do not have the highest levels of trade. And some of those with tariff cuts do not have the lowest tariffs. So changes in trade and tariffs do not match with levels of either (Samman 2005; Nye et al. 2002). The globalizers in terms of cuts in tariffs and growth in trade are often countries with lower levels of trade and relatively high tariffs, and so are not very globalized. When this is matched up with growth, many countries are those with high tariffs or low levels of trade and the least successful are those with lower tariffs and high levels of trade, even if these have changed a lot. When trade or tariffs are looked at in terms of level, rather than change, the opposite of globalization seems to be linked with growth.

5   *Other factors behind growth.* Dollar and Kraay mention that growth and reductions in poverty could be caused by factors other than trade or tariffs. One factor is foreign direct investment, a form of globalization which could affect growth but which is different from lower tariffs or more international trade. They say that they have controlled for factors such as geography and institutional change by looking at trade volume over time. Geography and institutions do not change over time, so any differences in growth must be linked to what does change, e.g., trade volume. However, even if geography does not change, its significance can. For instance, a landlocked country may find

itself in a better position because of improved transport and communications. And institutions do change, so controlling for institutional factors by looking at trade and growth over time does not rule them out as a factor. Furthermore, there is quite a lot of evidence that institutions are significant in trade, growth and the reduction of poverty, as mentioned below. As such, the trends towards increased growth with reductions in poverty in some countries, pointed out by Dollar and Kraay, could well have been due to such factors rather than to increased openness to the global economy.

6 *Does growth help the poor?* Dollar and Kraay suggest growth in average incomes enables the poor to gain in proportion. However, there are qualifications to this, some of which Dollar and Kraay make themselves (see also Nye et al. 2002).

(a) One is that it depends on who you mean by the poor. If you look at the bottom fifth of the population, as Dollar and Kraay do, this works better than if you look at those further down in deeper levels of poverty. The evidence for the latter is that their incomes do not keep up with average incomes, so the growth that Dollar and Kraay talk about does not help the poorest of the poor. In fact, this group seems to fall behind when there are average increases in income. If it is true that globalization leads to growth in average incomes it is not clear that the poor gain from this.

(b) An average of the bottom fifth across countries may keep up with average incomes. But this is an average. In some places the bottom fifth's income keeps up with average incomes and in some places it does not. As a mean, the poorest keep up with average incomes. But the mean is made up of cases which do better than this, alongside some doing worse, so the picture is a mixed one, with some of the poor gaining from rises in average incomes while in other instances this is not the case. So the evidence here is not that growth caused by globalization helps reduce poverty. It is that the outcome of globalization is uneven. Whether growth pulls up the poorest varies, and figures on the bottom fifth when disaggregated do not support the idea that growth from globalization is a solution to poverty. This is not to say that growth is not good for raising incomes, but that it is uneven and therefore not the solution, as more than growth is needed.

(c) What Dollar and Kraay discuss is the issue of the poor keeping up in terms of rates of growth. However, as discussed above, a high rate of growth for a poor person alongside a low rate of growth for a rich person can still lead to rising inequality between them, if the poor person's income is small enough that even with a high rate of growth its increases are smaller than a rich person's smaller growth on a larger income. Proportionate gains by the poor in rates of growth do not necessarily lead to proportionate gains in incomes; in fact, they often lead to greater inequality because of the higher starting point of the rich. These points apply both to incomes within countries and to differences between countries. One response to this, as I have mentioned, is that it is of little importance (Wolf 2004). If the poor are becoming better off, what does it matter if inequalities are growing? But, as we have seen, there may be reasons why inequality is as much of a problem as poverty. And, as we have also seen, it is not clear the poor are becoming better off.

Dollar and Kraay acknowledge some of these points themselves. But such points provide qualifications to the idea that growth from trade helps the poor and that 'globalizers' are best suited to improving growth and solving poverty. In fact, this is not case for the poorest of the poor, or for others who fall below average income improvements, and it may not help with inequality. More generally, discussions of Dollar and Kraay's research suggest that globalization may not be the key to growth and solving poverty. In fact, it could be non-globalizing factors or even protection from the global economy that can sometimes improve growth and help solve poverty. And in practice this has often been the case.

Are the globalizers globalizers?

We have seen that a country which is a globalizer in terms of trade volume may not be a globalizer on the indicator of liberal policies towards the global economy such as lower tariffs. Furthermore, a country whose tariffs are coming down fast or whose trade is growing may be a globalizer in changes like these whilst not being so in terms of levels of tariffs and trade at the end of the day. These can remain quite unglobalized in outcomes despite increases in openness.

An economy can be globalized in many different ways and the impact on growth and poverty can vary with different types of globalization. Globalization of the economy can include lower tariffs, more trade in imports or exports, or more foreign direct investment either outwards or inwards. Some countries have globalized more in some ways than in others, for instance, growing through increases in exports while being quite closed in terms of tariffs and imports, or being open in terms of investment more than goods moving in or out. So pointing to a growing exporter as a sign of the success of globalization should not be the basis for generalizing to other types of globalization, such as openness to imports or finance, as the basis for success. It could be good, for instance, to export goods but globalization of your economy in other ways, such as the ending of subsidies or limits on imports, could hinder rather than help with exports, growth and poverty.

Countries like Brazil, Mexico, Peru and Zambia have been liberal in allowing imports in, but have had mixed records in achieving growth and reducing poverty. Latin American economies have been leading liberalizers, but with varying results for growth and poverty and widening inequality. Places like Haiti and Peru found domestic livelihoods shattered and poverty increased when they opened up to imports.

Furthermore, when looking at the histories of the globalizers who are highlighted as successes, their routes have been in part on the basis of something different, even opposite, to globalization. So globalization may not be the best recommendation to make to the rest of the developing world.

We need to look at the bases for the success of some of the so-called globalizers. There is no doubt that many such countries have flourished when they have opened up their economies to the global market. But that is not necessarily how they got into the position to do that. Some have succeeded as much by restricting globalization at key points. China, South Korea, Taiwan and Vietnam have gained from integration into the global economy and strong export orientations. But they also placed restrictions on foreign investment, subsidized exports, and had tariff and non-tariff barriers on imports. Rather than the state being rolled back, it intervened to pick and choose where and how growth could be facilitated. In short, their successes in the global economy have come partly from non-liberal and non-globalizing measures, such as protecting their own industries from global competition and giving them special assistance. This is instead of opening up to free competition in which they would have had to compete with rich nations with huge advantages, as well as opening their markets up to the imports of those nations with the inevitable impact on domestic industries. The only people who would have gained from this would have been those keenest on it, and most selective about practising it themselves, namely, the rich developed countries.

China's growth began in the 1970s with an early emphasis on

export liberalization. Import liberalization was delayed, so that Chinese industries were protected from open competition on the global market. Openness came late and in partial ways. Rodrik (2000) argues that it was during the late 1980s and 1990s when trade liberalization started, by which time China was already growing fast on the basis of a semi-globalized strategy and in part through protection from globalization.

Indian growth increased substantially in the early 1980s, but serious trade reform did not happen until the 1990s. Tariffs that restrict inward trade were higher in the rising-growth period of the 1980s than in the low-growth 1970s. So protection seems to link with the periods of success. Like China, India participated in international trade in growth periods, so involvement in the global economy has been important to growth. At the same time, protection from it has been part of India's success as much as liberalization and opening up to globalization. Similar points could be made about Vietnam.

So globalization does not seem to be the complete story of the success of nations such as India and China where there has been growth with a reduction in poverty. From a postcolonial perspective, explaining the success of China, India and other Asian countries in terms of globalization is a resurrection of Western colonialism, exporting the idea that the Western system is the only way to succeed, a view that is based, as discussed, on suspect empirical evidence (Hutton and Desai 2007; Mishra 2006). This was a view popularized by some like Fukuyama (1989) but more recently put into doubt, as we have seen, by uncertainty regarding the success of the Washington Consensus.

Is globalization the problem?

This is not to say that globalization has not played a role in helping poor countries to grow. Some countries that grew under less than globalized conditions, with state involvement, subsidies and protection, then benefited when they opened up to the world economy. So openness is part of the story. But the evidence for globalization as a solution is mixed.

Success from globalization has been selective. In the globalizing period since the 1980s, developing countries increased their share of manufacturing, but this was mainly in East Asia, especially China. Latin America, the Caribbean and sub-Saharan Africa saw losses in their market shares of manufacturing, as did some parts of Eastern Europe. Some quite globally integrated countries did not benefit, for instance, sub-Saharan countries whose exports were more significant for their economy than was the case for rich countries. In terms of exporting, they are quite globalizing but these are the countries that have remained abjectly poor under globalization. Similarly Russia and Central and Eastern European countries have become poorer and more unequal, although a number of these were ones who ditched socialism to adopt the Anglo-Saxon neoliberal model which is the basis for globalization. Latin American countries have had a mixed record since the 1980s despite often adopting Washington Consensus style policies, against which there has been a backlash in that part of the world.

Robert Wade (2007) says we live in a 1:3:2 world as far as income and growth go. About 1 billion people live in high-income countries; 3 billion live in countries where growth has been faster than in high-income countries over the last twenty years, but still with low incomes; 2 billion people live in countries where growth has been lower than in high-income countries. Some of the latter are middle-income states, and some low income, and most developing countries fall into this bracket. Between 1993 and 2001, 50–60 per cent of the increase in world consumption went to the richest 10 per cent in the world. The other 40–50 per cent went to the next wealthiest bracket, the majority being the Chinese middle class. This left little for a bottom group earning under $1,000 (in purchasing power terms) a year ($2.73 a day). Most of these live in South Asia, Africa and China.

For those who have been successful, or hope to be, there may be *explanations other than globalization,* some of which have been tried more than others. For instance, development can be connected with technology, education, environmental sustainability, health care, democracy, peace, transport and communications, or civil society participation, not to mention global interventions of a non-neoliberal sort such as redistribution, debt relief and aid. There are other domestic factors in growth, natural resources, for example, in the case of oil-rich countries like Venezuela or Nigeria, having working political institutions, or cultural values and norms favourable to growth, including some which are occasionally quite contrary to liberal and competitive values, for instance, in Japan where collectivist norms such as loyalty and cooperation are seen to have been important to their success. Countries like Vietnam and Botswana have grown in part because of propitious internal factors, while others like Nicaragua and Mexico have not developed so fast for internal reasons. So there are solutions to poverty other than globalization. At the same time, that these factors are internal rather than to do with the liberalization of developing countries' economies does not mean external assistance cannot help with cultivating some of them (Birdsall et al. 2005).

Not only is globalization not always an explanation for success, but, Kaplinsky (2005) argues, *it may actually be going badly in some cases.* The purchase of manufactured goods is becoming concentrated amongst a smaller number of firms globally, and they are looking for the cheapest prices from the lowest cost producers. So there is strong competition for poor countries to offer low-price exports. Since the 1980s, the price of manufactured goods has been falling, especially for manufactures from lower-income groups and those with the least technological content, which tend to come from low-income countries. Prices of manufactures with higher technological content from higher-income countries have not fallen so fast. So the price of manufacturing exports has fallen most for those from lower-income countries, while the cost of their imports from higher-income countries has risen.

Development also has quite a negative effect on some areas. The expansion of industrial capacity can reduce the number of jobs available, because industrial technology often replaces human labour, and mobile capital tends to gravitate to faster-growing areas like China (and to the fastest-growing areas inside China) at the expense of poorer, slower-growing areas. Aid to low-income countries is falling, especially to countries of less geo-strategic interest to Asia and Europe. In 2008, the main recipients of aid from the USA were Israel, Egypt, Iraq and Georgia, all for political or geo-strategic reasons such as electoral lobbies in the US, their role in the Middle East or conflict with Russia. None of these has a case for top priority for aid on development criteria.

In short, exports for poorer countries are making less money, competition from other areas is strong and foreign investment is going elsewhere. Exports, overseas competition and flows of capital are all factors of globalization. In some instances globalization is having a negative effect on poorer countries, especially where it intensifies inequality and poverty amongst the poor who need to protect themselves from the world economy as much as increase their participation in it. At the present time, the success of China and other Asian economies is squeezing out space for other poorer countries to benefit from globalization.

Alternatives to globalization

Protectionism is still important in the global economy. Sometimes this is on the part of advocates of globalization itself, what could be called *hypocritical globalizers*. These advocate an open, competitive world economy when it is in their interests, but are protectionist when their industries may be under threat, as in the case of US steel tariffs and EU quotas on Chinese textile imports. Similarly, world trade talks cover a range of areas for liberalization – agriculture, manufactures, finance and services – but in one area, the free movement of labour, where liberalization would be of great benefit to developing countries through enabling incomes and remittances, rich countries are instead increasing the barriers, as we saw in chapter 6.

Advocates of free trade in rich countries put the highest tariffs on goods of the sort that happen to come from developing countries, such as agricultural goods, low-priced goods, and simple manufactures. In the 1990s, the average tariff in rich OECD countries placed on manu-factured goods from developing countries was 3.4 per cent, four times that on manufactures from other OECD countries. Not only are the globalization advocates of the rich world hypocritical, but their protec-tionism is greatest in relation to the poorest countries who need entry into their markets the most and less so to rich countries whose needs are less. 60 per cent of developing countries' imports to the richest countries in Europe, North America and Japan are subject to peak tariffs, which are tariffs above 15 per cent. OECD agricultural subsidies to their own farmers totalled $311 billion in 2001, dwarfing aid to all countries of $52 billion. The UN say there is greater subsidy per cow in Europe than aid per person in developing countries (UNDP 2003).

One solution to this is *global cosmopolitan agreements*, which I will discuss in chapter 10. These could be interventionist and egalitarian to agree debt relief, aid or redistribution. Or they could be more neo-liberal, agreeing on an open free trade economy, as in the Uruguay and Doha rounds of world trade talks that started in 1986 and 2001. However, such global negotiations often fail because of the material interests of the parties involved. Debt and aid agreements have been misleading, inadequate and linked to conditions that benefit rich countries, and remain unfulfilled, as in the case of the G8 summit at Gleneagles in 2005. There have been important initiatives to provide debt relief to heavily indebted poor countries but many targets have not been met. In 2006, ten developing countries spent more on repay-ing debt than on education, and in fifty-two countries repayment of debt costs more than the health budget. Official development assist-ance (ODA) declined by 4.7 per cent in 2006 and by 8.4 per cent in 2007. In 2007, the only countries to reach the UN target of 0.7 of their gross national income being given in ODA were Denmark, Luxembourg, the Netherlands, Norway and Sweden. The twenty-two members of the Development Assistance Committee of the rich country OECD gave 0.28 per cent of their combined income in ODA (UNDP 2008c: vii).

Those with the strongest case for being protectionist are poorer countries with the greatest needs and in the weakest position when opening up to global economic competition. However, global trade talks have broken down when rich states have not accepted the wishes of developing countries to maintain a point at which protection, such as tariffs, can be triggered if their industries face threatening levels of competition, for example, in agriculture. This was the case with the breakdown of the Doha round in 2008, although the USA and others (but not the EU negotiator) blamed China and India. Rich countries maintain the right to keep subsidies, on agriculture for example, or quotas and tariffs, for instance on textiles and clothing imports from developing countries, or they retreat from agreements to remove them. Solutions to global inequality are an area where an ideal solution, cosmopolitan global agreement, breaks down over divisions of material interest between rich and poor. Given some of the agreements that have been on the table, this may not always be a bad thing for developing countries. Developing countries should use these global fora as much as they can, but they may also have to fight for themselves outside them, in alliances with others in similar situations or with like-minded objectives. I will return to this theme in chapter 10.

An *alternative form of globalization* favoured by the global justice movement is based on open trade on a fair-trade basis. Workers in developing countries are paid a fair price and are not exploited in what is a genuinely free trade system. Openness includes free labour migration to developed countries with remittances sent home, a source of huge income for developing countries, far greater than Western aid, and in some cases greater than export earnings or foreign direct investment. This type of globalization involves the movement of people as well as capital or goods and services, while the agency of individuals and families bypasses corporations, governments and NGOs. Attempts by rich governments to tighten up on immigration threaten it.

There are also those who argue for greater localism and *self-sufficiency* for environmental reasons. For them, trade and transport in the global economy is wasteful and causes environmental problems such as climate change. This is a product of carbon emissions resulting from the transport of goods from one part of the world to another. Climate change can have negative economic effects, such as changing agricultural land into desert, especially in areas with already hot climates, where the poor are dependent on agriculture. This hinders economic development and can lead to conflict as people fight over declining water and fertile land. Societies should cut down on this trade and transport by relying more on what they can grow and produce in their own area, although this could have negative impacts on the poorer countries that need to export to rich countries to grow their way out of poverty.

There are more regionalist protectionists. Regional, bilateral or multilateral relations are set up between nations to trade more openly with one another. Through agreements to liberalize, countries can find markets, and competition with each other leads to dynamism and success. At the same time, blocs like the EU and ASEAN protect their trading area from outside competitors. This is *regionalism for the rich* in the case of groups like the EU. It has expanded to include poorer Central and Eastern European countries but still acts to protect its members from the wider global economy. It could also be *regionalism or multilateralism for the poor* as a semi-protectionist route out of poverty for the poorest countries. Selective protectionism and regional collaboration amongst poorer countries, rather than fully blown globalization, is an option, especially for low-income economies outside East Asia. For those who have found globalization to cause inequality and poverty, some disengagement may be necessary. Such a strategy, combined with protection, may ease the disadvantage in the global economy that causes problems for some poorer countries.

An alternative way of putting it is that engagement with the global economy is needed but through a route other than open liberal integration. For instance, assistance with some industries would help more than open competition with no protection, enabling poorer countries to compete with the wealthiest most hi-tech business from rich countries. Or poorer countries could enter global markets in particular ways, for example, in regional or collaborative deals with selected others rather than complete open competition. Some Latin American countries have followed this type of guided insertion into global markets, with protection maintained in some areas, alongside regional alliances with other related economies. Poorer countries, where markets at home are not large enough, can focus on trade with other low-income countries that are at a more equal level and find wider markets there.

In this way, competitive growth can be achieved on the more realistic basis of trading on equal terms with similar economies, rather than with much richer ones where the playing field is not level. This implies more of a regional or multilateral than global approach, for instance, through ASEAN in Asia or the regional grouping Mercosur in South America. Or it can involve bilateral or multilateral agreements by states with politically or economically like-minded countries beyond their own regions. Some sectors may need to be protected against imports to enable growth before they are exposed to wider competition. Initially, the industries of poorer countries could be favoured to give these a more equal chance, with measures including protection from the best-performing lower-income countries. This is an approach of selective engagement and disengagement with the global economy, in a gradual way. It could be argued that a strategy like this is similar to those that led to some East Asian success stories.

Table 8.3 shows an outline of different perspectives or approaches to

Table 8.3 Types of involvement in the global economy

Globalizers	Type of globalization	Protectionists	Type of protectionism
Free trade neoliberal globalizers.	Open competition to foster global integration of poor.	Isolationists, nationalists.	For example, US disengagers.
Fair trade globalizers.	Competition but arranged so poorer countries get fair prices and wages, and not low ones dictated by the market or power of richer more powerful companies.	New Social Movement isolationists.	For example, environmentalists, self-sufficiency, etc.; want retreat from globalization to more local scale to cut down trade and transport consequences of globalization for the environment, and, therefore, humans.
Tilting the unlevel playing field.	For globalization but with the chances of the poorer and less equal adjusted to give them more of a chance.	Hypocritical free traders.	Advocates of free trade when it is to their advantage, but who are protectionist to protect their own industries. Same as 'globalizers who are protectionists' – e.g., USA on steel, EU on textiles, both on agriculture.
Globalizers who are protectionists.	Either advocate or partially practise global integration when it benefits them, but protectionist when it benefits some of their industries.	Full-scale protectionists.	Subsidies, tariffs or quotas to protect domestic industries against competition in global economy.
Cosmopolitan democrats/ global governance.	See globalization of the world economy but under conditions of global regulation or reformism in more politically interventionist forms to foster redistribution, human rights and actively help the poor politically, e.g., Held, Soros, Stiglitz.	Selective, disengagers.	Disengage from global economy in areas where too unequal to be able to compete. Like 'tilting the playing field globalists'.
Alternative globalists.	Globalization based on alternative principles to neoliberalism, but from below rather than above as with cosmopolitans. Social Movements, non-capitalist globalization, peace, environment, equality, social justice.	Regionalists.	Rich regionalists, e.g., EU; regionalism for the poor.

the global economy. This separates approaches into different types of globalization and protectionism. It is schematic and there is overlap. For instance, 'hypocritical free traders' in the protectionist column and 'globalizers who are protectionists' in the globalization column are similar or the same. 'Selective disengagers' in the protectionist column overlap with 'tilting the unlevel playing field' category in the globalization column. I have discussed in a previous section factors internal to countries that can help with development as much as liberalization, and which external assistance can also assist with. These might fall into the 'tilting the playing field' category. Some commentators on global inequality may fall into more than one camp.

Further Reading

Held and Kaya's (eds) (2007) *Global Inequality* is a useful reader on this topic.

Representatives of the pro-global trade position include Dollar and Kraay (2001) in their 'Trade, Growth and Poverty', which is easy to find on the Internet and is discussed critically by authors such as Rodrik (2000), Nye et al. (2002), and Samman (2005).

Another useful introduction to the different positions is the debate between Martin Wolf and Robert Wade (2002), in *Prospect*. This can also be tracked down on the Web. Martin Wolf is also author of (2004) *Why Globalization Works*.

Raphael Kaplinsky's (2005) book *Globalization, Poverty and Inequality* provides a critical but balanced discussion.

The World Bank and UNDP publish regular reports on global poverty and inequality, many of which can be downloaded for free from their websites. The UNDP Human Development Reports are very informative.

CHAPTER 9

Politics, the State and Globalization: The End of the Nation-state and Social Democracy?

O NE of the central themes of globalization studies is the idea that the nation-state has been made weaker or even undermined or dislodged by globalization. Sociology has long been concerned about power. Its distinctive approach has been to embed studies of power in wider social processes rather than just looking at political institutions such as parliaments or parties by themselves (e.g., Bottomore 1993). So analysing the role of the state in the wider context of globalization is a distinctively sociological thing to do.

At the same time, those political institutions themselves are part of society and so should be the concern of sociology. To treat politics as not really sociological, as beyond sociology and the concern of political science, international relations or maybe even economics, is to leave major parts of society outside the realm of a discipline that is supposed to study society. It also divorces institutions such as culture, social norms or values, or civil society from politics, as if these spheres are separate from it. The classic sociologists, from Marx to Weber and Durkheim, made the state central to their sociology and it should be so today. Some of their themes are very relevant to this chapter – from Marx, the way the state is linked to the needs of capitalism and the capitalist class; from Weber, his concept of the nation-state.

A theme of this book is that economic motivations are primary determinants in globalization but that this is not the same as saying that the economy is. Economic motivations, especially capitalist ones, tend to drive a lot (but not all) of globalization, but it need not only or primarily be economic actors or impersonal economic structures that enact this. Other actors have relative autonomy and can pursue such motivations themselves. The economy is a key factor in putting pressure on what the nation-state can do and the state can be usurped or determined by economic forces. But it is economic motivations that put that pressure on as much as the economy. It can be actors such as states that are the key ones in pursuing economic motivations. Furthermore, states may operate with some autonomy within the constraints of economic motivations. As we shall see in this chapter, there is state agency and variation in state practices. This is consistent with a perspective that recognizes the power of economic motivations but also does not see all sovereignty or autonomy of the state having been swept away.

The nation-state and sovereignty

A key argument about the globalization of politics is that the nation-state has declined in significance. I will start this chapter by looking at what the nation-state is. A comparison with previous systems helps to show what is distinctive about it. And I will look at what it means to say that it is or was sovereign (Held 1995; Held et al. 1999: ch. 1).

For many of us who live within the borders of nation-states, this institution is a part of common-sense reality, and seems normal and natural such that we do not think of an alternative to it. But the nation-state is a creation of the modern era, fairly recent in human history, and there have been many alternative forms of political institutions.

Hunter-gatherer societies were roaming societies. They had no boundaries as they were on the move. They had no state as they were small self-regulating groups that didn't need a political apparatus to ensure order or infrastructure. So they lacked the two distinctive features of the nation-state – territory (the nation) and a political apparatus (the state). Empires (from Chinese to Roman to European imperialism centuries later, to take just some examples) also have unclear boundaries. These may be shifting as the empire extends. In some cases, especially of older empires, how far and effectively their rule extended is unclear. Their authority was limited. In pre-modern empires covering large areas, in particular, it is probable populations carried on with their own lives in a self-governing way despite ostensibly being under the sway of an imperial power – they were ruled but not governed. These systems had military power but lacked an administrative apparatus for governing what had been conquered. So they lacked the clear territory, administrative system and sovereignty that nation-states have been identified with.

Feudal systems lacked centralized power. Power was diffused from the monarch through other levels and secured through a system of loyalty from below in return for gifts from above. Power was invested in the monarch as a person as much as in the impersonal power of office. People supported the person who was king or queen as much as the office of king or queen. So feudal systems lacked key attributes of what defines nation-states – centralized and impersonal power.

Absolutist states went more in the direction of nation-states. They involved greater centralization and more of an administrative apparatus. Military power became part of the state. There had been no standing army under feudalism, and military force had to be called on by monarchs from civilians at lower levels when the moment arose, in return for tributes. Law and diplomacy developed but there were still strong aspects of personal power.

So these previous systems were different from nation-states – lacking clear territory, or centralized impersonal power, but, as we can see, some attributes of nation-states were evident. The nation-state has clear national territory, centralized power, a monopoly on legitimate force, recognized authority, sovereignty and impersonal power. Externally, nation-states are seen to have been part of a Westphalian system (named after peace treaties signed in 1648 Europe which are said to have recognized national sovereignty). In this model, states are free from external authority, have internal sovereignty and a balance of power between equal states, without a hegemon, with relations based on diplomacy.

In the nation-state system, the state is sovereign and international issues are ones that concern foreign policy rather than any other area of government activity. Sovereignty here refers to the absolute power of the state over what happens within its own territory. Empires did not have this as their remit was very wide – they ruled without necessarily having penetrating power in many places where they theoretically governed. In feudal systems, there was not centralized sovereignty because power was diffused across a number of levels. But in theory the nation-state's territorial boundaries are clear – they are the nation – and the state has centralized and absolute legitimate authority in that area. It is sovereign. International involvement in state policy comes only from the extent that foreign policy requires it to engage in relations with other foreign states. International interference does not extend to an effect on the rest of purely domestic policies on areas such as order, health, education and the economy.

The question is what does globalization do to these characteristics? Has globalization undermined this sovereign nation-state?

Globalization and the decline of the nation-state

A key theme in the globalization literature is that globalization has undermined the nation-state, specifically its sovereignty. I wish to look at a number of ways in which this is said to have been the case: (1) internal crises of the nation-state which have made the state open to being undermined by globalization; (2) aspects of economic, political and cultural globalization that usurp the nation-state; and (3) problems which are global and affect the relevance and efficacy of the nation-state by requiring global solutions. I will then turn to the theory of the competition state, which suggests that nation-states are compelled, or choose, to be subservient to economic globalization with an effect on what policies are possible or not.

1 Internal crises

Views on the globalization of politics usually focus on external links and the external context – on globalization. But I wish to start with internal problems of the nation-state that are relevant to the undermining of the nation-state by globalization. Some theories focus on the crisis of the welfare state. It is argued that political parties have promised expansions of welfare to win elections, leading to public expenditure commitments it is difficult to keep, and reinforcing spiralling expectations from the public that cannot be matched. As governments promise more welfare and expand the welfare state, the public's expectations are raised and they want more. As a result, the welfare state has become overloaded, administratively too complex and too expensive, and governments have lost legitimacy as they are unable to deliver welfare adequately. There are left versions of this theory such as Habermas's legitimation crisis theory, and right versions as in pluralist and neoliberal ideas of the overloaded state (Held 1989).

Support for this perspective has been reflected in the policies of neoliberal and right governments who have seen welfare as too big, crowding out investment that could go into the private sector, as well as encouraging dependency amongst welfare recipients rather than providing active incentives to get work and off welfare. Centre-left governments, such as Clinton's and Blair's, followed up such concerns with policies such as workfare or welfare-to-work which try to trim the welfare state and get welfare recipients into the workforce through a mix of incentives and harsher restrictions on benefits. More recently, a key focus has been on demographic change, especially an ageing population in the developed world, where there are more elderly people to be supported by pensions and healthcare, with fewer younger people in employment paying the taxes to support such services.

This may seem a long way from globalization but such internal crises can be seen to undermine the legitimacy and effectiveness of the nation-state, such that in a context of globalization this leaves an opening for new forms and alternatives to it. Similarly, if you live in a society where there is a failing state, or corruption or war, globalization may become an alternative source for opportunities over the nation-state. Other pressures from within which have disabled or diluted the authority of the nation-state have included sub-national or intranational pressures for devolution, secession and even the break-up of the nation-state. These are evident from Sri Lanka, the break-up of the former Yugoslavia, and in separatist movements, from a number of African countries to the Basque region in Spain. The list could go on. Again, these are not globalized movements but they may be partly encouraged by pressures from globalization that undermine the nation-state. Furthermore, they challenge the authority and legitimacy of the nation-state and make it more open to globalization.

2 Globalization and the nation-state

Economic globalization is said to have undermined the nation-state. An argument of this book is that developments in economic globalization affect other areas of society. Bringing the economy in as a determinant factor should not be dismissed as 'determinist', 'reductionist' or 'crude'. Equally, as we shall see, economic forces are not irresistible and it is economic motivations, sometimes pushed ahead by non-economic forces such as the state, which are the key thing, rather than necessarily the economy or economic structures.

A key factor is the *mobility of capital*. It is said that this undermines the nation-state and makes it no longer able to pursue polices it wants to autonomously. Governments have to pursue policies that will attract mobile capital or will stop it from leaving. A buoyant economy and growth are key objectives of government both for their own sakes and, if the government is a democratic one, for it to be re-elected. Attracting and keeping investment in the country are important to this process. When capital was not quite so footloose, partly because technology was less developed and did not allow it to move so freely, and because of political and legal limits on the movement of money, governments could, to some extent, follow policies that might sometimes alienate capital without the fear it might flee and adversely affect the economy of the country. But, with globalization, state policies have to be more subservient to the needs of business. Capital has more power of 'exit'. This is in part because the state actively created this situation by pursuing policies of liberalization that allow money to move more freely. Nevertheless, from this perspective, the autonomy and sovereignty of the state has been diminished because an outside unelected force is a factor in determining its policies (Crouch 2004). It is not sovereign, and does not have such complete control over its own territory and the policies it pursues there. Sovereignty is more shared with capital. Some of the key actors amongst capital are large multinational corporations which often control large parts of particular sectors of the economy, bring FDI and employment, and that can benefit or undermine an economy by outsourcing into it or out from it. But other financial investors are also important. I will come back to economic globalization and the nation-state in more depth below, in discussing competition state theory.

Globalized culture is also seen to have undermined the nation-state. This is partly because with globalization cultures become more complex and less clear-cut. The national identity that states appeal to for legitimation – as the national government for the national people – is more complicated and mixed and so, it is argued, less clear and maybe less strongly held. People may increasingly hold to a number of national, religious and other identities that compose society, as well as a more complex nationhood. This is partly because of migration, which leads to an intermingling of identities in society. Some of it is because of global communications, which give citizens greater access to global cultures and meanings and dilute the hold of national identity. Postmodernism talks about our identities being plural (for instance, in terms of sexuality, ethnicity, religion or consumption) rather than more singular and clear as in the past (for example, primarily class identity), and joins here with globalization to give a view of the complexity of identities today. Here is where culture can have power, in this case, possibly, the hybridization of culture loosening the simple national identity that underpins the nation-state.

Criticism of repressive states is also facilitated by global communications. Citizens can pick up messages on the radio, TV or Internet, although governments have tried to censor and restrict these. If a state tries to maintain control by internal repression of dissenting opinion this can be undermined by such opinion making its way in from outside via global communications. So global communications can undermine the nation-state.

If economy and culture are more globalized in a way which undermines the power and sovereignty of the state, then the obvious alternative for politics is to organize elsewhere, such as through international or transnational levels. In fact, *political institutions* have developed to quite an extent at such levels, in ways that further undermine the sovereignty of the nation-state by transferring some of its functions upwards. The United Nations is one example of an international body. It is an entity composed of many states, which has taken on important responsibilities in areas such as peacekeeping, arms reduction, development and health. There are powerful economic institutions such as the World Bank and International Monetary Fund, military organizations such as the North Atlantic Treaty Organization (NATO), and various treaties or processes of negotiation under the auspices of entities such as the Nuclear Non-Proliferation Treaty (NPT) and the World Trade Organization (WTO). There are many International Non-Governmental Organizations (INGOs), covering areas such as the environment, academia and professional bodies, religious and sporting organizations, welfare and global social movements. And there are regionally transnational organizations like the European Union (EU, an economic union with twenty-five members), the North American Free Trade Association (NAFTA, a free trade area which includes Mexico, the USA and Canada), the Association of South East Nations (ASEAN, a free trade area which includes South East Asian Countries, originally Indonesia, Malaysia, the Philippines, Singapore and Thailand, and now others too) and Mercosur (a South American common market which includes Argentina, Brazil, Paraguay, Uruguay and Venezuela).

What is described above is multilayered governance, including sub-national forms, states, regional and international bodies and organizations which are governmental, non-governmental and sometimes very informal, as in the case of some global social movements. This has some parallels with pre-modern feudal systems' overlapping arrangements. From one perspective, what is happening here is the governance of the world through multipolar and horizontal rather than vertical relations. Power is diffused amongst states and international organizations of governmental and non-governmental kinds. Rather than being contained and unified and centralized in sovereign bodies, it is spread about and non-hierarchical. Governing is done by states liaising in horizontal ways multilaterally with one another, and by them in combination with other INGOs and International Governmental Organizations (IGOs) globally (although we shall see in other chapters that power is not as diffused as this makes it appear).

Other areas where political functions have been supranationalized and are not in the hands of nation-states, or may even be used against them, include tribunals and trials over human rights and war crimes. The 1948 Universal Declaration of Human Rights allows interference in a state's affairs and in 1976, in combination with other rights treaties, became a bill that gained the status of international law. The European Court of Human Rights allows national governments to be taken to court for transgressing regional human rights rules. The ECHR has supported Chechnyan cases against human rights abuses by Russia, to give one example. The UNDHR and ECHR override and can, from a supranational level, be used against nation-states. The Nuremberg Trials after the Second World War broke Westphalian norms about non-intervention by applying international humanitarian standards that overruled state laws and individuals' obligations to the state. Similarly, international courts such as the International Criminal Court and the International Criminal Tribunal for the Former Yugoslavia are used to try individuals for crimes against humanity and war crimes.

In such cases, functions are passed to levels above the state, can override it or set standards at a level where they have priority over state sovereignty and obligations. At the same time, important states like Russia, China and the USA are not fully committed to such forms of international justice or the principle of overriding state sovereignty. These three have not been parties to the International Criminal Court, for instance. They are inconsistent on this issue and geo-strategic interests rather than principle determine where they defend state sovereignty or not. Powerful countries are averse in some cases to interference in states' affairs in the name of justice.

Such supranational developments are held to show that many state activities have passed up to other levels. World politics is less focused on the sovereign nation-state and more on multilayered politics where functions operate at a number of levels. These include the nation-state, and nation-states have created and constituted many of these centres of power. But, from this perspective, functions and sovereignty are shared at many levels and between different entities.

3 Global problems

The challenge to the role of the nation-state has been accentuated by the global nature of many economic, social and environmental problems in the world. These are in part what is said to have led to the international and transnational forms discussed above. We saw in chapter 7 that the world economy is quite interdependent and interlocking and does not function as a number of separate discrete economies. What happens in one place can impact on others. Therefore, if rules, standards or redistribution are going to be enacted this will have to involve globally coordinated action. So economic bodies are increasingly global in order to deal with what is a global rather than national entity.

Similarly, social problems such as crime, drugs, terrorism and environmental degradation are not contained within national boundaries and therefore solvable by states with territorial jurisdiction. Crime is sometimes carried out by international organizations, by gangs who are funded or supported internationally or who are globally mobile. As such, the international collaboration of police forces is needed. The drugs industry in one country is rarely contained within that country. Drugs in the US are often imported from places like Colombia and

Afghanistan. So action to curb the drugs trade needs action in those countries and collaboration with their governments. In theory, this means first doing things to ensure the friendliness and collaboration of those governments.

Environmental problems are often global too. Climate change is perhaps the most high-profile example. Climate change is caused by the combined emissions of CO_2 from many nations and has a global effect often far away from the location where the emissions were produced. About 42 per cent of global carbon emissions are produced by high-income OECD countries of the north, while many of the most severe consequences in terms of flooding, desertification and the social consequences of these are experienced a long distance away in sub-Saharan Africa or South Asia (which produce 9 per cent of emissions – UNDP 2008a: 310–12). No one nation acting alone can solve the problem because it is caused so internationally. Also, no nation alone is going to take radical steps to reduce carbon emissions unless it knows others will, because in the short term it involves significant costs (although long-term savings). Furthermore the knowledge and cooperation required is better pooled than carried out atomistically by lots of nations alone. So here we have global social problems that lead down the road logically to global politics above and beyond the nation, and usurping national sovereignty and autonomy by passing action on to international bodies. As we shall see in chapter 10, things do not always work out smoothly in global politics, but the point here is that global social problems push towards the constitution of politics from national to global levels.

The competition state and social democracy

One way in which globalization is said to have had a determinant power, economic globalization especially, is in driving states to particular sorts of policies. In particular, it is said that states pursue neoliberal policies because they have to under external pressure from the global economy, competing to attract capital, or because they choose to when under such pressure. Social democratic policies are progressively ruled out, again because they are impossible in the circumstance of globally mobile capital, or because that is how states choose to respond to such circumstances. So competition state theory applies globalization to the nation-state in a particular way – it is specifically about policy and within that it argues in particular that neoliberalism is favoured while the prospects for social democracy look dim. Competition state theory is in part about the death of social democracy (Huber and Stephens 2002; Cerny and Evans 2004).

I will give a brief outline of what social democracy means, so that we can look at ways in which it is supposed to have been affected by globalization. Social democracy is a democratic and parliamentary-oriented politics that arose out of socialism, breaking away from Marxism, although its socialist content has been diluted as the years have gone on. Nevertheless, it has put an emphasis on egalitarian and inclusive goals and a concern for poverty. In the past, means for achieving this were seen to be public ownership and redistribution, although as time has passed less transformatory means have been advocated – such as Keynesian demand management and the welfare state (on social democracy, see Esping-Andersen 1985; Przeworksi 1985). The argument of competition state theory is that state responses to globalization have shifted away from such a politics and that social democracy has been marginalized from politics (see also Hirst 1999 and Crouch 2004). The British Labour Party after the mid-1990s, New Labour, has been a significant example of a party that has moved away from social democratic tenets and given globalization as one reason for this.

How has globalization affected social democracy in this way (see Shaw 2007)? In a globalized economy, states are reliant on foreign capital to raise output and employment, invest in new technology and boost competitiveness. Finance, which is so crucial in this context, is mobile because of reductions in direct political controls on its movements, offshore locations it can go where taxes are lower, and developments in IT that allow it to be moved rapidly and easily. Large amounts of money are also moved around in a way that takes advantage of fluctuating currency values, movements in the stock markets and the changing prices of assets.

1 Social democracy

What are the effects on social democracy? To attract investment and capital, states have to do their best to prevent them from exiting to other places, and compete with other states for capital. To do this, they have to, or choose to, take steps which are amenable to the interests of capital. They weaken labour protection (regulations which protect the pay, conditions and security of workers and facilitate union representation) and cut social overheads. These can be burdensome and costly for businesses and investors. A weaker labour force costs less money and reduces the social costs that businesses may have to pay. States reduce taxes, both on corporations and income tax. They may minimize tax liabilities by offering offshore facilities (sometimes in onshore locations) and perhaps subsidies. This means that wages, labour protection and social support become under threat. High taxes and high wages, social democratic priorities, are ruled out.

The welfare state is undermined and inequality is likely to grow, as corporations reward their bosses while workers have to take losses in wages and protection. Government polices increasingly conform to market liberalization. Both state power, the instrument for introducing social democracy, and social democratic policies of tax, equality and welfare, which the state follows under social democracy, are undermined. Social democratic governments are reduced to pursuing supply-side policies, such as investment in education and training, to improve competitiveness and provide an inviting environment for transnational capital.

Social democracy cannot attempt to control capital too much to stimulate investment and employment, or it will flee. Because many capital controls have been removed, governments cannot control capital or pursue policies against its wishes or it will leave. To avoid currency problems or capital flight a social democratic government will feel obliged to keep the confidence of international finance and investors more generally and avoid spending policies that might affect the government's credit rating with investors or the interest rates charged by lenders. A government that pursues policies disapproved of by finance may receive a worse credit rating making it more difficult to attract investment or to do so on reasonable terms. Capital is charged at higher interest rates to governments whose policies are disliked by investors. Judgements about the credit worthiness of governments depend in part on the extent to which government policies coincide with the free market preferences of businesses. In this way, finance and capital become determiners of the policies of governments.

Budget deficits tend to be disliked by capital so governments cannot finance social spending by building up deficits, which means investors effectively decide policy in this area too. Additionally, governments cannot control employment or stimulate investment and growth through deficits. Nor can they pursue demand management, often financed by borrowing, and involving spending money in the economy to create an onward benign spiral, stimulating employment, then consumer demand from those employed, therefore leading to more jobs and more people with wages that can be taxed to support welfare and redistribution. Thus a classic strategy of social democracy, deficits and demand management, is ruled out, together with the aims it is intended to achieve, employment and growth that support workers and welfare.

2 Democracy

All of these steps away from social democracy are business-friendly and work against social democratic aims to raise taxes and regulations in order to protect workers and achieve social goals. They make capital, because it is a valuable resource and can easily flee, strong, and labour and the state weaker. In the balance of forces between capital, state and labour the latter more fixed and less globalized entities become weakened in relation to capital. Consequently, neoliberal goals gain a stronger foothold while those of social democracy become weakened. Government policy becomes accountable not to electors of the country but to unelected powers, maybe from outside the country. Governments have to sell policies to international investors as well as domestic voters. National government policy is heavily influenced by MNCs, investors and banks, while states, especially welfare states, are undermined and made less autonomous. For Crouch, this ushers in an area which is not only post-social democratic but post-democratic, as the state's own citizens have no influence over policies decided by unelected or overseas investors rather than the state's own citizens to whom it is democratically accountable (see Crouch 2004; Shaw 2007; and Mosley 2005).

3 Convergence

As well as undermining social democracy, the power of capital and finance leads to convergence. Because the same pressures are applied worldwide to governments subject to the power of capital and finance there is a homogenizing of policies. And the convergence is around a 'race to the bottom', towards minimal wages and labour standards (Mosley 2005). So governments (1) lose autonomy; (2) they become less social democratic; (3) they lose accountability to their electorates in favour of influence from external corporate agents, resulting in less democracy; and (4) in these respects, they become increasingly similar across the world. Autonomy, social democracy, democracy and convergence are four areas affected by the arrival of the competition state.

The survival of the social democratic state

There is a strong case here. But could these conclusions be wrong? Despite the power and accuracy in this account, what is described as often the case *is only true to some extent and with variation*. The evidence is that, while this picture does accurately portray the pressures and often the way things are, there is also resistance to this, and space for social democracy. I will discuss some of the resistance in chapters 10 and 11, but I will concentrate here on space for social democracy (see also Garrett 1998; Vandenbroucke 1998; Mosley 2005; Wickham-Jones 2000; Shaw 2007; Huber and Stephens 2002).

1 Empirical diversity

It is sometimes found, when plausible and persuasive theories meet empirical reality, that the test of the latter does not support the former. To some extent this is the case with the competition state thesis. Despite pressures from the global economy, there is empirical diversity, without convergence, and not all seem to be forced into, or choose, the death of social democracy.

Scandinavian countries pursue relatively social democratic policies (see, for example, Taylor 2005). They maintain fairly high taxes and substantial welfare states without calamitous consequences for economic prosperity – in fact, they are amongst the richest states in the world with high standards of living, and relatively low levels of inequality and poverty. They are not shirkers when it comes to globalization, having healthy exports and quite open economies. So their social democracy is achieved in the context of being quite globalized. Similarly, Germany is the world's leading exporter, so quite a globalizer, and one of the richest, largest and most successful economies in the world, yet it is noted for the strong role of trade unions and relatively high taxes and regulations on the economy and employers. There are not clear or consistent constraints on government spending or taxation in OECD countries. In fact, average social spending in OECD countries has increased in the last twenty years and overall takings from tax risen, especially in globalized economies (Weiss 2005). The liberalizing process that has taken place in some of these economies since the 1980s has not resulted in the death of the institutions and policies of social democracy.

It is debatable whether some states have ceased to pursue Keynesianism because of globalization. France and Germany have been reprimanded by the EU for building up deficits that went over EU limits. America has built up a large deficit without endangering its capacity to borrow, although this has more to do with war than neo-Keynesianism, and America's power puts it in a different category from other nations. Finance Ministers, such as Britain's Gordon Brown, when he held this office, are not averse to public spending to reflate economies and create bursts of growth, especially if there is an election in the near future.

Latin American countries such as Argentina and Venezuela have pursued policies that, according to competition state theory, would seem designed to alienate finance, but have still kept its confidence. Argentina offered 'take it or leave it' deals on defaulted foreign payments to lenders. Many investors accepted small repayments and the country continued to command the confidence of investors. Venezuela nationalized energy industries, offering investors the chance to leave with compensation or stay with minority stakes, and initially some accepted the latter. Despite President Chavez's advocacy of socialism and anti-Americanism, the US remains Venezuela's main trading partner. Venezuela is the fourth-largest supplier of oil to the US and the US provides a third of its imports, more than any other country. Many American companies have offices in Caracas and trade between the US and Venezuela rose 36 per cent in 2006 (Surowiecki 2007). Despite neoliberal reforms and external constraints, there are significant differences in welfare regimes in Latin America. Mosley (2005) argues that neoliberalism narrows the policy space but with room for variation. Variation is affected by domestic politics, for instance, whether the poor and the left are well organized, and the extent to which the party system is competitive. Where the poor have a stronger voice, or a competitive system requires greater accountability to the electorate, more welfarist policies may follow.

There does appear to be some convergence and conformity with the competition state thesis, in terms of inflation and deficits (although see the qualifications on government deficits above). States try to keep inflation and deficits down to maintain the confidence of capital and finance. But the same cannot be said of state spending on social provision and taxes to support this. Some states continue to pursue social democratic paths in such areas without alienating investors. While there are overall cross-national similarities on monetary and fiscal policies to do with inflation and deficits, there is variation in areas such as public spending, public sector employment, size of government, distribution of spending across different government departments and programmes, and taxation. Domestic factors – such as local needs, path dependency or historical cultural and institutional traditions, and government ideology – are important (Mosley 2005; Shaw 2007).

The way that Mosley puts this is that globalization produces a *strong but narrow constraint* in developed countries. Where it has an impact, in areas such as inflation and deficits, this is strong. But it has a narrow constraint. The strong constraint covers a selected range of policies. In other policy areas it is less powerful. However, in developing countries, the constraint is strong and wide, and the danger for the developed world is that such strength and breadth may become more applicable there also. In advanced capitalist states, capital takes into account governments' macro-economic policies in deciding on investment decisions, but is less attentive to their micro-economic policies. But, in developing countries, the constraint is on micro-policies too.

2 The compensation thesis

A liberal openness to globalization may lead to a social democratic response. Externally induced economic volatility, with reduced public spending and welfare spending, perhaps unemployment and drops in wages and labour protection, all follow from the model of the competition state set out above. This can create a situation where social democracy is called for to compensate for or respond to such effects. Globalization creates insecurity and hardship, which leads to demands for government intervention to respond to such problems resulting in typically social democratic policies – more spending and jobs, welfare for the excluded, unstable or insecure, protection of exploited workers, education to provide for adaptation to the changes demanded by globalization, and protection for the losers and those dislocated (Glatzer and Rueschemeyer 2005).

In some developing countries there seems to be a positive correlation between globalization and compensation. Trade openness is linked to size of the public sector, especially in democracies. Public spending is higher to provide compensation for volatility where there is globalization. Compensation can be maintained if public investment is compatible with or assists with competitiveness and economic growth (Mosley 2005; Weiss 2005). This leads to the next point.

3 Social democracy is good for business

Another argument puts the attractions of social democracy at the start of the process of attracting capital and business, rather than at the end as a consequence of the dislocations produced. For example, companies may respond positively to government investment in education and training, seeing it as equipping the workforce for globalization and new hi-tech industries, and saving them from paying for it. This was the justification the British New Labour government made to the electorate and business for increasing spending in this area, seen as good in social democratic terms of social justice and inclusion for workers but also something that can attract investment in a competitive global economy.

Social democracy can be a policy of the competition state. Labour mobilization (strategies for inclusion of the unemployed in the workforce) and human capital formation (making people equipped for work under globalization) assist global capital and appeal to the latter in their search for investment opportunities. Employment and education are also social democratic concerns, involving work for workers and routes to equal opportunity and inclusion in the economy. Human capital formation helps the poor and workers by getting them into work and also helps the economy by providing skilled and well-trained labour, with increased taxable income helping to finance public spending, another key concern for social democrats. Another characteristic of social democracy, higher total taxation, is positively related to work because it finances higher public sector employment, also a social democratic desire. Higher tax returns result from higher employment and can be the basis for higher employment.

Supply-side policies can underpin the equality and social inclusion dear to the hearts of social democrats, but also provide the skills and education that business needs. This combination of social justice and economic efficiency has been part of the third-way combination of left and right, justice and business-friendliness, that New Labour and Clinton's New Democrats in the US projected themselves as following. This is allied to the provision of economic stability as part of an attractive business environment.

Wage bargaining and strong labour organizations can be good for attracting business, contrary to the competition state thesis, because they help wage restraint to be accepted. Centralized wage bargaining with strong unions is identified with social democracy in some countries. Wage restraint is accepted by unions in return for government promises on other policies, such as welfare provision. It can also be beneficial for business. From this perspective, higher wages undermine companies' success because they are costly and lead to job losses, with a reduced taxable income base from which to raise revenue for public spending, together with the need for greater social spending due to unemployment. Centralized social democracy and wage bargaining can protect against this. Strong labour and wage restraint is good for social democracy and also attractive to business (Vandenbroucke 1998; Wickham Jones 2000; Garrett 1998).

4 Variation and mediation

So *different reactions* to globalization are possible. As we have seen, there are varying routes to attracting global capital. The low-tax, deregulated, low-spending race to the bottom is not the only one. Capital can be persuaded to respond to other types of policies, including social democratic ones, which may benefit them.

A key thing is that there are different *types of economic globalization* – from exports and trade to globalized capital. Globalization does not exert the same kinds of constraints in all these forms. So a big exporter (like Germany) may require different policies to a big importer of foreign investment (like the UK). A country with high trade openness may find demands for compensation are strong because of the tough competition imposed on domestic industries, which leads to higher public spending and maybe deficits to finance these. But capital openness may restrict the possibility for deficits because these are off-putting for investors. So it is too simplistic to see economic globalization as all-determining, because it depends in part on what sort of economic globalization is involved (Mosley 2005).

There are also different *amounts of globalization*. A country that is heavily reliant on external investment is more likely to succumb to the policies described in the competition state thesis than one that can generate its own investment easily. Norway, for instance, is an oil-rich, wealthy, small country. It can tax highly and spend a lot on a developed public infrastructure because it is not so reliant on global capital as some other places. It has more independence from globalization.

There are also *different kinds of state*. Some have historical national cultures or institutional set-ups that are likely to take them in a different direction from another kind of state facing the same situation. Not only does the type of globalization vary, leading to different policies, but so do types of states facing globalization. They make different choices according to what kind of state they are and what kind of history they have, or what context they operate in nationally.

Related to this, *domestic pressures and traditions vary*. Responses to globalization are not unilinear and predetermined. As we have seen, there are pressures towards some obvious neoliberal choices, but there are possibilities for more social democratic choices too. These can be affected by distinctive national cultures and traditions and ways of doing things. To put it more strongly, these national paths exert a pressure on states to go certain ways, just as globalization does. Globalization is filtered or mediated by local or national institutional or cultural configurations, which provide intervening variables between globalization and its local outcome. As well as just *allowing* different decisions in response to globalization, they may also pressurize towards them.

These differences in domestic traditions and paths feature in the literature on path dependency and varieties of capitalism. Path dependency refers to the idea that nations develop traditions and ways of doing things embedded in national cultures and histories, or resulting from institutional set-ups and previous decisions. These play an influential role in what decisions are made in particular countries. For example, Germany has placed a high cultural premium on negotiation and compromise between its main actors and collectivism and corporatism in decision-making. Alongside business, government and unions have a big role, as consultation is not just an artefact of culture; it is also part of the institutional set-up in Germany, where unions are incorporated into company governance and the political system devolves many decisions to regions that are also incorporated into national government. This means that national governments have to negotiate and compromise with other actors – partners in coalitions which are needed under the PR system to get a majority, and, with the regions, business and unions. This leads to a consensual form of democracy, maybe slow-moving and frustrating at times, but one that facilitates inclusive and collectivist political culture and outcomes in Germany. Decisions that are made ruthlessly in the interests primarily of capital are not so easy to make in Germany as they are in the UK whose political culture is more individualist and liberal, where parties rule alone even if they have below 50 per cent of the vote, and relations between actors in society, such as unions and business, are historically and institutionally based more on competition or conflict than consensus.

I have mentioned a couple of nations here but this model has been looked at more broadly in terms of types of capitalism (see, for instance, Hall and Soskice 2001; Albert 1993), although national differences are significant enough for this to be examined in more narrow terms of national types of capitalism. Nevertheless, the varieties of capitalism literature bring out some of the issues and is illuminating. In this literature, Japan and East Asian capitalism (with some variations) is seen as being based in part on state intervention and guidance, with collectivist cultures of loyalty and trust. It is the intervention of the state and the culture of collective input that has led to economic development. Then there is the Rheinish capitalism of Germany, which is different but has some similar emphases in its active state, corporatism and collectivist culture. These types of capitalism are more long term, less strongly based just on returns to shareholders but with sensitivity to a wider range of stakeholders in the economy and society.

Anglo-American capitalism, exhibited by English-speaking countries such as the UK and the US, emphasizes a lesser role for the state as good for competition and the free development of business, with an individualist ethic driving capitalism forward as much as collectivism. It has a lesser role for unions and other actors, shareholder profits being the incentive that makes businesses entrepreneurial. It is a more dynamic and competitive model, maybe even more exciting for some, often delivering greater flexibility and better employment levels. But it has a hard edge, a more competitive capitalism with greater inequality and poverty, and more winners and losers who are less well protected by the state. It is roughly this sort of model that the Washington Consensus sees as transposable to some developing countries and which has been pursued in a strong form in post-communist Central and East European countries with some adverse consequences.

Beyond these models the enormous and growing examples of China and India should be added, with their own distinctive economic systems and cultures. Across the world nations have distinctive patterns of inequality, cultural identity and traditions, and infrastructures of government, communication, transport, education and health. They have varying degree of openness to trade and investment and other forms of globalization.

A similar taxonomy is sometimes applied to types of welfare states (see Esping-Andersen 1989). As we saw in chapter 8, there are a variety of routes out of global inequality. So literature on the varieties of capitalism shows that the bases for responses to globalization vary, and how they vary may depend in part on types of domestic cultures and institutions, and whether these are historically embedded, and with a path dependency of their own. These affect the extent to which globalization develops, how much and what decisions are made in response to it.

The case for the competition state theory looks powerful and plausible at first. But once you start to dig beneath it, looking at evidence and contrary possible perspectives, it looks less solid. It is difficult to argue with the case for economic globalization putting strong pressures on states and influencing their decisions in important ways. But there are other pressures and influences as well as globalization and there may be a variety of ways that states, especially richer and more powerful ones, can deal with their position in the global economy, rather than just a 'race to the bottom'. The evidence backs up a thesis of a variety of possible responses. In fact, some analyses of the competition state thesis suggest that social democracy may become more attractive in a globalized economy, rather than being sidelined by it.

If the evidence for the competition state thesis is so contestable why does it have a hold? Governments claim they are in a straitjacket, and to compete they must reduce government intervention, lower taxes and relieve the burden of labour and environmental regulations, or business will go elsewhere. Developed countries fear the flight of investment to fast-growing developing countries where wages are low and regulations light. Mosley argues that these arguments endure in the face of equivocal evidence because governments use them to justify ideological choices and cover for past mistakes. Globalization is used to justify policies which governments have an ideological commitment to. However, rather than sell the ideological message behind these, sometimes it is easier to just tell the public they are necessary, that there is no choice and they are forced upon the government by external circumstances, the imperatives of the global economy. So governments push reasons for harsh policies away from themselves on to the private sector, and resulting from the hard choices they have to make to attract investment for the long-term good of the country. If fiscal deficits are run up, to say these have to be reduced to suit private investment provides distraction from government policies that have allowed these to grow.

Globalization and the nation-state assessed

I have discussed above theses about globalization's effect on the decline of the nation-state and, more specifically, the competition state thesis and criticisms of it. I will go back now to the more general thesis about globalization and the nation-state. This section sums up some of the main criticisms of the thesis. To some extent these overlap with the policy-focused competition state arguments, but it is worth returning to a more general level to look at how the globalization thesis on politics is contested as this raises further issues (critical assessments of the globalization and nation-state thesis include Mann 1997; Weiss 1998, 2005).

1 Differentiation by type of globalization

A first important qualification to make about the globalization of politics or usurpation of the nation-state, and about any area of globalization for that matter, is that globalization has differentiated effects depending on the area where it falls. But my point here is that it may be differentiated by *type* of globalization.

We have seen in other chapters that globalization is differentiated within types. So, within economic globalization, finance is quite globalized. It can move around easily because of deregulation and technological change. But production, while still quite internationalized, is more constrained in its mobility. Production and workers are more physical and rooted, less unencumbered and not so easy to move so speedily. MNCs are quite nationally located things with international dimensions. They are far from global in their extent or disembeddedness from the national.

Politics may also be less globalized than in some other areas. Culture and money are often de-physicalized things that can be transmitted electronically, frequently with less technological or political barriers to their movement. There may be higher levels of globalization in areas such as culture and finance than in politics. Why politics may be limited in its globalization I will come to shortly. But the point at the moment is that globalization is differentiated by area, and politics may be one area that is less globalized than some other more footloose and free types.

2 Political globalization varies by country

Globalization varies not only by type of globalization but also by context – where it is received or produced or disseminated. We saw in chapters 3 and 4 how context of reception can alter how one product is received differently in different places, or even in the form it takes when distributed to those places. Similarly, there are inequalities amongst producers in who has the most power and influence over the production and dissemination of global culture.

Globalization has such characteristics when applied to politics. When the relative power of states in the world is examined, the thesis that globalization has undermined or eroded the nation-state is insufficiently complex and sensitive to variation. There are some states in the world that are very powerful, and others less so. When the American state, or European states, or the Chinese state, are compared to others in, say, Africa, or to smaller states in many parts of the world, it becomes simplistic to argue that globalization has eroded the nation-state. Some of these have remained much more powerful in globalization than others.

And some of these retain more power than others despite globalization. They are rich and powerful enough to retain control over their own domestic circumstances. Other states are under much more pressure, because of their economic weakness or lack of political clout, to accept economic globalization and important global political decisions without having much influence over them, and allowing big corporations to sell global culture in their nation if they choose to do so. Some states, such as the US or many European states, have greater economic power to resist economic globalization or political decisions.

Not only is there inequality in the capacity of states to retain control over their domestic circumstances, but they also have differing capacity to shape globalization itself. Some have great power to shape economic globalization because of their wealth and large corporations and state power. Others are weaker in such areas and are the subjects rather than the shapers of economic globalization. So there is inequality in terms of both the capacity to retain autonomy under globalization and to shape it.

3 Divergence in response and mediation

Differentiation applies not only to (a) types of globalization, and (b) degree of power or autonomy in the production or reception of globalization, but also (c) to *type* of response to globalization. I will be brief, as I have discussed this in relation to the competition state thesis and in other chapters. But inequalities, power and autonomy of states aside, whether from globalization or to shape it, different nations have different cultures, or political institutions which affect *how* globalization is received or responded to. Some nations may have cultures that are more or less open to Westernized media and culture often defined as globalization, as we saw in chapter 4. Similarly, there are states more open to globalization economically than others or that shape it in different ways.

In short, states have different institutional set-ups – for example, the UK's is more centralized, while in Germany coordination with different levels and interests is part of its institutions and culture. This illustrates how globalization takes varying forms as a result of different political cultures and institutions in different states.

4 Nation-state powers

Theses of the decline or usurpation of the nation-state have to take into account the considerable powers that nation-states have. This varies between nation-states as we have seen above. But powers that many nation-states have, to varying degrees, remain over: the ultimate resort of force, military action and the capacity to use it internally or externally; spending on welfare and social services, the levels these are set at, and the type of system or services preferred; power over amounts of investment in education and health and choice of policies in these areas; powers to raise or lower rates of taxation; power over law and order and justice, what policies to implement in these areas, and how much and in what ways to invest in them; policies over culture and arts; not to mention a number of levels of macro- and micro-economic policy. There are up to 200 states in the world and every one of them intervenes in the economy and, to varying extents, in these other areas. Between different nation-states there remain differences in government investment and policies, resulting in varying systems and outcomes. Such variation is, in part, a sign of the autonomy of nation-states from external pressure such as globalization, of the remaining power and sovereignty they have in areas such as decision-making on investment and policies and of where states make different decisions in part according to domestic ideological choices or histories, institutions or cultures. It must be emphasized, though, that the power and autonomy of nation-states in these areas varies considerably, and is dependent on whether their wealth and political power enable them to stand up to economic globalization or pressures from other states. Some states have much less power here than others.

5 Nation-states as globalizers

One problem with the view of globalization as undermining the nation-state is that globalization is seen as the actor and the nation-state as the subject, rather than the other way round. In fact, nation-states are amongst the key agencies that have created globalization and are constitutive elements in it. Nation-states often constitute globalization or global political fora in order to retain or expand their power and promote their national interest. They were key actors in earlier forms of globalized politics, such as empires, colonization, world trade, warfare and diplomacy. They are the building blocks for contemporary global politics or are hegemons and dominant forces in the shape it takes. Economically, it is nation-states that have deregulated the global economy and allowed many aspects of its development, such as corporate globalization and the ensuing globalization of production, trade and consumption.

6 Nation-states being globalized

Nation-states are themselves entities that, it could be argued, are being globalized as much as swept away by globalization. They are institutions that have become more widely proliferated across the world in a form of globalization. The spread of the nation-state as a dominant form worldwide is a characteristic of the modern period. Furthermore, the spread of democratic forms of the state has also been seen as a type of globalization. For some, democratization, and the growth of the number of nations adopting democratic systems, is a form of globalization. So, in the postwar period (and long before, for instance, in the Americas), many colonized nations, for example, in Asia and Africa, fought for and achieved their independence as nation-states. In the post-communist period the aspiration to nation-state status came to the fore in many previously communist countries, such as the former Yugoslavia, in some cases leading to bloodshed and conflict, and in some leading to successful achievement of this status by secessionist movements. Generally, nationalist movements struggling for their own state within existing nation-states are common. Hobsbawm (1990) has argued that while the nation-state has been undermined by globalization (something which, as we have seen, is contested) nationalism and aspiration to nation-state status have not been.

7 The nation state as transformed rather than undermined

In chapter 1, I discussed the difference between globalist, sceptical and transformationalist views of globalization. *Sceptics* are critical about the idea of globalization overriding the sovereignty of the nation-state for reasons given above, for instance, that some nation-states are still mightily powerful in the world, including in processes of creating or constructing what is called globalization. In fact, globalization may be better called internationalization because of the continuing importance of relations between nation-states in global contexts, and of nation-states in constituting processes of globalization while undermining them by their differences and conflicts in global fora or wars, for example. Many conflicts in the world are between nation-states as much as other entities, such as religions or corporations. They continue to maintain autonomy and power over domestic policies of great importance. They vary in form and shape and are popular institutions globally that many aspire to who feel unrepresented by a state, for instance, those who feel themselves to be stateless nations such as the Kurds, Basques or Tamils. So, like it or not, cultural nationalism remains strong. Sceptics are realists – they see nation-states as key actors in the world, widely recognized as legitimate representatives of citizens, and the appropriate form to govern over territorial areas. The idea that they are dead is as much a discourse or ideological tool, to justify capitulation to global capital by neoliberals, as a genuine recognition of the power of nation-states to pursue reformist or redistributive policies. It is argued that the sort of neoliberal policies pursued by national governments are as much a matter of ideological choice, or domestically conditioned, as forced by globalization.

Transformationalists, however, have a slightly different picture, although it is doubtful whether it departs as much from scepticism as it claims, as argued in chapter 1. For transformationalists, what happens to the nation-state is not decided and is open-ended. Forces of nationalism or aspirations to nation-state status could reinforce the role of the nation-state in the world. And, for some, globalization is leading people to search for security in an insecure world, which can often mean holding on to national identity and the state apparatus that goes with it. This could involve nation-states taking strong steps to counter insecurity and change caused by globalization, so reinforcing and bolstering up their role. So the decline of the nation-state is something that could occur but also something that could be reversed.

Furthermore, insofar as nation-states are being transformed by globalization, this may indicate their sovereignty is eroded but it could mean they are transformed into more globalized forms, rather than lost or undermined. For example, European states have participated in the European Union and so given up some of their autonomy and sovereignty. But they have done so in part to reclaim power over their economic fortunes and other policy areas in a way that they would be unable to do if acting alone. They have pooled sovereignty at a regional level but in doing so not just eroded their role but found a transnational way of maintaining or reinforcing it in an entity which has more clout and can give nation-states power over things they would otherwise be merely buffeted and undermined by, for example economic globalization. So the nation-state is as much reconfigured as undermined. In fact, sometimes it has been reinvented to maintain influence.

Conclusion

Some of the themes of this book are relevant to this chapter. The state is part of society and affects it. Governments and their policies are part of society and shape it. Sociologists should be interested in this form and not shunt its role away as something not relevant to their discipline.

The role of the nation-state in globalization has a historical context. The nation-state differed from previous political forms in a number of ways, as well as developing out of them. It became what represented people, both politically and in terms of their identities in the modern period, and it is not clear that globalization has pushed this aspect out of the picture. Dicken (2007: 175) argues that states are containers of distinctive institutions and practices, and regulators of economic activities and practices. As far as the outside world is concerned, they are competitors with other states and also collaborators with them in international fora and relations. It is within and through states that these things happen.

The economy is important and is often a causal factor behind globalization, but non-economic actors, such as the nation-state, are agents in this process. Economic determinism need not imply determination by impersonal economic structures.

Power, inequality and conflict are a big part of the story of nation-states in relation to globalization – their autonomy from, or integration into, globalization is heavily affected by how powerful or weak they are. Some are proactive agents of globalization; others are passive recipients of it. Globalization undermines some but others more powerful are its hegemons or subjects. There are enormous inequalities between nation-states. Conflicts between them show the limits of globalization, and often their own needs and desire for self-preservation have led to their integration into transnational processes and structures in which they maintain power often in the same process that they give it up.

To be patronizing towards those who see possibilities in national social democracy, as out of touch with new globalization thinking, pays too much attention to theory over empirical evidence, and sometimes to culture over knowledge of economics and politics. And it is to give up on some of the most feasible means, like them or not, for pursuing solutions to problems such as injustice and hardship, sometimes in favour of global approaches which are misused or ignored by the powerful who are agencies of injustice and hardship.

Nations and conflicts between them are still significant. It is important to recognize and engage with this in the very real context of international and global forms being important, as will be discussed in the next and following chapters.

Further Reading

David Held has outlined clearly what the modern nation-state is, its antecedents and the implications of globalization for it, in (1995) *Democracy and the Global Order*, and Held et al. (1999), *Global Transformations*, chapter 1, amongst other places.

Layna Mosley (2005) and Eric Shaw (2007) have outlined competition state theories and discussed these clearly and critically. Both argue that there are reasons to suggest the social democratic state has not been undermined by globalization.

Colin Crouch's (2004) *Post-Democracy* gives a more pessimistic view of how social democracy has been out-manoeuvred by global capital.

CHAPTER
10 Global Politics and
Cosmopolitan Democracy

WE saw in the last chapter that nation-states are still important in the world, both in their own domestic spheres, despite globalization, and in the constitutive role they play in globalization. Some have the capacity to resist, to some extent, the dominant policy choices of neoliberalism that are favoured by globalization, or at least by global capital and businesses. Nation-states are and will continue to be an important part of world politics. This means that the type of inequalities, conflicts and power imbalances that occur between nation-states will continue to be significant.

At the same time globalization has a big impact on states. Even Mosley (2005), whose main argument is that nation-states have 'room to move', argues that the constraints of economic globalization on states are strong and sometimes broad. So it is important for politics to be organized at a global level to be more effective in relation to globalization. In fact, the recognition that many issues require global coordination has already led politics to be organized globally on quite a scale. Those who advocate global politics do so on the basis of drawing on a globalization of politics that to some extent has already happened. On this descriptive empirical basis, observing how the world *is*, they make prescriptive statements about how they think it *should be* in terms of the global organization of politics.

In this chapter and the next I will look at two main types of global politics. The first is called cosmopolitan democracy and refers to the establishment of political institutions at an international level in a cosmopolitan form. This focuses mostly, but not entirely, on formal political institutions that can be set up globally, and is often fired by social democratic and liberal impulses to counter or regulate global neoliberalism and attack problems such as world poverty, conflict and abuses of human rights. As such, it relates to concerns discussed elsewhere in this book, for example, the desire to pursue social democracy, and problems of global poverty and war.

This chapter looks critically at cosmopolitanism but also looks for positive bases for its success. I wish to break away from *polarized arguments* either for or against cosmopolitanism. *Material interests* may be the key to both critical and positive approaches to cosmopolitanism, seeing where its problems are but also where it might succeed. The debate on cosmopolitanism can be quite divided. Those who have mixed feelings tend not to have a very analytical basis for dealing with this ambiguity. Supporters who see ambiguities in cosmopolitanism but want to continue with it may acknowledge these as problems but put their faith in hope and strength of vision in overcoming them (e.g., Fine 2006; Archibugi 2004).

Fine (2006), for instance, talks about a cosmopolitanism that reconciles an awareness of violence in the world with a normative vision of perpetual peace, and sees cosmopolitanism providing a mode of understanding as much as a legal and institutional order (49). He argues for keeping in mind the normativity of cosmopolitanism in the face of violence (51). Fine endorses both Kant's view that cosmopolitanism is right even if the public and state are not cosmopolitan (52) and Arendt's argument for taking bearings from the idea of cosmopolitanism rather than its actuality (58). Similarly, Archibugi argues that in the face of the obstacles and reality facing cosmopolitanism, it should be defended on the basis of being visionary (2004: 452, 454). In short, both argue for maintaining cosmopolitanism as a hope or ideal even if reality seems to be going against it.

In addition, I also wish to provide a less polarized perspective but more of a material basis for assessing the ambiguities of cosmopolitanism. Material interest is a basis on which cosmopolitanism is problematic, but also one on which it can be advanced. It is important to be critical of cosmopolitanism because in some forms, and adopted in certain ways, it can be dangerous. At the same time there are severe global problems that need tackling, together with international political structures that should be used rather than bypassed. Trying to find forms of global politics in such structures that can solve global problems is too important to be dismissed.

Some are sceptical about global politics, or turn their attention to other spheres. Global social movements are another form of global politics, beyond the formal political sphere in world civil society. Social movements have become more organized at global levels and many of their main concerns are about global problems – for instance, the implications of international neoliberalism for social justice and the environment. I will discuss global social movements in the next chapter. Further forms of politics are important – national state power discussed in the last chapter, and international level politics below the global level, that I discuss later in this chapter.

Social movements have long been of interest to sociologists – as a form of politics embedded in society outside political institutions, expressing social identities, such as gender or sexuality, or addressing social issues such as peace, social injustice and identity. But sociologists should be concerned about politics at this level and also in formal political institutions. Political institutions are a part of society. They express divisions, conflicts or problems in society and are one force amongst others that are constitutive of society. Sociologists should not see politics as beyond their boundaries and as the concern of others.

Why global democracy?

Cosmopolitan democrats include writers such as Held (e.g., 1995, 2000), Kaldor (2003), Archibugi (2004), Archibugi and Held (1995), Fine (2007), and Beck (2006). Their perspectives vary. But a core argument is that many matters that require governance have moved from a national to an international form, requiring governance and democracy to be organized at this level. In particular, such governance should be organized according to principles of cosmopolitan democracy – democratically and through the input of interests and actors worldwide. In this way, key issues can be dealt with: economic and environmental challenges; crime, including drug-trafficking; terrorism and weapons of mass destruction; and human rights, amongst other internationally constituted areas of human activity. The aim is to globalize democracy and democratize globalization. The social basis for this includes changes, outlined below and in other chapters of this book, which have led actors worldwide towards a common cosmopolitan consciousness (Archibugi 2004: 438).

One major imperative behind advocacies of global or cosmopolitan democracy is the *decline of the nation-state*. Rumours of the nation-state's demise have been exaggerated, as we have seen, but globalization has created transnational and international dimensions to economic, social and political life, which call for political organization at that level. Nation-states cannot govern alone; they need to combine and create forms that operate at more international levels to deal with issues at those levels.

A number of *challenges* that face the world are transnational and can only be countered by international action. *Environmental problems* such as climate change are caused by the combined action of many countries, often with effects far distant from where they were created. Individual states are not likely to curb their carbon emissions radically, given the costs and disadvantages involved, unless they know others are going to do the same. The scale of the problems also needs more action than that of individual states. The combined action of many is essential. Hence the problem of climate change needs to be pursued by states acting together, requiring international treaties or negotiations and the involvement of international bodies. Some of the most important negotiations on this issue have led to international treaties, such as the 1997 Kyoto protocol on tackling climate change, ratified by 137 developing countries and most developed countries, the US being an exception. This has been followed by further agreements and talks on the same issue under the auspices of the United Nations Framework Convention on Climate Change.

There is a similar aspect to the development of *weapons of mass destruction* (WMDs). Many states own WMDs capable of huge destruction. The US used two atom bombs against Japan in 1945, eventually killing over 200,000 people, mainly civilians, and causing ongoing serious health problems such as cancer and leukaemia for generations. Another seven atom bombs were planned, but not used, as the Japanese surrendered. Modern nuclear weapons are far more powerful than the Hiroshima and Nagasaki bombs. Other nations feel threatened by this and wish to develop their own WMDs as a means of defence, and maybe also to do with reasons of status and power. This global development of WMDs increases the risk of catastrophic consequences due to error or conflict. But individual states are reluctant to be deprived of what they regard as their right to WMDs, unless reassured that others will give up theirs in an equal and mutual way. For negotiations to be possible, where this can happen, good relations between states are necessary and these are best pursued multilaterally through economic relations and other agreements. International collaboration of many states is needed. Solutions to the global proliferation of weapons capable of great devastation rely on international relations and international agreements and institutions. Since 1968, 189 countries have signed the Nuclear Non-Proliferation Treaty, although several nuclear weapons powers are not signatories and there remain huge inequalities in the ownership of nuclear weapons, with non-proliferation to new nuclear weapon powers taking priority over disarmament of existing ones.

The *economy* is interdependent globally in terms of trade, finance and production. If one country goes into recession it has wider ramifications. Those exporting to it will have fewer buyers, workers abroad may lose their jobs, and finance globally can lose confidence, investing less, and leading to loss of value in shares and companies. This itself has spiralling knock-on effects, with problems in one place quickly having repercussions elsewhere and leading to a volatile and unstable situation in a world economy that is fluid, open, global and interdependent. Consequently, stability and security in the world economy needs action in more than just one country. It requires governance at an international level (Held 2000).

Some consider that without this the world economy is out of control. Humans do not have the capacity to ensure it works for their benefit and that they are protected against negative effects. Greater global governance is needed not only to ensure stability but also more accountability to citizens, rather than the economy being in the hands of powerful corporate elites unaccountable to anyone (or, if you see the global economy as out of control, in the hands of no one). Cosmopolitans propose bringing together the current fragmentation of bodies such as the IMF, WB, OECD and G8 into a more holistic agency that coordinates investment, production and trade, on a global level rather than the national one of state intervention. It is difficult to establish capital controls at a national level if other states do not do the same – otherwise capital can just go to places where it has more freedom. But controls could be established at global levels. Cosmopolitans also aim to establish regulation and transparency in accounting at such levels (Held 2000).

In addition to their aims of stability and democracy, cosmopolitans are concerned that the global economy should be regulated for reasons to do with social and environmental protection and equality (Held 2004). Cosmopolitanism aims to regulate markets to protect both the environment and labour, for instance, in developing countries, and to ensure a role for trade unions. The argument is that global governance can alleviate world poverty through measures to tackle debt, ensuring development and offering international credit. Suggested policies to fund redistributive programmes, aimed at the world's poorest, include taxes on turnover in foreign exchange markets, as proposed by ATTAC – the Association for the Taxation of Financial Transactions for the Aid of Citizens (see Ramonet 1997).

Problems such as *crime, drugs and terrorism* are international. They often involve actors who are globally mobile, from many parts of the world, and in international networks. The solution to these problems requires collaboration among governments, which in turn requires that they have good relations with one another. Disease, too, can be global. It spreads across national boundaries. To prevent this, as with drugs, crime and terrorism, a state needs to collaborate with others where the disease is coming from, often with those who do not have the resources to tackle it in their own area, and to pool resources, skills and knowledge for the maximum positive effect. AIDS, SARS and Asian flu are examples of health problems that have globally spread and where solutions have resulted from international collaboration.

Human rights are sometimes transgressed by individual states. Citizens of such states have no protection unless others step in from outside. Hence international intervention in human rights abuses is often required. From a globalization point of view, state sovereignty and mutual non-intervention do not fit with the fact that humans are a global species that have responsibilities to one another across national boundaries. Regardless of national boundaries, the obligations of the human race include everyone, not just those who happen to be citizens of a specific nation-state. This may sometimes involve overseas states or international bodies intervening to protect fellow humans against their own states.

Many see the world as having moved away from one where states are self-determining and able to define their own ideas of justice on the basis that interference, whether between states or by global actors in states' affairs, is ruled out. Now there is a stronger emphasis on universal ideas of justice, such as human rights (e.g., Beck 2006). Interference in the affairs of states in the name of such ideas is seen as more justified, for instance by major powers in contexts such as Kosovo or global institutions enforcing human rights.

The Nuremberg trials of Nazis for crimes against humanity and other offences after the Second World War has influenced subsequent developments in international human rights and criminal justice. International law overruled state laws or obligations, although the validity of the trials as genuinely international, just or legal is disputed. The 1948 Universal Declaration of Human Rights applied international standards across state boundaries. The European Court of Human Rights and International Criminal Court are examples of transnational legal bodies concerned with human rights across nation-state lines. Some cosmopolitans want to defend military humanitarian interventions to prevent human rights abuses and genocide, justifying attacks such as those by NATO in 1999 to prevent ethnic cleansing by the Serbian army in Kosovo, or arguing that such interventions should have been enforced in Rwanda and Sudan to defend people against genocide or large-scale killing. They campaign for international legally sanctioned cosmopolitan intervention to protect human rights militarily (Kaldor 2001; Beck 2006; Fine 2006; but see Zolo 1997, 2002).

There are further bases for the erosion of the nation-state and the growing pertinence of global politics. There may be internal reasons why states face problems and lose legitimacy, such as crises of the welfare state or secessionist movements at sub-national levels. Migration and developments in the technology of international communications lead people to have more complex or diluted identities, minimizing clear national identifications, with an increasing adoption of identities that are more transnational or relate to things other than nation or territory, such as religion, gender or sexuality.

Another basis for global cosmopolitan democracy is that people have a greater *subjective sense of global citizenship,* partly because they have an increasing range of global identities. But in part it is also due to the psychological consequences resulting from global risks, whether environmental, economic or military. We have a sense of vulnerability to such risks and more of a shared global risk consciousness where we feel we face the same threats as those on the other side of the world and feel we have the same interests as them (see Beck 2000).

Terrible events of the *twentieth century* have influenced the development of global governance. Two world wars which caused enormous death and suffering, followed by the possibility of nuclear conflict during the cold war, have led to a desire for global institutions which bring nations together in cooperation, to prevent such possibilities in the future. This is partly what was behind the development of the UN and the EU. The *end of the cold war* has turned a world divided into two hostile camps to one where greater unity is possible. Societies are less divided between communist and capitalist, or democratic or socialist states, and more, from this perspective, based on common norms of capitalism, liberalism and democracy.

There is a *democratic deficit* caused by this situation. Democracy is based primarily around nation-states, national citizenship and freedom to vote in national elections. It is through nation-states that citizens have a democratic say, with political authorities being held accountable. However, power is shared by diverse forces that include but are also beyond nation-states. The forces and processes that affect our lives operate across nations and many bypass democratic control where it is located, at the nation-state level.

Problems in areas such as health, environment and security are not specifically domestic. So traditional instruments of policy need to be relocated at the transnational levels where these occur. But while transnational bodies may be composed of nation-states they are not themselves accountable to democratic decision-making. Important decisions in the world are made by corporations, by foreign states such as the US, or by international organizations and treaties. States accountable to us are involved in the latter. But, by and large, many key actors at these levels are not accountable to citizens, and even international political actors have no direct line of representation to people. So there is an issue of election, representation, consent and legitimacy being organized nationally, while political decisions are made at other levels. Cosmopolitanism is not only about finding the most relevant levels at which governance should occur but also re-establishing democracy at these levels.

Measures are needed to extend democratic forms across national boundaries. Held argues that this can start by enhancing transparency and accountability in decision-making centres, such as the EU and the UN Security Council. More significantly, it can bring together global fora that there are into a more democratic set-up to establish global democratic institutions where they do not yet exist. The solution proposed here is *cosmopolitan democracy*, democracy organized at global levels and composed of many actors from around the world. Cosmopolitan democracy is global in the level at which it is situated and the wide and plural scope of actors included; equalizing because actors with different powers in the outside world have an equal vote in cosmopolitan fora; and dialogic and deliberative in the way decisions are made.

The idea of worldwide governments and political actors from around the world coming together and making decisions collectively for the benefit of humankind may sound a bit utopian. However, cosmopolitan democrats argue that their proposals are *realistic*, and point to the basis in political reality and consciousness for global politics. I wish to argue that, while existing political and cultural bases for cosmopolitanism are important, a really non-utopian cosmopolitanism would also have to look at bases in material interests. But let us focus on political and consciousness factors first.

Already, there are numerous important international governmental (IGOs) or non-governmental organizations (INGOs) in the world that have jurisdiction over many areas, not to mention regional organizations where decisions are made at a supranational as much as national level. Areas where international bodies exercise jurisdiction or play an important role include human rights and the environment (e.g., some UN organizations and others mentioned above), economic development (e.g., the World Bank and IMF), markets and trade (e.g., the WTO, regional economic entities such as the EU and ASEAN, and OPEC) and international security (e.g., the UN Security Council and NATO). International non-governmental organizations include examples such as Oxfam, the Ford Foundation, Amnesty International, church organizations and professional associations, to give just a few examples of the various types from the tens of thousands that exist. There are well-developed bodies of international law on matters such as the conduct of war, human rights, the environment, conflict, jurisdiction between states and governance of the seas.

What this is said to lead to is a multilayered system as much as a centralized hierarchical one, with horizontal networks of nations combining in international fora along with INGOs. These networks make up a system of global governance. So cosmopolitans argue that what they advocate is not utopian. It builds more deliberately and holistically on networks of global governance that have developed in the postwar period. And such global networks have spread because they are necessary in a world where problems can increasingly be solved only at global levels.

Cosmopolitans argue that there is not just an institutional basis for cosmopolitan democracy but also a cultural or social basis. There are foundations for global consciousness or for a culture of transnational citizenship that can be translated into formal citizenship with lines of accountability and legitimation of global political fora. For Beck, this lies in world risk consciousness. The unintended outcome of things like shared ecological risks and the development of WMDs has been that people the world over have a sense of shared fate and common risks. Because of migration many people have multiple or transnational citizenship, so readily identify with transnational identities rather than single nations. On the basis of this, there are opportunities for cosmopolitan citizens and politicians who can engage in dialogic democracy and empathize with global others. Cosmopolitan democracy is based on the idea of cosmopolitan citizens and politicians who cross national traditions and styles of life, with dialogic skills to mediate between them, expand their own framework to that of others, be members of different communities, have multiple citizenships and think in terms of the overlapping communities of fate in the world. The possession of transnational as much as national identities enables identification with transnational institutions of governance, and for these to gain legitimacy (e.g., Held 2000; Beck 2006).

In this way, cosmopolitanism is seen as both aspirational and having a basis in real developments. I have focused on existing political institutions and cultural consciousness as foundations for cosmopolitanism. But we need to look at another and perhaps more important basis to assess whether cosmopolitanism can work – material interests and the political articulation of these.

Problems of cosmopolitan democracy

The issues that need tackling are global, and national bodies are not up to the job. So governance needs to be established globally to provide institutions that operate at the right transnational level for what needs to be done. Furthermore, this would democratize world processes which are either in the hands of unaccountable elites or out of control altogether. And it would provide mechanisms to deal with volatility and instability, as well as assisting social goals related to equality, poverty, justice and rights. Some economic liberals will disagree with this as too interventionist. But, if we believe that political intervention is needed for the purposes just outlined, what cosmopolitans say seems to make a lot of sense and even to be urgent and desirable. Why would anyone who has such a perspective disagree with this?

There are a number of criticisms of cosmopolitan democracy. These are to do with interconnected issues such as – *the nation-state, Westernization, power and inequality, conflict, stalemate, material interests and cosmopolitan consciousness*. Some are mentioned by critics such as Zolo (1997 and 2002), or by cosmopolitanism's own advocates such as Archibugi (2004) and Fine (2006, 2007).

Global politics and democracy are good goals. But envisaging these as operating in a cosmopolitan manner may be unrealistic in some ways and liable to undermine global politics through underestimating the power, inequality and conflict involved. Global levels of politics are important and should be engaged with. Cosmopolitans are right to direct us down this line. But they are infused with the national and international powers and interests as much as with global consciousness, and are best pursued through a sense of the inequality, power and conflict involved rather than just a belief in cosmopolitan consciousness. A cosmopolitan approach can allow those who pursue global politics for motives of enhancing their own interests to take advantage of situations involving conflicts of power and inequality. Those with social, cosmopolitan and social justice goals need to be ready to participate in global politics with the same approach of interests, conflict, inequality and power to be able to achieve these goals.

A key element of this perspective is the focus on material interests and conflict as part of global politics, together with global consciousness and shared mutualism. I will look in more detail now at some problematic areas of cosmopolitanism mentioned above.

1 The nation-state

One issue I will only touch on because I discussed it in the last chapter is the enduring importance of the nation-state.

(a) Nation-states still have considerable importance in terms of what goes on within their own boundaries. If economic globalization does not undermine politics and the capacity to pursue social justice at state level, then global democracy may not be as necessary as it appears. The state has influence within its own borders, for instance, in terms of spending and policies on issues such as education and welfare. The differences between nations, in terms of economic culture and political systems, lead to variations in policies despite globalization. Scandinavian countries and Germany, for instance, have had relatively high taxes and big welfare states despite being globalized. Latin American governments have been able to default on loans or nationalize major energy companies yet maintain the confidence of investors. Convergence on inflation and deficits is greater than on spending, social provisions and tax. Electorates may seek compensatory social democratic policies of welfare and education to protect them from the effects of globalization. In fact, a social democratic infrastructure of health, education and welfare may be attractive to businesses if it gives them a better workforce and lowers their costs in such areas. So the nation-state may be able to pursue social justice under economic globalization, making cosmopolitan politics at a global level seem less necessary. Cosmopolitanism needs to be an addition to nation-state government rather than a replacement for it, as the nation-state government still plays a strong role.

(b) The globalization of politics has happened, to some extent, through nation-states becoming globalized. They are more sought after as a form throughout the world and by groups seeking to expand their influence and involvement globally. The role of the state in globalization is as pertinent today as is the fact of the state being undermined by globalization. Nation-states are constitutive building blocks in global fora. They are what such fora consist of and are active agents in them. So they are likely to have a big influence in cosmopolitan structures. As such, motivations and interests geared around states will feature strongly in international fora as much as cosmopolitan feeling. Nation-states bring clashing interests to global politics as much as cosmopolitanism, and inequalities between nation-states globally are transferred into the cosmopolitan fora. So global institutions are as dominated by conflict and the predominance of the interests of some over others as by consensus. In global negotiations on issues such as climate change, nuclear proliferation, human rights and free trade we have seen nation-state interests and conflicts, as much as cosmopolitan feeling, dominating outcomes.

(c) Furthermore, there is great inequality in the power of nation-states in the world. Many have a large and disproportionate influence. This undermines cosmopolitan democracy. Powerful nation-states can get their own way in global democratic fora, in a way that is very uncosmopolitan. Despite the supposed equalizing effect of cosmopolitan institutions, this is not so where some have more sway because of greater economic, military and political power, for instance, in the case of the US.

It would be better to regard global democracy as a combination of the national and international, comprised of states relating and combining, rather than as global, above and beyond states and transcending them. It is just as likely that cosmopolitan fora made up of states, with unequal power and different material interests, will be a site of conflict and contestation as of cosmopolitan mutuality. The emphasis placed by cosmopolitans on global fora is a positive one, but it may be better to see these fora as sites where actors, including nation-states, will have to strive in conflictual situations of diverging interests for objectives such as social justice or equality, as much as focusing on a cosmopolitan consciousness about these. Such a consciousness may exist alongside actors geared around their own interests, but the former is unlikely to be generalized while the latter is prevalent.

States that have cosmopolitan goals will need to act alone, or in alliances and multilateralism with others that have similar interests and are like-minded, most likely states or actors disadvantaged in the global order, or their supporters in NGOs and social movements. This will involve conflict politics, engaged in by those with egalitarian or social justice goals, in international alliances and global fora but with a consciousness that, regrettably, this needs to be done in conflict with those with opposite objectives, perhaps those of neoliberalism or global hegemonic power, rather than on the basis that cosmopolitan mutualism will occur. This is international but short of global, and conflict politics as much as cosmopolitan.

2 Westernization

In cosmopolitan fora, some actors, as mentioned, will have greater economic and military and therefore political clout. Cosmopolitan fora can give everyone an equal vote but some will be more influential in determining which way votes are cast, or, in the world beyond voting, in how much power they have to ignore international democracy. And this power to have greater influence in international democracy or to bypass it comes from factors such as superior economic wealth or military force.

Hence cosmopolitan fora are likely to reflect the views of some actors more than others. At the moment the most powerful actor in the world is the US, along with like-minded powers in other Western states in North America and Europe. In a world where hegemonic power reflects a unipolar rather than a multipolar balance of power cosmopolitanism is especially likely to reflect that. Equally, cosmopolitanism can be undermined where the hegemon decides to act in a unilateral, and thus not very cosmopolitan, way.

Furthermore, the type of values that cosmopolitans propose, desirable as they may be, are distinctly Western ones – such as democracy and human rights. With the dominance of Western powers, they are also likely in practice to include free markets and capitalism (even if some cosmopolitans, such as Held (2004), are more social democratically inclined towards redistribution and regulation). In addition, specifically Western conceptions are seen by the West as universal – as applicable and desirable everywhere, a form of Western domination.

There are different types of democracy, human rights and capitalism and especially western versions of these are proposed or likely to dominate cosmopolitanism. For instance liberal ideas of human rights – of individual rights against political repression – are highlighted by cosmopolitans or are likely to be in Western-dominated cosmopolitan fora, rather than social or economic rights, or other concerns such as development or poverty. The latter rights are more positive ones which require the sort of state intervention and equality western liberal ideas of rights can conflict with.

These values are then said to be universal. For those on the receiving end of supposedly universal but Western-influenced values, it feels like Westernization exported. For some in the Muslim world, Western versions of individual human rights are insensitive to aspects of the values and culture of Islam. Furthermore, that human rights discourses favour individual rights over state self-determination is seen as justifying Western powers' intervention in foreign states, to overturn them and dominate other parts of the world. Countries such as Russia and China are wary of intervention on the basis of universalist ideas, and incline towards favouring the rights of states to self-determination.

Western powers do not always live up to the values they present as universal. So their interventions are discredited not only for western domination but also for inconsistency and double standards. There is a lack of self-practising of cosmopolitan and global values such as human rights, environmental protection, free trade and democracy. This has happened for instance in Guantanamo Bay, the reluctance of the US to participate in the International Criminal Court and climate change agreements, US and EU protectionism, the role of money in elections in America, non-recognition of elected authorities like Hamas in Palestine, and the bypassing of the UN in the Iraq War. The US, the world's leading power, has been unwilling to subject itself to cosmopolitan norms unless this is in their own interests. In such cases cosmopolitan values that are advocated are not always practised or are done so inconsistently.

Western cosmopolitanism sometimes appears to be geo-strategic intervention due to the tendency to intervene in states where there is a Western interest or special relationship, rather than primarily to prevent human rights abuses in those countries. The amount of aid the US gives to Israel compared with more needy countries is one example. Other instances are interventions in Afghanistan and Iraq, attributed to motivations such as oil, WMDs or terrorism, rather than in Sudan or Rwanda where terrible human rights abuses had fewer implications for Western powers' interests.

Some cosmopolitans advance cosmopolitan ideas but reject Western domination and so see their theory as not vulnerable to some of the points just made. However, these criticisms still raise issues for cosmopolitan theory, as some concern aspects of cosmopolitan theory or how it is likely to be dominated by Western powers in practice, something that the theory has to take into account. Cosmopolitan values (a) are likely to, or actually do represent Western views more than others; (b) are presented as universal when in fact they are Western; and (c) are not practised by the Western powers that have proposed them as universal.

Whether democracy, rights, capitalism and markets, and the particular sorts envisaged, would be good for societies generally across the world is one question. In some societies such institutions have been a force for the good, as well as having negative effects and not being equally desirable in the same form everywhere. But my key point here is not the normative defensibility of these values and institutions globally, but the way they fit into the politics of cosmopolitanism.

Because of structures of power and the institutions and values of cosmopolitanism, it will probably be western dominated, be seen as such and suffer a lack of legitimacy because of this. It is not likely to be very cosmopolitan and its cosmopolitan credentials will be doubted. It will also lose legitimacy for presenting itself as not western-dominated, as cosmopolitan and universal, and if cosmopolitan values are held to inconsistently by their advocates.

3 Power, inequality and conflict

These two points so far, on nation states and westernization, draw attention to the fact that cosmopolitanism in practice, and in theory given the westernized definition it has of rights and democracy, is likely to be marked by inequalities, power relations and conflicts. Cosmopolitanism is likely to be made up of nation-states with their own interests which will come into conflict with each other when these diverge. The states with more economic and military power consequently have more political clout. Furthermore, the imposition of so-called universal but in fact Western values, represented by cosmopolitanism, is likely to be resented.

Power and inequality are key themes of this book. I have argued that there is a danger in seeing globalization as plural and equalizing (despite the real potential it has along such lines) without also seeing the structures and relations of globalization that mean it is character-ized by inequality, power and conflict. This is nowhere more relevant than in relation to the plural and equalizing system of cosmopoli-tanism. Cosmopolitan democracy is plural because it is inclusive in political representation, and equalizing because all have a vote, such political equality supposedly overriding inequalities of a material, economic or military nature. But, in reality, cosmopolitanism is domi-nated by especially powerful actors in their relations of inequality with others less wealthy or influential, despite equal integration into cosmopolitan fora. Thus, even within politically equal fora, actors have unequal power dependent on the amount of economic and military weight they possess. This initial basis for conflict is further provoked by the Western bias in some cosmopolitan proposals or in those likely to be propounded in cosmopolitan fora. This makes for a system of power, inequality and conflict, rather than one that has the plural and equalizing character of cosmopolitanism.

4 Stalemate

I think power, inequality and conflict are likely to be major features of cosmopolitan fora that need to be taken into account when thinking about cosmopolitanism, rather than having well-intended but ineffec-tual aims to avoid this. But we can also look at what cosmopolitanism might be like if it was a more equal system. If cosmopolitanism were to be plural and equal but with the many perspectives that come from a complex and diverse world, with cosmopolitan fora composed of multiple actors of global origins there may be other problems. One is that views may be so diverse that these outcomes are possible – impo-sition, stalemate or agreement:

(a) A resolution may be achieved by some actors forcing their will on others. In this way, the impact of a great diversity of inputs could be solved by the imposition of some views over others.

(b) Another possibility is that no views win out and the result is stalemate. Views are so diverse and different, and backed up by such different material interests, that agreement cannot be found.

(c) In smaller communities, a possibility is that agreement is reached through negotiation because some actors agree to lose on some issues or are persuaded to change their minds by other actors.

A smaller range of interests, greater homogeneity and the closeness of reduced scale may make (c) possible. But on a wider global scale with greater diversity and where the issues involved (such as weapons of mass destruction, climate change and economic development) are so hugely important this seems less likely. So aside from the imposition of power to resolve diversities of views (a), another possible outcome seems to be stalemate (b).

So far we have seen various possibilities in cosmopolitanism – (1) inequality and the imposition of power (e.g., Westernization); (2) conflict (e.g., resistance to dominant power or conflicts from clashing views); (3) stalemate; (4) consensus or agreement. These last two under (4) are not quite the same thing: consensus means everyone holds the same view, but agreement is where people hold diverse views but through negotiation accept a final decision even if it may not be quite what they all want or believe. But the most likely outcomes seem to be those of conflict and domination, given: the scale of global diversity, inequality and power; the major issues at stake, over which compromise is less likely; that politicians will do the negotiations; and that their record of agreeing effectively is discouraging so far on issues such as climate change, free trade, nuclear disarmament and global poverty.

5 Cosmopolitan consciousness and material interests

Cosmopolitans are hopeful about what can be achieved because of the possibilities for shared consciousness, cultural dialogue and agreement. But the difficulties I have suggested arise because of differences in the material interests of the actors involved.

Ulrich Beck identifies shared risk consciousness about ecological problems as a basis for cosmopolitan democracy. This could also extend to weapons of mass destruction, which he is also concerned about, and to economic volatility. These are globally shared problems and involve global interdependency. It is said that there is or could be a shared risk consciousness about these. We feel jointly exposed to risks with those on the other side of the world. We feel we have problems and interests in common which makes it more likely we will talk together and negotiate mutual solutions to the same problems we share. Shared risk gives us something in common and creates a commonality and mutuality that can be the basis for cosmopolitan discussion in a cosmopolitan democracy. Archibugi (2004: 444) argues that 'human rights, concern about natural catastrophes, conditions of extreme poverty and environmental risks ... increasingly unite this planet's various populations. Human beings are capable of a solidarity that often extends beyond the perimeters of their state.'

But moving beyond the level of consciousness and culture, once such problems are embedded in political and economic interests, structures and relations, the possibility of shared consciousness and agreement looks less likely. A shared consciousness about nuclear weapons (if it exists, which is questionable on this and other issues) is undermined by the political and economic interests underlying it. Those with nuclear superiority are primarily concerned with reducing the nuclear capability of nations that they see as a threat. This is evidenced by the maintenance and renewal of nuclear weapons by states such as the UK and the US, and by the tolerance of the US towards India's nuclear programme. while intolerant of the nuclear weapons programmes of North Korea and, allegedly, Iran. It is difficult to see this as being for any reason other than that the US has been concerned about WMDs when they are perceived to be a threat to the US but not in more cosmopolitan terms worldwide.

Similarly, a major state responsible for substantial carbon emissions may see the costs of reducing these as significant. It might view itself as not affected by the worst consequences – desertification, flooding, and wars over declining fertile land and water – especially if it is in the northern hemisphere, and sees these as affecting mainly other parts of the world. So the costs of change may appear great and the benefits mainly elsewhere. It is not clear that a cosmopolitan consciousness about climate change will emerge while a sense of shared material interest globally is not perceived by all, and with the state in question seeing itself as free from the worst problems.

Affluent populations or politicians may not see themselves as having a shared consciousness with people in developing countries about global poverty and inequality. They themselves are not generally poor or losers from global inequality. There is no material interest for them in global equality; nor are there material benefits to be gained from eradicating global poverty, according to this point of view. As such, there cannot be shared consciousness of a problem that is experienced by poorer countries but not shared by the richer ones.

This may seem to be a dated 'realist' perspective, which sees states as the main actors in world politics and their actions as governed by material self-interest, out of touch with globalization. If you focus on something like intellectual culture amongst contemporary European elites you may find evidence for cosmopolitanism (although my experience is that they are often not cosmopolitan in consciousness of the world beyond their rich areas or in meaningful commitment to other parts of the world). But, as mentioned above, in global negotiations over the world's most serious problems such as climate, trade, poverty and nuclear weapons, states have been the key actors and their actions and the outcomes of negotiations have been in accordance with diverging material interests. The empirical evidence bears out this interpretation more than it provides evidence for cosmopolitan consciousness at a global level in politics. So it is not surprising that Archibugi (2004: 438), a cosmopolitan, says that since the end of the cold war the governments of Western liberal states have made no major institutional reforms in a cosmopolitan direction apart from the International Criminal Court. War, he says, continues to be a mechanism for 'tackling controversies', international law is violated and aid to developing countries has decreased.

If material interests are seen as dividing actors and undermining the possibility of cosmopolitan consciousness, we should also look to see whether there can be *shared material interests providing a basis for cosmopolitanism* in a more positive way. When material interests coincide and political actors articulate these, there may be a basis for cosmopolitanism. For some time the Bush administration in the US would not support climate change initiatives because it did not see them as in its interests. But, if climate change is seen as something that adversely affects US interests, then it is possible the US might come into line with international negotiations to deal with this problem, and this is more likely now than in the past. For instance, if it is predicted that there may be changes to the US climate such as flooding, hurricanes, warming or colder temperatures, then the US can see itself as having material interests to engage in cosmopolitan fora on this problem. Concern about the effects of climate change in the US may also be heightened by the rapid growth of China and India, who are fast adding to the global carbon emissions currently dominated by rich developed countries.

Similarly, if it is perceived that the effects of US carbon emissions on other nations could lead to hostility towards the US, with the possibility of violent conflict that might involve WMDs, then the US may see it as being in its interests to engage in cosmopolitan agreements on the problem. Democrats argue that the US should not be using just the hard power of sanctions and military action to protect itself. It should also use the soft power of persuasion and attractiveness. This includes recognizing the bases for animosity towards the US and dealing with the causes, such as carbon emissions and their effects, rather than carrying on in ways which arouse antagonism, then dealing with this by force (Nye 2002).

My argument has been that the assertion of shared risk consciousness is insensitive to political-economic differences of power and inequality. But where shared economic and political interests emerge then cosmopolitanism becomes more possible. This could be the case as global understanding develops regarding climate change, global poverty and WMDs. Sometimes rich countries have not seen these as issues they have an interest in taking action on. But, as developments and debates reveal the implications these have for richer countries, this may change. For instance, they may become more conscious of the consequences of climate change for the North and how this will be accentuated as China grows, or of the implications of global poverty in terms of hostility towards rich countries.

Optimism about cosmopolitanism should not be based on being utopian, visionary or hoping for it to work (e.g., Fine 2006 and Archibugi 2004). It should be founded on material bases for it. This approach is better than being merely pro- or anti-cosmopolitanism. It involves being critical about bases for cosmopolitanism, yet also open to possibilities for it, but in ways that go beyond utopianism by looking for a material basis.

Material interests do not automatically develop into cosmopolitan consciousness. They *have to be perceived and articulated*. That there have been political differences in the US on whether it should be more unilateral or multilateral shows that shared material interests do not by themselves develop into cosmopolitanism but have to be mobilized.

This is not to say that there cannot be altruistic cosmopolitanism, advanced even if not in someone's own interest. But for global cosmopolitanism to work there needs to be widespread mobilization of material interests as well as pools of altruistic cosmopolitanism. At the same time, although material interest is often a hindrance to cosmopolitan solutions to world problems, this need not always be the case. It can also be allied with altruistic motivations to further cosmopolitanism.

Cosmopolitans and anti-cosmopolitans

(a) This perspective departs from mostly *utopian cosmopolitans* who argue for cosmopolitanism because they see it as necessary and desirable: (i) Material interests can divide and undermine cosmopolitanism; utopian cosmopolitans are merely hopeful in the face of this problem that cosmopolitanism must and hopefully can overcome it; (ii) the perspective I have outlined argues that there have to be shared material interests for cosmopolitanism to develop, so it tries to be positive about cosmopolitanism on real material bases rather than determinedly hoping for cosmopolitanism because it is important, an idealistic rather than a material aspiration.

(b) The perspective I have outlined also departs from *refuseniks about cosmopolitanism*; saying that material interests are at the basis of cosmopolitanism not only means that they undermine

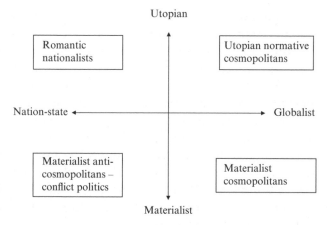

Figure 10.1   Materialist and utopian cosmopolitans and anti-cosmopolitans

it where there are conflicting interests but also that where material interests are shared, or overlap, they can provide a foundation for it; global problems are so acute and globally agreed solutions so potentially valuable that it is wrong to dismiss these – we should look for possibilities for them.

Utopian nationalists

Utopian nationalism is not a concern of this chapter. But it includes appeals to an idea of national identity or nationalism, on the basis of mythical shared characteristics such as shared language, history or ethnicity, which often lack a real material basis. Cosmopolitan shared global identity is an alternative to nationalism but may also appeal to a shared identity that is not real.

Utopian cosmopolitans

Cosmopolitans are conscious of being utopian and argue for this (Fine) or say they are not utopian on the basis that global political institutions (Held) or cosmopolitan cultural consciousness (Beck) already exist. The focus on existing political institutions, as providing a real rather than utopian basis for cosmopolitanism, identifies political bases for cosmopolitanism as far as institutions go. But it does not identify common material interests in cosmopolitanism within those institutions. The focus on shared cultural consciousness is empirically open to challenge, and diverging material interests and political decisions by different world powers suggest there may not be such a shared consciousness, despite the potential for it. In these senses, cosmopolitans who see political and cultural bases for cosmopolitanism are more utopian than materialist, as shown in figure 10.1 where an attempt is made to summarize some of the cosmopolitan and anti-cosmopolitan perspectives, with cosmopolitanism analysed in terms of material interests and their political articulation.

Sometimes utopian cosmopolitans, from the top right in figure 10.1, argue against the anti-cosmopolitan conflict politics of the bottom left, while themselves having a conflict view at the level of domestic politics. They have a cosmopolitan view of politics at the global level but a view of conflicting interests where global capital meets state and labour nationally. Beck (2000), for instance, sees German politics as characterized by a conflict between the interests of state and labour in protection, security and equality, against mobile global capital which is a force for insecurity and liberalization, and which, because it is mobile, is winning out in the struggle between these different interests. Yet the conflict perspective on politics at this domestic level is not transposed to the global level where it would show antagonistic interests there too, challenging cosmopolitanism.

Materialists

It is possible to be materialist and both positive and negative about the prospects for cosmopolitanism, depending on material interests at the time and the extent to which material interests for cosmopolitanism are perceived and articulated by political actors. Being a positive materialist cosmopolitan is not a once and for all position. Someone can vary from this, depending on material interests and the political articulation of them. The same applies to those who have a negative perspective on cosmopolitanism because of material interests. Materialist cosmopolitanism is open to different conclusions because it depends on the state of material interests at any given time.

6 Institutions or policy

Cosmopolitans sometimes propose policies to solve global problems. For instance, Held favours a tax on foreign exchange markets, regulations to protect workers, and measures to tackle debt and global poverty. On the whole, though, cosmopolitans' proposals are about democratic and political institutions at a global level more than the specific policies those institutions should follow. Such institutions are open to different kinds of decisions being made. The assumption of cosmopolitanism is that they will be cosmopolitan-minded institutions. We have seen that this may not be the case. If it is, this still leaves open what policies would be the best to solve problems connected with global inequality, climate change or WMDs. Such issues need substantive policy solutions as much as institutions that can bring actors together to negotiate these.

Solutions to major world problems highlighted by cosmopolitans need to go beyond formal institutions of democracy at a global level, important as these are, also to substantive policies. Or substantive policy choices need to be made prior to choosing the political institutions for carrying them out. Solutions can be decided on and then varying forms of politics for enacting them weighed up.

Conclusions

A number of criticisms I have mentioned fall into *realist or Marxist perspectives* on international relations. These contrast with cosmopolitan perspectives. Realists see international relations as the interaction of states trying to further their own interests on the global stage. Cosmopolitan democracy or institutions of global governance are, therefore, an extension of state interests in international institutions. These are dominated by the most powerful states. Marxists have a similar perspective to this, but link the state to economic interests and the imperatives of capitalism. From a Marxist point of view, realists have a reasonable perspective on world politics but do not match their description with enough of an explanation for the bases of state interests. State interests are based in economic interests, specifically the imperative of capital towards accumulation and economic expansionism. States act in the interests of the capitalist economy's pursuit of profit. Both of these perspectives cause problems for cosmopolitanism because rather than seeing commonality and agreement they see interests and conflict.

I have outlined problems with cosmopolitan democracy. These are mostly linked to political-economic issues of power and inequality and conflicting interests. However, I have also made some more positive points and I will conclude on that note.

1 Globalism

It is right to focus on global institutions to solve problems which are global. Falling back on state sovereignty alone as a method of politics is not adequate when many problems are of a global nature and important supranational structures exist which can be engaged with. It is wrong to stand aside from such institutions where things can get done or which, if just left to others, could be misused.

2 Normative cosmopolitanism

A cosmopolitan outlook is desirable. I have argued less against being cosmopolitan but more about why cosmopolitanism is unrealistic given political-economic differences, or not very cosmopolitan in practice given the biases of what it proposes, such as Western ideas of human rights and democracy and maybe capitalism and markets. Inclusiveness, negotiation and agreement to solve huge world problems are desirable.

3 Actual cosmopolitanism

As far as cosmopolitanism in practice goes, whether it works or takes a cosmopolitan form is dependent on the material bases for it, and whether or how these are politically articulated. Where mutual material interests for cosmopolitanism exist, and political actors articulate and mobilize these, it can work. Where they do not, the opposite is the case. Aspirations to common consciousness will fail because different actors have diverging material interests, or have mutual material interests that political actors have failed to mobilize.

This perspective is better than (a) being positive about cosmopolitanism purely on the basis that it is desirable and should be hoped for. I have argued for a positive approach to cosmopolitanism not just on the basis of hopefulness, but also in terms of material interests and political mobilization. This perspective is also better than (b) being completely against cosmopolitanism on the basis of conflicting political-economic interests, because these could change to being more mutually similar and thus enable cosmopolitanism to be effective if articulated by political actors. And (c) I have tried to put forward a perspective that does not favour a utopian approach to cosmopolitanism, or complete negativity on material grounds. Instead, such a perspective sees material interests as a basis for being critical or sceptical, but also sees bases for positivity on grounds of material interests.

4 Global conflict politics

Even if cosmopolitanism does not emerge on such a basis then political participation in global or cosmopolitan institutions is still important, given that global solutions are needed to what are global problems. What will be required in such circumstances is for these to be secured through a politics of conflict, where like-minded nations form bilateral or multilateral alliances in favour of things like social and economic as well as individualized ideas of rights, for more regulated and less liberal markets, more protectionism and fair trade for poorer countries, or serious reductions by rich nations in WMDs and carbon emissions as a basis for more global action on these. Where there is not a material and political basis for cosmopolitanism this should not lead to sceptics ruling out institutions of global politics. These will still operate at a level that make them important for tackling global problems, and if they are not engaged with then other powers will take advantage of them. But if they lack a material and political basis for cosmopolitan politics, this will have to be pursued through conflict politics, recognizing real material and political divides, and taking the side of those whose interests favour the poorer and more exploited. This will involve multilaterally forging alliances with those who have shared material and political interests and orientations, and trying to secure objectives against those who have opposed interests and orientations. This is an international politics but on the basis of conflict rather than cosmopolitanism and at a lower, less inclusive level than the fully global.

An *example of global conflict politics* can be seen in Latin America where there is a history of experiments with neoliberalism that turned out harshly. This experience is combined with a tradition in the region of nationalist-populism, pan-South Americanism and anti-imperialism, at first against European imperialism and then towards US involvement in influencing the politics of the region. Politics at this level can be through cross-South American cooperation, for instance, in institutions such as Mercosur. President Chavez of Venezuela recognizes that anti-neoliberal and anti-US imperialism cannot be pursued by his government alone and that international alliances are needed, either with other South American countries, or with those who are like-minded politically, including neighbouring Latin American countries with left-leaning leaders, or countries such as Iran and Russia, hostile to US imperialism. Chavez has formed economic links, arrangements involving mutual assistance and political bilateralism with such states. For him, global institutions represent the interests of neoliberalism and US imperialism, so he does not see these as cosmopolitan. He has a conflict perspective on operating through them, and he recognizes the need for international politics and alliances but at a lower level than globalism.

Hence there is a role for state, conflict and sub-global politics in achieving ends such as social justice, as well as for global cosmopolitan deliberation.

1 *Nation-states* still matter. There are national differences in state policies and there is space for politics like that of social democracy at state level. So the politics of issues such as social justice, rights and environment still involve nation-states strongly, and these are one alternative to cosmopolitan democracy.
2 Nation-states are building blocks for globalization and, if the interests of nation-states clash, this undermines cosmopolitan democracy and leads to *conflict rather than cosmopolitan politics* at a global level. It is right to be oriented to global institutions but this may need to be on the basis of conflicting interests rather than deliberative cosmopolitanism.

3 A third alternative is *international politics at sub-global level*. States may be better off organizing outside globalization because of the sway of more powerful states. Actors can form international alliances regionally, bilaterally or multilaterally, trading agreements, for instance, with other nations that are like-minded ideologically or where there are resources of mutual interest. Chavez recognizes that politics needs to be international and beyond the nation, but based on conflicting interests between some powers globally, rather than cosmopolitanism at that level, while interests in common with others are established on a sub-global international level.

It is right to reorient from national to global politics because many serious problems are global and require global coordination. It is worth attempting to pursue aims such as social justice through liberal political institutions at a global level and this chapter is not an argument against that. But cosmopolitanism may be too optimistic about pluralism and dialogue and insensitive to conflicting economic material interests which counteract political and cultural bases for cosmopolitanism. Other forms of politics are equally possible, such as state and international forms of politics, which are short of fully blown globalism. There needs to be a certain amount of scepticism about possibilities for dialogic deliberation in cosmopolitan fora and an awareness of the importance of state and conflict politics

Further Reading

Many of David Held's publications advocate cosmopolitan democracy, including the article (2000) 'Regulating Globalization', and his book (1995) *Democracy and the Global Order,* but also many others.

Ulrich Beck's (2006) *Cosmopolitan Vision*, amongst other publications of his, advocates cosmopolitanism at sociological, political and military levels.

Daniele Archibugi's (2004) article is an outline of cosmopolitan democracy and criticisms of it.

Like Archibugi, Robert Fine (2006) is a cosmopolitan who sees ambiguities and problems in cosmopolitanism but argues for it as a visionary aim.

Danilo Zolo (1997 and 2002) is a critic of cosmopolitanism, especially of some of its philosophical, legal and military dimensions.

Anti-globalization and Global Justice Movements

M ANY people are sceptical about what politics can achieve through states or global fora comprised of state actors, as discussed in the last chapter. States and international institutions do not have a great record in solving problems such as global poverty, environmental degradation and the proliferation of weapons of mass destruction. Many such institutions were set up to solve problems like this in the second half of the twentieth century yet they can hardly be said to have diminished or contained them. International institutions often seem to be the problem as much as the solution. Sometimes states on the international stage have been the actors behind global problems and it is the pursuit of their own interests that has led to such problems. So attention turns away from state and international elite politics to social movements in civil society, more popularly based movements of activists and ordinary people.

Developments in globalization such as the global nature of the world's main problems and global communications, facilitate international political action from the grassroots. Social movements have been a traditional concern of sociologists interested in politics, civil society and popular values and action. This is because they are based outside conventional political institutions in wider society. They are more about society than the polity.

What is going on in global social movements is exciting and provocative. These movements have raised important and original questions about some of the world's most significant problems which politicians have seemed relatively uninterested in, unwilling or unable to tackle in a firm enough way. Corporations have often been causes of such problems or too concerned about profits to want to use their wealth and power responsibly to tackle them. Global social movements are able to put on the agenda in a fresh, imaginative and critical way questions concerning problems reproduced by other sectors of society, which these sectors turn away from.

At the same time critical questions have been asked about global social movements. It is clear what they are against but do they have a vision of what they are for? Is what they are against so diverse and contradictory that they are too fragmented to be any sort of social force in the world? Are the key global actors not still states, corporations and international organizations, and so the entities that should be the focus of analyses of power in the world?

The movements I am looking at in this chapter are sometimes called anti-globalization movements. We shall see shortly why, and how this name may have some limitations. They are also sometimes referred to as global justice movements, a narrower term that obviously applies better to anti-globalization movements with specifically social justice concerns, than to others that are, say, nationalist or protectionist. The movements are also sometimes referred to as alter-globalization.

Anti-globalization

The oppositional character of the anti-globalization movement is captured by the 'anti' in its name. What specifically are its concerns, what is global or anti-global about it, and how has it come about (see Gill 2000)?

The movement is principally against *neoliberal globalization*. This is seen to give power to big corporations and the state in rich countries so that they can gain access to developing world markets, exploit cheap labour and loosen environmental standards, with outsourcing also bringing negative consequences for domestic workers in rich countries, such as unemployment. The actions of big corporations globally lead to cultural globalization and a loss of cultural diversity globally, as argued in chapter 4. These corporations override the rights of indigenous peoples and can exploit local areas and then move on if, say, local environments are exhausted or polluted, leaving the consequences for the local inhabitants. Some anti-globalizers want greater equality of mobility, with free movement for people as well as capital, perhaps even more mobility for people and greater constraints on capital. I gave some reasons why this is beneficial in chapter 6. However nationalist anti-globalizers want more restrictions on immigration. Free trade is seen to occur in a relationship of inequality between rich and poor countries, and inconsistently, as rich countries maintain protection or subsidies for their own industries and agriculture while expecting openness from the developing world. As far as capital mobility goes, anti-globalizers want to see greater fairness and justice in corporate behaviour, especially towards people in developing countries. Organizations or treaties which are seen to facilitate free trade and the freedom of capital to exploit local communities are strongly opposed, for instance, the World Bank, International

Monetary Fund, agreements of the G8 and World Trade Organization, the North American Free Trade Area, and the OECD's Multilateral Agreement on Investment.

A related key concern is with *democracy*. Anti-globalization movements want to rescue democratic control for ordinary people. They say it has been taken from them and put in the hands of states, unaccountable corporations and international bodies. These constitute an alliance that is pushing for global neo-liberalism, privatization, deregulation and open markets. These favour corporations and states from rich countries as they give them access to developing countries' markets and to cheap labour which can be exploited for a profit. The democratic aspect is that neoliberalism has almost been locked in by these actors, who are unaccountable, as a common-sense norm and basic part of the organization of economic and political life. So, in institutions such as the EU, WTO and NAFTA, bodies have been established whose *raison d être* appears to be based around the constitutionalizing of neoliberalism (Gill 2000). Actors who have established neoliberalism in this way are mostly not accountable, or they have put neoliberalism beyond accountability as an issue not up for democratic debate. Power has been monopolized by state-corporate elites beyond mechanisms of popular consent, ruling out the possibility of choices other than those such elites favour. The rights they entrench are those of corporations to act freely and so represent particular class interests. Anti-globalization movements want to open this issue up to debate, to argue that alternatives are possible and that this should be a matter for democratic choice, not established as taken for granted.

Aside from democracy, a key concern of anti-globalization movements is the substance of what gets pursued by these unaccountable actors. One aspect is that *labour* is more constrained because it has to make itself amenable to mobile capital. There is a rising rate of exploitation as capital can move its operations to areas where it can pay workers the least, so also driving down wages in the developed world where workers have to compete with cheap labour from developing countries. This divides international workforces and makes them less able to cooperate for their common interest against capital. There is a 'race to the bottom', as far as labour, the environment and social interests are concerned. States lower standards in such areas to attract mobile capital.

Anti-globalization movements also campaign on the way that globalization has impacted on *social reproduction*, the upbringing and support of people beyond the labour force. The effects of structural adjustment policies and economic liberalism, as we saw in chapter 8, have fallen on the poorest in society, often excluded from the workforce or integration into society, and women who carry a disproportionate burden in the family. Institutions concerned with social reproduction – welfare, health and education – lose out from policies against deficits, state expenditure, and too big a role for the public sector.

A key concern of anti-globalization movements is *human rights* for those in social reproduction, for labour, or for communities in their own environments, especially indigenous people, who are faced by the power of big states and large-scale capital. They criticize forced migration and the exploitation of migrant workers. At the same time, many are for rights of free movement for people to match capital's rights to move freely. In this sense they are pro-globalist and more concerned by inconsistency and inequality in globalization, although more populist nationalist elements of the movements are anti-immigration.

Global social movements have an agenda which goes beyond labour and social reproduction and encompasses other areas, perhaps most noticeably *human health and the environment.* They tend to be concerned about food security, health risks, genetically modified crops, the privatization of water, and patenting. Some argue that human interference in the natural environment is risky and full of unknown possible consequences, as well as some now well-known consequences. Biodiversity in nature is being replaced by a monoculture caused by human manipulation for its own ends – for instance, in the genetic modification of crops. Those pushing humankind down this road are corporate elites, backed by science and technology bent on their interests, backed up by international and state power that supports such directions of change. Anti-globalization movements see monoculture being created globally, at the expense of biodiversity and the environment, for the interest of large corporations and at the expense of indigenous people and humankind generally. Big corporations can over-exploit local environments but then move on when resources there are exhausted, while local people are left behind with the consequences.

Running through all these issues is a concern for *development.* It is especially the consequences of neoliberalism for developing countries that anti-globalization movements are concerned with – debt, aid, and the role of developed world governments and corporations in developing countries are themes that are raised. The labour rights of sweatshop workers and exploited migrant workers, the effects of SAPs, the consequences of climate change and other environmental problems are developing world issues that the anti-globalization movement is concerned about. Anti-globalizers have suggested that the liberalization of world markets, promoted as being in the interest of developing countries, is pursued more because it is in the interest of the rich states and corporations, giving them access to developing world markets and cheap labour, than because it helps developing countries.

The concerns of global social movements have been summarized as being anti-debt, anti-sweat (referring to sweatshops in developing countries), and anti-war. Opposition to global cultural homogenization through the domination of Western or even American culture, media and consumerism, at the expense of local cultures or cultural diversity, is also voiced. Anti-globalization concerns are debated and expressed in meetings of entities such as the World Social Forum or European or Asian Social Forums, alternatives to the World Economic Forum held in Davos, and in the campaigning of INGOs such as Oxfam, Care International and Save the Children. Much discussed movements have included the Zapatistas in Mexico (Morton 2002), the protesters at the 'Battle of Seattle' at the WTO in 1999 and similar protests at G8 meetings (often organized through the Peoples' Global Action network), the Chipko Indian movement and the MST (the Brazilian landless workers' movement). It is identified with writers such as Naomi Klein (2001, 2002, 2008), although the movement has many other spokespeople who are not celebrities, or would rather see itself as not having individual spokespeople at all. The French newspaper *Le Monde Diplomatique* has championed the anti-globalization movement and was behind the ATTAC initiative to tax financial transactions to fund help for developing countries (Ramonet 1997; Birchfield and Freyberg-Inan 2004; Cassen 2003 and 2005).

Positive perspectives promoted by the movement have included, as we shall see, environmentalism, and political ideas from social democracy to socialism and anarchism, and even populist nationalism, all with a common antipathy to neoliberal globalization. Development and feminist perspectives have been influential.

Many anti-globalization protesters are sceptical about mainstream or institutional politics, but there is some crossover with anti-neoliberal state politics. For instance, in Latin America, alternatives to neoliberalism have played a large part in the agenda of state actors. The Brazilian President Lula's roots were in the trade union movement and Workers Party in Brazil and he has been supportive towards radical social movements. At the same time, he is on the moderate left and seen as too subservient to neoliberalism for many in the anti-globalization movement. President Chavez in Venezuela has tried to set out an alternative to what he sees as neoliberalism and American imperialism, and in doing so has attempted to create multilateral alliances and mutual relationships with other states opposed to American power, from Iran to Cuba to Bolivia. The president of Bolivia, Evo Morales, a radical with concerns like those of Chavez, comes out of Bolivian social movements and indigenous people's rights. I will return to these statist anti-globalizers in evaluating anti-globalization later in this chapter.

Anti-globalization movements

As should be clear now, the anti-globalization movement is diverse, and, as we shall see shortly, this is highlighted by critics. I wish to say something in this section about what the anti-globalization movement is composed of and, having focused so far on its critique of society, what some of its more positive proposals may be (Gill 2000 is a collection on anti-globalization, and *New Left Review* from issue 9 onwards has published a number of articles on 'the movement of movements').

Some elements of the anti-globalization movement come from the *traditional left*. They are anti-capitalist, critical of corporations and of the states that support their interests. They attempt to advance the interests of labour and the excluded and dispossessed against such interests or classes. These elements represent the more materialist aspects of the movement as against other parts which are more about symbolic than material politics. These traditional left strands can be internationalist, but some are also domestically oriented, concerned with protecting home workforces against globalization. The latter (some in the left join the right on this issue) presents itself as fighting against globalization and for home workers' jobs. Having said this, what they are fighting is not unemployment but the movement of employment from rich countries to needy poor countries. The exploitative nature of some outsourced work is a problem, but often the work is more needed in poor countries than rich ones.

There are also more *postmodern expressive* elements to the anti-globalization movement. These see anti-globalization less as a political cause and more about the expression of identity. They may not have specific political goals. In fact, having such goals can be looked down upon. For this strand of the movement, the idea is to let plural identities be discovered, flourish and develop, and to see where this takes us, in a way that is not predetermined. The process is the key thing, a democratic and open-ended movement, rather than the end. This part of the movement is more interested in symbolic and representational politics than material goals or political ends. The meetings, demonstrations or street performances are as important as any political changes these methods are calling for.

Some parts of the anti-globalization movement are more formally organized than this, acting as pressure groups on politicians to pursue alternatives to neoliberal globalization with policies which are environmentally concerned and oriented to solving global poverty through means other than free trade. These are *INGOs* and are concerned with issues such as sweatshops and fair trade. They often have hierarchical structures and salaried staff. Examples include organizations such as Oxfam, Care International and Save the Children.

Environmentalist parts of the anti-globalization movement may be at this more organized end of the movement or more *radical and anarchist* in their approach. They are often in favour of self-sufficiency rather than globalization, to cut down on the trade and transport that leads to carbon emissions and climate change. In and beyond environmentalism there are broader more anarchist elements to global justice movements, who are autonomist, seeking separation from both formal institutional politics and capitalism, and more localist in their approach. These sometimes cross over in these ways with left or postmodern parts of the anti-globalization movements. There is an emphasis on radical democracy in the more anarchist parts of the movement.

Anti-globalization movements also sometimes share things in common with anarchism in their types of action. They sometimes use direct action, and anti-politics, meaning an opposition to established mainstream formal political institutions. Anti-globalization has grown, to some extent, through disillusionment at efforts to persuade governments to adopt policies on important global issues, turning instead to politics outside conventional political fora. Rather than try to persuade governments, or to participate in the state to change it from within, many have turned to oppositional action against the state. These elements of the anti-globalization movement are less about seizing state power than delegitimizing it, dismantling mechanisms of rule and winning greater space or autonomy from it (Graeber 2002: 62, 68).

The question that arises is: if change is not going to be achieved through state power, then how else? One answer is through the establishment of alternative spaces based on different ways of living. These are the start of change. Rather than trying to change politics or people, you lead the way by initiating change yourselves in your own separate spaces. This may seem a big project in a world that is highly integrated into capitalist, industrialist and state forms of organization and activity. But anti-globalization is a prefigurative form, aiming to set up alternative forms of organization and live them out as a way of providing an example that can be followed. In this sense the movement itself is, again, the end as much as something trying to achieve an end (see Holloway 2002; Holloway and Callinicos 2005).

An absence in this plan is that it is about democratic forms when the problems of the world need not only different forms of politics, but also substantive policies. Substantive solutions are not evident in these alternative political forms themselves. More anarchist types of organization are open to different sorts of policy or substantive ends. Anarchist proposals are deliberately open to where they will go, and the problem is that the urgency of global problems requires a decisive direction, with speedy implementation of policy solutions. Furthermore, some of these are likely to require centralized regulation and redistribution. The dismantling of centralist forms of political organization, well meant as it is, will undermine as much as enable such changes. Decentralist political forms would, if generalized, be as likely to undermine solutions to global problems as facilitate them. If such forms do not become generalized, as seems possible, then they can act as imaginative guides to alternative ways at local levels, if not to the best mechanisms for solving large-scale global problems in the shorter and more urgent term. In this role, alongside more conventional politics, they are valuable as a source of alternative thinking and imagination.

I have described this movement as anti-globalization and those who are against globalization include also *protectionists and nationalists* of both left and right. Those on the left are concerned with workers' rights in their own country and the effects of globalization and competition from developing countries, through businesses relocating abroad and taking jobs with them, or through lower wages abroad driving down the wages of their own workers. Paradoxical as it may sound, there are internationalist protectionists who see protectionism in developing countries as a better route to growth than openness to free trade, as we saw in chapter 8. At the same time, there are right-wingers who fall into the protectionist camp, who are opposed to immigration and, outside the US, to what they see as the swamping of national cultures by Westernization or Americanization. There is often a populism to their rhetoric. The French National Front is an example of a party that represents this strand. Many, for instance in the US, are opposed to outsourcing because they say it leads to unemployment at home and lowers domestic workers' wages as a result of competition from low-paid labour in developing countries. These strands have many things which differentiate them from previous anti-globalization groups mentioned, and that they can be considered part of a movement whose other members hold great antipathy to them is questionable, but they share in common the ideas of anti-globalization.

As can be seen from this there is a mix of very different bedfellows in the anti-globalization movement (Worth and Abbott 2006 outline this diversity, as do many other commentaries). There is no doubt that many of these actors will not get on well together. Equally,

Table 11.1 Anti-globalization movements	
Strand of the movement	Ideas/perspectives
Traditional left	Labour; anti-neoliberal, anti-corporate; socialist; global reformist.
Postmodern expressive	Process not end; identity more than material.
INGOs	Anti-debt, anti-sweat; fair trade over free trade; environmentalism, development; global solidarity.
Anarchist	Autonomist, self-sufficiency; radical democracy; localization.
Protectionists, nationalists	Domestic workers and agriculture; protectionism; anti-immigration, populist; anti-Americanization; right-wing or worker-oriented left.

individuals and groups cross over the categories I have given. Table 11.1 is intended to help understanding of the different perspectives, but for reasons just mentioned should be seen as an aid to understanding strands and perspectives rather than a hard and fast categorization of anti-globalization movements into different types. This table does not include cosmopolitan democrats, discussed in the last chapter. These are more oriented to international political fora in which states and formal actors are or would be integrated. Nonetheless, some cosmopolitan democrats are interested in the politics of civil society also.

I have used a number of names for the movement, or movements, that I have been discussing, from global justice movement to anti-globalization movement. In relation to the latter term, one question that could be asked is whether this movement is actually *anti-globalization*. It may be against only a certain sort of globalization. And some parts of the movement are actually quite globalist and globalized (Ashman 2004). One of the reasons for looking at these movements in this book is not just that they are critical of globalization, but that they are also globalized and products of globalization themselves – examples of globalization as much as opponents of it. To what extent, then, does it make sense to talk about them as anti-globalization?

Many of the parts of the movement are primarily against what they see as neoliberal globalization, rather than globalization per se. Globalization for them means neoliberal globalization. The anti-globalization movements tend to be against free trade proposals for developing countries. As we saw in chapter 8, developed countries often expect free trade from developing countries that they do not intend to practise themselves in relation to their own industries, if this will cause problems for them. They are seen as imposing an economic model on developing countries that suits the rich, for instance, by opening up developing countries' markets to the developed world. And, as we saw, policies are expected in return for financial assistance which include rolling back the public sector and price restrictions, the consequences of which can include great hardship. The organizations that come under attack are those such as the World Bank and the IMF. And anti-globalizers are against the role of big corporations and neoliberal treaties and organizations, such as the EU and NAFTA, in other parts of the world. So it is the neoliberal policies and their imposition that is seen to be problematic, rather than globalization per se.

At the same time some of the movements have quite a globalized character (e.g., Graeber 2002: 62–5). The international non-governmental organizations are international, with offices and operations in many countries. Trade unions are becoming organized globally, through international links with one another and with global associations, even if they are well behind capital in terms of globalization. Social movements are increasingly globalized – from environmental to peace movements and others, they are located multinationally and organize with each other through global networks. There have been prominent international conferences of the women's movement, for instance, large UN conferences on women in Beijing in 1995 and, in previous years, in Mexico City, Copenhagen and Nairobi. Protests at Seattle and G8 meetings have been composed of activists from around the world, organized globally by using new global communications technologies such as the Internet – see, for instance, the international websites of Indymedia.

As well as having a global composition, the demands of the movement are also often quite internationalist. There is a concern for global issues such as environmental problems and an internationalist concern by developed world movements for the developing world. Some of the movements are not so much against open free trade as against hypocrisy where its proponents require it for others but not themselves. Or they are against free trade on an unlevel playing field. Greater equality in free trade is called for and fair trade, rather than no trade. It is argued that the free movement of capital should be matched with the free movement of people, information and ideas. In short, they are for globalization in ways that are genuinely free and equal.

So anti-globalization movements are not so much against globalization as economically liberal globalization (with the caveat of one complaint that it is not very liberal or open, for reasons given above).

At the same time, this could not be said of all anti-globalization movements. There are strands that are against globalization beyond neoliberalism – protectionist, nationalist and anti-immigration – against globalized culture and in favour of localism and decentralized self-sufficiency. These encompass green, anarchist and far-right anti-globalists. No one would suggest these movements have all that much in common. But they are, with different ideas, critics of globalism beyond just its neoliberal form.

Some parts of the anti-globalization movement disavow conventional forms of politics and also, in some strands, institutions such as growth, capitalism, liberal democracy and the state. They are less about material, economic or political goals as they stand and more about developing alternative ideas. Much of their work is ideological as much as material, aiming to displace dominant *ideas* of capitalism, and global relations. This involves quite a bit of persuading of actors to look at things in a different way. As such their politics aims to be *counter-hegemonic*. The word 'hegemonic' in this context, refers to the work of the revisionist Italian Marxist Antonio Gramsci. Gramsci tried to move Marxism away from economic determinism towards an approach that favoured the capacity of politics and ideology to shape society. It means moral or ideological leadership and is often accompanied by counter-hegemony, the attempt to establish alternative ideological frameworks for explaining and organizing society. The anti-globalization movement has been in part about establishing alternatives to conventional ideas such as growth, neoliberalism, representative democracy and capitalism. In many ways this is the great contribution that anti-globalization has to make. While its successes in actually changing policies can be debated, as we will see below, it has the imagination and creativity to put alternative ideas on the agenda.

Consequently, Gramscian ideas have often been used to explain the anti-globalization movement (e.g., Cox 1999; Rupert 2003; Worth and Abbott 2006). Along with the idea of hegemony comes another Gramscian idea – *transformismo*. This refers to cooption, that the ideas of anti-globalization can be absorbed into neoliberal globalization and transformed into a form that supports or is integrated into or legitimates it, resulting in anti-globalization losing its power as an alternative counter-hegemony. Sustainable development and debt might be examples here. Sustainable development is the idea that societies can develop economically but in an environmentally sustainable way. It is a concept that has been adopted by many mainstream agencies, such as the World Bank, and used to describe development through market forces and freedom of enterprise (Gill 2000: 139). This is not quite what was meant by many of its popularizers in the green movement and has been used to endorse what they were criticizing as institutions that are a threat to sustainability. Similarly, the cancellation of third world debt has been a campaign aim of INGOs and others for a long time. In recent years, this aim has been adopted by governments of some of the world's richest countries, with some debt being cancelled. However, campaigners have complained that the extent of debt cancellation has been exaggerated and tied to conditionalities such as economic liberalization and partnership, as in the case of the 2005 G8 Gleneagles agreement. Debt relief has been coopted by rich country governments to justify policies that are a long way from those proposed by anti-debt campaigns, so taking the edge off debt-cancellation campaigns without their aims being achieved. Sustainable development and debt cancellation have been appropriated by mainstream politics, legitimating policies that are seen as unsatisfactory by many, behind the public appearance of sustainable development and debt cancellation.

Anti-globalization evaluated

There have been a number of criticisms of the global social movements literature. This literature tends to be quite normative. It is an attempt at advocacy as well as description, and many of the criticisms of it are about the extent to which global social movements are real or viable movements. Other criticisms are that the movement is dominated by activists from the North, or that it has been too violent. The former is probably true and inevitable, given the areas of the world with the resources to participate politically in such actions. There has been violence from some parts of the movements on some occasions, but it is far from generalized, and anti-globalization activists have been on the receiving end of violence too. Far more destructive violence has been used by states to achieve their ends than by the movements they criticize for this.

I wish to concentrate on three more substantive criticisms of anti-globalization movements: (1) that they are too diverse to be a movement; (2) that they are mainly oppositional without much of a positive framework; and (3) that they operate outside spheres where decisions are really made and so have limited effectiveness.

The first criticism mentioned is that anti-globalization movements are too diverse to constitute a movement. As we have seen above, anti-globalization extends from far-right nationalists, to left protectionists, to environmental and development INGOs, and to more radical and innovative social movements, to take just some examples. In terms of ideology and mode of organization, these movements are too varied to count as one movement. Some elements are more social-ist and some are more right-wing, while others are protectionist, or at least concerned with the domestic consequences of globalization for rich countries, and others internationalist and concerned with developing countries. Some are against globalization and some for a different kind of globalization. Some are oriented around quite con-ventional formal types of political organization; others around more informal, decentralized, pluralistic, symbolic expressive politics. It could not even be said that what they share in common is that they are civil society movements operating outside the state, as some of the left and right versions have a party political aspect, for instance, in the case of far right nationalist parties.

A possible answer to this criticism is that it makes a fair point, but that it is based on the grouping together of dissimilar movements fol-lowed by an argument that they are dissimilar. Such criticism groups strands which are too diverse to be a movement and then makes an argument out of the fact that they are not a movement, which is a fake and manufactured criticism. A more meaningful way of analysing the anti-globalization movement might be to see these as movements in the plural, oriented towards globalization in one way or another, quite different yet with some things that overlap. If you look at them separately as different kinds of movements with varying agendas and types of organization, while all oriented towards forms of globaliza-tion, then there is not a false grouping of them. Anti-globalization should be seen as an umbrella term rather than one social movement, and even this may be positing too much commonality. The criticism of false homogeneity only works by falsely grouping them all together and then pointing out this does not work. This is why I have some-times used the terminology of anti-globalization movements in this chapter.

The second criticism mentioned above is that anti-globalization is purely oppositional and lacks a positive agenda (Worth and Abbott 2006; Graeber 2002; Scholte 2000). To some extent this is linked to the previous criticism. Anti-globalization movements lack a positive agenda because they are too fragmented to produce anything coher-ent in a positive sense. Even if these movements are broken down as I have suggested, to be looked at separately, there still appears to be mainly an oppositional politics. There is a lot of what the movements are against, with less of a positive agenda – specifically detailed sug-gestions of what they would put in place of globalization.

For Worth and Abbott, the combination of these two problems – diverse movements grouped together and the lack of a positive agenda – leads to a situation where anti-globalization movements are broadly linked and end up being allied with, and so legitimating, partners with objectionable ideologies, such as far-right parties. They are mainly negative and share this across the political spectrum, lacking a clear and concrete enough positive agenda to differentiate themselves from other anti-globalizers in that spectrum, thus giving legitimacy by association to some unpleasant and dangerous parts of the movement. More progressive anti-globalization movements need less inclusive alliances and more of a clear positive message if they are to mark themselves off from reactionary anti-globalization movements and prevent themselves from giving the latter credence.

Where there is no clear positive agenda there is also the danger of *transformismo*. If an anti-globalization movement lacks a positive alternative, and primarily defines itself by what it is against, it is easier for it to be coopted or disarmed by mainstream political actors putting forward their own positive agenda. It is difficult for anti-globalization movements to resist this if they allow a negative viewpoint to dominate without presenting a clear concrete positive alternative. Insofar as there is an agenda amongst anti-globalization groups it is contradictory. Some parts advocate protectionism, others want free trade that is really free, others open trade but structured so the playing field is more level or oriented more to fair trade, and some are more concerned about matters other than trade altogether, for instance, migration, culture, the (dis)organization of politics or symbolic expressiveness.

However, this last point gives the game away on the criticism that anti-globalization movements lack a positive agenda. It would be fair to say that some are more oppositional and less positive, or that there are diverse and sometimes contradictory concrete proposals. But it is not accurate to say that anti-globalization movements lack clear positive proposals. INGOs concerned about development and environment have clear suggestions about fair trade, semi-protectionism in developing countries, energy alternatives that can help prevent climate change, protectionist measures to support domestic workforces in rich countries, policies on migration and culture to limit globalization from the outside, and domestic or multilateral alternatives to neoliberalism based around nationalization, regulation and redistribution. These are diverse and sometimes contradictory because they come from different movements. To some, they may appear to be unpalatable, unrealistic or wrong policies. But there are clear positive agendas here.

To others, the lack of a positive agenda is a good thing (Graeber 2002; Holloway 2002). The movement is about the process, reinventing radically democratic forms where the ends are not finalized in advance but determined by the movement as it goes along. Ends should not be predetermined, so the situation is open for initiatives to rise from below. Or the movement should not be oriented around specific policy alternatives but only concerned with creating its own separate forms of life, which, in terms of goals, are prefigurative at best. Here, the concern is for horizontal, networking, decentralized, consensual forms rather than top–down hierarchical decision-making.

For me, the response that anti-globalization movements have concrete proposals, but diverse ones, is better than the argument that they should not formulate such proposals because they should be concerned with radical democracy. It is good to be imaginative and think about alternatives to formal organized politics and forms of decision-making. At the same time, this underestimates the problems of decisions being reached in a consensual, decentralized way, or how all can be included in large-scale formats, and what would happen in terms of disagreement and stalemate if they were. As I mentioned in the last chapter on cosmopolitan democracy, stalemate is a problem and the way it can be solved can also be problematic – dominant powers imposing decisions to break the impossibility of plural actors agreeing. Consensus or decisions are reached by dissent being marginalized and this is what might happen in social movement democracy. Also, radically decentralized and participatory democracies are open to similar problems as those experienced by formal centralized democracy, such as being dominated by leaders. In fact, these problems can be worse because of the more informal nature of this form of decision-making without formal rules to ensure all are treated equally – what is sometimes called the tyranny of structurelessness – and with decisions made in a less rational way through the passion and feeling of the participatory meeting.

I have looked so far at two criticisms of the anti-globalization movement: that it is too diverse to be a movement; and oppositional without a positive agenda. What about the idea that it is too far outside mainstream politics to have any effect (Halliday 2000; Scholte 2000)? Despite a very visible role for the anti-globalization movement since the 'Battle of Seattle' at the WTO in 1999, corporations and major IGOs still seem committed to a broadly neoliberal perspective on globalization. There have been victories in bringing issues like debt on to the political agenda. But government and corporate action to tackle problems such as global poverty, climate change and the possibility of major nuclear war seem sufficiently far away for these to remain major threats to human life on a large scale.

Halliday (2000) argues that where historically there have been changes on issues that international social movements protested about, these were more to do with political and economic factors than the social movements. The Seattle talks broke down more because of differences between states than noisy protests outside the venue.

The US withdrew from Vietnam because it was unable to win the war and suffered large losses, not because of the anti-war movement. Communism collapsed because of the economic decline of central planning, with political changes towards greater liberalism in the Soviet Union. The 1960s student movement was followed by a period in which conservatism and neoliberalism, initially under Ronald Reagan and Mrs Thatcher and then as a more generally accepted framework, took hold, and in fact became an element in globalization. For Halliday, international social movements have not been key factors in global change.

A key explanation is that those who have the power to make decisions in the world are big corporations and the most powerful states. Global social movements can make issues more visible and even help to set the agenda to some extent, for instance, on debt relief. But they do not make the decisions that matter. Furthermore, Halliday feels that if they were included in decision-making processes there would be paralysis because of the divergences of views and their principally oppositional stance.

Anti-globalization as a political alternative

Halliday has a point, but there are reasons to have a more positive view of the possible effectivity of anti-globalization movements. First, they are visible and it could be said that they have helped to put important issues such as debt and climate change higher up the political agenda of important states. Power is not just about taking decisions but is also about influence over what things decisions are made about, and over what types of alternative possible decisions on those issues are put on the agenda.

Second, historically, workers' movements started out from an oppositional position outside mainstream politics and, in many parts of the world, became political forces to be reckoned with, forming political parties and winning political, economic and social rights for workers. If the global justice movement is outside spheres of power where important decisions are made this does not mean it, or its members, will stay there. Anti-globalization movements may be suspicious of becoming involved in formal politics because of the compromises this involves. But it may help them have more direct effect in power.

Third, the anti-globalization movement has the capacity to ally with more 'political' movements in the world – anti-neoliberal and anti-imperialist states, such as (at the time of writing) Venezuela and Bolivia, that are forming alliances with other like-minded political actors and setting up mutually beneficial trading arrangements and other types of economic and political links. This could be allied with increasingly vociferous governments in poorer countries, many of whom have resources that are in demand by the West and by developing countries like China, such as oil in some African countries, or that are growing and becoming more economically and politically important.

Many anti-globalizers have deep suspicions about becoming involved with more formal politics in the conventional sense, and the feeling may be mutual on the part of state actors. But there are similarities and crossovers with some of the anti-globalization movements. We have seen so far that one political limitation of the anti-globalization movement is its lack of decision-making power, in the form that corporations and states have this, and also that historically social movements have turned into political actors in the more narrow sense and achieved gains that way.

I wish to mention briefly here some anti-globalization states in the world and in the next chapter come back to other alternative centres of power to the USA that do not fall into this category. Hugo Chavez, the President of Venezuela, has provided one of the most high-profile alternatives to what he sees as neoliberalism and American imperialism. Chavez has received a number of large mandates in elections and referenda during his term in power through votes for himself or his platform or supporters and is very popular, especially amongst the poor. He has halted planned privatizations and nationalized key energy resources in his country, putting money into 'missions' to increase education and health and tackle poverty in poorer parts of the country. Chavez is more committed to socialism than democracy and there have been question marks over human rights under his rule. He first tried to come to power in a military coup against a democratic (but corrupt and repressive) government, and was later elected as President. There have been reports of harassment or discrimination against citizens who do not support him and threats towards institutions that do not support his programme. At the same time, there are not political prisoners in Venezuela and Chavez has an electoral mandate, within a competitive party system where independent monitors have endorsed his successes as representing the will of the people. His supporters and critics can both find evidence for or against his democratic credentials. Foreign media have been hostile to Chavez and often reported things which are problematic about his government but in a way which is often out of context, selective and misleading.

Chavez aims to provide a 'twenty-first century' socialist alternative to more neoliberal forms of capitalism. He has tried to build international alliances in this project, partly through using his country's oil wealth and partly through deals with other nations – whether political agreements or economic exchanges – with like-minded powers, from Cuba to Russia. This is in the tradition of Bolivarian pan-Americanism. So there is an internationalist element to his anti-globalization. Recently, there have been other more moderate or radical left leaders in Latin America, from Lula in Brazil, who has built links with global justice movements, and Bachelet in Chile, to the more radical Cuban government, and Morales in Bolivia. Other countries in the region such as Uruguay, Ecuador and Argentina have elected left-leaning leaders. Chavez has exchanged cheap oil for doctors from Cuba, and has offered similar deals involving subsidized oil to other countries, as well as bilateral mutual aid and trade agreements with states such as Argentina, Bolivia and China. He arranged an exchange of subsidized diesel in return for political advice with the Greater London Authority in the UK. And he has arranged other such joint deals with countries critical of America, such as Iran.

Chavez has had warm relations with Fidel Castro, the former President of Cuba. Cuba is another country that has provided a socialist alternative to capitalism and a voice against American power, since the revolution there in 1959. It survived the collapse of communism globally in the late 1980s, but only after a period of exceptional hardship. Mistakes have been made in Cuba. The state is repressive and dissidents have been executed or imprisoned often for very long terms. There is not freedom of speech or competitive party elections. The country and its people are poor and this is in part because of a dogmatic resistance to any corrupting influence from overseas private investment or the use of market incentives. At the same time, Cuba has shown that an alternative to capitalism can work, even in the face of the opposition of the world's most powerful nation, the US, which has supported military action and assassination attempts against Castro as well as a long-standing economic embargo which has failed to unseat the socialist government and has succeeded only in keeping the country poor. The government has prioritized social goals such as high standards of free health care and education, with widely acclaimed success, and Cuba is a peaceful society and one in which there are low levels of inequality or destitution. In such areas Cuba is more successful than many richer countries. It has, for instance, life expectancy and infant mortality levels that are as good as those in rich developed countries with far greater resources.

So there are a range of countries - such as Venezuela, Cuba, Bolivia, Iran and Russia – that provide alternative systems or centres of power to what is seen as US-led neoliberalism and imperialism. The global justice movement has concerns in common with the Non-

Aligned Movement of governments, founded in 1955 with currently 118 members. This supports democratic cooperation in support of anti-imperialism, disarmament, alternative approaches to development, cooperation with the Group of 77 developing nations founded in 1964, and human rights within the context of respect for cultural diversity. A number of these concerns are marked by a critique of Westernization and Western power. More specifically, the NAM has been critical of US foreign policy and supported a Palestinian state and reform of the UN. This is an example of a cooperative governmental forum where there can be cooperation with the non-governmental but like-minded global justice movements. Large, rapidly developing countries and some European states, as we shall discuss in the next chapter, as well as poorer developing countries, can be added to those who might have an interest in joining alliances and mutual agreements with anti-neoliberal, anti-imperialist social movements.

Can anti-globalization movements be effective? They have an agenda-setting capacity and there are historical and current reasons to suggest they can move from social to more political movements, more integrated into structures of actual decision-making and with greater power than they have at present. At the same time, much as some participants may react against this, there are bases for mutual interests with state actors who have shared concerns, criticisms and objectives. These actors have powers of decision-making, the authority of office, and financial and bureaucratic weight. The anti-globalization movement could be made up of combinations of global social movements and state actors with similar social justice objectives. For some in global justice movements, this will only lead to cooption and a loss of radicalism. But it is also a form through which such movements can have an effect in the spheres of those who have power and make decisions.

Further Reading

David Graeber's (2002) article 'The New Anarchists', and Stephen Gill's (2000) 'The Postmodern Prince', provide nice outlines of the forms and arguments of global justice movements.

New Left Review's articles on the 'The Movement of Movements?' feature in various editions from issue 9 onwards, including pieces by Klein, Wallerstein and others.

Gill's article is in a special issue of the journal *Millennium* 29/1 (2000), which is on anti-globalization movements after the Battle of Seattle and includes useful contributions by a number of advocates and critics.

Much anti-globalization activity is organized through the Internet, and websites such as open Democracy (DIY world section) and Znet, amongst others, cover the arguments and practices of global justice movements. Searches with keywords such as 'World Social Forum' and 'People's Global Action' will find more of these.

The Future World Order: The Decline of American Power?

Pᴀᴇᴠɪᴏᴜѕ chapters looked at the power of American culture globally and the significance of US corporations in the world economy and media. The US is also internationally powerful in politics and as a military force. It can affect agreements on nuclear proliferation, climate change and international justice by its opposition, in a way no other state can. Because of its economic resources and military might it can intervene in places economically, politically or militarily to alter the direction of events. The US has the world's largest economy ahead of its nearest rivals Japan, China, Germany, the UK and the EU as a collective entity. Its economic weight in the global economy is very significant, despite the competition and the likelihood it will be overtaken by China as the world's biggest economy. US military might, in terms of extent of deployment, expenditure and technological advancement, hugely exceeds that of any other country. The US is confident it can defeat any national army it chooses to in a war. In Afghanistan and Iraq it has been unable to beat insurgency and make the peace, but it was never in question that it would overcome the state armies of these countries.

Table 12.1 is an adaptation of Nederveen Pieterse's (2003) table on American characteristics and their international ramifications. This includes economic and cultural dimensions discussed in previous chapters, as well as the political and military power that this chapter focuses on. The latter cannot be separated from economics and culture. Economic strength is a basis for political and military power. And cultural or 'soft' power is a basis for political influence and an alternative to 'hard' military power. Nederveen Pieterse discusses American unilateralism and empire as combining economic neoliberalism with political, military and cultural forms (e.g., Nederveen Pieterse 2003, 2004b; for an historical view, see Wallerstein 2006).

Why should sociologists be concerned with American power? The

Table 12.1 American exceptionalism (AE) and international ramifications	
Dimensions of AE	Contemporary international ramifications
Free enterprise capitalism	• US-style capitalism as the norm of capitalism • Washington Consensus, structural adjustment, IMF and World Bank conditionalities • Deregulation of international finance • The role of US MNCs.
Free trade	• Trade policy as a foreign policy instrument • WTO and neoliberal global trade rules • Free trade policies in NAFTA, APEC • Double standards on free trade.
Minimal state and political conservatism	• Non-participation in international treaties • Non-compliance with International Court • Double standards in regional affairs (Middle East) • Promotion of narrow form of democracy – liberal/political • Reduction of government in development policies.
Hegemony of military	• Cold War spillovers – regional intervention and legacies from past ones • Policies of embargoes, sanctions • Unilateralism; acting outside UN Security Council mandate • Militarization of international affairs • Promotion of enemy images (rogue states, axis of evil etc.) • 'Humanitarian militarism': coercive approach to local conflicts • Network of military bases and intelligence surveillance • Nuclear proliferation • Health and environmental hazards of military operations (Gulf War, Balkans, Afghanistan and within the US) • Arms sales, training and fostering regional arms races.
Americanism	• Presenting other states as deviant • Promotion of the 'American way'.
American culture	• Car culture, fossil fuel dependence • Marketing as dominant cultural style • Star and celebrity system • McDonaldization, Disneyfication, Barbiefication • CNN effect and sound-bite culture • Internet, Microsoft, dot.com • African American culture (jazz, hiphop).

Source: Abridged and adapted from Nederveen Pieterse 2003: 310–11

latter is often analysed in terms of hegemony or the balance of power of states in the world, whether America is too unilateralist or pays too much attention to 'hard' power. Surely this is about governments and foreign policy and, as such, to do with political science and international relations rather than sociology. Many sociologists see it this way.

Sociologists have always been concerned about power. This is from Marx who focused on class and ownership of the means of production, to Weber who saw the struggle for power as also about other forms of advantage on the market and non-economic bases, such as status or political organization. Weber added studies on tradition, charisma and bureaucracy as sources of legitimacy for power in society and developed a concept of the modern nation-state. Sociological contributions have included Lukes's study of dimensions of power beyond observable decision-making. Foucault analyses the positive power of discourse through which the world is defined in our knowledge, being as important as the negative and narrower power of sanction. The power of economic ownership, the nation-state, agenda-setting and discourse have all featured in this book.

One characteristic of these approaches is that they do not see power as purely in terms of the state, government or military might. They see it also outside the institutions of government. Political sociology is distinguished from political science, narrowly defined, by an idea of power as located not only in politics but also in wider structures in society, the economy and culture. Power has been a key theme of this book and the focus has been on the way it is exerted through the economy or culture, and the role of US corporations in this, as well as the role of states, something which sociology, rather than a narrowly political perspective, is equipped to expose.

But if sociology wants to understand power at a global level it has to look at American power, including in the state and military. It is self-defeating to see these dimensions as 'not sociological' and the preserve of other disciplines. This indicates a lack of interdisciplinarity and effectively removes the study of some of the most important forms of power in the world from the sociological arena. Sociology is the study of society, and international state power is part of society and has a huge impact on it. It cannot be seen as outside the sociological remit because it is economic or political. The economy and politics also affect other spheres such as culture, as we have seen throughout this book. Sociology needs to get involved here, and it is good that sociologists such as Wallerstein (2003), Harvey (2003) and Mann (2003) have done so.

Some dimensions of American power are specifically sociological. They involve not just 'hard' military or state power but also culture and political legitimacy, 'soft power'. These concerns are close to the heart of sociology as a discipline historically. Sociology has a role to play by looking at social and cultural bases of power but also needs to branch out to areas such as international politics and the military, which are of enormous social significance.

Models of global power

In this section I will look at different ways of conceptualizing how power is divided up globally between actors, especially nation-states. I will look at models that see power as divided along imperial, hegemonic, bipolar, unipolar, triadic, or multipolar lines.

One model of global power is to see it as following an *imperial* or empire model. Into the twentieth century the major imperial power was Britain. Its empire was built on economic expansionism and had tentacles throughout the world, in North America, Asia, Oceania, Africa, parts of Europe (Ireland) and small parts of Latin America. Its imperialism involved different forms of rule, not as direct as French imperialism when colonies were directly appropriated within the French state, but more direct than US power is now.

Whereas the British installed rule in distant states, the US generally relies on more indirect influence, supporting opposition movements or governments economically or by supplying arms. This has happened, for instance, in Latin America, sometimes in support of anti-democratic and repressive movements or governments. The US has also exercised domination through economics and the spreading of capitalism, opening markets to US investment and exports, or through culture, as we saw in previous chapters. In well-known cases, from Vietnam to Iraq, intervention has been military and direct even if aiming to eventually install an indigenous (if preferred) government – 'regime change'. The US interferes in other countries, but it does not incorporate them within its own rule in the way previous empires did. It is better to see the US not as an empire or a form of colonialism, as in the more direct rule of European colonies, but as imperial or hegemonic (Colás and Saull 2006).

The US took over from Britain as the world's leading power in the mid-twentieth century. Supporters of US imperialism see it as providing security, for instance, for Japan in the East and Israel in the Middle East, as a global policeman ensuring order, and protecting or trying to spread liberal freedoms, democracy and the prosperity that comes with capitalism. Its opponents argue that American imperialism imposes power in pursuit of US interests, for instance, through involvement in strategic areas such as the Middle East or East Asia, and by protecting its access to resources such as oil and overseas markets. It is probable that the Afghanistan and Iraq invasions would not have happened without the 9/11 attacks, or if there had been a Democrat President. At the same time, there was a historical predisposition and orientation to such types of intervention.

Imperial and *hegemonic* views of world power are not the same, although they are related and sometimes conflated. Hegemony involves a leadership role, in this case globally, often mobilized through ideological means, rather than actual intervention in others' affairs as suggested by imperialism. So, in this context, the US could be seen as a world power representing liberalism, capitalism and democracy, trying to mobilize support for these through influence rather than actual imperial intervention.

For some, US empire or hegemony is about defending capitalism, by securing resources abroad, spreading neoliberal globalization and getting access to overseas markets (Harvey 2003). For others, such as Nederveen Pieterse (2006), the explanation is less about capitalism alone and more a combination of factors, including a geo-strategic presence overseas, having a superpower syndrome and a long-standing security state approach internationally, in the vein of path dependency theory mentioned in chapter 9. Here, American imperialism is more to do with the influence of interests within the state, and institutional factors, than with ideology or economics. This is reinforced by other internal factors, what Nederveen Pieterese calls the 'American bubble', intense discussion about politics within insular borders, and a lack of knowledge about the rest of the world and how America is perceived globally. This allows the US to continue with an imperial, unilateral attitude and global intervention. For Hardt and Negri (2000), 'empire' is broader than the US and includes other powers such as the G8 and international organizations, the WB, WTO, IMF, NATO and so on, as well as non-state actors such as MNCs, and its mode of rule is more total than just military or economic control.

Imperial or hegemonic views of the world after the collapse of Eastern bloc communism in 1989 give a picture of a *unipolar* world. This is where power is concentrated in one dominant set of hands. British rule was not unipolar because it was in competition with other major European imperial powers such as the French, Spanish, Portuguese and Dutch. US power between 1945 and 1989 was not unipolar because of a cold war split between the US and capitalism on the one hand and the USSR and communism on the other. This divide between two superpowers was *bipolar*. Both sides penetrated across the world, including in military conflicts in Asia (most famously Vietnam and Korea) and in Africa, where the USSR aligned with socialist forces and the US with anti-communist forces, both supplying arms to their sides. This entanglement was a major drain on resources, and is a reason for the collapse of over-extended USSR socialism (Lane 1996) and for the US's large budget deficit which President Clinton tried to tackle, only for George Bush to build it up again through military expenditure.

Bipolarity is said to have ended with the collapse of socialism and the victory of the US and capitalism (Fukuyama 1989). For some, this is where globalization started – with the end of a two-system world to one dominated by a single, more unified, expanding core. While the world has changed with the collapse of many of the most significant socialist (or nominally socialist) regimes, socialism has not disappeared completely. States like Cuba are still socialist and others such as North Korea nominally socialist, while China has a one-party system dominated by the Communist Party, although its economic policies are increasingly capitalist. Elsewhere, socialism as an ideology has not died, either because of its power in explaining capitalism and providing an outline of an alternative, or because of its hold on people's beliefs. In former communist countries, socialist parties still get significant votes, including from those who have experienced socialism and capitalism and are nostalgic for the former, because of the security and greater equality it provided. In the former East Germany, the precursor to the Left Party, Die Linke, was the second biggest party in the 2005 elections, gaining 8.7 per cent of the vote in the unified country and 25.3 per cent in the former GDR. In states such as Venezuela and Bolivia, democratic socialist governments, opposed to neoliberalism and US imperialism, have commanded substantial support, especially from the poor. In elections and referenda, Venezuela's President Chavez, espousing a 'twenty-first century socialism' for the poor, has repeatedly won a clear majority of the vote.

Rivalry to the US comes from economic and political as well as ideological forms. Chinese claims over Taiwan have been an ongoing source of tension between the nuclear power and the US, with many US troops stationed in the region and a pledge from the US to support Taiwan in the event of conflict with China. There have been ongoing tensions between the US and North Korea and Iran over the latter's attempts to develop nuclear weapons (alleged in the case of Iran; admitted in the case of North Korea). There have been tensions between the US and Russia over missile defence and Russia flexes its muscles in surrounding areas militarily and via controls over supplies of energy resources like gas. Both Russia and China dispute US intervention in other states' affairs. These show tensions between the US and rival powers. The rivals do not make a coherent bloc of the sort that occurred in the bipolar split of the cold war era but they provide opposition to US power.

The world, as we saw in chapter 8, is also divided by wealth and income into a number of strata, perhaps most simply seen as developing countries, newly industrializing countries and the developed world. Very big nations in the developing camp are India and China, nuclear powers and homes to about a third of the world's population. Developing or newly industrializing countries have the possibility of organizing to provide collective alternatives, for instance, through regional groupings (such as the South American economic bloc Mercosur), organizations like the Non-Aligned Movement or bilateral alliances. The world is not clearly unipolar or multipolar, more a case of dominant power in a context of rising competitors, opposition and alternatives.

Unipolarity and bipolarity should not be confused with *unilateralism* and *multilateralism*. Unilateralism happens when a nation acts by itself without the agreement or cooperation of others. This is what the US was accused of in the Iraq War where it went ahead despite lack of multilateral endorsement through the UN. But, in a unipolar world, the most powerful actor can act in a multilateral way, seeking agreement with others before it goes ahead with its actions. The US under George Bush was often (but not always) unilateral, bypassing, defying or opting out of the United Nations, the International Criminal Court and agreements on climate change, and pursuing double standards in nuclear proliferation agreements. The US was behind the development of many multilateral institutions but has also seen some of these, such as the UN, as rivals. President Obama, on the other hand, wishes to pursue unipolarity in a more multilateral way.

Two other alternatives to unipolar or bipolar views of the distribution of world power see it as triadic or multipolar. *Triadic* views of the world usually refer, as we saw in earlier chapters, to the way in which economically there are three main blocs in the world, Japan and East Asian NICs, North America, especially the US, and Europe, especially EU states. Much trade and investment goes on within and between these blocs to the relative exclusion of other parts of the world, especially Africa. The triadic model does not include the rise of a different economic type, China, which is becoming a hugely influential presence on the global economic stage in its own right. Nevertheless, it shows the limits of the view of the world as global because the economy is focused in three rich, developed areas. This model is primarily economic. It shows the important issue of the distribution of economic weight in the world but not necessarily power more generally, to which there are political, cultural and military aspects, albeit related to economic factors. As we shall see, the restriction of some blocs in the world to mainly economic functions, with a lesser emphasis on political or military aspects, restricts, for now, their capacity to be countervailing centres of power to the US.

Another view, sometimes associated with the realist perspective in international relations in which nation-states are important, is of a *multipolar* world. Multipolarity sees power not as residing in one place but as distributed amongst many sites. So it involves a pluralist view of power. Power need not be equal but it is spread amongst many. Order is maintained by a balance of power between actors. Multipolarity is different from multilateralism. Different states in the world can operate independently and unilaterally in a balance with one another. Multipolarity can also coexist with multilateralism, for instance, in the case of European Union states combining to make agreements on common economic policies. In such cases the possibility arises that the merged unit will take over the multilateralism of its components.

These models of world power highlight different perspectives on

Table 12.2 Models and perspectives on world power	
Models and perspectives on world power	Definition
Imperial	Dominant power by a state over other countries.
Hegemonic	Leading role, possibly ideological, of a state.
Unipolar	One power dominant in the world.
Bipolar	World split between two dominant powers or blocs.
Multipolar	Power in the world divided between many centres.
Unilateral	Power acting alone without consultation or agreement.
Multilateral	Powers acting in consultation and agreement with others.
Triadic	Three way split of power in the world, e.g., economically.
Cosmopolitanism	Global deliberation and agreements made together by plural cooperative actors.
Realism	State interests dominate.
Marxism	Economic interests, conflict and inequality are behind state and global forms of power.

what motivates actors in such orders. As we saw in chapter 10, one model is of *cosmopolitanism* amongst world actors, where they can multilaterally forge a common or agreed consciousness around norms such as democracy and human rights. Although well meant, it is not clear how viable this perspective is. There are different ideologies and interests in the world. Evidence from negotiations on some of the most serious problems facing humanity – climate change, nuclear proliferation and world trade – suggests that states and other actors tend to act according to what they can gain for their own interest rather than in a more other-regarding way.

This is how the *realist* perspective sees it, with states pursuing their interests, order being maintained by their powers balancing out one another or by a hegemonic power that acts as a global policeman amidst the multiplicity of self-interested actors. *Marxism* tends to take a realist view but with the economy emphasized. States, but also corporations, act in a self-interested way, capital accumulation and profit being the main guiding force for their actions. Marxists are less sure about the prospects of this being maintained in a benign balance, putting more emphasis on contradictory interests and inequalities of power in which conflict and change is likely.

The US as strong

I will focus now on American power. States in the world have been differentiated into pre-modern, modern and postmodern (e.g., see

Cooper 2003). *Pre-modern states* are states that don't really work. Often this is in postcolonial nations which were left by imperial powers with a Western-style state which did not fit to borders or groupings with a meaningful shared identity of a national type. In these countries the most powerful actors can be non-state agents, such as armed militias associated with warlords or insurgent groups. These are sometimes called 'failed states' and have been found in places like Somalia, Afghanistan, Liberia, Sierra Leone, Sudan, Congo and Chechnya.

Modern states are not interested in conquering or intervening in pre-modern states unless they become a threat, for instance, in Afghanistan because of the harbouring of al-Qaeda. They operate with a balance of power or hegemonic state view of the preservation of order. The ultimate guarantee of security is force, for example, against an intervening state or by the hegemonic state keeping the peace. The US has been classified as a modern state and the only one in the world that has a global strategy. In this model it is a guardian of security through armed force.

From this point of view, the biggest threat to the US is from weapons of mass destruction (WMDs). America can counter other types of physical threat with its military power. Hence the US desire to develop missile defence systems and its interventions against nuclear proliferation in countries seen to be unfriendly, alongside attempts to maintain nuclear superiority. In most states, the imperial urge is dead and the US is as much a hegemonic state as imperial because it does not rule directly. It has worries about places where the balance of power looks endangered and threatening to its interests, for instance, in the Far East where China is becoming more powerful, or in the Middle East. In such places the US has a large military presence or has been a direct military intervener. The US has not accepted rules of mutual surveillance or mutual restrictions, on issues such as nuclear proliferation (e.g., it allowed an exception to nuclear restrictions for India), international justice (e.g., it has not joined the International Criminal Court which adjudicates on war crimes, crimes against humanity, and genocide), or energy use (it has in the past resisted international agreements on tackling climate change) unless it sees them as in its own interests.

These rules of mutual surveillance and interference are character-istic of *postmodern states*. In such states relations are sustained not by a balance of power or hegemony but by mutual openness, treaties and pacts. These go across states and make borders less important. Some European countries are postmodern states with mutual inter-ference agreements on arms inspections, international crime and justice, and common environmental and economic agreements. The European Union is not a military pact but was formed in part to create mutualism between countries to prevent conflicts like those of the two world wars. Postmodern states do not want to go to war with one another or, unlike modern states, to conquer. But some postmodern states do not apply these standards to outsiders, for instance, in the case of the UK in Iraq.

Robert Kagan (2003) has tried to explain why America fits the modern mould while European states are postmodern. In his words Americans are from Mars and Europeans from Venus and represent, respectively, power and paradise. For Kagan, these identities are longer running than September 11 and George Bush's foreign policy. The US's approach, Kagan says, is coercion and unilateralism, and for America the world is divided into friends and enemies. It is less patient than Europe and less inclined to pursue solutions to overseas issues through multilateralism. Europeans favour diplomacy and persuasion; they are more patient and tend to go through international agreements and institutions. They use commercial and economic ties to bind themselves together as postmodern states, the EU being the obvious example.

Why are there these differences between the US and Europe? Kagan says Europeans and Americans have similar values. Both believe in democracy, individual freedom and capitalism. Europe does not have more of a moral consciousness. For Kagan, the difference is psychological. Europe had a psychology of the strong when its major nations were imperial military powers. The US had a psychology of the weak. But the roles have been reversed. The US uses strength to secure order because it is the strong global actor. Europe's reliance on multilateralism is the result of its weakness.

Europe has to be multilateral because it cannot resolve issues through force. This is less a difference of culture or philosophy than capability. The US can exert unilateral force, but Europe has less power so it is in its interest to pursue multilateral solutions to restrain the US. Europe is inclined to be more tolerant because it faces fewer threats, in part because it is weaker and so less of a threat to others. Europe has a security guarantee from the US which protected it in the Second World War and cold war, and allows it to develop a non-military outlook in the knowledge it will be protected by the militarily strong. These reasons for Europe's more multilateral approach of peaceful diplomacy and patience are based on weakness.

Can the US keep up its unilateralism and hard economic and military power? Kagan is confident that it can and must. It is the world's policeman and keeper of order and the only state powerful enough to be so. The US has immense military superiority. It spends 45 per cent of the world's military expenditure. The next biggest spenders are the UK and China with 5 per cent of world expenditure each (SIPRI 2008:

11). America has the capacity to continue going it alone. In Iraq and Afghanistan other nations sent soldiers as part of the US-led alliance, but the US did not need them in military terms and took on the main burden of the fighting itself. In the Afghanistan war, the US did most of the war-making with other partners coming more in security roles after the initial conflict had been won.

Kagan's analysis can be questioned. The US does not always do what it says it does as a hegemonic protector of world order. It advocates the promotion of democracy but has mixed democratic credentials itself. Money plays a big role in American elections and the US has undermined democratic governments in other parts of the world, for instance, Latin America. Its record in supporting international human rights is problematic, both in governments it has supported that have abused human rights and in its own practices, for instance, in Guantanamo Bay. It has contradicted its promotion of free markets by expecting economic access and openness from others while itself maintaining subsidies and restrictions on imports. While under the protection of the US, in its role as global policeman and protector of security, hundreds of thousands of civilians have died, and insecurity and conflict have increased in many of the places it has been involved, Iraq being the most prominent recent example.

This has been exacerbated by the effects of climate change. The US is a chief contributor to this and it has an effect on the security of poor people in other parts of the world. Climate change causes desertification, loss of fertile land and flooding. This leads to hardship, migration and conflict over declining resources. The US has undermined nuclear disarmament by expecting non-proliferation from states such as Iran and North Korea, but not from friends, such as Israel and India, and by maintaining huge nuclear superiority while expecting others to give up nuclear weapons. In places like the Middle East, US power seems oppressive and unfair, and a cause of insecurity and violence rather than a protector. Many countries and groups fear or resent the US's role. In response, insecurity for America is increased by the prospect of what Chalmers Johnson (2004) calls 'blowback' against it.

There may, contrary to what Kagan says, be value differences between the US and Europe. Europeans may have different values concerning conflict and multilateralism as a result of their experience as the site of large-scale war and death in the twentieth century, rather than because of a psychology of weakness. Some European societies put a stronger emphasis on social values, welfare, the state and collectivism than the US. These are likely to feed into a less unilateralist and more peaceful attitude to external relations. And it is possible that America's exercise of power in such a unilateral and 'hard' way has threatened its own power. Being Mars could as much contribute to

America's downfall as maintain its strength, as critics of 'hard power' argue.

The US as too hard: hard power and soft power

A key proponent of the soft power thesis is Joseph Nye (2002). It has become more popular since the wars in Afghanistan and Iraq, and has been supported by Democrats such as John Kerry and President Obama. The US beat the armies it fought against but has not been able to defeat guerrilla action and has alienated allies and others for the unilateral and military approach it took. This approach lost the US government popularity domestically, amongst allies and more widely, and it is perceived that the US needs to persuade more and use force less. Nye agrees with Kagan's interpretation of the US as a hegemonic power but argues that it relies too much on hard power and needs to use soft power more.

The US has discovered it cannot solve all the problems it wants to by itself. For instance, finding al-Qaeda in Afghanistan needs the cooperation of others, intelligence from other parties locally, and neighbouring and friendly countries. Cooperation in terms of intelligence and political support is needed to solve problems of terrorism, drugs, disease and environment. These problems are global, have origins in various countries and require others' actions for solutions to be effective. Terrorism can be cross-national and many actors have intelligence about it and sovereignty over relevant territories. Drug supplies come from countries such as Afghanistan and Colombia. The US has found that military force can have severe costs – political (loss of support from other nations and domestically if there are heavy casualties and ongoing resistance), social, human and economic. America has also found that it cannot make peace after wars on its own. It needs cooperation, and it is easier to get support after military action if this is established before the conflict. Making peace in the former Yugoslavia, for instance, required multinational support from regional government (i.e., the EU) and NGOs from around the world, and involved mobilizing their support as early as possible. All of these add up to show that military action is limited in what it can achieve, costly in a number of ways or even counterproductive. Furthermore, it shows the value of multilateral rather than unilateral action. President Obama has argued that the US needs to rethink its commitment to military unilateral action to solve problems and aim for more peaceful and multilateral actions.

Nye and Ikenberry argue that the US has the attractiveness and multilateralism to move away from hard power. For Ikenberry (2004), the US is multilateral. Other advanced industrial democratic states have not tried to pull away and counterbalance its power. Amicable relations with powers in Europe and Japan in trade, investment and political alliances have been maintained. The US has been behind international rules-based institutions such as the UN and WTO, so it is not straightforwardly a unilateral and militaristic power alone. Its unipolar power is experienced positively by some, such as Japan, as well as negatively by others, and within all states public views of America vary and respond to different aspects of its policies, depending on who is in government, the state in general or American culture. Antipathy to the US is not straightforwardly the only clear issue. It varies according to whether it is capitalism and democracy that people are integrated into, or political-military power globally, or US policies in various areas that may change over time. So the US's relations with other parts of the world are variable and, while it is often unilateral and militaristic and opposed, this is by no means the only shape and meaning its power takes.

Ikenberry argues that the advantages possessed by the US mean its power is likely to be maintained beyond hard power. The US has massive military power and states trying to build up equivalence may face opposition from neighbours who feel threatened by this. So military counterbalancing is unlikely. Some countries value the security provided by American military protection and the large market the US provides for exports. In a nuclear age, war against the US does not make much sense because of the devastation modern nuclear weapons would cause. The eras of overturning great powers by war have gone. People are more likely to relate to the US via peaceful and multilateral means.

For Ikenberry, the US is geographically remote from other great powers and this makes it less threatening. Historically, it has been drawn into world affairs as a balance to other powers rather than a dominator, for instance, in the two world wars and after that as a presence in Europe, Asia and the Middle East. In the latter cases its involvement has been as guarantor of security, for instance, through NATO, as a protector of Japan and restraint on its military development, and a mediator between Israel and others. These make it seem less threatening, and states fear being abandoned by the US more than dominated by it. Ikenberry says that US power expanded after the years of European imperialism in a way that was more about access to other parts of the world than outmoded territorial control. So the US did not appear coercive or imperialist.

Ikenberry argues that the US is democratic and integrated with other democratic states. Democracies are unlikely to use power against each other. They feel less threatened by other states that are democratic. The US shares with Western states a belief in civic nationalism (national identification with common political institutions such as the rule of law, democracy and rights), rather than ethnic nationalism based on race, religion, language or ethnicity. The US's democracy, rule of law and liberalism make it more predictable, cooperative and transparent, and so easier to build relations with. It is easier for outside powers to have access to influence on America, and the US is integrated into international institutions such as the UN, IMF, World Bank, NATO and WTO, in which it has surrendered itself to restrictions by the international community. In the international sphere, the US is in synch with other nations' drive to modernization and industrialization. Its model fits with where other countries in the world are going. Ikenberry says that the US may become more entangled in multilateralism because of economic interdependency, which requires greater multinational coordination of policies. This signals restraint and cooperative will, both likely to encourage the cooperation of other states.

Nye sees the attractiveness of the US to other parts of the world as also already in place. Soft power involves attraction and persuasion, based in values and culture, or the appeal of economic or political systems. People will do things because they are persuaded they are right or because of the desirability of what is possible (e.g., capitalism, freedom and democracy). Soft power achieves things through persuasion to the course of action, rather than it being forced on them by economic sanctions or military force.

Nye feels the US can take action via international institutions, not just because multilateralism is right in principle but also because it will do more to legitimate its actions. Furthermore, he is confident in the attraction of the US, and of its values and institutions, which can win people over. This includes values and practices of democracy, personal freedom, the upward mobility of the American dream, and openness. The US has dominance in the media, where such attractive images are disseminated, whether in Hollywood film or American TV programmes. Images of American life are beamed across the world. There is a sociological approach here to understanding power. It is secured not just by unilateral action or force. Social dimensions of power are important – collective action and power secured through the attractiveness of institutions and values, culture and image. Power is not just about force but also about culture, media and legitimation.

Nye's analysis of the importance of soft power makes sense. But it is not clear that soft power and multilateralism have existed in all the ways that Ikenberry and Nye suggest, although this could improve under President Obama. Ikenberry is right that the US is integrated into multilateral military and economic relations – through organizations like NATO and combined operations in post-war Afghanistan, and through economic agreements, for instance, on trading relations. In military invasions in Iraq and Afghanistan it sought Western allies, as well as allies within these countries – the Northern Alliance and warlords in Afghanistan and militia in Iraq who switched from resistance to alliance with the US against al-Qaeda.

But the US is not in principle multilateralist. These military operations would have been pursued with or without allies and they sidestepped UN approval. The US has engaged in multilateralism when it is to its advantage and undermines or bypasses it when it is not. How unilateral or multilateral the US is depends in part on who is governing. It is difficult to see how Ikenberry's case for the US as a multilateral power at a structural level over time and one which has the credibility to attract the soft power of legitimacy holds up. Ikenberry's case comes from within American ideological views of itself and is symptomatic of an inability for America to see itself from an external point of view. A number of the multilateral credentials that Ikenberry presents may seem plausible theoretically and from a US point of view, but do not match up with evidence from US foreign policy and how it is perceived globally.

To take some examples from Ikenberry's analysis, the US has not been a good practitioner in international rules-based institutions. As we have seen in this book, it has tended to go along with these when it suits them, while disregarding them in relation to human rights, nuclear proliferation and climate change, for instance, when it does not. Its record as a multilateralist in such institutions is disparaged in other parts of the world. Many postwar multilateral organizations that are backed by the US promote a US point of view more than that of other countries – for instance, the WB, the IMF and the WTO. It favours friends but not its enemies in such institutions – for example, Israel and India when it comes to nuclear proliferation, but not Iran and North Korea. To some nations not under US protection, its global military deployment seems more interference or threat, rather than protective. The geographical distance of the US does not make it less of a danger – distance has not been an obstacle to US interventions, whether in Latin America, Asia or Europe, or against military threats on the other side of the world in Russia. The nuclear balance is no guarantee against threats to, or from, the US – during the Cuban missile crisis the world was on the verge of nuclear war, held back only by Soviet Union and US political leaders who resisted pressure from advisers to launch nuclear attacks. Evidence does not coincide with beliefs the US has about itself – it has not been perceived as multilateral, and therefore as a state that can be trusted to be benevolent and engaged with cooperatively. The US is multilateral when it can achieve what it wants in that way, as in cases mentioned above, but equally it often sidesteps multilateralism when it cannot achieve its ends that way and is more unilateral. Its multilateralism is dependent on whether this will work for it, rather than principled or consistent (see Colás and Saull 2006).

It is also difficult to see that the US has the power of global attractiveness and therefore potential for soft power to the extent that Nye argues. If what Nye says about American values and achievements is true, many states and societies around the world do not find these desirable. American-style capitalism, individual freedom and democracy are sometimes seen as challenges to local religious and collective values and to more social or economic ideas of freedom and democracy. The actuality of American values and achievements is not plausible to some. America seems to be a politically corrupt, undemocratic, unequal society, with poverty and violence, both internally and in relation to other parts of the world. America is not a land of opportunity, freedom and openness for all, for instance, for poorer Americans and for people in other parts of the world affected adversely by the American dream – such as those affected by climate change due to US energy use, or by US interventionist attempts to maintain influence elsewhere.

Much US power comes from its position as the world's largest economy, rather than its meritocratic appeal. Its wealth secures domestic consent from the majority at the expense of a poor disenfranchized and excluded minority. The US is prosperous but with inequality, poverty, violence, easy access to guns, a large prison population and often flawed use of the death penalty. Its wealth funds its military power and is in part the basis for its political power, as much as its external credibility as a free and democratic society is. There is an inconsistency between US appeals for democratization globally and itself as a model of democratic attractiveness. Political corruption is a major issue for voters in elections. Voter registration has been weaker amongst poor black voters who support the Democratic Party. In the 2000 presidential election, crucial votes were questioned, some electors were unable to vote and the winning candidate had fewer votes than the loser. Huge (often corporate) funding is necessary for election to Congress or the presidency, unlike in most other democratic states, and is often gained in return for contracts or favourable policies to funders. The critical media is quite small and not widely accessed, so there is a narrowness to political debate. Critical voices are often treated as pariahs and tarred as unpatriotic. Externally, the United States' commitment has been to friends rather than democracy – it has attempted to undermine democratic governments though support for military opposition, attempted assassinations or coups against democratic leaders, from Chile and other Latin American states in the past to Palestine and Venezuela more recently. Its record on human rights has been questioned, for instance, in Iraq and the illegal prison camp at Guantanamo Bay where prisoners have been held for years without a trial or access. The US has been unwilling to join international criminal fora like the ICC because it does not wish to be subjected to their jurisdiction. In other words, it has expected to be excused from human rights transgressions for which it condemns others.

So it is difficult to see how the US meets the criteria of multilateralism, legitimacy and attractiveness that Nye and Ikenberry say it has or can achieve on the basis of its current society. This may improve under President Obama, but many of these problems are longstanding and pre-date the Bush administration. So there are indications they are, to some extent, structural. But, if we can overcome these doubts and agree that soft power is the answer, Michael Mann's view is that the US is already in decline as an imperial power across a range of spheres.

The US as a declining imperial state

Mann (2003, 2004) separates American power into economic, military, political and ideological dimensions. *Economically*, the US has been dominant since 1945, especially in production and trade and increasingly finance. However, in production and trade now, the US is (or is the major part of) one bloc amongst three. Inequalities and imperialism in trade are constituted as much by the dominance of the three blocs as by America alone. As mentioned in other chapters, some poorer countries are increasingly resistant and form blocs and alliances through mutual agreements, sometimes (if not always) in opposition to US imperialism. What America has economically in the world, for Mann, is power more than hegemony, domination or legitimacy. It is a powerful actor, but does not dominate because economic power is divided with a number of other significant nations and fast-developing blocs. With such abridged power it is not able to dominate alone, even if it is very important.

Militarily, the US is more unrivalled. It shares its military position less with other powers than in the case of the economy. As mentioned above, the US spends 45 per cent of the world's military expenditure, with the next highest spender contributing 5 per cent. For Mann, the key feature of American military power is not nuclear weapons. Many states have these, albeit not such advanced models as the US. Neither is it sheer number of soldiers – China has more, and India, North Korea and Russia nearly as many. One key factor behind the US's military power is its global deployment. In 2008, the US had 290,000 of its 1.3 million troops stationed abroad in 39 of the world's 195 or so countries; 150,000 were in Iraq, 85,000 in Europe (mostly Germany), about 60,000 in Japan and Korea, and 31,000 in Afghanistan (US Department of Defense 2008). Another factor is the strikepower of its planes, missiles, ships and smart (i.e., self-guided) and robotic weapons. What has been called the Revolution in Military Affairs (RMA), primarily big technological advances in the computerization of weaponry, has been exploited by the US. What it allows (for instance, precision bombing from the air and offshore ships) is a large impact on opposed forces with minimal casualties to US forces (Shaw 2005). So while the US is powerful rather than dominant in the economy, it is difficult to say something as restrained for the military, where the US is in a dominant position over all other forces globally. However, while it can win wars against other armies, it is less able to pacify populations in peacetime, as shown in Iraq and Afghanistan, and it is not so able to secure its political objectives through or after war. This brings us from the economy and military aspects to the position of the US in political and ideological power and dominance.

It would be wrong to downplay the *political* power of the US. The US can either get its way in international organizations like the UN Security Council or NATO or, when it does not, bypass them and act unilaterally. It is economically and militarily powerful enough to do so without having to fear severe retribution of the type it is able to impose on others through, say, sanctions or military action. But US political power is limited in that it is not easy for it to pacify or impose political order on other states. The attempt to do so militarily in Iraq and Afghanistan has been difficult to accomplish. There are obstacles to the US enforcing, for instance, nuclear non-proliferation in states it sees as threats, certainly by itself and without the cooperation of allies. No actions – whether those of persuasion, economic sanctions or military force – seem assured of success in terms of the US achieving its political objectives abroad, securing energy resources, preventing the development of weapons of mass destruction in hostile hands and being sure of friendly regimes in strategically important places. So politically the US is powerful. But whether this power allows it to get its way in the world is less certain.

That it can do so through *ideological* means is in doubt, despite power and the increasing global penetration of American (or Americanized) media and culture. The globalization of communications has not only been to the advantage of the US. Transnational TV stations and the Internet have also helped the spread of alternative ideologies of nationalism, anti-imperialism, racial equality and human rights, against the US. Here, the spread of literacy has helped, as has the availability of TV and of wireless communication and mobile telephony in areas without a highly developed fixed-line infrastructure for communications. The Arab TV station Al-Jazeera is one example of an international media outlet where alternative perspectives to that of Western powers and the US can be found.

The ideological appeal of the US is self-undermining in some respects. One problem is when the US propounds values of democracy, freedom and human rights. Global communications help it to spread these as US ideas but also to show that the US undermines them in its own actions, in ways mentioned above. Flaws in US society attract negative evaluations – inequality and poverty, democracy, environment, unilateralism, militarism, the US bias to Israel in the Middle East, the Iraq War and war on terror, and inconsistency in its stipulations about restricting weapons of mass destruction and condemning state terrorism. In many parts of the world the actual record of the US on what it condemns seems poor and global communications are used to draw attention to this.

In the 2007 Pew Global Attitudes Survey, majorities in 20 out of 47 countries surveyed (including America) gave more unfavourable than favourable opinions of the US. This was especially the case in the Middle East and Asia, including allies such as Turkey and Pakistan, and European countries such as Germany, France, Spain and the Czech Republic. In many places, favourable views of the US have been in decline. One reason given for anti-Americanism is the US's unilateralism, with 90 per cent of Swedes, 89 per cent of the French, 83 per cent of Canadians and 74 per cent of the British seeing this as a problem, as do majorities in all European countries surveyed. Majorities in 30 of the 47 nations surveyed say the US does not take into account the interests of countries like theirs, and 39 of 47 countries have majorities who do not support the US war on terror. In 32 of the 47 countries a majority feel that the US makes global inequalities worse. Many people express opposition to American ideas of democracy. This has increased in nearly all the 33 countries where trends are available for the period 2002–7. Majorities in 43 of the 47 countries, including 63 per cent in the US itself, say the US promotes democracy only when it is in its interests rather than wherever it can. American science, technology and popular culture are popular, but in 37 of the 47 countries majorities say they do not welcome the spread of American customs. In 34 out of 37 countries where data is available the US is the nation blamed most for environmental problems (Pew Global Attitudes Project 2007).

So the US is economically powerful but not dominant. US hegemony seems to be in decline or precarious. Economically, it faces strong and growing competition from the Far East, Europe and maybe in future from other quarters. China is the world's third largest economy behind the US and Japan. It will soon overtake them. Economic success underpins political and military power and ideological legitimacy, so this could have knock-on effects in these areas. Militarily, the US outflanks all other states and can win wars, but pacification of populations and achieving political objectives through military action are a different matter. Politically, the US is powerful but faces obstacles in achieving its objectives globally. It does not have the final word and some of its political importance rests on its economic weight, which is becoming more contested. The US has access to media dissemination and what is an attractive message and image to some. But it has failed to secure legitimacy as widely as might be expected from this. In global civil society there are mixed feelings towards the imperial role of the US, and without ideological or soft power it is difficult for the US to achieve all of its objectives. For Mann, it is still a very important power but a failed empire whose best hope is as a leader in a multilateral framework. Alternative powers include the EU, Japan, Russia, India and China, in most cases economic clout being an important basis for their importance.

American power and the alternatives

What does the future hold, then, in terms of the distribution of world power? A multipolar balance of power model seems unlikely because of inequalities in power. There are too many huge powers at the core, richer, militarily stronger and politically more influential, for others more peripheral to have a status that comes near to that required for a really multipolar world.

As I discussed in chapter 10, global democracy – cosmopolitan multilateralism in global institutions – seems unlikely at present given inequalities in power and the way such global institutions are either used by Western powers to impose their will or bypassed. Global institutions exist and may well develop further. Because they are there and correspond to the global nature of problems, actors should engage with them and use them to the best of their ability. The decision by the UN Security Council to send troops to Darfur to prevent large-scale killing is an example of where such institutions can be used for positive ends (albeit belatedly and weakly in this case). At the same time these institutions are governed by power that is structured unequally, and marked by divergent ideologies and interests that stymie consensus (as was the case with the Darfur decision). This makes a conflict perspective better for understanding where possibilities exist in global politics. The aspiration to consensus, while well intentioned, can supply a tool for Western power to use or ignore, and may also give false hope of common worldwide agreement when other political paths may be more fruitful.

Collective security and multilateralism might increase in Europe and other regional blocs and alliances as US power wanes. The US and Europe may feel that they have a lot in common as they face economic competition from China. But the EU is more advanced than other regional blocs, and more on economic than other bases. One perspective sees Europe, or the EU, as a countervailing power to the US that can restrain US foreign policy and provide an alternative centre of power (Leonard 2005; Haseler 2004; Rifkin 2004; also Garton Ash 2004; Peterson and Pollack 2003). To some extent this is a response to European opposition to the Iraq War from states such as Germany and France, and the idea that invasions such as the one of Iraq could be held back by opposition. Both as an important economic bloc and politically, Europe could provide competition with the US economy and a counterbalance to its foreign policies.

But there are reasons to be dubious about such a possibility. Europe was divided over the Iraq War. The UK, some Central European states such as Poland, which tend to be pro-American because of US support for them in the Second World War and cold war, supported the invasion of Iraq, as did other European states such as Italy and Spain. While the EU has created common economic agreements, it has not forged a common political identity or foreign policy stance. Difficulties in negotiating economic treaties and the collapse of the European Constitution show some of the problems with establishing a shared political identity. Constituent states have different histories, national cultures and traditions (e.g., from state/collectivist to liberal/individualist, more egalitarian and less so) and varying interests, so that a common bloc would be difficult, including in foreign policy. Furthermore, governments change within the states that make up the EU. Having said this, EU countries have created a common economic area and have been involved in Israel and Palestine, and in relation to nuclear proliferation in Iran. Although there are reasons for doubt, it would be mistaken to rule out the EU as having a role in politics globally.

Conflicts within and between nations, as much as cooperation, are likely to escalate, within a changing but still unequal world order. These will be over resources, declining oil, the control of gas, and declining water and fertile land in Africa caused by climate change. Technological alternatives will lag behind the loss of traditional sources of energy. There are ongoing tensions in parts of the world where states' military power is so great that a conflict could have severe consequences, for example, in Taiwan, Korea and Kashmir. For observers such as Hirst (2001) and the US National Intelligence Council (2008), the world is becoming more conflictual and chaotic, with Western democracy challenged and conflict over scarce resources. International institutions are too weak to respond, and nuclear proliferation makes major catastrophe more likely. States are as important as ever, especially after the financial crisis, with the US less dominant and so forced more into multilateralism, especially under a president more committed to this. Responses to the financial crisis have been made mostly by governments and have varied nationally.

With the decline of the US, one question is whether *China* will emerge as a dominant power. A number of contenders for global leadership have been mentioned, with Europe or the EU suggested as a possibility, as just discussed. Russia has a strong state, is a large country with military power, energy resources that many are reliant on and a belligerent attitude towards the US. One possibility is that it could go back in the direction of the superpower status it had when the dominant part of the USSR. Some in the US fear this. India is a big and fast-growing economic power, with nuclear weapons and the US as a friend. Nevertheless, it does not carry the same economic and political clout or global ambitions as other current or rising powers. China seems to be most likely contender for the most imposing global power of the future. It is a huge, fast-growing and economically mighty power.

China is on track to becoming the world's largest economy, currently the third largest in the world and catching up with those ahead of it. This has happened under the centralized control of the Communist Party, rather than through political pluralism and democracy. It has developed gradually and in an experimental way via zones of capitalism, private property and profit retention being allowed. Over time China has opened up to the world economy, becoming a major exporter. Much of the development has happened in urban areas, especially on the east coast. As we saw in chapter 8, this involved globalization in terms of export production, for instance, of electrical goods and textiles, but not initially through openness to the global economy in other ways such as imports. Chinese growth was driven by a strong state, managed initially behind protectionist barriers, rather than through open competition.

China has been an astute political operator, developing more capitalism while maintaining an undemocratic one-party system and repression of dissent. It has established mutual relations with oil-producing African nations to ensure ongoing oil supplies. China buys oil from African countries and in return provides expertise and workers for projects such as road-building. There is a large Chinese diaspora and many Chinese study at universities in other parts of the world, bringing back what they have learned to their home country.

Development has been unequal and inequalities have risen. There have been severe environmental effects from China's growth that will be exacerbated as rapid development careers ahead. China is starting to rival the US for the status of world's leading carbon emitter, and this will increase as resource use grows and car ownership spreads, although historically the US is much more responsible for the stage climate change has reached so far. Pollution is acute in some areas of China and the country is building a new coal-fired power station every week. Populations have been displaced for economic development and construction, leading to local protests that are sometimes responded to in a draconian way. There is political and economic corruption, which China has shown its concern for by severe punishments. Those sceptical about China's rising power argue that such problems and conflicts could stem this rise. For some, an undemocratic and illiberal state is incompatible with economic success, a view regarded by others as too Western-centric (Hutton and Desai 2007).

Economic power is at the basis of other forms of power. Political weight in the world comes in part from having energy resources, a large market, being the source of foreign investment, or having products that provide tough economic competition for other nations. So China's huge and growing economic weight will be at the basis of its role outside the economic sphere, in political influence and mightier military power. China has a massive population, about 1.3 billion, the largest in the world, and one-fifth of the world's population. This gives it a large labour force and domestic market to whom it can sell more consumerist goods as affluence spreads, even before it sells to international markets where it is already successful. Taking on board capitalism and consumerism has led to a Westernization of Chinese culture in some areas. But China has also been an exporter of its own cultures through its diaspora and in forms such as food, martial arts, religion, medicine, exercise, art and film. China has the largest number of Internet users in the world, partly a product of its size, and as this rises the movement of culture and information in and out will increase. Censorship is only partly effective in preventing this.

China's population gives it the potential for a large army. It has the largest in the world with over 2 million personnel and nuclear weapons. It does not rival US military expenditure, power, deployment and advanced technology, and the US acts as a protector in the local region for Taiwan and Japan. But nuclear weapons and its army make it a country that can deter powers in its own region and elsewhere, and its growing wealth and size will allow it to expand its military capability in the future. Sometimes China has strategically contrary interests or stances to the West, on issues such as Western military intervention, on the UN Security Council, in its local region in relation to Taiwan, and its arms sales to countries such as Pakistan and Iran. At present Russia is more awkward politically and militarily for the US, and China is showing no clear signs of serious military intentions beyond its own borders. Militarily, it is a regional presence that does not yet match the global presence it has achieved economically. But China's stances on foreign policy issues and its potential in the future could change that. There are regional tensions between China and others such as Russia, India, Taiwan and Japan, over historical, sovereignty or border issues, territorial disputes or oil and gas claims. America is a friend of some of these states, with large numbers of troops in the area. This may deter China but would also make it a serious situation should China in the future use military force to tackle any of these issues.

There are reasons to be doubtful about China's rise and whether the country will continue to become the major world power, and an alternative or replacement for the US (Segal 1999; Buzan and Foot 2004; Breslin 2005; Hutton and Desai 2007). China is running away as an economic globalizer, but politically and militarily it is committed to state sovereignty and self-determination rather than global power and is more regionally than globally significant. China may stumble because of inequality, environmental problems, a repressive and corrupt government, internal conflict, separatism, or popular opposition to the one-party state. Economic liberalization could open the doors for greater political liberalism and democratization. Many Chinese travel abroad to be educated and return home with experience of other systems and societies, such as that in the US. If not done carefully and gradually, as with economic liberalization, political liberalization could undermine economic development and social and political stability because of dissent and upheaval, currently stifled by a repressive state. But without some opening up of the political system resistance could grow in a way that is disruptive.

As China becomes more globalized in terms of exports and investment then it becomes increasingly vulnerable to the decisions of financiers or slumps in countries it is investing in or exporting to. Its exports were affected by the post-2007 financial crisis. China may not be the economic powerhouse it appears at first sight – many of its exports are comprised of components from other countries or made by foreign companies located in the country so not as much benefit to China as they may seem. Its growth is partly a product of its size – if calculated per person it falls down the league table of productivity and income compared to other countries. Its rates of growth are very high but starting from a low point. High growth on a poor income can still leave a poor person quite poor. Segal (1999) argues that, as a market and in terms of its output, share of exports and FDI, China is not hugely significant, and the case is similar for its political influence, military power and cultural influence globally.

Not all of these points are convincing. China's population size is as much an advantage as a reason to count down the significance of the economic data. If China does become vulnerable to global forces, it has growing domestic demand to fall back on at a level no other countries have. Its potential domestic consumer force is large, likely to get much richer, and tending to save a lot at present so providing potential to be bigger spenders in the future. China is showing adaptability in its reliance on the global economy, for instance, through its deals with African countries that supply oil. It may be more an economic power globally than a political or military one, but the latter are dependent on the former and it is likely they will develop if China continues to be economically successful.

So, if America is declining, what are the alternatives? Genuine multipolarity is unlikely because of greater power in some states and blocs compared to others. Power stays disproportionately at the core, even if that core may change, at the expense of the poorer and less powerful. Global democracy is unlikely for similar reasons – that it would involve an equality and inclusion of participants that the most powerful will not accept, together with clashes of ideology and interests that make conflict more likely than common consciousness. Conflicts over resources seem likely to escalate, including violently, climate change being one basis for this, eroding fertile land and the availability of water. There has been a war in Sudan, in which hundreds of thousands have died, in part over such resources. Against this background of increasing conflict and war, China has the rapidly growing economic clout to emerge as the world's hegemon in the foreseeable future, economically quickly, and politically, and perhaps militarily subsequent to economic dominance.

Conclusions

The diagram in figure 12.1 sums up some of the discussions of this chapter. In the centre is the status quo, American hegemony. Around the edges are alternatives. The vertical axis shows a continuum from formalized arrangements at the bottom to informal ones at the top. The horizontal axis shows centralized set-ups to the left and more diffused arrangements to the right.

The top left alternative shows the US continuing as an imperial power, as advocated and predicted by Kagan but seen as failing by Mann. For Nye, the US can be a dominant power in this sector but

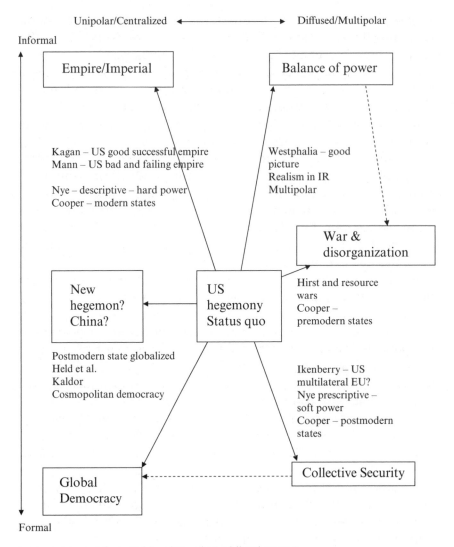

Unipolar/Centralized ←————————→ Diffused/Multipolar

Informal

Empire/Imperial

Balance of power

Kagan – US good successful empire
Mann – US bad and failing empire

Nye – descriptive – hard power
Cooper – modern states

Westphalia – good
picture
Realism in IR
Multipolar

War &
disorganization

New
hegemon?
China?

US
hegemony
Status quo

Hirst and resource
wars
Cooper –
premodern states

Postmodern state globalized
Held et al.
Kaldor
Cosmopolitan democracy

Ikenberry – US
multilateral EU?
Nye prescriptive –
soft power
Cooper – postmodern
states

Global
Democracy

Collective Security

Formal

Source: Adapted from Held and Koenig-Archibugi 2004: 3

Figure 12.1   The future of world power

based more on soft than hard power. Also presented here is the pos-sibility of an alternative global hegemonic power, China. The bottom left portrays a more institutionalized and centralized system, unipolar but multilateral. This is exemplified by the cosmopolitan democracy outlined by advocates such as Held, Kaldor and Beck.

The right-hand column gives a more diffused multipolar scenario. At the top is the balance of power portrayed in realist pictures of power dispersed amongst many states or actors in the world. Adjacent to this is a more extreme diffused situation, with multipolarity in a situation of conflict rather than balance. The conflict is exacerbated by a disorganized world system, without a clear hegemon, and competition over declining resources. Some rule out the possibility of war between advanced states, but I think this is too optimistic given tensions between states in the Far East, Middle East and former Soviet Union. The bottom right part of the diagram shows a more formalized situation of diffused and multilateral power, with Ikenberry's view of the US as multilateral, greater soft power, agreements between states, and arrangements such as blocs like the EU.

American power brings out a number of themes of this book. It has a lot to do with politics and the military. But it cannot be reduced to this. US power also resides in more sociological bases – multilateral cooperation, the wider economy and the legitimacy of soft power. A state's political clout depends on its economic significance globally and on having the money to finance advanced military technology and deployment. Rich and powerful nations are in a position to get what they want politically, against poorer less powerful countries. To say that a focus on the economy is too reductionist or determinist may sound theoretically sophisticated. But it is not empirically so. It ignores the evidence of economic power and glosses over unequal power. Finally, if there are inequality and power differences, then seeing the world of states as globalized is less plausible. Some states lead the world, while others are more sidelined and have less or little input. This is a world of exclusion and conflict as much as one of integration and convergence.

Further Reading

Jan Nederveen Pieterse discusses features involved in America's global role in *Globalization or Empire?* (2004b), which includes articles also published elsewhere.

Held and Koenig-Archibugi's (2004) *American Power in the 21st Century* is an edited book that includes contributions by Kagan, Cooper, Nye, Mann and Ikenberry that I have mentioned in this chapter.

Kagan's (2003) *Paradise and Power* focuses on why the US is and should be a strong hard power. It can also be found on the Internet. Joseph Nye puts forward his views on soft power in a number of places, including (2002) *The Paradox of Power*.

Michael Mann's argument that the US is a declining power is in (2003) *Incoherent Empire*, and in an article in *Review of International Studies* (Mann 2004).

Some evocative critiques of American power include Harold Pinter's (2005) acceptance of the Nobel Prize for literature in 2005, and Vladimir Putin's (2007) speech at the 43rd Munich conference on security.

Barry Buzan and Rosemary Foot's (2004) book, *Does China Matter? A Reassessment*, includes contributions on China's global role, economically, politically, militarily and culturally.

CHAPTER
War and Globalization **13**

As discussed in the last chapter, one of the ways that power is maintained is through military force. It is in the military sphere that American power has its strongest basis. As we saw, America's military might is greater than most of the next most militarily powerful nations added together. The case for unrivalled American power is greater for the military sphere than for economic power, political power or ideological legitimacy.

Military power is important. If economic or political power or cultural or ideological persuasion does not work, there is ultimately physical force, by the threat or use of destruction and power over life and death. Many books on globalization do not say much about war. Sociologists' concerns in general have tended to be with other forms of conflict – for example, class or gender conflicts at work, or in the family or state. When looking at the exercise of power or the maintenance of order, they have tended to look at cultural, social, political or economic bases for these. Why should we pay attention to war and killing, and why should sociologists look at something which is normally the concern of war studies or international relations rather than apparently to do with *social* conflict?

War and sociology

In rich developed countries which are relatively peaceful democracies, such as those in Western and Northern Europe and North America, wars and large-scale violence seem distant and not a big part of people's lives. People are sheltered from them, and allow themselves to be so. Even when they are citizens or residents in a country at war it has little obvious effect on their society. For the soldiers involved, and for their friends and families, it has a great impact, but for the vast proportion of society there is little direct impact of the war itself. This is unlike the experience of the First and Second World Wars, when casualties were extremely high and many people were affected by bereavements in their families or communities. Economies were war economies – civilians were conscripted into the armed services, women replaced the men who were in the army, industries were turned over to arms manufacture and goods were rationed. In the post-1945 period, there was a constant threat in the background of major nuclear war between the USSR and the US, with Europe being stuck in a battlefield in the middle.

Contemporary wars for Western powers are mostly available through the media. It is not something that most of us have close or direct experience of and the media adds even more distance by sanitization of what we see. Air strikes are portrayed through the radar sights of planes and there is very little film shown of fighting, deaths or the remains of victims. Most people in a country at war, such as the UK or the US, would know little about it if they did not follow the news. It is not noticeable in everyday life, unlike in the mass total wars of the twentieth century. So war may not seem an important part of daily life in rich Western democratic societies, and this is true in many other places. Why should sociologists pay attention to it relative to apparently more immediate concerns such as welfare, the family, education, crime, the media and so on?

But in other societies, beyond the 'West', war – or the threat of being on the receiving end of it – is a major fact of existence and continues to define social lives and power relations. It is easy for people in rich democratic developed worlds to make themselves unthinking about how significant war is for the daily social lives of many people throughout the world. When you are a citizen in a state which is killing in a war, but not in your territorial area, it is easy to make yourself subconscious about this fact. In the face of such adversity we are often more concerned with self-oriented issues such as status or salary. If you bring up the subject of war with sociologists there is often irritation or distraction, from people concerned with matters more important to them, to do with their own or developed countries, where violent conflict is not a daily threat. To Beck's (2007) credit, he acknowledges this:

> I do take the criticism of Anthony Elliott and Charles Lemert (2006) in their inspiring book *The New Individualism* about the violent nature of the risk society which is underdeveloped in my writings: 'Risk is too gentle a word in a world where so many are caught without hope (. . .). The worlds today are not so much risky as they are deadly, and especially for those on the social and economic margins. Deadly worlds are violent worlds (. . .). There is a risk to be sure, but the ubiquity of violence in the world is something more.' (702–3)

When looking at conflict sociologists have tended to look at social conflict, or perhaps economic or political conflict, for instance, to do with identities such as class, gender or ethnicity and in sites such as the workplace or family. There has been less attention to violent conflict over issues such as territory, resources or security. When looking at order sociologists have tended to focus more on law, legitimacy and ideology, but have paid less attention to violence, or the threat of violence, as a mode of maintaining order and power within societies and between them. Weber is an exception to this rule and these are absences that Giddens, for one, has pointed out.

Violence has social causes, effects and solutions and so is a matter of sociological concern. It has varying social effects on warring societies and changing social actors are involved, as we will see below in discussions of recent wars, post-military society and new wars. The arms trade which underpins war is a major part of the economies of the world and, apart from the direct effect it has on people's lives by providing arms for killing them, it also has social implications in terms of the economic wealth of a society, and employment. To be blunt, the act of killing or being killed is as decisive an event in our social lives as it is possible to have. That sociology does not very often incorporate this fact into its studies, or that sociologists bypass it or somehow leave it to the edges of their consciousness, seeing this as beyond their disciplinary remit, or outmoded and out of date with the new global world, is not excusable.

For Barkawi (2006), globalization studies have tended to see globalization as separate from war, leading to a view of globalization as pacifying. Globalization is equated with the end of the cold war, when the world became more unified and the threat of nuclear catastrophe retreated. War was equated with a bad old world of states clashing, and of communism and capitalism threatening each other. The new dominant ideas became free trade and democracy, and cultural hybridity developed. As far as war and peace goes, globalization is about international security regimes, peacekeeping and international human rights protections.

But Barkawi argues that globalization is tied up with war as much as it is a form of peace. Globalization can cause war. The attempt to impose neoliberalism or American foreign policy, and, previously, European imperialism and its version of 'free' trade, has caused hostility and conflict against such impositions and let nationalism and ethnic strife loose. Global inequality breeds conflict. As we shall see shortly, the globalization of the arms trade has enabled war and the development and spread of ever more dangerous and destructive weapons, sold by richer, more peaceful countries to poorer more conflict-ridden ones. States are intrinsic to the pursuit of war and the processes that underlie it.

As well as being about clashes of states, war is often a form of globalization and furthers globalization by force. For Barkawi, it is as much about interconnection as about the defending of boundaries and national allegiance. It leads to interconnections between societies, even if this comes about through people on both sides doing their best to kill each other. Soldiers travel and literally do get to see the world, as the recruiting posters used to say, and the world gets to experience them. Barkawi tells of how Indian soldiers in the Second World War fighting with Britain experienced cultural and political values and systems amongst the British and took this information home, if they were lucky enough to survive. War is a channel through which the circulation of goods, people and ideas happens, as with other types of globalization. It is through military intervention that other flows then happen – economic, cultural, political and so on. Globalization through war is not restricted to elites. Many ordinary people are soldiers or are those in invaded countries, especially in the mass wars of the twentieth century. After the Second World War, global ideas about human rights and the prevention of genocide, crimes against humanity and a focus on peacekeeping came to the fore. Many local conflicts have global ramifications – the Israel–Palestine conflict, for instance, and the US 'war on terror'.

Barkawi says that those who study mainly military matters tend to leave society out of it. But when you look at war and globalization together society is very important. Conflicts that extend in a globalized way change the society that is making the war as well as the society it is being waged on, and also change the relations between those societies. War transforms the societies that make them, especially in the case of total wars where the domestic population are mobilized. But it also transforms noticeably the society at the receiving end, as in wars to establish empire. These were transformed by the imperial powers, but imperialism also forged anti-colonial nationalism. Rather than being wiped away by globalization or replaced by a benign cultural hybridity, nationalism here is fermented by it. Violent conflict reproduces and transforms national identities and their counterposition to other opposed identities, for instance, between West and East or North and South in the world.

Barkawi uses the example of British imperialism in India, backed up by military force. This changed Britain, part of the process of making it into an imperial power with all the economic, political and social effects this had for the country. It transformed India. And it led to a changing and enduring relationship between the two nations over time. Militarily, the British Indian army played a significant role in the Second World War, and the use of the Indian army was a factor that led to the decline of British rule in India. War also changes global politics – for instance, after the Second World War when Europe was carved up between communism and capitalism and international institutions were set up, in part to prevent mass conflict happening again.

At the time of writing this book there were a number of wars or violent conflicts going on in the world:*

- Ongoing conflicts in Iraq and Afghanistan. Estimates on fatalities in the former vary, but many calculate them to be in the hundreds of thousands since 2003.
- A civil war in Sri Lanka between the government and Tamil separatists, which had been going on for twenty-five years or more and caused tens of thousands of deaths.
- A war in the Darfur region of Sudan which in five years has led to the death of about 2–300,000 people, in part over land, water and resources which are in decline partly because of climate change.
- In the Democratic Republic of Congo there are continuing conflicts from a war which officially ended in 2003, leading to the deaths of over 5 million people in the war itself or during its after-effects.
- A recent war in Somalia between the Somalian transitional government backed by Ethiopia with US involvement against opposed militias; so far thousands have died and probably hundreds of thousands have been displaced, with the risk the conflict may suck in further neighbouring countries such as Eritrea.
- This goes alongside a longer-running war in Somalia, started in 1988, in which more than 300,000 have died, a civil war involving warlord and clan militias and in which UN and US troops have also been involved.
- There are conflicts between government and other forces (e.g., FARC) in Colombia, seemingly at present on the decline.
- And there is war between the Turkish army and the Kurdish nationalist PKK, with tens of thousands of deaths.
- In Kashmir, war over territory disputed by India and Pakistan, in which tens of thousands have died.
- Regional and ethnic conflicts in Nigeria, for reasons including rights to the benefits from oil production.
- Ongoing conflicts in Chechnya between Russia and rebel Chechens, with deaths in the tens of thousands since 1999.

---

* I have used multiple news and media sources to obtain figures on fatalities in these conflicts. These themselves have used independent NGO figures. Where higher figures seem to be reasonably disputed I have given lower or more flexible figures (e.g., 'tens of thousands'), so as not to overestimate casualties.

- Ongoing intermittent conflicts in Israel/Palestine, between the Israeli army and Palestinians, and between Palestinian groups.

There are many other ongoing violent conflicts: in Burma between the government and other groups, with thousands dead and hundreds of thousands displaced; between the governments and insurgents in the Philippines; in Peru (in which about 70,000 died before the conflict became more low level); in Laos between government and the Hmong; a drug war in Mexico; conflict over land in Western Kenya; several conflicts within both India and Pakistan aside from the Kashmir dispute; in Niger and Mali over the benefits of mineral mining; and civil war in Chad connected to the Darfur conflict mentioned above. There is a separatist insurgency in Southern Thailand (with thousands of deaths), and insurgencies and separatist conflicts in Yemen, Saudi Arabia, Ethiopia, Senegal, Uganda, and the Maghreb region across Algeria, Mauritania and Morocco. The latter is connected to the earlier Algerian civil war in the 1990s, in which more than 150,000 died, itself preceded by the Algerian war of independence in the 1950s and 1960s in which probably over 150,000 died.

There have also been recent wars in Lebanon and Georgia. Going back to the 1990s, there was a previous war in Iraq and Kuwait in 1990–1, war and genocide in Rwanda (probably close to a million died), wars in the former Yugoslavia (in which tens of thousands at least died) and Sierra Leone (with tens of thousands of deaths), and previous wars in Afghanistan, involving Russia, and resulting in tens of thousands of deaths. There was a civil war in Tajikistan in which up to 100,000 died, a civil war in Burundi in which about 300,000 died, a civil war in Nepal in which thousands died, a war between Ethiopia and Eritrea, with between 50,000 and 200,000 deaths, a civil war in Liberia (with about 150,000 deaths) and civil war in the Ivory Coast.

Between 1990 and 2001, there were fifty-seven major armed conflicts in forty-five locations with sub-Saharan and other developing countries disproportionately affected, with the impact this has on poverty and inequality. Since 1990, conflicts have killed as many as 3.6 million with 90 per cent of the deaths and injuries being civilians and half of these children (UNDP 2003: 45). Of course, there has been enormous bloodshed during the last hundred years across Europe, Asia and the rest of the world, in world wars and other mass killing, with the deaths of tens of millions, but I won't continue the list of wars to before the 1990s.

Most people, including many sociologists of globalization, it seems, are unaware of the majority of recent wars in the rest of the world, even though the proportion of civilian deaths reveals how much they penetrate into ordinary society. The locations of these wars and conflicts should not mislead. They are often in poor countries and not in Europe or North America. But countries from the latter regions have been very involved in them as military forces or as funders and providers of arms to parties involved. Or the wars are connected with the foreign policies of the richer and most powerful countries. For instance, the deployment of US troops and US support for Israel in the Israel–Palestine conflict has been one factor prompting insurgent movements to take up arms. Many of the conflicts appear to be ethnic, tribal or national but are equally often over the decline of resources due to climate change caused by emissions mostly from rich countries. Many of them are interconnected, conflicts arising because of injustice felt about another situation of conflict (e.g., in Palestine), with overlapping or interlinked forces, or spilling over borders and sucking in neighbouring, or not so neighbouring, countries.

It is difficult to see, following this list, how sociologists of globalization can see the world as one defined, as Barkawi also laments, by cosmopolitanism and a benign mixing of cultures. As we have seen above and will see more below, much of this violence comes from processes of globalization. This is unless you keep your focus on societies beyond those which are poor and war-afflicted, or narrow it to culture, and keep out economics, politics and violence. Alongside the mass poverty and inequality discussed in chapter 8, which in some respects is getting worse, there is widespread war, violent conflict, death and dislocation throughout the world, involving many different states and actors. Such evidence does not support more theoretical and pleasing assertions of a growing cosmopolitanism. Frequently, the wars are over resources, economic and material interests and power. This does not square easily with approaches which see analyses of power, conflict and the importance of the economy as outmoded and crude, with the world as one of emerging cultural cosmopolitanism and universal human rights.

The globalization of war

In this section I will look at the way that war has changed in the world since about 1500, the extent to which military relations have been globalized, and at how far war is a phenomenon of globalization.

Worldwide and historically, the experience of humankind has been run through with conflict through organized violence. Humans have had an astonishing capacity throughout their history to carry out mass killing against one another through war, as well as other means. Genocidal phenomena such as the Holocaust and Rwanda often get much attention in this context. But organized legitimized killing in war throughout the time humans have been on earth has been another form through which this has happened. Theories that globalization is bringing us together in a way which can be more culturally communal and based on universal rights need to back this up in relation to the history and continuing record of mass violence by humans on humans.

Globalized forms of war developed from the late fifteenth century onwards with the expansion of *European powers* as they tried to construct imperial orders, where necessary through the military subjugation of indigenous populations or in competitive wars with other imperialist nations. These were global forms of war because they were carried out by the major European powers across the world, in Asia, Africa and the Americas. The conflicts between European states, and by them on indigenous populations, rewrote the world order for centuries, globalizing European power and carving the world up between the territories of different imperial powers. After colonized states became independent, both before and during the twentieth century, many problems they faced were due to the way imperial powers had constituted and left them. This was the case, for instance, in the war for the independence of Bangladesh from Pakistan, conflict between India and Pakistan over disputed parts of Kashmir, and the conflict between Israel and the Palestinians, not to mention ethnic, tribal and border conflicts in Africa. European powers were able to be victorious in the colonial period in part because of the firepower gap between them and what became their colonies, that is, the technological advancement of their weapons. This military gap led others to try to acquire the same sorts of technologies. In this way military technology became more globalized. I will come back to the globalization of the arms trade.

Global war happened in the *two world wars between 1914 and 1945*. These encompassed Europe, Asia, Africa and North America. In part, this was a continuation of competitive imperialist wars. Imperial possessions were fought over, for instance, in Africa. As mentioned above, they were mass 'total' wars that required huge quantities of armaments and people. War was industrialized to meet these demands. And for the wars to be fought many nations had to combine and mobilize money, humans, arms, and supplies such as food. No state alone had the capacity to win. So the wars were multinational and fought between international alliances of nations.

After 1945 the global character of war did not go away. The era of British or European imperialism finished and the imperial *superpowers of the US and USSR* became dominant in a bipolar world. They entered into bilateral and multilateral relations with other states throughout the world. These often involved promises of military protection by the superpowers, as well as commercial agreements, such as the supply of subsidized goods by the Soviet Union to communist allies. Both superpowers had deployments of bases and troops throughout the world in friendly countries, as the US still has. Conflicts by the superpowers have been characterized as a cold war stand-off, with nuclear missiles pointed at one another but never fired. However, there were hotter elements to it. Proxy wars between capitalist and communist powers were fought in other countries, for instance, in Vietnam, where Americans fought with the South Vietnamese against the communist North Vietnamese backed by China and Russia. In African and Latin American countries, the US and USSR backed and armed the respective pro-Western and pro-communist sides. As such, the superpower conflict was globalized, in bilateral and multilateral agreements, deployments and distant proxy wars. Furthermore, it was luck as much as anything else that prevented the nuclear balance teetering into nuclear war.

War after the cold war

With the collapse of one of the two superpower blocs, under the leadership of the USSR, one perspective on the world military order is that it has become more multipolar. I discussed how credible such a description is in the last chapter. Leaving aside economics, politics and culture, multipolarity cannot be said to be an accurate way of characterizing the distribution of military power in the post-cold war period. The *US is a sole superpower militarily*, hugely in advance of everyone else as far as military strength goes. It has greater military expenditure and more weapons. In 2007, the US spent $547 billion on the military, nearly half of the world's military spending. The next two biggest spenders were the UK and China, each at just over $59b and $58b respectively, followed by France, Japan, Germany, Russia, Saudi Arabia and Italy spending 3–4 per cent of global military expenditure (SIPRI 2008: 11). The US has about 1.3 million military personnel in active service. Many are deployed outside the US. Major deployments (in tens of thousands) are in Iraq, Afghanistan, Germany, South Korea, and Japan. Its global deployment is more extensive than any other nation. It has hi-tech weapons that allow it to win wars with fewer casualties than its opponents. An example of this is the ability to fire relatively accurate weapons from planes or ships at a distance. These are not so accurate that they can avoid the death of civilians in the enemy area, but they can be fired from such distance that casualties amongst US forces are minimized.

Rivalry between the biggest powers in the world is less one of mutual military threat than it was in the cold war. Competition between states such as the US, Japan, China, EU members and Russia is more to do with economics and trade. There is also political conflict, for instance, with Russia and/or China sometimes having a different policy to the US, and with some EU states on issues such as war in the former Yugoslavia and intervention in the Darfur region in Sudan. Because Russia and China are on the UN Security Council, this has stymied some of the aims of the US and European allies such as France and the UK. For some, security issues of a military kind are confined mostly to regional or local tensions, for instance, in the former Yugoslavia, North Korea, between China and Taiwan and India and Pakistan, and in secessionist or insurgent conflicts going on globally in various states, from Sri Lanka to India and China.

Having said this, *military tension* between the US and other great powers of the cold war era is not absent. It cannot be said that the cold war is completely over or that rivalry between great powers is devoid of military threat. In the Far East, Taiwan, a province of China, is claimed by China but is self-governing, and an ongoing issue is the possibility of its complete independence. However, China recognizes Taiwan as part of One China with two systems (comparable to the status that capitalist Hong Kong gets, as a former British territory that reverted to China in 1997). China says it will not accept a declaration of independence by Taiwan and the US, who have many troops stationed in the region, say they will not accept Chinese military intervention in Taiwan and will back it if such a situation were to arise.

There are tensions between Japan and China over history, territory and resources, and Japan moved away in small steps under prime ministers Koizumi and Abe from its postwar pacifist standing. India and Pakistan have fought a war and are in ongoing disagreement over the disputed part of Kashmir that lies between the two nuclear power nations. The US has contemplated stationing missile defence systems in Central Europe. They said these were to protect them from 'rogue' states like Iran and North Korea, but Russia saw them as a hostile threat to itself. A defensive system can be seen as hostile because it makes it easier for the state that installs them to launch an attack, knowing that, if the system works, it can protect itself from retaliation. So the old cold war conflict with Russia simmers on, with Russia trying to exert an influence in surrounding nations such as Georgia that the US feels it should not, and with vital supplies, such as gas, that it can withdraw or increase the price of as a way of exerting pressure on its neighbours.

A number of the powers involved in these tensions have nuclear weapons. Japan is one exception. However, some argue that war between such advanced states, because they are so militarily advanced and often nuclear powers, would be so destructive that none would engage in it. It is thought that war between advanced states, of the sort experienced in the twentieth century with such devastating effects, will not reoccur.

In fact, one development in the postwar period has been mutual, cooperative, *multilateral security agreements*, such as the Warsaw Pact, that bound together communist countries in the cold war, and NATO that bound together the US and its allies and that, since the cold war, has been enlarged to encompass others. Because these are transnational they are seen as a sign of globalization. Although members have fought offensive wars through such mutual pacts, for example, the NATO intervention in Kosovo, these agreements have been as much to avoid war between members as to secure mutual agreements about making war. The European Union was also in part an attempt to bring European nations together in greater mutualism, after the terrible world wars of the first half of the twentieth century, to prevent them fighting each other again.

With the development of more formal and institutionalized multilateral organizations, security has become less about nations defending national territory from invaders and more about collective defence, or ensuring international security. As well as the fora mentioned, other developments of regionalized bodies or agreements have included the Western European Union, Organization for Security and Cooperation in Europe and the European Rapid Reaction Force. The UN is involved in peacekeeping operations around the world, for instance, after the 2006 Israel–Lebanon war and in the Darfur region of Sudan. Alongside UN peacekeeping there have grown international organizations intervening not just to stop crimes against humanity and war crimes (such as in Darfur), but also to bring to justice those guilty of them, for instance, former presidents Milosevic of Yugoslavia and Charles Taylor of Liberia. There have been international agreements on the conduct of wars and attempts to restrict the types of weapons used, for instance, landmines and cluster bombs which kill and maim a disproportionate number of civilians during and after wars. There are mutual arms restrictions treaties, such as those negotiated between the US and USSR in the cold war and the Nuclear Non-proliferation Treaty. In short, there have been international dimensions to security, the rules of war and human rights, and to arms restrictions and peacekeeping.

I have mentioned the possible devastation and mutual agreements that hold back advanced states from attacking each other. Such states may not have the same reservations about attacking less advanced states with inferior military capabilities. Those beyond the most advanced states, for instance, in the Middle East and Africa, are now seen as sites of instability and rising militarism, where conflicts internally or between states or other forces are most likely to happen. This view may be over-sanguine about the prospects of war between advanced states. If what was said above is true, that the absence of nuclear conflict in the cold war was as much luck as deterrence, then warfare between major military states cannot be ruled out in the longer term, given a situation of US military superiority and missile defence systems, with tensions between states such as China, Russia and the US.

Increasingly, debates see *threats to security* as wider-reaching than war and the military. Economic instability and volatility can lead to insecurity for many in ways that are out of their control. Crime, for instance, drugs and violent crime, affect the basic security of people. Terrorism, especially of an international sort, receives attention as a threat to human security, especially since 9/11. Similarly, environmental problems such as climate change which lead to essential resources such as water and fertile land declining, as well as flooding and possibly volatile weather conditions, are now seen in this light.

These are all problems which have global dimensions and cannot be solved by military means or by nation-states alone, even if there have been counterproductive attempts to stop some of them by force (e.g., the war on terror). They have to be solved by the global cooperation of states. I have argued that all-inclusive global cosmopolitanism based on common consciousness is unlikely in many circumstances, as there are divergent interests and ideologies in the world and relations of power and conflict. But, through coalitions of the willing, probably necessarily in conflict with those who are opposed, solutions to such problems need to be established as far as is possible at more international levels. And soft as much as hard power is needed to solve these problems. For example, some problems of international terrorism are in part responses to US imperialism and problems in the Middle East, such as the predicament of the Palestinians. Hence solving these root causes will be more helpful than military action on the symptoms. Drugs and violent crime often (if not only) result from underlying economic or social problems, such as a lack of alternative opportunities for making a living or finding fulfilment. Many of these problems are international and as such require international solutions; clearly, human security is threatened by more than military force, and more than military power is needed to solve the underlying causes which require economic, political and social solutions.

I will return shortly to current forms of war and the future of war. But, first, let us turn to the armaments industry that underpins war and look at how this relates to themes about globalization.

The arms race and globalization

The arms trade has increasingly been globalized. As we have seen in other chapters, for instance on the media, globalizing trends are often linked to developments in regulation (or deregulation), technological development and the possibility of making money by globalizing. The state, technology and capitalism are important.

What has often happened with the globalization of the arms trade is the development and acquisition of new military technologies in some countries, which then leads to their spread to other parts of the world. *Innovation becomes more globally generalized.* The arms trade is a profit-making enterprise in which capitalist corporations develop products for sale on the market to be bought by states or other actors. This capitalist production and trade becomes globalized as new producers seek to make profits from the industry and markets are sought out globally. The arms trade is a form of capitalist globalization.

Held et al. (1999) discuss four tiers in the arms trade. In the first tier is the United States, standing alone as innovators to develop new military technologies. Then come other rich developed countries, like the UK, France and Germany, which adapt these innovations and produce the same sorts of arms technologies themselves, but their own versions. Third come those who copy and produce the innovations, for instance, China, India and Israel. Finally, there is a tier that does not produce arms but generates buyers, for instance, many African and developing countries.

A key development in the *early modern arms trade* was the gunpowder revolution. The mechanization and industrialization of arms allowed some armed forces to leap ahead and have weapons with reach, accuracy and effect superior to others. In this early modern period arms were sold mostly regionally rather than globally, and often privately and in an unregulated way.

Since then, the state has become more often the intermediary through which arms are sold even if they are produced by private companies, and sales have become more regulated and controlled by governments, for instance, in terms of to whom it is allowed to sell. Having said this, many governments have had few qualms about allowing sales to states that use them for repression or aggression (rather than just defence), even if they are governments that emphasize human rights and humanitarianism themselves and have criticized the actions of the states they sell to. The *modern arms trade* involves industrialized mass production of arms, for profit, often for export, with overseas production being established and with more licensing of production but limited regulation. There has been a global diffusion of arms so that more and more actors are able to obtain them.

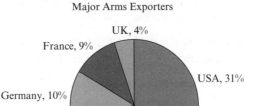

Major Arms Exporters

UK, 4%

France, 9%

Germany, 10%

USA, 31%

Russia, 25%

Exporter	Main buyers
USA	South Korea, Israel, UAE, Greece
Russia	China, India, Venezuela, Algeria
Germany	Turkey, Greece, South Africa, Australia
France	UAE, Greece, Saudi Arabia, Singapore
UK	USA, Romania, Chile, India

Source: Data from SIPRI 2008: 14

Figure 13.1   Major arms exporters – share of arms exports 2003–2007

The *contemporary arms trade* grew until 1987, with the superpowers and Warsaw Pact and NATO members being the biggest spenders. It shrank thereafter, with the end of cold war tensions. In recent years it has accelerated again. Developing countries' share of arms spending, especially on imports, has increased since the 1960s. The number of producers and buyers has grown, although there are still great inequalities between producers and importers. In the post-cold war period the US has dominated the arms trade, with the UK, France, China, Russia and Germany doing most of the rest of the supplying. Despite Germany adopting a non-offensive stance since 1945, it has been a major arms supplier.

In the immediate postwar period the rich North was the main focus of trade, with the Middle East being a region of increased buying from the 1960s onwards and, more recently, with an increase in arms buying in Asia. As can be seen in figure 13.2, the world spent $1,339 billion on arms in 2007, and arms spending is on the rise across the world. This should be seen in the context of the needs of the one in six globally in poverty, discussed in chapter 8. Stiglitz and Bilmes (2008) put the cost of the Iraq War at $3 trillion, not including indirect and hidden costs. They argue that the money could have been spent with a huge effect on social and economic programmes globally, which would have done more to increase American security in non-violent ways, quite apart from improving the life chances of the one billion or

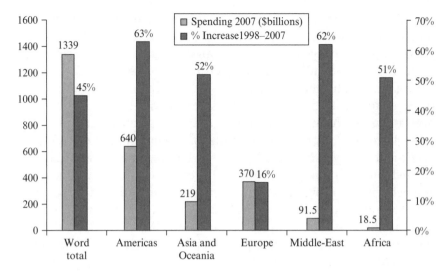

Source: Data from SIPRI 2008: 10

Figure 13.2   Global military expenditure, 2007

Table 13.1 Largest arms-producing companies, 2006		
Company	Arms sales 2006 $m	Profit 2006 $m
1. Boeing USA	30690	2215
2. Lockheed Martin USA	28120	2529
3. BAE Systems UK	24060	1189
4. Northrop Grumman USA	23650	1542
5. Raytheon USA	19530	1283

Source: Abridged from SIPRI 2008: 12

more living on a dollar a day. The arms trade has become more commercial and privatized, and increasingly the contractors are agencies
other than governments. As can be seen in table 13.1, some companies
make a lot of money from selling arms.

Supplying arms has been a *part of the politics* of the powerful for
a long time. Powerful states supply arms to states or organizations
that are deemed friendly or will fight for their side, or to buy favours.
This was the case in the cold war when the Soviet Union and USA
armed forces in distant countries that were more pro-communist or
pro-Western respectively. Often military support can be to temporary allies from whom allegiance shifts quickly later on, such as the
Mujahideen in Afghanistan, who were fighting against the Marxist
government and Soviet troops in the 1980s, supported by Bin Laden
and the US amongst others. The US has supplied India with material
for the production of nuclear power, in contravention of nuclear proliferation agreements, in return for India's support in the 'war against

terror', whilst trying to halt other countries' development of nuclear weapons, for instance, in Iran and North Korea. In 2007 the US did a series of deals with countries in the Middle East, involving arms sales to the Sunnis in Saudi Arabia who felt the US were being too hard on Sunnis in Iraq, followed by increases in arms aid to Israel that effectively compensated for their arms sales to Saudi Arabia and other Arab states. So the arms trade is part of the game of power politics.

We have seen that the arms trade is a major source of capitalist profit and is driven by this incentive. It has become increasingly globalized, but very unequally so in terms of who gains from producing and who is spending, and which countries are militarily the most advanced and superior. There has been a diffusion and proliferation of arms globally, including nuclear weapons. As we shall see shortly, there has also been a technological leap forward to more of an information age in arms technology.

New wars and the future of war

In this section I wish to look at current and future wars and whether they are taking a new form or what form they may take in the future.

Looking sociologically at current wars from the perspective of the most powerful nations, and compared to the wars of the twentieth century, these may nowadays be called *post-military societies* (Shaw 1991). Western states can go to war but, because of the technological means that are used, with minimal casualties on their side compared to deaths inflicted on enemies (Shaw 2005). These are asymmetric wars in which one side may have very superior strength, leading the other side to adopt alternative tactics to fight back, for example, guerrilla fighting as in Vietnam or Iraq. Conscription in advanced states is not required, there is no mass mobilization of industry and people, and multinational alliances are sought for military or political reasons rather than to pool enormous resources. The wars of the current eras are, for the advanced powers, not total wars of mass mobilization. Politically, wars may be controversial and affect the fortunes of politicians. This happened to George Bush and Tony Blair in relation to the Iraq War, although it was not an election-loser for either. But sociologically, in its narrow sense, their effect on society is almost unnoticeable in the daily lives of many people in rich warring nations, apart from the supply of sanitized media coverage that does not show the human effects, even if it does sometimes report these selectively. Human and social resources are not fundamentally reorganized as they were in the two world wars of the twentieth century. So advanced states, even if involved in wars, have been defined as post-military societies.

For Mary Kaldor (2001), there has been a shift from older to *newer forms of war*, and she argues for cosmopolitan solutions to such wars (see also Münkler 2005). Old wars, she argues, were between nation-states and often over national territory. In new wars, however, the actors are frequently entities other than nation-states. They are less about state-building or expansion; in fact, they often (but not only) take place within failing or weak states. They may be private actors rather than state actors – warlords, militias, insurgents or terrorist organizations – and often more local or global than national, for instance, in Somalia, Afghanistan and Iraq. These actors fund their weaponry and war-making through participation in a criminal economy. War-making is more decentralized and less total. It may be less between symmetrical state armies than asymmetrical forces, and less focused on full-scale wars than sometimes on-and-off simmering or intermittent conflicts, as in the Israel–Palestine conflict. And the wars are not necessarily expansionist over national or other forms of territory. They may be to do with resisting imperial domination, or around identities, such as ethnic or religious identity, as in conflicts in the former Yugoslavia that are to the fore in Kaldor's thinking. Terror directed at civilians is part of these wars, as much as conflict with armies. Civilians are killed or brutalized as an instrument of war, to prevent them assisting the enemy, as a form of proxy attack on enemy forces, or may be the very aim of war as in the case of 'ethnic cleansing'. For Kaldor, the solution to situations such as these is cosmopolitan humanitarian intervention. This involves cosmopolitan ideals to bring warring parties together, for example, conflicting ethnic or religious groups, and/or intervention by Western powers who have the military might to do so, on the basis of humanitarian concerns and human rights.

There are some reasons to be a bit sceptical about parts of Kaldor's analysis, although it should be stressed she is talking of a shift from old to new wars rather than a clean break between the two types. For instance, direct attacks on civilians and the terrorizing of civilian populations is not new. This was a tactic used by the Americans and British in the Second World War against Germany, in the bombing of cities such as Dresden, as well as by many other powers in wars. Similarly, although the argument for cosmopolitan solutions is well meant and, where such solutions are possible, should be pursued to prevent large-scale human death and tragedy, there are reasons (as we saw in chapter 10) to be doubtful about how realistic such global cosmopolitanism is. One reason to doubt the possibility for such cooperation is that a lack of mutual global cosmopolitan ideals or consciousness, combined with the degree of conflicting interests and use of power in the world, makes it unlikely that there will be cooperation on a significant enough scale in the foreseeable future. Actors may forge agreements if they have coinciding material interests in doing so, but there is not much evidence of a cosmopolitan consciousness that can be the basis for this.

So interventions may have to come from a more limited range of powers where there are coalitions willing to pursue them. These will often have to occur in non-cosmopolitan situations, against opposition, as has been the case in international interventions in violent situations so far, for instance, by NATO in the former Yugoslavia. As Kaldor has noted, such interventions may have to involve conflict where outside interveners take one side against another, rather than acting as neutral peacekeepers, staying in the middle to keep the sides apart or attempting to forge a cosmopolitan consensus in which all are agreed on the intervention. Wars happen because one side is attacking the other and sometimes the solution is for one of these sides to be defeated rather than for a buffer zone to keep them apart, which is not to say the latter is not valuable in some cases. Cosmopolitan interventions, desirable and possible as they may be in some cases, often in practice meet with opposition, for instance, from China and Russia. They are seen, consequently, as Western imperialism, and may aggravate as much as resolve problems.

Since the American use of the atom bomb against Japan in 1945, a key and frightening development in military technology has been the development and diffusion of *weapons of mass destruction*, from that initial bomb to contemporary nuclear weapons, together with other weapons of mass destruction such as chemical and biological weapons. These can kill hundreds of thousands of people on or very soon after impact, with many people for decades afterwards being effected, for example, by nuclear radiation, as was the case in Japan. The focus in public debate is sometimes on the development or acquiring of WMDs by 'rogue' states or terrorist organizations. But many advanced states in the world have had such weapons for a long time and, as we have seen, have been the ones so far who have been willing to use them with terrible consequences.

Since 1945 many more states have developed or acquired nuclear weapons, or are trying to develop these. In some cases this is, in part, in response to the military power of major states, and in contexts where there is tension between nuclear powers, for example, between India and Pakistan over Kashmir. In 2008, eight nuclear weapon states had over 10,000 operational nuclear weapons, thousands of which can be launched within minutes. Including other nuclear weapons, these eight states have over 25,000. It also seems likely that non-state actors will at some point be able to acquire such weapons, perhaps from a state that sponsors them or from individuals who for financial

Table 13.2 World nuclear forces, 2008		
Country	Strategic warheads	Operational nuclear weapons (including non-strategic warheads)
USA	3575	4075
Russia	3113	5189
UK	185	185
France	348	348
China	161	176
India	-	60–70
Pakistan	-	60
Israel	-	80
Total		10,183

Source: Abridged from SIPRI 2008: 16

or ideological reasons will help them acquire the knowledge to make WMDs.

The Nuclear Non-Proliferation Treaty and other arms agreements were designed to stop the spread of nuclear weapons. However, these do not work as well as would be hoped. Some states do not join and advanced states put pressure on some (such as Iran and North Korea) not to develop nuclear weapons, while being more relaxed about others (such as India) and unwilling to disarm on a major scale themselves. They try to prevent others developing or acquiring nuclear weapons whilst wishing to retain the right to have them themselves. This damages the effectiveness of non-proliferation and undermines the legitimacy of attempts at it. The US is developing missile defence systems that would allow them to deter nuclear attacks. This would make it easier for them to launch nuclear attacks because there would be less fear of reprisals getting through, should the technology work. At the same time, President Obama has made the reduction of nuclear weapons an aim of his period in office.

Hirst (2001) points to the Revolution in Military Affairs (RMA) a significant aspect of which is the development of hi-tech weaponry. He raises the prospect of computer or robot wars in the future, at least on the part of richer advanced states that can afford to develop such technologies and use them against their enemies. Drones or robots, such as unmanned planes or other vehicles, can do remote-control fighting, lessening the casualties for the advanced state and, as such, perhaps making them more willing to go to war. The US has used drones to fire missiles in places like North Pakistan and Somalia. Greater use of space, mobility and intelligence are also part of what are seen as new developments in war-making, replacing large mass armies. Smaller units capable of responding quickly, having the intelligence to know where to strike and where threats may come from, are increasingly emphasized.

Nevertheless, lesser technology – from planes on September 11th to roadside bombs, rocket-propelled grenades and AK47s – can cause serious problems for a hi-tech force like the US, and there is a limit to the type or amount of information that can be gathered with even the most complex information technology systems (Boot 2006). The war in Iraq, waged by the most technologically sophisticated power in the world, still involved old methods of fighting. There were quite precise missiles fired from great distance with minimal casualties to the US. These did not prevent substantial civilian deaths, or the civil bloodbath that followed Saddam Hussein's fall, but they were able to hit targets from a distance without direct risk to those firing them. However, a great deal of the Iraq War also involved men on feet or in vehicles entering towns and cities, patrolling and being attacked by insurgents guerrilla-style. The latter forms of warfare, with echoes of the tactics used successfully against the US in the Vietnam War, has been the biggest military challenge faced by the US in Iraq. In 2004 the Iraqi town of Fallujah was taken by American and Iraqi forces in urban fighting, with the loss of over 100 lives on their side and more than a thousand amongst insurgents in the city.

Hirst also emphasizes new bases for war. *Climate change* leads to desertification, the loss of fertile land and water, especially in hot climates such as parts of Africa where these resources are already in short supply. Consequently, there is competition over declining resources that are vital for the very bases of life, and to this can be added the threat of declining oil reserves, at present combined with a lack of alternative fuel development by states and societies. Hirst predicts that competition over declining resources such as land, water and oil will lead to military conflicts. Migration to escape from such conflicts or from the loss of land and water will provoke its own conflicts as societies resist immigration to protect their own resources. Such conflicts already exist. The war in Sudan has been portrayed as a war between ethnic or religious groups, or between the government and some of its citizens. But it is also a war over declining water resources and land. About a quarter of a million people have died as a result of the conflict, at the time of writing. While advanced powers have invested trillions of dollars in the war in Iraq, arguably related in part to oil, there has been less willingness and slow progress in developing a 'cosmopolitan' intervention in the Sudan conflict (with echoes of the West's unwillingness to intervene also in the genocide in Rwanda despite its military capacity to do so). So, for Hirst, the future is one where we will face increasing violent conflicts over water, oil and fertile land. He argues that states are still key actors in these scenarios, as they control energy resources and land and provide armies. And the firepower revolution of the sixteenth and seventeenth centuries is still the most important – that is, the move by societies to the mechanized weaponry that remains the mainstay of many conflicts today. At the same time, the ability of advanced states to put up missile defences and use drones and robotic technology, so minimizing their own casualties, only increases the likelihood that they, the forces with the most destructive power, will go to war.

Conclusions

For sociologists to turn their face away from international war shows a narrow and blinkered view of the world and of the study of society. In advanced industrial states we are sheltered from the significance of militarism, and can easily allow ourselves to be so, but war is a major fact of life and death in many parts of the world. If you want to understand society you need to understand the role of military action. And war has social causes and consequences. Consequently, sociology has a reason to be interested in it and to cast light on it.

War has been a quite globalized phenomenon: as far back as the European imperialist powers, this has been the means through which many parts of the world have been conquered, and military power has maintained the domination of one state over another. The world wars of the twentieth century and the cold war were internationally extended conflicts, and showed the global nature of military conflict. In the post-cold war situation, the world's greatest military power, the US, has demonstrated a unipolar version of globality in its military deployment. Nevertheless, in these global military situations war-making power is highly unevenly distributed. If globalization is consistent with very powerful actors defeating the distant and less powerful then this is globalization. But if it involves a more equal integration of different parts of the world, then it is difficult to see these examples as globalization.

So, power is an important part of the history of modern war. Capitalism also plays a large part in it. War is a business, out of which corporations and states can make a lot of money, and in which the most advanced states are the major producers from whom other poorer countries purchase military technology. The arms industry that underpins global military capabilities is driven by profit incentives, reproducing power and inequalities between the core and periphery. As we have seen, the role of state regulation (or lack of it) is significant, as are technological developments in weaponry.

Capitalism, economic incentives, the state and technology are important factors in global war and arms.

I have suggested that there are reasons to be worried about the future of warfare. The most powerful states have immense military capability, including the WMDs they seek to deprive others of, and, in the case of the US in Japan, have shown they are willing to use them. During the cold war, it was mainly due to good fortune that nuclear weapons were not used, but missile defence systems make the use of nuclear weapons more likely in the future. The development and siting of defence systems themselves increase conflict and tension of the sort that can spiral into military action. Russia has spoken out strongly on the basing of US missile defence systems in central Europe. Powerful states will be able to wage war, minimizing casualties on their side through other technological advancements such as the computerization of military capability. Furthermore, climate change produces new and developing sources of conflict in the world, on top of existing ones, with competition for declining water and land resources and over the ensuing migration from desertified areas. As nuclear proliferation widens to include more states and possibly non-state actors, the chances of hugely devastating war and great human tragedy increases. The onus in this situation lies with the most powerful not to aggravate the situation by building up arms or threatening other parts of the world, as was the strategy in the early years of the twenty-first century. The alternative is that the most heavily armed states lead the way in making radical arms reductions, especially of WMDs, and seek to resolve sources of tension and conflict in the world which increase chances of military conflict – for instance, the Israel–Palestine situation in the Middle East, climate change, global poverty and resented overseas interventions.

Further Reading

Tarak Barkawi's (2006) book, *Globalization and War*, explores the interconnections between war, globalization and society. I have summarized some main points from this book towards the start of this chapter.

Paul Hirst (2001), *War and Power in the 21st Century*. This is a readable short book by Paul Hirst who, with Thompson (1996), wrote the sceptical book *Globalization in Question*. Hirst provides a knowledgeable historical perspective on the development of military technology and war, seeing the gunpowder revolution and the nation-state as vital developments. He has a bleak view of the potential consequences of developments in military technology and competition over declining resources caused by climate change, to which cosmopolitan solutions do not provide a realistic response.

Held et al.'s (1999) *Global Transformations* is a few years old but, nevertheless, chapter 2 on organized violence is a good introduction to the globalization of war, security and the arms trade, historically and up to the late 1990s.

The *Stockholm International Peace Research Institute* has a website and many publications on the state or conflict and arms proliferation globally, including an annual yearbook.

Conclusion

SOCIOLOGY has a good record, at least in the past and in some countries, of taking a critical approach to what seem common-sense
ideas. It looks at the theoretical coherence in what is said, and at the
empirical evidence, to test what seems intuitively the case. It is an
interdisciplinary subject that does not focus just on social relations
in abstraction from economic and political divisions and power.
It has a history of looking for power, inequalities and conflicting
interests – from class, through to gender and ethnicity, and beyond.
For a long time it has done so at an international level, from Marx
and Wallerstein, to the sociology of development, to take just some
examples. As well as discussing traditionally sociological areas of globalization, such as culture and migration, I have also tried to bring
these aspects of sociological approaches to the process of understanding globalization.

Doing so shows limitations in some sociologies of globalization.
These are sometimes focused on culture and migration, but less so
on other areas such as economics and politics, often deliberately so
in the name of anti-economic determinism and an alleged outmoded-
ness of approaches which see nation-states as central. But, leaving out
the economy and the way economic motivations, economic power
and inequality structure globalization gives an over-benign, harmoni-
ous and equalized picture of globalization. 'New' approaches which
see globalization in this cosmopolitan way do not pay enough attention to some of the old approaches – many of which have enduring
explanatory power but are seen as out of touch with changing times.
Consequently, a key element is left out, that is, the way that globalization is based on and reproduces power, inequality and conflict. A
world that has such characteristics is then validated by being defined
in terms of the more benign category of globalization.

An objective of this book has been to test ideas of globalization. A
few will see some of its conclusions as conservative and not looking for
new ways of thinking in a rapidly changing world. My conclusions are
mixed. They are doubtful about some aspects of globalism, but not all,

and sceptical in some ways, but not others. However, the aim is not to come up with new ideas but rather the best ideas for understanding the world. If new ideas are needed then we should look for them, but sometimes they are celebrated too much for their newness and imaginativeness instead of being tested for their quality in understanding the world. The latter criteria can lead us towards existing or old ideas. This is not conservatism or lack of imagination, but a matter of finding the perspectives which are right. New theories cannot just be advocated as theories. They need to be tested against empirical reality. Too often a benign cosmopolitan sociology of globalization gets its power from theoretical elegance, and disproportionately represents the experience of European elites, rather than being grounded in empirical evidence with a worldwide scope. We should not fetishize the new, and we should also not fetishize theory in abstract from the broadest empirical reality.

Looking at the criteria for globalization, some of these issues arise. It is important to *define* globalization and measure whether what it describes matches up to the definition. This is partly because globalization is a powerful discourse and idea that can give a picture of multiple inputs, equalization, hybridity and convergence. When the word is used it can reinforce the appearance of these features in the world. So it is important to set out criteria for globalization and to test whether this is what it is really like. At the start of the book I argued that for something to be globalization it has to involve global extent, inputs from worldwide rather than just some parts of the world, interdependency, stability and regularity in global relations.

Historically, globalization is a process. In the pre-modern past, structures and relations in the world failed to meet such tough criteria. But it is fair to say that globalizing developments can be seen then, which came closer to realization when capitalist incentives and industrial technology drove this forward with a qualitative leap. To some extent, more recent developments in globalization, such as the end of the cold war divide and the introduction of the Internet, build on the globalization established by capitalist industrialism rather than by providing their own qualitative globalizing leap.

At the same time, studies that look for hard empirical evidence rather than pleasing theories show that on the criteria mentioned above arguments for globalization fall down. Global relations are not globally inclusive. Agency in and subjection to globalization is unequal and well short of convergence. The evidence for this can be found as much in pro-globalist theories as in those that are explicitly sceptical. It is important to define and test the theory of globalization, otherwise its power as an idea and discourse hides enduring and accentuating divisions of power, inequality and conflict. These give some in the world great advantages and subject large numbers at the opposite end to circumstances in which it is difficult to even stay alive, let alone achieve life chances beyond this.

There is potential in globalization to overcome such relations of power, inequality and conflict. *Cultures*, coming from around the world and fusing together in localities, produce exciting and dynamic hybrids, new experiences and the possibility for greater commonality between divergent groups. New forms of identity emerge, made up of diverse global inputs from media and migration, and found in areas such as consumption, style and music. In the media, the technology of the Internet, with a wide range of websites and blogs, allows individuals and groups to access information, and, more importantly, produce and disseminate content without corporate or political backing. Equally, the most popular accessible and prominent media content is controlled by corporate power, increasingly concentrated in the hands of a few rich and powerful Western interests that have gained ownership across media sectors.

The freedom for *people to move* is also unequally distributed, with those least in need, rich elites, being the most free, while those most in need of mobility, the poor and those beyond the rich core, are most restricted. The benefits of migration – for improving people's life chances and assisting their home countries through remittances, as well as providing labour and tax income to receiving countries for the support of public services and the ageing population, not to mention the input provided by cultural diversity – are not realized as much as they could be because of restrictions on migration. Resistance to inward migration in rich countries cannot be due to lack of benefits because the gains are, on the whole, clearly revealed by empirical evidence. Prejudice and racism must play a role.

One area in which the opportunities of globalization remain unfulfilled or even actively countered is in *economic globalization*. It is important to have a pluralistic understanding of globalization that does not reduce explanations to economic or other single factors. At the same time, it is also important to see the links between different factors in globalization and look at the extent to which some have causal power over others, rather than just seeing all as equal, separate or unaffected by one another. The search for resources, trade, production or investment, and the wealth that can be made from this, has been a driving force in globalization, from pre-modern trade to European imperialism and global capitalism. One result has been global economic interdependency such that small occurrences like the 2007 US sub-prime crisis can have ramifications for economic, political and cultural life globally. Similarly, aspects like culture and migration are not autonomous from economics, often being motivated, unequal or structured by power on economic bases. To dismiss economic explanations as too economistic leads to such causes, power relations and inequalities being ignored.

Deregulation and technology have allowed for massive and fast financial flows. This, along with the globalization of production and trade, can bring investment, jobs and exporting possibilities to developing countries. Giants like China and India have seized such opportunities, although on the basis of insulation from globalization until they were strong enough to enter the global economy. However, economic globalization is not as globalized as it seems. The *poorest* have been locked out of such opportunities, with financial flows con- centrated amongst the richest triad, and world trade being conducted on a basis in which they are hugely disadvantaged. Efforts to open up world trade are followed by rich countries when it benefits their industries but obstructed when it does not. Approximately 20 per cent of the world's population live on what a dollar a day could buy in the US, and 40 per cent on two dollars a day or less. For many in these groups, hunger and early death is normal and there is a dispro- portionate likelihood of experiencing war and suffering the effects of climate change.

Such experiences are inextricably linked to the advantages that rich countries have. The growth that produced prosperity in rich coun- tries produced the carbon emissions behind climate change. Climate change leads to the loss of fertile land and water, with ensuing con- flicts over these in developing countries. Rich countries profit from wars by selling arms, and wars are often rooted in conflicts or differ- ences left behind by imperial powers – in the Israel–Palestine conflict, for example. Poverty in developing countries is linked to the advan- tages that rich countries ensure for their own industries, despite their expectations of free trade on the part of the poor. The pleasing image of globalization as a cosmopolitan process that generalizes human rights and provides equalization, convergence and integration fails to match with empirical evidence about such issues. It reflects a view of elites that is mostly theoretical and focused on rich countries and culture.

Global politics, which brings people together to forge agreed solu- tions to climate change, economic regulation, world poverty, war and human rights abuses, is an ideal solution and should be pursued where possible. However, power imbalances, inequalities and conflict- ing interests amongst actors in the world make this a difficult way to achieve success. For some, the suggestion that corporate power and powerful nation-state interests undermine global political solutions shows an outmoded and discredited Marxist economic determinism with an unreconstructed view of nation-states. But the evidence from economic globalization, and from the global politics of world trade, international human rights, environmental protection, nuclear proliferation and miserable attempts to help the world's poor, suggests that nation-state interests and the material interests of the wealthy are blocks to globalization at this level.

One key nation-state, *the US*, has asymmetrical power economically, politically, culturally and militarily. If the power of America in world affairs is on the decline, it could arrest this by the greater soft power or multilateralism favoured by President Obama. If not, it looks most likely to be replaced not by a multipolar order or global cosmopolitanism but by another state, such as China, or other powerful states. But if China were to take over from the US as the leading power in economic and other spheres it is not clear whether this would change the structure of the world order to favour the poor. China may join or replace the core in globalization as much as end a core-periphery division. At the same time, some mid-ranking and poorer countries have resources, a critique of the current world order and of imperialism, and things in common with each other. These could be built on in a politics aimed at equalizing power and wealth.

Global social movements have exposed the lack of globalization in globalization, and have put important world issues on the agenda and brought them to wider attention. They have an imaginative and critical attitude which has enhanced understandings of globalization and the world of global politics, on issues such as labour, corporate power, neoliberalism, imperialism, development, inequality, democracy and rights. Yet they lack the political clout to achieve their goals. The agencies that do have clout are *states* with a critique of globalization and the resources, power and material interests to ally with one another. States operate at an international level, pursuing their own interests. They can ally internationally with other nation-states, if below the level of fully global politics, and with others that have shared interests or ideologies.

States have the resources and power to tackle problems within their own borders. The diversity of national policies and practices, and varying records in addressing poverty, suggests that governments have not lost the capacity to provide social democracy, welfare, redistribution and alternative policies to neoliberalism. This is evident from Scandinavian countries through to leftist governments in Latin America. Such forms of politics come as much from states' own resources, domestic traditions and alliances as from globalization. Beyond their borders, international state action by anti-globalization governments, from outside the rich core and in alliance with global justice movements, provides a forum where global politics to tackle world poverty, climate change, human rights and war seems to have the most chance. Ideology, material interests and bilateral links provide a basis for this sort of global politics. This can put pressure on a Democrat President in the US, open to such concerns, but also part of a core of rich states with their own interests and preferred type of globalization to pursue.

Acknowledgements

Thanks for their advice on chapters to Ozge Aktas, Erica Consterdine, Matt Dawson, Jake Martell, Katie Martell, Kevin McCormick, Julien Morton, Alison Phipps, and to others for important advice at the start which was remembered and incorporated. Thanks to the excellent students on my Sociology of Globalization course over the years for their good company and ideas. I'm grateful to others who have made suggestions, been encouraging and supportive, told me about good things to read or discussed the topic with me in ways that were helpful. Thanks to all at Polity Press for their work and to their readers for very helpful suggestions.

References

Abercrombie, Nicholas et al. (1980) *The Dominant Ideology Thesis*, London: HarperCollins.

Abu-Lughod, Janet L. (1989) *Before European Hegemony: The World System AD 1250–1350*, Oxford: Oxford University Press.

Acker, Joan (2004) 'Gender, Capitalism and Globalization', *Critical Sociology*, 30/1: 17–41.

Albert, Michel (1993) *Capitalism against Capitalism*, London: Whurr.

Albrow, Martin (1996) *The Global Age: State and Society beyond Modernity*, Cambridge: Polity.

Anderson, Benedict (2006) *Imagined Communities*, London: Verso.

Archibugi, Daniele (2004) 'Cosmopolitan Democracy and Its Critics: A Review', *European Journal of International Relations*, 10: 437–73.

Archibugi, Daniele, and David Held (eds) (1995) *Cosmopolitan Democracy: An Agenda for a New World Order*, Cambridge: Polity.

Ashman, Sam (2004) 'Resistance to Neoliberal Globalization: A Case of "Militant Particularism"', *Politics*, 24/2: 143–53.

Bales, Kevin (2004) *Disposable People: New Slavery in the Global Economy*, Berkeley, CA: University of California Press.

Barber, Benjamin (1996) *Jihad Versus McWorld*, New York: Ballantyne Books.

Barkawi, Tarak (2006) *Globalization and War*, Lanham: Rowman and Littlefield.

Bauman, Zygmunt (1998) *Globalization: The Human Consequences*, Cambridge: Polity.

Bayly, C. A. (2004) *The Birth of the Modern World, 1780–1914: Global Connections and Comparisons*, Oxford: Blackwell.

Beck, Ulrich (2000) *What is Globalization?*, Cambridge: Polity.

Beck, Ulrich (2006) *Cosmopolitan Vision*, Cambridge: Polity.

Beck, Ulrich (2007) 'Beyond Class and Nation: Reframing Social Inequalities in a Globalizing World', *British Journal of Sociology*, 58/4: 679–705.

Beck, Ulrich, Natan Sznaider, and Winter, Rainer, eds (2003) *Global America? The Cultural Consequences of Globalization*, Liverpool: Liverpool University Press.

Birchfield, Vicki and Freyberg-Inan, Annette (2004) 'Constructing Opposition in the Age of Globalization: The Potential of ATTAC', *Globalizations*, 1/2: 278–304.

Birdsall, Nancy et al. (2005) 'How to Help Poor Countries', *Foreign Affairs*, July/August 2005.

Blair, Tony (1997) *Speech to the Party of European Socialists' Congress*, Malmo, Sweden, 6 June.

Blanchflower, D. et al. (2007) *The Impact of the Recent Migration from Eastern Europe on the UK Economy*, London: Bank of England.

Boot, Max (2006) 'The Paradox of Military Technology', *The New Atlantis*, Fall: 13–31.

Bottomore, Tom (1993) *Political Sociology*, London: Pluto Press.

Bourdieu, Pierre (1984) *Distinction: A Social Critique of the Judgment of Taste*, New Haven, CT: Harvard University Press.

Bourdieu, Pierre (1998) *Acts of Resistance: Against the New Myths of our Time*, Cambridge: Polity.

Bourdieu, Pierre (1999) *The Weight of the World: Social Suffering in Contemporary Society*, Cambridge: Polity.

Bourdieu, Pierre (2003a) *Firing Back: Against the Tyranny of the Market 2*, London: Verso.

Bourdieu, Pierre (2003b) 'Culture is in Danger', in *Firing Back: Against the Tyranny of the Market 2*, London: Verso.

Breslin, Shaun (2005) 'Power and Production: Rethinking China's Global Economic Role', *Review of International Studies*, 31: 735–53.

Broad, Robin (2004) 'The Washington Consensus Meets the Global Backlash: Shifting Debates and Policies', *Globalizations*, 1/2: 129–54.

Bruff, Ian (2005) 'Making Sense of the Globalization Debate when Engaging in Political Economy Analysis', *British Journal of Politics and International Relations*, 7: 261–80.

Buzan, Barry and Foot, Rosemary (eds) (2004) *Does China Matter? A Reassessment: Essays in Memory of Gerald Segal*, Abingdon: Routledge.

Cameron, Angus, and Ronen Palan (2004) *The Imagined Economies of Globalization*, London: Sage.

Cassen, Bernard (2003) 'On the Attack', *New Left Review*, 19 January/February: 41–60.

Cassen, Bernard (2005) 'ATTAC Against the Treaty', *New Left Review*, 33, May/June: 27–33.

Castells, Manuel (2000) *The Information Age: Economy, Society and Culture: Volume I: The Rise of the Network Society*, Oxford: Blackwell.

Castles. Stephen and Miller, Mark (2003) *The Age of Migration*, Basingstoke: Palgrave.

Cerny, Philip G., and Evans, Mark (2004) 'Globalization and Public Policy under New Labour', *Policy Studies* 25/1: 51–65.

Chen, Shaohua, and Ravallion, Martin (2007) *Absolute Poverty Measures for the Developing World, 1981–2004*, Washington, DC: World Bank.

Chen, Shaohua, and Ravallion, Martin (2008) *The Developing World is Poorer than We Thought, But No Less Successful in the Fight against Poverty*, Washington, DC: World Bank.

Chow, Esther Ngan-Ling (2003) 'Gender Matters: Studying Globalization and Social Change in the 21st Century', *International Sociology*, 18/3: 443–60.

Colás, Alejandro, and Saull, Richard (2006) Introduction, in *The War on Terrorism and the American 'Empire' after the Cold War*, edited by Alejandro Colás and Richard Saull, London: Routledge.

Cooper, Robert (2003) *The Breaking of Nations: Order and Chaos in the Twenty-First Century*, London: Atlantic Books.

Cox, Robert (1999) 'Civil Society at the Turn of the Millennium: Prospects for an Alternative World Order', *Review of International Studies*, 25: 3–28.

Crouch, Colin (2004) *Post-Democracy*, Cambridge: Polity.

De Swaan, Abram (2001) *Words of the World: The Global Language System*, Cambridge: Polity.

Dicken, Peter (2007) *Global Shift: Mapping the Changing Contours of the World Economy*, London: Sage.

Dirlik, Arif (1994) 'The Postcolonial Aura: Third World Criticism in the Age of Global Capitalism', *Critical Inquiry*, 20/2: 328–56

Dirlik, Arif (1996) 'Review of Frederick Buell "National Culture and the New Global System"', *Journal of World History*, 7/2.

Dodd, Akram (2008) 'Migrant Crime Wave a Myth – Police Study', *Guardian*, 16 April.

Dollar, David, and Kraay, Art (2001) *Trade, Growth and Poverty*, Washington, DC: World Bank.

Esping-Andersen, Gøsta (1985) *Politics Against Markets: The Social Democratic Road to Power*, Princeton, NJ: Princeton University Press.

Esping-Andersen, Gøsta (1989) *The Three Worlds of Welfare Capitalism*, Cambridge: Polity.

Fine, Robert (2006) 'Cosmopolitanism and Violence: Difficulties of Judgment', *British Journal of Sociology*, 57: 49–67.

Fine, Robert (2007) *Cosmopolitanism*, London: Routledge.

Flew, Terry (2007) *Understanding Global Media*, Basingstoke: Palgrave.

Foucault, Michel (1979) *The History of Sexuality: Volume 1*, London: Viking.

Frank, Andre Gunder (1998) *ReOrient: Global Economy in the Asian Age*, Berkeley, CA: University of California Press.

Frank, Andre Gunder, and Gills, Barry K. (eds) (1993) *The World System: Five Hundred Years or Five Thousand?* London: Routledge.

Friedman, Jonathan (1999) 'The Hybridization of Roots and the Abhorrence of the Bush', in Featherstone, M. and Lash, S. (eds), *Spaces of Culture: City-Nation-World*, London: Sage.

Fukuyama, Francis (1989) 'The End of History', *The National Interest*, summer.

Garrett, Geoffrey (1998) *Partisan Politics in a Global Era*, Cambridge: Cambridge University Press.

Garton Ash, Timothy (2004) *Free World: Why a Crisis of the West Reveals the Opportunity of our Time*, London: Allen Lane.

Giddens, Anthony (1990) *The Consequences of Modernity*, Cambridge: Polity.

Gill, Stephen (2000) 'Towards a Postmodern Prince? The Battle in Seattle as a Moment in the New Politics of Globalization', *Millennium: Journal of International Studies* 29/1: 131–40.

Gills, Barry K. (ed.) (2000) *Globalization and the Politics of Resistance*, London: Palgrave.

Gills, Barry and Thompson, William (eds) (2006) *Globalization and Global History*, London: Routledge.

Glatzer, Miguel and Rueschemeyer, Dietrich (2005) *Globalization and the Future of the Welfare State*, Pittsburgh: University of Pittsburgh Press.

Glick Schiller, Nina et al. (1992) *Towards a Transnational Perspective on Migration*, New York: New York Academy of Sciences.

Globalizations journal, mission statement, available at: <http://www.tandf.co.uk/journals/journal.asp?issn=1474-7731&linktype=1>.

Glyn, Andrew (2004) 'The Assessment: How Far Has Globalization Gone?', *Oxford Review of Economic Policy*, 20/1: 1–14.

Graeber, David (2002) 'The New Anarchists', *New Left Review*, 13, January/February: 61–73.

Gray, John (1996) *After Social Democracy: Politics, Capitalism, and the Common Life*, London: Demos.

Guinness Book of Records 2008, London: Guinness World Records.

Hall, Peter and Soskice, David (eds) (2001) *Varieties of Capitalism: The Institutional Foundations of Comparative Advantage*, Oxford: Oxford University Press.

Halliday, Fred (2000) 'Getting Real about Seattle', *Millennium: Journal of International Studies*, 29/1: 123–9.

Halpern, David (2004) *Social Capital*, Cambridge: Polity.

Hardt, Michael and Negri, Antonio (2000) *Empire*, New Haven, CT: Harvard University Press.

Harris, Nigel (2001) *Thinking the Unthinkable: The Immigration Myth Exposed*, London: IB Tauris.

Harvey, David (1991) *The Condition of Postmodernity: An Enquiry Into the Origins of Cultural Change*, Oxford: Blackwell.

Harvey, David (2003) *The New Imperialism*, Oxford: Oxford University Press.

Haseler, Stephen (2004) *Super-State: The New Europe and its Challenge to America*, London: IB Tauris.

Hay, Colin and Marsh, David (eds) (2000) *Demystifying Globalization*, Basingstoke: Palgrave.

Held, David (1989) *Political Theory and the Modern State*, Cambridge: Polity.

Held, David (1995) *Democracy and the Global Order*, Cambridge: Polity.

Held, David (2000) 'Regulating Globalization? The Reinvention of Politics', *International Sociology*, 15/2, 394–408.

Held, David (2004) *Global Covenant: The Social Democratic Alternative to the Washington Consensus*, Cambridge: Polity.

Held, David et al. (1999) *Global Transformations*, Cambridge: Polity.

Held, David and Hirst, Paul, (2002) *Globalization After 11 September: The Argument of Our Time*, Open Democracy, at: <http://www.opendemocracy.net/globalization institutions_government/ article_637.jsp>.

Held, David and Ayse Kaya (ed) (2006) *Global Inequality: Patterns and Explanations*, Cambridge: Polity.

Held, David and Koenig-Archibugi, Mathias (eds) (2004) *American Power in the Twenty-first Century*, Cambridge: Polity.

Held, David, and McGrew, Anthony (eds) (2002) *Governing Globalization: Power, Authority and Global Governance*, Cambridge: Polity.

Held, David and McGrew, Anthony (eds) (2003) *The Global Transformations Reader*, Cambridge: Polity.

Herman, Edward and McChesney, Robert (1997) *The Global Media: The New Missionaries of Corporate Capitalism*, London: Cassell.

Hirst, Paul (1999) 'Has Globalization Killed Social Democracy?', *Political Quarterly* 70, Special Issue: 84–96.

Hirst, Paul (2001) *War and Power in the 21st Century*, Cambridge: Polity.

Hirst, Paul, and Thompson, Grahame (1996) *Globalization in Question*, Cambridge: Polity.

Hirst, Paul, and Thompson, Grahame (2000) 'Globalization in One Country? The Peculiarities of the British', *Economy and Society* 29/3: 335–56.

Hobsbawm, Eric (1990) *Nations and Nationalism since 1780*, Cambridge: Cambridge University Press.

Hobson, John (2004) *The Eastern Origins of Western Civilization*, Cambridge: Cambridge University Press.

Hoerder, Dirk (2002) *Cultures in Contact: World Migrations in the Second Millennium*, Durham, NC: Duke University Press.

Holloway, John (2002) *Change the World without Taking Power: The Meaning of Revolution Today*, London: Pluto Press.

Holloway, John and Callinicos, Alex, (2005) 'Can We Change the World Without Taking Power?', *International Socialism*, 16 August.

Holton, Robert (1998) *Globalization and the Nation-State*, Basingstoke: Palgrave.

Holton, Robert (2005) *Making Globalization*, Basingstoke: Palgrave.

Holton, Robert (2007) *Global Networks*, Basingstoke: Palgrave.

Home Office (UK Government) (2007), *The Economic and Fiscal Impact of Immigration*, London: Home Office.

Hoogvelt, Ankie (2001) *Globalization and the Postcolonial World: The New Political Economy of Development*, London: Palgrave.

Hopkins, A. G. (2002a) 'The History of Globalization – and the Globalization of History?', in *Globalization in World History*, edited by A. G. Hopkins, London: Pimlico.

Hopkins, A. G. (2002b) *Globalization in World History*, London: Pimlico.

Hopkins, A.G. (ed.) (2006) *Global History Interactions between the Universal and the Local*, Basingstoke: Palgrave.

Hopper, Paul (2007) *Understanding Cultural Globalization*, Cambridge: Polity.

House of Lords Select Committee on Economic Affairs (2008) *The Economic Impact of Immigration*, London: House of Lords.

Huber, Evelyn and Stephens, John, D. (2002) 'Globalization, Competitiveness and the Social Democratic Model', *Social Policy and Society*, 1/1: 47–57.

Huntington, Samuel P. (1996) *The Clash of Civilizations and the Remaking of World Order*, London: Simon and Schuster.

Hutton, Will (1995) *The State We're In*, London: Vintage.

Hutton, Will and Desai, Meghnad (2007) 'Does The Future Really belong to China?', *Prospect*, 130, January.

Ikenberry, G. John (2004) 'Liberal Hegemony or Empire? American Power in the Age of Unipolarity', in Held, D. and Koening-Archibugi, Mathias (eds), *American Power in the Twenty-first Century*, Cambridge: Polity.

International Commission for the Study of Communication Problems (1980) *Many Voices, One World*, Paris: UNESCO.

International Telecommunications Union (ITU) (2008) *World Telecommunication/ICT Indicators Database*: <http://www.itu.int/ITU-D/ict/statistics/ict/index.html>.

Johnson, Chalmers (2004) *Blowback: The Costs and Consequences of American Empire*, New York: Owl Books.

Kagan, Robert (2003) *Paradise and Power, America and Europe in the New World Order*, New York: Knopf.

Kaldor, Mary (2001) *New and Old Wars: Organized Violence in a Global Era*, Cambridge: Polity.

Kaldor, Mary (2003) *Global Civil Society: An Answer to War*, Cambridge: Polity.

Kaplinsky, Raphael (2005) *Globalization, Poverty, and Inequality*, Cambridge: Polity.

Keane, John (2003) *Global Civil Society*, Cambridge: Polity.

Kennedy, Paul, and Catherine J. Danks (eds) (2001) *Globalization and National Identities: Crisis or Opportunity?*, London: Palgrave.

King, Russell (1995) 'Migrations, Globalization and Place', in Massey, D. and Jess, P. (eds) *A Place in the World?*, Oxford: Oxford University Press.

Klein, Naomi (2001) *No Logo*, London: Flamingo.

Klein, Naomi (2002) *Fences and Windows: Dispatches from the Frontline of the Globalization Debate*, London: Flamingo.

Klein, Naomi (2008) *The Shock Doctrine: The Rise of Disaster Capitalism*, London: Penguin.

Kofman, Eleonore, and Youngs, Gillian (eds) (1996) 'Introduction: Globalization – The Second Wave', in *Globalization: Theory and Practice*, edited by Eleonore Kofman and Gillian Youngs, London: Pinter.

Kraay, Aart (2006) *Trade, Growth and Poverty: A Response to Nye, Reddy and Watkins*, Washington, DC: World Bank.

Krugman, Paul (1996) *Pop Internationalism*, Cambridge, MA: MIT Press.

Kumar, Krishan (2004) *From Post-Industrialism to Post-Modern Society*, Oxford: Blackwell.

Lane, David (1996) *The Rise and Fall of State Socialism*, Cambridge: Polity.

Larrain, Jorge (1983) *Marxism and Ideology*, Basingstoke: Palgrave.

Legrain, Philippe (2006) *Immigrants: Your Country Needs Them*, London: Little Brown.

Legrain, Philippe (2007) Don't Believe this Claptrap: Migrants are No Threat to Us', *Guardian*, 15 January 2007.

Leonard, Mark (2005) *Why Europe Will Run the 21st Century*, London: Fourth Estate.

McChesney, Robert (1999) 'The New Global Media: It's a Small World of Big Conglomerates', *The Nation*, 29.

McKeown, Adam (2004) 'Global Migration 1846–1940', *Journal of World History*, 15/2: 155–89.

McPhail, Thomas (2006) *Global Communication: Theories, Stakeholders and Trends*, Oxford: Blackwell.

Mann, Michael (1997) 'Has Globalization Ended the Rise of the Nation-State?', *Review of International Political Economy*, 4/3: 472–96.

Mann, Michael (2003) *Incoherent Empire*, London: Verso.

Mann, Michael (2004) 'The First Failed Empire of the 21st Century', *Review of International Studies*, 30: 631–53.

Martell, Luke (2008) 'Beck's Cosmopolitan Politics', *Contemporary Politics*, 14/2: June, 129–43.

Martell, Luke (2009) 'Global Inequality, Human Rights and Power: A Critique of Ulrich Beck's Cosmopolitanism', *Critical Sociology*, 35/2: 253–72.

Marx, Karl and Engels, Friedrich (1998) *The Communist Manifesto*, London: Verso.

Massey, Doug et al. (1998) *Worlds in Motion: Understanding International Migration at the End of the Millennium*, Oxford: Oxford University Press.

Messina, Anthony M. and Lahav, Gallya (2006) *The Migration Reader: Exploring Politics and Policy*, London: Lynne Rienner.

Milanovic, Branko (2003) 'The Two faces of Globalization: Against Globalization as We Know It', *World Development*, 31: 667–83.

Mishra, Pankaj (2006) 'The Western View of the Rise of India and China is a Self-Affirming Fiction', *Guardian*, Comment is Free section, 10 June.

Modelski, George (1972) *Principles of World Politics*, New York: Free Press.

Moghadam, Valentine (1999) 'Gender and Globalization: Female Labor and Women's Mobilization', *Journal of World-Systems Research*, 1/2: 367–88.

Moghadam, Valentine (2000) 'Transnational Feminist Networks: Collective Action in an Era of Globalization', *International Sociology*, 15/1: 57–85.

Moghadam, Valentine (2005) *Globalizing Women: Transnational Feminist Networks*, Baltimore, MD: Johns Hopkins University Press.

Morton, Adam David (2002) '"La Resurrección del Maíz": Globalization, Resistance and the Zapatistas', *Millennium: Journal of International Studies*, 31/1: 27–54.

Moses Jonathon (2006) *International Migration: Globalization's Last Frontier*, London: Zed Books.

Mosley, Layna (2005) 'Globalization and the State: Still Room to Move?', *New Political Economy*, 10/3: 355–62.

Motta, Sara (2006) 'Utopias Reimagined: A Reply to Panizza', *Political Studies*, 54: 898–905.

Münkler, Herfried (2005) *The New Wars*, Cambridge: Polity.

National Intelligence Council (2008) *Global Trends 2025: A Transformed World*, Washington, DC: US Government Printing Office.

Nederveen Pieterse, Jan (2003) 'Hyperpower Exceptionalism: Globalization the American Way', *New Political Economy*, 8/3, November: 299–319.

Nederveen Pieterse, Jan (2004a) *Globalization and Culture: Global Melange*, Boulder, CO: Rowman and Littlefield.

Nederveen Pieterse, Jan (2004b) *Globalization or Empire?*, London: Routledge.

Nederveen Pieterse, Jan (2006) 'Beyond the American Bubble: Does Empire Matter?', *Third World Quarterly*, 27/6: 987–1002.

Nye, Howard et al. (2002) 'Dollar and Kraay on "Trade, Growth and Poverty": A Critique': <http://www.maketradefair.org/en/assets/english/finalDKcritique.pdf>.

Nye, Joseph (2002) *The Paradox of American Power: Why the World's Only Superpower Can't Go It Alone*, Oxford: Oxford University Press.

OECD (2008) *International Migration Outlook*, Paris: OECD.

Office for National Statistics (2001) *UK Census 2001*, London: ONS; also available at: <http://news.bbc.co.uk/1/shared/spl/hi/uk/05/born_abroad/countries/html/overview.stm>.

Ohmae, Kenichi (1990) *The Borderless World*, London: Collins.

Ohmae, Kenichi (1996) *The End of the Nation-State*, London: HarperCollins.

O'Rourke, Kevin H., and Jeffrey G. Williamson (1999) *Globalization and History: The Evolution of a Nineteenth-Century Atlantic Economy*. Cambridge, MA: MIT Press.

Osterhammel, Jürgen and Petersson, Niels, P. (2005) *Globalization: A Short History*, Princeton, NJ: Princeton University Press.

Outhwaite, William (2006) *The Future of Society*, Cambridge: Polity.

Parkin, Frank (2002) *Max Weber*, London: Routledge.

Perrraton, Jonathan and Goldblatt, David (1997) 'The Globalization of Economic Activity', *New Political Economy*, 2/2: 257–78.

Peterson, John and Pollack, Mark A. (eds) (2003) *Europe, America, Bush: Transatlantic Relations in the Twenty-first Century*, London: Routledge.

Pew Global Attitudes Project (2007) *Rising Environmental Concern in 47-Nation Survey: Global Unease with Major World Powers*, Washington, DC: Pew Research Center.

Pew Research Center for the People and Press and the Pew Hispanic Center (2006) *No Consensus on Immigration Problem or Proposed Fixes: America's Immigration Quandary*, Washington, DC: Pew Research Center.

Pinter, Harold (2005) *Art, Truth and Politics*, Stockholm: Nobel Foundation.

Porter, Bernard (1996) *The Lion's Share: A Short History of British Imperialism 1850–1995*, Harlow: Longman.

Przeworski, Adam (1985) *Capitalism and Social Democracy*, Princeton, NJ: Princeton University Press.

Putin, Vladimir (2007) *Speech at the 43rd Munich Conference on Security Policy*: <http://www.securityconference.de/konferenzen/rede.php?sprache=en&id=179>.

Putnam, Robert (2001) *Bowling Alone: The Collapse and Revival of American Community*, New York: Simon and Shuster.

Putnam, Robert (2007) 'E Pluribus Unum: Diversity and Community in the Twenty-first Century, The 2006 Johan Skytte Prize Lecture', *Scandinavian Political Studies*, 30/2: 137–74.

Pyle, Jean and Ward, Kathryn (2003) 'Recasting Our Understanding of Gender and Work during Global Restructuring', *International Sociology*, 18/3, September: 461–89.

Ramonet, Ignacio (1997) 'Disarming the Markets', *Le Monde Diplomatique*, December.

Rantanen, Tehri (2005) *The Media and Globalization*, London: Sage.

Ray, Larry (2007) *Globalization and Everyday Life*, London: Routledge.

Reed, Howard and Latorre, Maria (2009) *The Economic Impacts of Labour Migration on the UK Labour Market*, London: Institute for Public Policy Research.

Reich, Robert (1992) *The Work of Nations*, New York: Vintage.

Rifkin, Jeremy (2004) *The European Dream How Europe's Vision of the Future is Quietly Eclipsing the American Dream*, Cambridge: Polity.

Ritzer, George (2007) *The McDonaldization of Society*, London: Pine Forge Press.

Robertson, Roland (1992) *Globalization*, London: Sage.

Robins, Kevin (1997) 'What in the World's Going On?', in *Production of Culture/ Productions of Culture*, edited by P. du Gay, London: Sage.

Rodrik, Dani (2000) *Comments on Trade, Growth and Poverty* by D. Dollar and A. Kraay. Available at: <http://ksghome.harvard.edu/~drodrik/Rodrik%20on%20 Dollar–Kraay.PDF>.

Rosenau, James N. (1997) *Along the Domestic-Foreign Frontier*, Cambridge: Cambridge University Press.

Rosenberg, Justin (2000) *The Follies of Globalization Theory*, London: Verso.

Rupert, Mark (2003) 'Globalising Common Sense: A Marxian-Gramscian (Re-) vision of the Politics of Governance/Resistance', *Review of International Studies*, 29: 181–98.

Samman, Emma (2005) *Openness and Growth: An Empirical Investigation*, New York: UNDP Human Development Report, UN.

Sassen, Saskia (2001) *The Global City: New York, London, Tokyo*, Princeton, NJ: Princeton University Press.

Sassen, Saskia (2007) *A Sociology of Globalization*, New York: WW Norton and Co.

Schiller, Herbert (1969) *Mass Communication and American Empire*, Boston, MA: Beacon Press.

Scholte, Jan Aart (2000) 'Cautionary Reflections on Seattle', *Millennium: Journal of International Studies*, 29/1: 115–21.

Scholte, Jan Aart (2005) *Globalization: A Critical Introduction*, 2nd edn, Basingstoke: Palgrave (1st edn, 2000, Basingstoke: Palgrave).

Scott, John (1990) *Ideology and the New Social Movements*, London: Routledge.

Segal, Gerald (1999) 'Does China Matter?', *Foreign Affairs*, 78/5: 24–36.

Shaw, Eric (2007) *Losing Labour's Soul? New Labour and the Blair Government 1997– 2007*, London: Routledge.

Shaw, Martin (1991) *Post-Military Society: Militarism, Demilitarization and War at the End of the Twentieth Century*, Cambridge: Polity.

Shaw, Martin (2005) *The New Western Way of War: Risk-Transfer War and its Crisis in Iraq*, Cambridge: Polity.

Simon, Julian (1989) *The Economic Consequences of Immigration*, Oxford: Blackwell.

Sklair, Leslie (2002) *Globalization: Capitalism and Its Alternatives*, Oxford: Oxford University Press.

Smith, Anthony D. (1990) 'Towards a Global Culture?', *Theory, Culture, and Society* 7: 171–91.

Soros, George (2005) *On Globalization*, New York: Public Affairs.

Sriskandarajah, Dhananjayan (2006) 'Pulling up the Drawbridge will Damage Our Economy, *Guardian*, 23 August.

Stiglitz, Joseph (2003) *Globalization and its Discontents*, London: Penguin.

Stiglitz, Joseph and Bilmes, Linda (2008) *The Three Trillion Dollar War: The True Cost of the Iraq Conflict*, London: Penguin.

Stockholm International Peace Research Institute (SIPRI) (2008) *SIPRI Yearbook 2008 Summary: Armaments, Disarmament and International Security*, Stockholm: SIPRI.

Strange, Susan (1996) *The Retreat of the State: The Diffusion of Power in the World Economy*, Cambridge: Cambridge University Press.

Strange, Susan (1997) *Casino Capitalism*, Manchester: Manchester University Press.

Surowiecki, James (2007) 'Synergy with the Devil', *The New Yorker*, January 8.

Taylor, Robert (2005) *Sweden's New Social Democratic Model: Proof That a Better World is Possible*, London: Compass.

Thompson, John (1995) *The Media and Modernity*, Cambridge: Polity.

Tomlinson, John (1999) *Globalization and Culture*, Cambridge: Polity.

Trade Unions Congress (2007) *The Economics of Migration: Managing the Impacts*, London: TUC.

Tunstall, Jeremy (1977) *The Media are American*, New York: Columbia University Press.

Turner, Bryan (2006) 'Classical Sociology and Cosmopolitanism: A Critical Defence of the Social', *British Journal of Sociology*, 57/1: 133–51.

UNCTAD (2006) *World Investment Report: FDI from Developing and Transition Economies: Implications for Development*, New York: UN.

UNCTAD (2008a) *The Least Developed Countries Report 2008: Growth, Poverty and the Terms of Development Partnership*, New York: UN.

UNCTAD (2008b) *World Investment Report: Transnational Corporations and the Infrastructure Challenge: Overview*, New York: UN.

UNCTAD (2008c) *World Investment Report: Transnational Corporations and the Infrastructure Challenge*, New York: UN.

UNDP (2003) *Human Development Report 2003: Millennium Development Goals: A Compact Among Nations to End Human Poverty*, New York: UN.

UNDP (2007) *Annual Report 2007: Making Globalization Work for All*, New York: UN.

UNDP (2008a) *Human Development Report 2007/2008: Fighting Climate Change: Human Solidarity in a Changing World*, New York: UN.

UNDP (2008b) *Annual Report 2008: Capacity Development: Empowering People and Institutions*, New York: UN.

UNDP (2008c) *Delivering on the Global Partnership for Achieving the Millennium Development Goals*, UN MDG Task Force Report, New York: UN.

UNESCO (2005) *International Flows of Selected Cultural Goods and Services, 1994–2003*, Montreal: UNESCO.

UNFAO (2008) *The State of Food Insecurity in the World: High Food Prices and Food Insecurity: Threats and Opportunities*, Rome: UN.

UNHCR (2000) *The State of The World's Refugees*, Geneva: UNHCR.

United Nations (2007) *Urban Population, Environment and Development*, New York: UN Population Division.

UNWTO (2008) *Tourism Highlights*, Madrid: UN.

Urry, John (2000) *Sociology beyond Societies: Mobilities for the Twenty-first Century*, London: Routledge.

US Department of Defense (2008) *Active Duty Military Personnel Strengths by Regional Area and by Country*, Washington, DC: US DoD.

Vandenbroucke, Frank (1998) *Globalization, Inequality and Social Democracy*, London: Institute for Public Policy Research.

Wade, Robert (2007) 'Globalization: Emancipating or Reinforcing', *Open Democracy*, 29 January, at: <http://www.opendemocracy.net/globalization-institutions_government/globalization_inequality_4292.jsp>.

Wakeham, John (2008) 'The £6 Billion Fallacy', *Guardian*, 1 April.

Wallerstein, Immanuel (1974) *The Modern World System, Volume I: Capitalist Agriculture and the Origins of the European World-economy in the Sixteenth Century*, London: Academic Press.

Wallerstein, Immanuel (1980) *The Modern World System, Volume II: Mercantilism and the Consolidation of the European World Economy, 1600–1750*, New York: Academic Press.

Wallerstein, Immanuel (1989) *The Modern World System, Volume III: The Second Great Expansion of the Capitalist World Economy, 1730s–1840s*, San Diego: Academic Press.

Wallerstein, Immanuel (2003) *The Decline of American Power: The US in a Chaotic World*, New York: New Press.

Wallerstein, Immanuel (2006) 'The Curve of American Power', *New Left Review*, 40, July/August: 77–94.

Waters, Malcolm (2001) *Globalization*, London: Routledge.

Weiss, Linda (1998) *The Myth of the Powerless State: Governing the Economy in a Global Era*, Cambridge: Cambridge University Press.

Weiss, Linda (2005) 'The State Augmenting Effects of Globalization', *New Political Economy*, 10/3: 345–53.

Wickham-Jones, Mark (2000) 'New Labour in the Global Economy: Partisan Politics and the Social Democratic Model', *British Journal of Politics and International Relations*, 2/1: 1–25

Wilkinson, Richard (2005) *The Impact of Inequality: How to Make Sick Societies Healthier*, London: Routledge.

Wilkinson, Richard and Pickett, Kate (2009) *The Spirit Level: Why Equal Societies Almost Always Do Better*, London: Allen Lane.

Wolf, Martin (2004) *Why Globalization Works: The Case for the Global Market Economy*, New Haven, CT: Yale University Press.

Wolf, Martin, and Robert Wade (2002) 'Are Global Poverty and Inequality Getting Worse?', *Prospect* 72 (March). Available at: <http://www.prospectmagazine.co.uk/article_details.php?id=4982>.

World Bank (2002) *Globalization, Growth and Poverty: Building an Inclusive World Economy*, Oxford: Oxford University Press.

Worth, Owen and Abbott, Jason (2006) 'Land of False Hope? The Contradictions of British Opposition to Globalization', *Globalizations*, 3/1: 49–63.

Wright, Anthony (1987) *Socialisms: Theories and Practices*, Oxford: Oxford Paperbacks.

Zolo, Danilo (1997) *Cosmopolis: Prospects for World Government*, Cambridge: Polity.

Zolo, Danilo (2002) *Invoking Humanity: War, Law, and Global Order*, London: Continuum.

Index

Abbott, Jason, 246, 249, 251–2
Abu-Lughod, Janet, 45, 46, 66
Afghanistan, 61, 92, 107, 196, 227, 259, 260, 262, 267, 269, 270, 273, 276, 291, 292, 295, 301, 303
Africa, 21, 30, 44, 47, 51, 56, 58, 61, 69, 71, 73, 74, 75, 78, 80, 86, 93, 96, 106, 107, 108, 109, 114, 115, 116, 117, 127, 128, 145, 147, 153, 165–71, 180, 181, 192, 196, 208, 210, 255, 262, 263, 265, 279, 280, 283, 294, 295, 297, 299, 301, 306
agency, 13, 20, 23, 24, 32, 40–1, 55–7, 59, 60, 65, 101, 103, 110–11, 115, 131, 137–9, 184, 189, 210, 212–13, 224, 311–12, 314
aid, 128, 181–4, 227, 231, 242, 256, 302
air travel, 73, 79, 109, 116, 117
Algeria, 75, 292, 300
Americanization, 10, 22, 24, 44, 62, 70, 76, 80, 91, 95, 143, 243, 246, 247, 259–86
   see also USA and Westernization
anarchism, 243, 245–6, 247, 249
Anglo-American capitalism, 75, 154–5, 181, 205
   see also neoliberalism and types of capitalism
anti-globalization (and global justice movement), 35, 63, 95, 126, 163, 184, 239–58, 314–15
   see also social movements
Archibugi, Daniele, 34, 215, 216, 223, 229, 231, 238
Argentina, 148, 168, 174, 194, 200, 256
arms trade, 9, 260, 262, 263, 282, 289, 293, 294, 299–302, 307, 308, 309, 313

Asia, 21, 26, 28, 30, 44, 45, 47, 49, 53, 56, 60, 62, 70, 71, 73–5, 80, 96, 97, 109, 113–16, 127, 144, 145, 151, 153–6, 165, 166, 168–70, 180–2, 194, 196, 205, 210, 243, 262, 263, 265, 271, 273, 277, 292, 294, 300, 301
Association of South East Nations (ASEAN), 63, 152, 185, 194, 221
Australia, 56, 74, 83, 86, 107, 116, 121, 124, 125, 127, 148, 300

Bangladesh, 116, 124, 125, 294
Barkawi, Tarak, 289–91, 293, 308
Bauman, Zygmunt, 98, 101
Beck, Ulrich, 3, 4, 20, 54, 67, 97, 98, 100, 122, 216, 219, 220, 222, 229, 233, 234, 238, 284, 288
belle époque (1870–1914), 26, 29, 31, 32, 33, 57, 59, 62, 114, 117, 151, 156, 157
bilateralism, 35, 50, 62, 63, 118, 184–5, 236–8, 256, 264, 294–5, 315
   see also multilateralism
Bilmes, Linda, 300
bipolarity, 1, 30, 60, 61, 64, 71, 261, 263–6, 294–5
blogging, 63, 77, 80, 95–6, 312
Bolivia, 243–4, 254, 256, 264
Bourdieu, Pierre, 3, 17, 85, 88
Brazil, 23, 115, 144, 148, 168, 170, 171, 179, 194, 243, 256
Bruff, Ian, 36, 40–1, 42
Burma, 292
Burundi, 292

cable technology, 2, 54, 70, 74, 75, 76, 78, 82, 83, 84, 90, 93, 94, 96